LPIC I

Ross Brunson

LPIC I Exam Cram 2

Copyright © 2005 by Que Publishing

International Standard Book Number: 0-7897-3127-4

Library of Congress Catalog Card Number: 2003116155

Printed in the United States of America

First Printing: August 2004

07   06   05   04   4   3   2   1

Trademarks

Warning and Disclaimer

Bulk Sales

Que Publishing offers excellent discounts on this book when ordered in quantity for bulk purchases or special sales. For more information, please contact

U.S. Corporate and Government Sales

1-800-382-3419

corpsales@pearsontechgroup.com

For sales outside of the United States, please contact

International Sales

international@pearsoned.com

Publisher
Paul Boger

Executive Editor
Jeff Riley

Acquisitions Editor
Carol Ackerman

Development Editor
Michael Watson

Managing Editor
Charlotte Clapp

Project Editors
Tricia Liebig
Dan Knott

Indexer
Ken Johnson

Proofreader
Jessica McCarty

Technical Editors
Luke Crow
Sean Walberg
Brian Bork
William Rybczynski

Publishing Coordinator
Pamalee Nelson

Multimedia Developer
Dan Scherf

Interior Designer
Gary Adair

Cover Designer
Gary Adair

Page Layout
Bronkella Publishing

CERTIFICATION

Que Certification • 800 East 96th Street • Indianapolis, Indiana 46240

A Note from Series Editor Ed Tittel

You know better than to trust your certification preparation to just anybody. That's why you, and more than 2 million others, have purchased an Exam Cram book. As Series Editor for the new and improved Exam Cram 2 Series, I have worked with the staff at Que Certification to ensure you won't be disappointed. That's why we've taken the world's best-selling certification product—a two-time finalist for "Best Study Guide" in CertCities' reader polls—and made it even better.

As a two-time finalist for the "Favorite Study Guide Author" award as selected by CertCities readers, I know the value of good books. You'll be impressed with Que Certification's stringent review process, which ensures the books are high quality, relevant, and technically accurate. Rest assured that several industry experts have reviewed this material, helping us deliver an excellent solution to your exam preparation needs.

Exam Cram 2 books also feature a preview edition of MeasureUp's innovative, full-featured test engine, which is trusted by certification students throughout the world.

As a 20-year-plus veteran of the computing industry and the original creator and editor of the Exam Cram Series, I've brought my IT experience to bear on these books. During my tenure at Novell from 1989 to 1994, I worked with and around its excellent education and certification department. At Novell, I witnessed the growth and development of the first really big, successful IT certification program—one that was to shape the industry forever afterward. This experience helped push my writing and teaching activities heavily in the certification direction. Since then, I've worked on nearly 100 certification related books, and I write about certification topics for numerous Web sites and for *Certification* magazine.

In 1996, while studying for various MCP exams, I became frustrated with the huge, unwieldy study guides that were the only preparation tools available. As an experienced IT professional and former instructor, I wanted "nothing but the facts" necessary to prepare for the exams. From this impetus, Exam Cram emerged: short, focused books that explain exam topics, detail exam skills and activities, and get IT professionals ready to take and pass their exams.

In 1997 when Exam Cram debuted, it quickly became the best-selling computer book series since "...*For Dummies*," and the best-selling certification book series ever. By maintaining an intense focus on subject matter, tracking errata and updates quickly, and following the certification market closely, Exam Cram established the dominant position in cert prep books.

You will not be disappointed in your decision to purchase this book. If you are, please contact me at etittel@jump.net. All suggestions, ideas, input, or constructive criticism are welcome!

Ed Tittel

Taking You to the Solaris 9 System Administrator Finish Line!

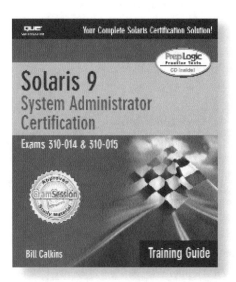

Many thanks to all the trainers and training folks I have ever been involved with, particularly Andres, Ken, Arnold, and the boys and girls who over the years understood that it was all about the attendee and whatever you had to do to make it real for them—you know who you are. "We few, we happy few, we band of brothers..."

&

About the Author

Ross Brunson is currently the director of Linux/Unix education for The Training Camp and an LPI-US (Linux Professional Institute) board member. He began his IT career in the U.S. Army in the 1980s working with battlefield simulation systems running on Unix platforms.

Prior to joining The Training Camp, Ross authored several books about Unix/Linux integration with Windows, including *The Linux and Windows 2000 Integration Toolkit*.

Ross began his formal training and consulting career with Learning Tree International as a courseware technical editor and was his area's second-highest scoring instructor.

After a number of years conducting TCP/IP, Unix, Linux, and networking courses for Learning Tree, Mastering Computers of Scottsdale, and other companies, he took a courseware and development position at Computer Associates developing and delivering Windows 2000 and Linux courses for many U.S. and international companies.

Ross then took a position with Thomson Learning's Sair Linux certification and courseware division as the director of courseware development and instruction. He built an excellent instructor force spanning 13 countries and 110 instructors in little over a year, delivering many T3 (trainer preparation courses) to current and prospective instructors in the United States and overseas.

He lives in Coeur d'Alene, Idaho, with his wife, baby daughter, and dogs and enjoys canoeing, fishing, and hiking in between teaching and consulting gigs.

About the Technical Editors

Sean Walberg is a network engineer and Linux administrator. He discovered Unix while at university in 1994 and began working at an ISP as an administrator soon after. After graduating with a degree in computer engineering, he spent some time as a Unix developer before moving into networking. Currently, Sean makes extensive use of Linux for network management and security tasks. Sean lives in Winnipeg, Canada, with his wife, two sons, and two cats.

Luke Crowe has been in the IT industry for 10 years, working with a wide range of systems from CAD/CAE systems to data center servers with operating systems from SGi and Microsoft. He joined the Linux revolution when he started working as a technical manager at OCF, a company that designs, builds, and installs Linux Beowulf clusters on various architectures for educational and corporate environments. Currently, he divides his time between working for The Training Camp in the U.K., where he teaches LPIC and CompTIA Linux+ certification courses, and his own business, which includes IT consultancy and support services for small businesses.

Acknowledgments

. . . .

I'd like to acknowledge the wonderful support of my wife Monique and daughter Rose, especially when Dad was holed up with vi, sed, and the kernel for days at a time.

Gratitude to LPI and its wonderful crew for their support and tolerance; your vision made this possible in the first place.

Many thanks to Carol Ackerman for believing in this book and for her support of the free/open-source community.

Contents at a Glance

Table of Contents

Chapter 9
Software Installation **217**

We Want to Hear from You!

As the reader of this book, *you* are our most important critic and commentator. We value your opinion and want to know what we're doing right, what we could do better, what areas you'd like to see us publish in, and any other words of wisdom you're willing to pass our way.

As an executive editor for Que Publishing, I welcome your comments. You can email or write me directly to let me know what you did or didn't like about this book—as well as what we can do to make our books better.

Please note that I cannot help you with technical problems related to the topic of this book. We do have a User Services group, however, where I will forward specific technical questions related to the book.

When you write, please be sure to include this book's title and author as well as your name, email address, and phone number. I will carefully review your comments and share them with the author and editors who worked on the book.

Email: feedback@quepublishing.com

Mail: Jeff Riley
         Executive Editor
         Que Publishing
         800 East 96th Street
         Indianapolis, IN 46240 USA

For information about the Exam Cram 2 series, visit www.examcram2.com. Type the ISBN (excluding hyphens) or the title of a book in the Search field to find the page you're looking for.

A note from the author: If you have any questions or comments you want to direct to me, you can email me at ross@brunson.org. I welcome your feedback—it's all about you and your journey to certification and its benefits.

Introduction

Terms you'll need to understand:

✓ Radio button
✓ Check box
✓ Careful reading
✓ Exhibits
✓ Multiple-choice question formats
✓ Simulation questions
✓ Process of elimination

Techniques you'll need to master:

✓ Preparing to take a certification exam
✓ Researching and understanding topics
✓ Recognizing areas that will be tested
✓ Marking and reviewing questions
✓ Handling fill-in-the-blank questions
✓ Finding answers online and in man pages

Plenty of people have taken the Linux Professional Institute Certification (LPIC) exams, but only approximately 40% make it through a given LPIC exam the first time. That's a pretty slim margin, but it helps keep the certification worthy and respected in the exam industry.

Realistically, people prepare for the LPIC exams in several ways—some advisable, others not quite cheating but not recommended. The following list is a (recommended) set of things you should do to prepare for this set of exams (and others):

- Study the objectives, thoroughly.

- Understand every command listed in the objectives.

- Try everything mentioned several times on a live machine.

- Read every study guide in existence.

- Buy books like this one and read them thoroughly.

- Search the Web to find answers (known hereafter as *Googling*).

- Take a class, do all the labs, and use it as a springboard to learn more.

- Acquire your own Linux guru to bug incessantly with questions about how things work.

- Join your local Linux user group (LUG) and geek out regularly, or start the local LUG if it doesn't already exist.

- Read every study and article (TCO, implementation, and so on) published on the topic.

- Regularly learn a new topic and focus on measurable steps.

Try to avoid the following practices:

- Surfing the "braindump" sites; most of the answers are fallacious at best, and fantasy and criminally wrong at worst.

- Using test-preparation guides that purport to "guarantee" your passing. Several vendors offer what (at least to this author) look like *exact* copies of the questions. This is illegal.

- Using study-buddy situations in which a group of candidates serially take the exam, slowly building a pool of questions for later examinees.

Taking an exam can be a very nerve-wracking experience. When I do boot-camps, part of the introductory briefing is to take everyone to the testing center and let them see the "torture chamber" so it's not unknown when exam time comes.

The LPIC exams are one of the most difficult in the industry, and I'm not just telling you this to make you uncomfortable, either. The usual Microsoft or Cisco question can be quite wordy, with a lot of fluff and distracters—not the LPIC. LPIC questions are rarely more than a couple of sentences and are usually as blunt as a two-by-four to the knees.

Rather than worry about the environment and how the testing center will be, concentrate on the exam questions, the types and strategies, and how you'll prepare for the exam.

Good preparation makes the rest of the experience take a back seat. You're there to take the exam, not worry about whether they'll give you enough paper or pens.

This chapter—besides explaining the LPIC exam environment and software—describes some proven exam-taking strategies you should be able to use to your advantage.

The Exam Situation

When you arrive at the testing center to take your exam, you need to sign in with an exam proctor. He will ask you to show two forms of identification, one of which must be a photo ID, preferably government issued. After you have signed in, you are asked to deposit any books, bags, or other items you brought with you. Then you are escorted into the closed room that houses the exam seats.

All exams are completely closed book, open mind. In fact, you typically aren't permitted to take anything with you into the testing area.

Some centers are a little more relaxed than others; shop around to find one that suits you. Some gladly give you extra paper or laminated sheets, but others might seem stingy or suspicious of your motives. Try to understand what might have caused those behaviors—for instance, the center might have been plagued by cheaters and questionable examinees in the past.

You will be furnished with a variety of possible note-taking materials, all of which must be surrendered upon exiting the exam room. Possible scenarios include: a pen or pencil and blank sheets of paper; a notepad of paper and writing implements; and a laminated sheet of paper and an erasable felt-tip pen.

Here's the key to using the writing materials you have been given: Write down anything you want to remember for the exam, starting from the moment they sign you in. Take a few minutes before you hit the exam start button to write down all the items you memorized and think you'll need.

They (the mythical *they*) say that humans only use 10% of their brain's capacity, with no one quite sure what the other 90% is taken up with. I can tell you something that no scientist will agree with, but I know to be true for techies: It's all operating system overhead! We use it for motor skills, surfing games, and finding the nearest Starbucks. You have only a limited amount of mental RAM, so use it wisely and commit things you know you'll need to paper as a way to free up that 10% of your brain so it can all be used for the purpose of taking the exam.

You are allowed to write down any information you want on your writing tablet or whatever. You should memorize as much of the material that appears on the Cram Sheet (inside the front cover of this book) as you can, so you can write that information on the blank sheets as soon as you are seated in front of the computer.

Typically, Exam 101 takers need to remember the serial and parallel port information and Exam 102 takers always try to memorize the **man** page sections.

Typically, the room will be furnished with anywhere from 2 to 30 computer stations, each of which should be separated from the others by dividers designed to keep you from seeing what is happening on someone else's computer.

Most test rooms feature a wall with a large picture window. This permits the exam proctor to monitor the room, prevent exam takers from talking to one another, and observe anything out of the ordinary that might go on. The exam proctor will have preloaded the appropriate LPIC certification exams—for this book, either the 117-101 RPM or 117101 DPKG, and the 117-102. You're permitted to start as soon as you sit down in front of the computer. Ensure that you agree to the testing agreement, as refusing to do so will void your exam.

The Actual Exams

The LPIC exams are all 90 minutes in length. A reminder of this time amount is the ticking clock on the screen that lets you know how much time is left before they kick you out of the exam, or you're done.

Both of the major testing vendors use similarly functioning systems, so anywhere you take the LPIC exams will have the same methodology of exam generation. LPIC exams are randomly generated at the time of registration and then downloaded to the testing center on the day of testing. Each and every exam is randomly generated, with the questions doled out based on the weights and section. *Weights* on an exam topic denote how many questions are likely to appear on the exam, not how much is scored for each question.

If, by chance, two people register at the same time, they might get vaguely similar exams, but it should be noted that even between the two exams the order of the questions and the order of the answers for the questions will be randomized. It's extremely unlikely that two examinees will get an identical exam or get the same exam mix and questions for a retake. Don't bother trying to figure out what will appear the next time; be sure to look at the second sheet of your test results and study further for the sections you didn't do well on.

Taking the exam is quite an adventure, and it involves real thinking as well as skill and time management. This book shows you what to expect and how to deal with the potential problems, puzzles, and predicaments you are likely to encounter.

One of the strategies that attendees seem to have great success with is skipping and marking questions they don't know or that will take a lot of time to answer. This requires a lot of discipline, contrary to conventional wisdom. I've heard of people getting the answers to previous questions from reading and answering later ones—several people who experienced mental vaporlock had their memories jogged by a question and were able to navigate back and change a wrong answer.

This isn't cheating, no matter what a purist might say. It's intelligent use of the interface and your own skills; the testing environment is stressful enough without having your brain lock up on you. Additional stressors include a boss who said, "Don't come back without your certification," and knowing that everyone else is waiting for you to emerge victorious before they take the exam! Nothing like being the point man or woman....

The next-to-last screen presented at the end of the exam is the Review screen. This is where you can see whether you've missed a question (denoted by a red mark next to it), left any multiple-choice questions with too few answers (same red mark), or marked any questions for review (black check/X next to it). It's essential that you revisit the incomplete or marked questions before you click the End Exam button because it's too late then!

 A certain number of attendees will try to outguess the interface and leave the choose-all type of questions with a single or no answer. This does not generate a red mark next to the question, and you might well forget the question, getting it completely wrong.

The exam ends when you click the End Exam button. The system will print out two sheets; the section scores will be on the second sheet. Table I.1 shows a sample for the 101 RPM Exam.

Table I.1 Sample for 101 RPM Exam		
Section	Items	Score
Hardware and Architecture	7	71%
Linux Installation and Package Mgmt.	14	66%
GNU and Unix Commands	20	100%
Device, File Systems, and FHS	16	75%
X Window System	8	50%

You're not informed of your score until you get out of the exam room or to the printer! This is stressful and can give your evil-minded instructor a chance to mess with you! We've never teased our attendees about failing the exam, such as giving them a long face and a conciliatory pat on the back and then springing the winning score on them! Never, ahem, cough.

Exam Scoring

The exams are scored on a scale from 200 to 890. Very few people I know have scored above a 700, and 890 (perfect) scores are almost unknown, with that level of intelligence and retention seemingly being incompatible with corporeal existence. Seriously, many a darned good sysadmin has scored in the mid 600s, even if they did fantastic on the exam prep and in class. A pass is a pass. Take it and drive on to higher heights, I always tell them.

If you get the chance to take an exam over again(!?), be certain to keep the detailed percentage report that makes up page 2 of your printout, shown in Table I.1. This can be a valuable resource in studying for the next time.

If you need to retake an exam, you have to schedule a new test with Prometric or VUE and pay for another exam. (The amount of the retake exam is determined by what you paid for the original exam.) Keep in mind that, because the questions come from a pool, you will receive different questions the second time around.

LPI Retake Policy

LPI has recently instituted a retake policy, summarized herein:

If you fail a given exam the first time, a full week must pass before it can be scheduled again.

If you fail that same exam a second time, 90 days must pass before it can be scheduled again. Subsequent failures of the same exam must wait an additional 90 days.

LPIC Exam Question Types

In this section, you learn more about how LPIC test questions look and how they must be answered. Several types will be unfamiliar to those used to Microsoft and Cisco exams; these are covered in detail along with the usual question types.

The LPIC exams are the most like the Sun Solaris exams; they feature the same question types and similar styles of answers. LPIC questions are short, blunt, and easy to answer if you've done the action or item being tested. I have seen grown-ups cry in frustration, particularly if the requisite labs and studying haven't been performed.

Multiple-choice Questions

Multiple-choice questions are single-answer, as opposed to a Choose Two or Choose All That Apply question. LPIs are much the same as any other vendor's multiple-choice questions. The main difference consists of long command strings and a lot of options to parse through. There is only one answer, and this question type is the easiest to get through.

 An important tip for getting through multiple-choice questions is to read all the possible answers and discard any that are silly, obscure, or outright wrong. It's possible to not know the answer and get the question right through the process of elimination. This is a main reason the LPIC exams have so many of the other question types—they don't want us to guess our way into a certification!

Sample Multiple-choice Question

Which of the following commands shows the full listing of normal files in the current directory?

- ○ A. `ls -l`
- ○ B. `ls -1`
- ○ C. `du .`
- ○ D. `df -h`

Answer A is correct because the `ls` command and `stat` are the only utilities to show a full set of inode information about a file. Answer B is incorrect because the `1` option shows files in a single column and shows just the filenames. Answer C is incorrect because the `du` command doesn't show the full file information. Answer D is incorrect because the `df` command shows only the free/used disk space.

Choose Two/Three Questions

These are a little tougher than the multiple-choice questions because there are usually five or six answers and the question has you choose two or three answers from the available choices. Not selecting enough of the answers marks this question in the review screen as incomplete. If the exam wants you to choose all the correct answers from the list, the question states, "Choose all that apply."

Sample Choose Two/Three Question

Which steps must be performed before a newly installed hard drive is available for use by a normal user account? (Choose three.)

- ❑ A. `mkfs`
- ❑ B. `mount`
- ❑ C. `scsi_info`
- ❑ D. `dd`
- ❑ E. `fdisk`

Answers A, B, and E are correct. For a disk to be used by a standard or normal user, it must have at least one partition put on it (`fdisk`), have a file system of some type on that partition (`mkfs`), and be mounted by the root user or an entry in the `/etc/fstab` file that enables users to mount it without the root user's help. Answer C is incorrect because the `scsi_info` tool gathers information about SCSI devices but is not necessary to the process of a user gaining access to a disk. Answer D is incorrect because the `dd` command transfers one file format to another but has no effect on users accessing disks.

Choose All That Apply Questions

More difficult than the previous types, these actually make you think through all the possible answers because any of them might be right. LPI is the only vendor to my knowledge that uses these questions with only a single answer in some cases. The best strategy is to read all the answers and mark the correct ones. Use your note paper to keep track if it's confusing.

Sample Choose All That Apply Question

Which of the following commands creates a second file that is identical to the first? (Choose all that apply.)

- ❑ A. `cp file1 file2`
- ❑ B. `cat file1 ¦ file2`
- ❑ C. `cp < file1 > file2`
- ❑ D. `dd if=file1 of=file2`
- ❑ E. `cat file1 > file2`

Answers A, D, and E are correct. Using the `cp` command to copy one file to the other is normal; the difference between answers B and E is the incorrect use of the ¦ symbol to another file. It must be followed by a program, and the unusual usage of the `dd` command will work in this case. Answer B is incorrect because files may not be redirected via a pipe symbol (¦). Answer C is incorrect because the use of the < and > characters produces a syntax error.

Fill-in-the-Blank Questions

This question type has been nicknamed by attendees of my bootcamps as *TFQs* (those fine questions). Fill-in-the-blanks are the most difficult of the types because the possibility of guessing your way through one is about zero. There is just the question and a large, long text box to type your answer into. Typically, the exams contain 6–11 of these questions, by my estimation.

 Rule: If it works on the command line, it should be correct. Don't get tricky, though, and try to show off your skills—simpler is better. Always double-check exactly what the question wanted. Don't type in a long command string for a question that asks just for the command name.

Sample Fill-in-the-Blank Question

What command with necessary switches shows you the information page and a complete listing of files for a downloaded RPM package file named `pkg1.rpm`? (Type in the answer below.)

Answer `rpm -qpil pkg1.rpm` is correct. When typing in answers, be sure you use that standard order of options, such as the *q* character coming first in queries, followed by the rest of the options. Long options, such as `--nodeps`, are typically entered right after the short options. There are multiple correct versions of these answers. For example a `tar` command that uses the - before options is correct, and one that has the same options without a - is correct, too. LPI has a table in the exam software that contains all the right strings; your answer is matched against this table when you click Next.

Identify-the-Component Questions

Very few of these appear on the LPIC exams, but the odd one has been sighted by a few people, including the author. Essentially, you're shown a graphic and asked to identify the component or to select the correct component from a list of graphics shown as answers. Don't get excited about how Linux-like this type of question is; very few of them appear on the LPIC exams.

Sample Identify-the-Component Question

What is the component in the exhibit?

Figure 1 Exhibit for question.

❏ A. PCI card
❏ B. VLB card
❏ C. PCMCIA card
❏ D. Async I/O card

Answer C is correct. The card is obviously a PCMCIA card due to the size, style, and connector type on the left side. Answer A is incorrect because the exhibit shows a PCMCIA card. Answer B is incorrect because the exhibit shows a PCMCIA card. Answer D is incorrect because the phrase Async I/O Card is too ambiguous and doesn't mean anything.

 Watch out for questions about SCSI connectors or cable ends; counting the pins is the best option.

If you are not finished when 95% of the time has elapsed, use the last few minutes to guess your way through the remaining questions. Remember that guessing is potentially more valuable than not answering because blank answers are always wrong, but a guess can turn out to be right. If you don't have a clue about any of the remaining questions, pick answers at random or choose all As, Bs, and so on. The important thing is to submit an exam for scoring that has an answer for every question.

 Be extremely careful when changing previously answered questions! Many an attendee has missed the exam by 10 or 20 points, and when queried how many questions they weren't sure about and changed, the typical answer is "one or two." Don't change answers unless you are certain you have found a better answer in a later question—go with your gut.

Mastering the Inner Game

Knowledge breeds confidence, and confidence breeds success. If you study the information in this book carefully and review all the practice questions at the end of each chapter, you should become aware of those areas where you need additional learning and studying.

Follow up by reading some or all of the materials recommended in the "Need to Know More?" section at the end of each chapter. Don't hesitate to look for more resources online. Remember that the idea is to become familiar enough with the concepts and situations you find in the sample questions that you can reason your way through similar scenarios on a real exam. If you know the material, you have every right to be confident that you can pass the exam.

After you have worked your way through the book, take the sample tests in Chapters 20 and 22. This will provide a reality check and help you identify areas you need to study further. Answer keys to these exams can be found in Chapters 21 and 23.

Be sure you follow up and review materials related to the questions you miss on the sample test before scheduling a real exam. The key is to know the why and how. If you memorize the answers, you do yourself a great injustice and might not pass the exam. Only when you have covered all the ground and feel comfortable with the whole scope of the sample test should you take a real one.

Pre-exam tips include drinking at least a liter of water, eating potassium-rich foods such as bananas, and working silently on your "war face" in the mirror. Whatever works for you, stick with it; others will have their own little rituals that seemingly make a difference.

Attitude is very important when taking these exams. Indeed, all exams require a good attitude and a healthy dollop of confidence. It always amuses us when attendees seem to plan for failure, with the first questions being how much additional exams cost and what the retake policy is. Give yourself a chance to be a hero in this field; the knowledge will last you a long time and might help you in not only your present job, but any future ones you might seek.

Need to Know More?

A good source of information about the LPIC certification exams comes from the LPI site itself. The site is relatively simple and appealingly laid out.

Visit the following links to get more information on how to become LPIC certified:

 The LPIC Program at http://www.lpi.org/en/lpic.html

 Task List and Sample Questions for Exam 101 at http://www.lpi.org/en/tasks_101.html

 Detailed Objectives for Exam 101 at http://www.lpi.org/en/obj_101.html

 Task List and Sample Questions for Exam 102 at http://www.lpi.org/en/tasks_102.html

 Detailed Objectives for Exam 102 at http://www.lpi.org/en/obj_102.html

 IBM has a wonderful selection of study guides and sample exams, but it moves them around a lot on its Developerworks site. Check out the main page and search for *LPI* with the site search function at http://www.ibm.com/developerworks/linux/.

 Be very careful about where you get your exam prep materials. Almost all the resources except this book, LPI's site, and IBM's resources are outdated and cover only the previous version of the exams. There is a dearth of information about the current revision of these exams, which this book seeks to change.

Coping with Change on the Web

Sooner or later, all the information we have shared about Web-based resources mentioned throughout this book may develop link rot, get moved around, or be replaced by newer information. There is always a way to find what you want on the Web if you are willing to invest some time and energy.

Good Luck!

Self-Assessment

How ready are you to take and pass the LPI Level 1 exams? This self-assessment section is designed to give you an overview of who the ideal candidates for the LPIC Level 1 certification are and how to adjust your current skills and mindset to the correct level to make this certification valid and meaningful for you.

You will be taking two exams as a part of this certification: the 117-101 and 117-102. You actually have two choices for the first exam: 117-101 RPM and 117-101 DPKG. The two 101 exams are identical, except that the RPM exam covers the RPM package style, whereas the DPKG exam focuses on Debian's .deb packaging style.

There is only a single version of the 117-102 exam, but it's more than enough for most examinees. The 117-102 is about 15% more difficult than the 101 series. So if you barely pass the first exam, you'll have some studying and work to do before you should attempt the second exam.

LPI Exam Sections

It's good to know the breakdown of sections and questions for the exams before you take them. This information is not proprietary; it's just not something you'll see unless you take the exams and don't pass them the first time around.

The 117-101 RPM and DPKG exams are broken up into the five sections shown in the following listing, with the number of questions in each topic area shown on the right side:

Section	Number of Items
Hardware and Architecture	7
Linux Installation and Package Management	14
GNU and Unix Commands	20
Devices, File Systems, and FHS	16
X Window System	8

The 117-102 exam is broken up into the nine areas shown here, with the number of items on the right:

Section	Number of Items
Administrative Tasks	15
Networking Fundamentals	10
Network Services	18
Security	6
Kernel	5
Boot, Initialization, and Runlevels	4
Printing	3
Documentation	6
Shells, Scripting, Programming, and Compiling	6

As you can see, some of the more prolific topics have an interestingly smaller number of exam questions. For example, while you'll only get an average of 8 X Window System questions, because X is what it is, it'll seem like you're getting 20 or so. Study hardest on the topics you're weaker on and study the ones that will have more exam questions, and you'll do fine.

NOTE   I have been keeping track of the number of questions attendees have gotten in each topic area and haven't noticed any variation from what is shown here, but reportedly there is the possibility of the randomization producing an exam with one or two questions more or less. Again, I haven't seen this, but it could happen.

LPIC Level 1 Professionals in the Real World

I deal with so many types of skill sets in my classes and consulting that it's hard to say, "Oh look, *that* is an LPIC!" (We tend to mark ourselves as geeks and techies anyway, what with our belt-gadgets, modern eyewear, and t-shirts that have "rm -rf /win" instead of "I'm with Stupid" on them.) A typical class has about 15 people, approximately one third of which are the usual techie sysadmins and recovering MCSEs and the rest being programmers, VARs, and CIO/CTOs trying to figure out what their contractors are getting away with.

On the consulting front, I find more and more government and industry customers are beginning to use Linux for everything from files and printing to clustering. The majority of what I find myself doing in the consulting practice is helping plan out a roadmap around the potholes that will slow down an implementation or rollout, and using lots of Samba.

The Ideal LPIC Level 1 Candidate

The minimum requirement for being a candidate in the LPIC Level 1 world is a decent set of basic computer skills at the power user level. I've seen a number of normal users try to get their heads around this topic, with poor results. This is a hard certification to get if the thought of breathing server fan exhaust isn't one of your goals.

On the other hand, if you are gregarious, dig explaining hard things to rooms of skeptical people, and love the people aspects of your job, maybe you should become a trainer....

Here's a basic LPIC candidate checklist:

➤ Wants to be a system administrator

➤ Has some command-line skills

➤ Isn't unduly confused by details

➤ Has functional study skills

➤ Has a couple of machines to blow up or break repeatedly for learning

➤ Has good reading skills, with particularly good comprehension and decent speed

➤ Has time to try everything several to many times

Degrees and certificates of higher learning are fine and all, and might tip the scales for you in a close interview situation, but they aren't a requirement for being an LPIC. As a matter of fact, those who are intensely academic will actually have a slightly harder time with the plethora of options and possibilities presented to them during a class situation.

Most of all as an LPIC candidate, you should have a very strong sense of curiosity and a desire to learn and experience things that are not only fun, but also useful and that will keep you firmly employed!

The LPI-based requirements for the exams are somewhat formidable—a lot of files, commands, and options must be understood to gain this certification. Don't be put off by this because many have gone before you, and if I can do it, certainly the majority of you can do it. I see groups of attendees all the time emerge mostly victorious from the testing center.

Although getting this certification is not impossible, you should be keenly aware that it does take time to learn these skills and it can cost you a couple of retakes for the exams. But most of all, you need a commitment to learn Linux in a deep and broad sense that most won't experience unless they undertake a certification.

If you're willing to undergo the discipline of really learning this level of Linux, both the reading and the practice, you can take—and pass—the exams.

This book, and the Exam Prep Questions in each chapter in particular, are designed to make it as easy as possible for you to prepare for these exams, but nothing can take the place of your determined involvement.

After you've taken and passed the Level 1 exams, you might want to consider the LPIC Level 2. These are significantly more difficult than Level 1, so beware.

Putting Yourself to the Test

What follows next is a set of questions you should honestly answer to determine how ready you are to take these difficult exams.

Don't focus on what you think I might want or what the right or wrong answer might be; in some cases there is no right or wrong answer.

If you're not ready to take an exam, you'll just waste your money and time, so take care to meet all the objectives and have adequate knowledge of the items you see there. If there is anything on the objectives that you are not familiar with or can't hold a conversation with someone about, you're not ready.

Educational Background

1. Do you have any command-line skills? (Yes or No)

2. Do you have any Unix/Linux skills, or have you taken any classes on these topics? (Yes or No)

   If you have Unix/Linux skills already or have taken classes on the topic, that will be key to your success in this area because you already will understand how commands are constructed and what options and arguments are. If you don't have any Unix/Linux skills already or haven't taken any of these classes, you might want to consider an online learning or classroom-based course to get you up to speed in a hurry. I recommend boot camps for those who have the budget and are short on time, particularly those who can't be out of the office for multiple weeks just to get a certification.

3. Do you have any networking skills? (Yes or No)

Linux networking is similar to Unix networking, and even Windows networking skills will serve you well. It's mainly a matter of the names and the tools that differ between the platforms. One thing I do in class is build a Windows/Linux map that attendees quickly start to add to—it really seems to help!

4. Have you done any reading or studying of Linux/Unix concepts or practices? (Yes or No)

If you have, please continue to use those resources in conjunction with this exam preparation book. Much as I'd like to write a book that includes everything you need, there are constraints of space and time. If you haven't read about or studied Linux/Unix yet, look closely at the Need to Know More? file on the CD. I've taken great care to put my favorite and most succinct resources in this file.

Hands-On Experience

It's absolutely and unequivocally a requirement that you have hands-on experience with Linux and each of the topic areas that appear on the objectives and in this book. Reread the previous sentence again, will you? I have had a number of attendees dash themselves against this requirement. I always tell them up front how nearly impossible it is to pass these exams if you can't do what is being tested, but some have to learn the hard way.

If I convince you of nothing else, you should be fully aware by the end of this book that the easiest way to get your certification is to know these topics, both in your head and with your hands.

5. Have you installed and settled in to using a distribution (or two or three) of Linux? (Yes or No)

If yes, make sure that you have used at least Red Hat, Debian (I recommend using Knoppix, which is a Live-on-CD bootable distro of Debian), and Novell SuSE.

If you haven't installed and used on a daily basis any or all of these distributions, go to http://www.linuxiso.org and start downloading, or buy a copy of the products and install them. I frequently use VMWare because it's much easier to run different distributions inside VMWare or even Virtual PC.

You can also use Colinux, which can be found at **http://www.colinux.org**. It's an Open Source (GPL) program much like VMWare or Virtual PC and works quite well.

Testing Your Exam-Readiness

Some will wait until they have studied a long time to take practice exams, which is fine, but they're missing out on the continuous feedback that taking the chapter sample questions will give them. To get completely traumatized, before you read any of the load-bearing chapters about the exams, take the 101 and 102 sample exams just to see how you do.

I recommend keeping a couple of distributions running nearby, this book, and a Web browser for research—oh, and a cup of some caffeinated beverage to keep you sharp. Spend at least a couple of hours a day studying and trying the things you read. And don't slack off; it's easy to forget and not study for a while.

I empathize with my fellow parents particularly; it's hard to get time alone to do this. But think of how much better a life you can provide for your little darlings if you get your certification and get a better job or a raise. It makes it all seem more than worthwhile, doesn't it?

And as I always recommend, consider taking a class if you've tackled self-study materials, taken the test, and failed anyway. I doubt that you will take these exams more than once or twice at the most after the preparation I have gathered between these covers. I've given more than 300 classes and seminars, many of them on Linux/Unix, and done more LPI-related classes than anyone else I can find in the training world. You're getting the distilled essence of all that in this book. You could say that I wrote the book that I wanted to use in my classes and now it's available for everyone else to use.

If you want to know more about my classes, email me at **ross@brunson.org**. (I answer in a timely fashion.) Also feel free to check out the Linux trainers site at **http://www.linuxtrainers.biz**, my Web site, and the Unix/Linux Training Blog that I update fairly frequently.

Assessing Your Readiness for Exams 117-101 and 117-102

More than 330 exam questions appear in this book's chapters and the exams at the end of the book. Those questions represent the distilled experience of more than 1,000 exams' worth of preparation and working with attendees afterward to get their knowledge tuned up.

Various exam prep engines and sites area available; some are decent and others are outright rips of the exams.

There are a number of choices for exam preparation questions on the Web. Some of the questions seem to have been taken from other copyrighted sources, and I have licensed some to a third party years ago that were picked up by another vendor. This is legal, but I recommend that you work your way through the many questions in the book and on the CD-ROM as your main study guide. I'm more familiar with the exam's questions than the other vendors by far.

Onward, Through the Fog!

Grab this book, fire up the Linux boxes, crank up the `man` pages, open a Web browser, and get down to business! This is a fascinating topic and we've worked very hard to put all this together in a single place for you. Enjoy it and let me know what you think, like, and don't like.

—Ross

PART I

LPIC Exam 101

Linux Installation

Terms you'll need to understand:

✓ Distribution
✓ Kernel
✓ GNU/GPL
✓ Multitasking
✓ GRUB
✓ LILO
✓ MBR

Techniques you'll need to master:

✓ Installing a Linux distribution
✓ Determining and fixing device conflicts
✓ Viewing conflicts via the **/proc** file system
✓ Partitioning disks for installation
✓ Using the installation consoles
✓ Creating installation and boot disks
✓ Viewing boot messages

Linux Distributions

A distribution or packaging is usually performed by the group or company that puts out a product, such as The Debian Project, Red Hat, SuSE, and many others. If the company or organization wants to make it easy for people to get and use the distribution, it's normally made available via ISO files, a method of making a large binary file out of a CD-ROM. These ISO files are found on the Linux distribution vendor's site, on mirrors of that site, and in stores if they make a box product that is sold at retail outlets.

A Linux distribution is the packaging together of a Linux Kernel, the needed supporting GNU and other utilities, an installation program plus customization with Logos, and GUI management tools.

You can expect to be asked questions that test your knowledge of what a distribution consists of.

LPI Certification and Distributions

How does LPI treat the plethora of distributions? LPI is truly vendor-neutral and distribution-agnostic, but it does recognize that currently Red Hat and Debian are the dominant strains.

For the majority of the objectives and exam questions, the focus is on Linux, not distributions. If a feature is one way in Red Hat and another in Debian, you're expected to know both.

This is true except in the case of package management. LPI has split the first exam (101) into two identical exams, one focusing on the RPM (Red Hat Package Manager) style and the other on DPKG (Debian Package Management). The exam-taker must specify at scheduling which version he wants to use for the 101 Exam.

If a specific distribution is mentioned in the exam, it's mostly in the areas of packages, installation options, partitioning tools, file or directory placement for configuration files, and X configuration tools.

Which Version of Red Hat and Debian to Use?

The most direct mapping to the exams seems to be the Red Hat 7.3/Red Hat AS 2.1 tree and Debian's 3.0 or Woody/Knoppix 3.x. In the future, the plan is to use the Filesystem Heirarchy Standard (FHS) and Linux Standards Base (LSB) as the guidelines, so it will be even more distribution-neutral than it is now.

Preparing Hardware for Installation

Unlike the Microsoft HCL, where hardware is tested by a lab to determine compliance, the Linux hardware compatibility lists that exist are either on a vendor-by-vendor basis or by interested groups or organizations. One of the most obvious places to look is the Linux Documentation Projects Hardware-HOWTO, located at http://en.tldp.org/HOWTO/Hardware-HOWTO/.

Additionally, you can check the following sites and vendors to see whether these distribution HCLs are current and have the systems in question listed:

➤ Red Hat's Hardware Compatibility Lists—http://hardware.redhat.com/hcl/

➤ SuSE's Linux Component Database—http://hardwaredb.suse.de/index.php?LANG=en_UK&PHPSESSID=5dac6af3ddc8b8c18919f3ca16fae260

➤ Mandrake's Hardware Database—http://www.mandrakelinux.com/en/hardware.php3

Problem Peripherals

Older IDE CD-ROMs can cause a lot of problems, although most work fine with current distributions. If they don't, just toss and replace them because they're relatively inexpensive.

8-bit NICs are PIO-bound (meaning they depend on the CPU way too much), and should be tossed, too. Despite that feeling of adrenaline you'll get from getting an old SMC IRQ 3 and IO 280 card to work, it's way too slow for today's networks.

The subject of Winmodems can cause a lot of discussion and controversy for Linux. These modems were developed to depend on the Windows OS for parts of the needed processing and software drivers. Fortunately, some bright people in the Linux community have taken this problem to heart and have produced a lot of drivers that run on Linux. These drivers can make certain Winmodems function at least to a certain level and often to full functionality. Take a look at http://www.linmodems.org, and please download and use the

ScanModem tool before posting to the list or asking questions. ScanModem can be found at http://linmodems.technion.ac.il/packages/scanModem.gz.

Resolving Conflicts

A conflict is when devices vie for resources, and the main areas in which conflicts can occur are

➤ **Direct memory access (DMA)**—When devices need access to memory sans the CPU.

➤ **Interrupt request (IRQ)**—Interrupts alert the CPU when a device needs an attention or action.

➤ **I/O**—Base addresses define the memory address used to communicate with the system for a particular resource.

Viewing Configuration Addresses

When planning an installation of Linux, the easiest way to find out what a particular machine has that might cause a conflict is to investigate another, similar machine.

The two methods of viewing the possible conflicts on a Linux system are

➤ Mining the /proc subsystem

➤ Using the ls tools

The /proc subdirectory under the root directory contains a hierarchy of directories and files that are a representation of the running kernel. Such subdirectories as /proc/ioports, /proc/dma, and /proc/interrupts can show the investigating user or sysadmin a lot of pertinent information about the system's configuration.

When errors or conflicts occur, the following commands are essential to resolving the conflicts that will be shown in the output. Viewing that information straight from the /proc directory is accomplished with the following commands:

```
cat /proc/interrupts
cat /proc/ioports
cat /proc/dma
cat /proc/usb
cat /proc/pci
```

The `ls*` commands show you what `/proc` can do but are much easier to run in scripts and control the output of.

The pertinent commands are

➤ `lsmod`—Shows the modules loaded, along with any dependencies for those modules

➤ `lspci`—Shows a lot of information about your PCI bus and devices

➤ `lsscsi`—Shows information about the SCSI devices on your system, if the system supports SCSI

➤ `lsdev`—Shows the devices that are recognized by your system

➤ `lsraid`—Displays the RAID devices on the system

➤ `lsusb`—Displays the USB information and devices for your system

Expect to get questions about the output of these programs, such as which one will show the most comprehensive information about your system's IO ports, DMA, and IRQs. The **lsdev** command shows the most definitive set of information in one stream of output.

Partitioning Disks

Partitioning differs with the system's role. A server uses more partitions than a user's workstation for a variety of reasons, mostly to separate data that changes often from that which is more static. A useful acronym to remember for real-world needs is PIBS:

➤ Performance

➤ Integrity

➤ Backup

➤ Security

Performance

Performance is increased if as many as feasible of the system's heavy usage directory trees are put on another disk. Good candidates for a move to another disk are the `/home` directory or the swap partition.

Integrity

The system's disk resources can be corrupted or damaged, and having all the files and data on a single partition can disable a system for hours if a complete fsck check is needed. Distancing risky portions such as an FTP upload folder from the traditional root of the system is a good idea. If an FTP user fills up the system partition with uploads, the system will crash.

Backup

The tar command is used to back up sets of files and directory trees. It can be used to back up an entire file system, but there is a more efficient tool for backing up partitions and complete disks: the dd command.

Security

When placing partitions and directory trees on the system, be aware that it's much easier to isolate or jail a risky portion of your server if it's contained on a separate partition or disk.

Understanding Partition Limitations

For the purpose of the installation section, understanding just which types of partitions are allowed is critical. Many people believe that the four primary partition rule is DOS- or Windows-oriented, but it's really a firmware limitation.

NOTE An excellent description of many disk-related topics is available at **http://www.storagereview.com**.

When the decision that defined the use of four primary partitions per PC disk was made, it was somewhat short-sighted, much like Bill Gates's famous quote, "Who would ever need more than 640K of RAM?" The size of disks kept increasing while the limitation of four primary partitions remained. After review, an extended partition was defined, and only one of those is allowed per disk. For example, if you needed the structure shown in Figure 1.1 for your system, you would need more than four partitions.

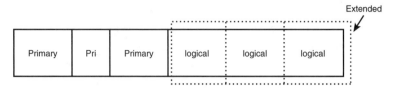

Figure 1.1   A sample partition structure.

An extended partition takes up a primary partition slot and acts like an empty container that, once defined, can contain from 0 to 16 logical partitions. Logical partitions behave just like primary partitions, with the exception that the boot files must exist on a primary partition.

One of the artifacts of having such a disk configuration and the resulting limitations is the 1024 cylinder boundary. Originally, disks were very small; an early limitation of 540MB is an example. The cylinders a disk contains are a static number, whereas the amount of MB and GB has grown drastically over the years. The 1,024th cylinder is a boundary that affects the booting of various operating systems, including Linux and Windows.

The reason we're discussing this is simple: Many sysadmins have installed Linux on a larger hard disk only to find that it won't boot properly. This has lead to the use of a smaller /boot partition that contain only the files needed to boot the OS on the much larger / partition. The recommended size for the /boot partition is usually 200MB, just in case you compile or upgrade your kernel and need some extra room.

Another thing you need to know about is the /home partition and why you should isolate users and their data from the rest of the system. You should do so because users can and will do terrible things to the server, such as backing an entire laptop drive up to their home directory on the server and filling up the server hard disk, causing at the very least a kernel panic and a system crash.

Partitioning Applications

Linux has several possible disk partitioning tools available, with nearly every distribution using fdisk. Debian usually includes cfdisk, and only Red Hat uses Disk Druid.

fdisk

The fdisk tool is line oriented and somewhat cryptic. When you issue commands to the fdisk tool, your choices and the output scroll upward over time and disappear from view, making it hard to see large sets of disk information and even to remember where you are in a complex configuration.

It's very important to remember that fdisk destructively alters the partition table, with the writing taking place after you press the w key and Enter. Up to that point, pressing the Q key and Enter helps you escape an fdisk configuration gone bad.

A typical fdisk session that creates a typical workstation disk layout is described in the following, step-by-step list. The partition layout consists of 200MB /boot, 750MB swap, and 6GB / (root). It then makes a single extended partition and a 1GB data partition in that extended partition.

Please note that output from the fdisk program is shown to support what the user will see. Anywhere you need to type or enter something, we've noted it:

1. Start the fdisk tool, specifying the disk to configure the following.

```
# fdisk /dev/hda
The number of cylinders for this disk is set to 2088.
... (text deleted)
   (e.g., DOS FDISK, OS/2 FDISK)
Command (m for help):
```

2. Type m for the menu:

```
Command action
   a   toggle a bootable flag
   b   edit bsd disklabel
   c   toggle the dos compatibility flag
   d   delete a partition
   l   list known partition types
   m   print this menu
   n   add a new partition
   o   create a new empty DOS partition table
   p   print the partition table
   q   quit without saving changes
   s   create a new empty Sun disklabel
   t   change a partition's system id
   u   change display/entry units
   v   verify the partition table
   w   write table to disk and exit
   x   extra functionality (experts only)
Command (m for help):
```

3. Issue the **p** command to see the partition table, and assume it's blank:

```
Command (m for help): p
Disk /dev/hda: 17.1 GB, 17179803648 bytes
255 heads, 63 sectors/track, 2088 cylinders
Units = cylinders of 16065 * 512 = 8225280 bytes
   Device Boot    Start       End    Blocks   Id  System
Command (m for help):
```

4. To create a 200MB /boot partition, issue the following commands:

```
n
p
1
(Press Enter)
+200MB
```

5. Check your new partition with the **p** command.

6. To create the 750MB swap partition, issue the following commands:

```
n
p
2
(Press Enter)
+750MB
```

7. To create the 6GB root partition, issue the following commands:

```
n
p
3
(Press Enter)
+6000MB
```

8. Enter the **p** command again to check the layout again:

```
Device Boot      Start      End    Blocks   Id  System
/dev/hda1            1       25    200781   83  Linux
/dev/hda2           26      117    738990   83  Linux
/dev/hda3          118      847   5863725   83  Linux
Command (m for help):
```

9. To create the extended partition, issue the following keystrokes:

```
n
e
4
(Press Enter)
(Press Enter)
```

10. To create the data logical partition, issue the following keystrokes:

```
n
(Press Enter)
+1024MB
```

11. Lastly, set the 750MB partition to the type **82**, which is used for Linux swap partitions with the following:

```
t
2
L
82
```

12. Check your partition layout with the **p** command:

```
Device Boot     Start     End   Blocks     Id  System
/dev/hda1           1      25   200781     83  Linux
/dev/hda2          26     117   738990     82  Linux swap
/dev/hda3         118     847   5863725    83  Linux
/dev/hda4         848    2088   9968332+    5  Extended
/dev/hda5         848     972   1004031    83  Linux
```

13. Write the changes to the disk with the **w** command and press Enter.

 NOTE

The system might require a reboot at this point because you've altered the drive on which the system's root (/) partition exists.

Also note how the first logical partition becomes **/dev/hda5** for IDE drives.

Disk Druid

Red Hat's Disk Druid partitioning tool comes in two modes or styles. The text-mode, or TUI, tool is present during a text-mode installation of Red Hat and is visually similar to the true GUI-mode tool. The X GUI Disk Druid tool is just that—it runs in X and is present in the GUI install of Red Hat. Disk Druid offers a one-stop shop of partitioning, formatting, and choosing the mount points for the various partitions. It also has some advanced features, such as software RAID, that can be configured with multiple disks.

cfdisk

The cfdisk menu options are context-sensitive, so when you've highlighted the free space, only the create, quit, and write options are selectable. When focused on an existing partition, the appropriate options, such as delete, type, and bootable, are available.

Red Hat Installation Console Options

Malfunctioning or apparently driverless peripherals are a common reason to have to use the shell during installation, as is the case when a machine boots the installation process from the CD-ROM and then refuses to recognize that exact same CD-ROM for the rest of the installation process! In this situation, and with certain peripherals in times past, getting to the installation console shell prompt and typing the command depmod -ae was necessary to have the machine's CD-ROM recognized.

Consoles can be invoked by using the key combinations indicated in Table 1.1.

Table 1.1 Console Key Combinations		
Console F-Key Number	**Function**	**Key Combination**
1	Text install	Ctrl+Alt+F1
2	Shell prompt	Ctrl+Alt+F2
3	Install program log	Ctrl+Alt+F3
4	System messages	Ctrl+Alt+F4
5	Miscellaneous other messages	Ctrl+Alt+F5
7	GUI (X11) install	Ctrl+Alt+F7

Creating Installation Disks

When the CD-ROM installation method isn't functioning, or the hardware cannot be detected by the installation program, a boot disk might be the only option. The exam requires you to know how to make a boot disk from both Red Hat and Debian distributions.

If you are on a Linux machine, it's relatively easy. You just insert CD 1 of your Red Hat distribution, mount the CD, and then run the following command to take the boot.img file from the /images directory on the CD-ROM. Then, you write it to the first floppy device. (Put a blank or scratch floppy in the drive first.) Here's the command:

```
dd if=/mnt/cdrom/images/boot.img of=/dev/fd0
```

If you're using a Win9x/Me machine or DOS, insert CD 1 in the CD-ROM and navigate to the \dosutils directory; then run the rewrite.exe command to start the process of writing the `\images\bootdisk.img` image to the A: drive, like so:

```
D:\dosutils\rawrite.exe d:\images\bootdisk.img
```

When you're using NT, Win2k, or XP, you need to get the rawwritewin.exe tool from the following link:

```
http://uranus.it.swin.edu.au/~jn/linux/rawwrite.htm
```

This application allows the writing of the boot disk images to the floppy. Windows NT and higher won't normally allow direct access to hardware from a DOS program such as rawrite.exe.

Boot Loaders

A Linux computer has the boot loader in one of two places: the master boot record (MBR) or the first sector of the Linux partition. Because many other operating systems use the same methodology—particularly Windows claiming the exact same MBR location as Linux—conflicts can occur.

Dual-booting Linux and Windows can be a challenge, but if you install them in the correct order and use LILO or GRUB to manage the boot loader environment, it's not difficult. I recommend installing the Windows product first because it's pickier about the MBR. Then, after the final reboot, install the Linux system in the prepared free space, allowing LILO or GRUB to notice and configure the Windows partition in the boot loader setup.

LILO—The Linux Loader

The LILO package consists of the `/sbin/lilo` command, the `/etc/lilo.conf` configuration file, help documentation, and boot loader files. The relationships between the `/sbin/lilo` command, its configuration file, and the MBR/First Sector targets are as follows:

1. The `/sbin/lilo` program is invoked.

2. The `/etc/lilo.conf` file is read and parsed.

3. The salient files mentioned in the file are located and errors are produced if they're not found.

4. The resulting binary image is written by default to the MBR.

5. The `/sbin/lilo` program exits.

The LILO configuration file, /etc/lilo.conf, is a two-part file. The first and top section is the global section, which contains settings that affect all the images and the behavior of the LILO environment. The images section is next; an image is simply a set of configuration parameters that make up a boot reference and options for a selection that appear in the LILO menu or prompt. Listing 1.1 shows a sample /etc/lilo.conf file.

Listing 1.1   A LILO Configuration File

```
prompt
timeout=50
default=win
boot=/dev/had
map=/boot/map
install=/boot/boot.b
message=/boot/message
lba32

image=/boot/vmlinuz-2.4.7-10
    label=lin
    initrd=/boot/initrd-2.4.7-10.img
    read-only
    root=/dev/hda5

other=/dev/hda1
    optional
    label=win
```

Several parameters bear mentioning from Listing 1.1, particularly for troubleshooting and the exam questions:

➤ timeout—This is in 1/10 of a second, not seconds.

➤ default—The value for the default parameter *must* match a label in an image, or the system cannot boot properly.

➤ lba32 versus linear—If using a larger hard disk, or if the /boot or / partitions are not below the 1,024th cylinder of the disk, the lba32 keyword is recommended. If using SCSI or certain types of other disks, the linear keyword is recommended.

➤ vga—The vga option doesn't always exist by default, and if it does, it might be set to vga=normal. If you're configuring a laptop or LCD monitor with Linux, using the vga=2 option makes the monitor X friendly and usable.

Entering Options at Boot

Because Red Hat uses a GUI LILO screen, you might need to press Ctrl+X to get to a LILO: or Boot: screen. The exam asks questions about how to enter boot-time options from the LILO or boot prompt, and answering them correctly demands having seen this change happen when you press Ctrl+X. So remember, LILO: and Boot: are the same for our purposes.

Entering options at boot time is necessary to troubleshoot or correct a problem that causes the machine to be unable to boot as configured. For example, if you have a system that, right after bootup, has a problem with the GUI, the system might hang for a long time and then become unusable, requiring a reboot. Typically, this system will have the default runlevel in the /etc/inittab set to 5 and will experience the same problem every reboot until fixed. To fix this, the system should be rebooted and at the LILO: or Boot: prompt, you should enter linux 1 to boot it into single user mode or linux 3 to boot it into text mode. Here's the syntax:

```
LILO: linux 1
```

Or

```
Boot: linux 3
```

If your system won't boot into runlevel 5 (the X GUI login screen), you should specify the runlevel as shown and then run the X configuration tools again.

Important LILO boot options include

➤ root=/dev/hda1—Sets the root device and is good for rescue

➤ mem=#—Sets the RAM amount to access older machines

➤ maxcpus=#—Is good for troubleshooting bad CPUs

Troubleshooting LILO

Another issue that causes some confusion is how LILO records the kernel location on disk for use in the MBR code, rather than the /directory/filename information. Only 512 bytes of space is available into which to cram all those options and parameters.

Therefore, if you move the files in the /boot directory or the directory itself, or upgrade the files (even with the same name), it's not the same location on disk and LILO throws an error.

Always, always rerun LILO after

➤ Updating kernel or other /boot files

➤ Changing the disk size

➤ Changing the partition size

➤ Moving the /boot directory

If you encounter errors, examine the /etc/lilo.conf file for mistakes. The /sbin/lilo command does some syntax and file-presence checking, but it can miss something.

Always rerun the /sbin/lilo command after you've made any changes to the /etc/lilo.conf file, and particularly after you've updated or created a new kernel, even if you name it the same name as the existing one.

 Overwriting your only existing kernel file with a new untested one is a quick way to stop all productive work and gain some troubleshooting experience. Watch for questions about this on the exam.

LILO Command Options

LPI likes to test the LILO command options, probably because you'll end up using them fairly often and troubleshooting is a very important part of the job for many sysadmins.

These options are used for troubleshooting with the /sbin/lilo command in the following format:

```
lilo -options
```

➤ -b—Sets the boot device (such as /dev/hdb).

➤ -c—Specifies a configuration file other than the default /etc/lilo.conf.

➤ -D—Boots a particular kernel (lilo -D label, where label is the corresponding name of a kernel's image label).

➤ -l—Makes the system use linear or 24-bit addresses when accessing the disks.

➤ -L—Makes the system use 32-bit or LBA32 addressing, allowing access to all disks that are larger than 1,024 cylinders.

➤ -q—Queries the /boot/map file for the names and locations of the kernels that can be booted. It can be combined with the -v verbose option to give more detailed information.

➤ -R—If followed by a discrete command sequence, that sequence is run at the next boot.

➤ -s—A copy of the MBR or first sector is saved when LILO is rerun. The saved contents are put in /boot/boot.NNNN, where NNNN depends on IDE or SCSI for its naming.

➤ -t—Tests the configuration only; doesn't write it to the MBR or first sector. Essentially, this is a dry run.

➤ -T—This is arguably the most useful option for LILO; its keyword values can be used to bring back information about the disk and video, among others.

➤ -T help—This shows help for the -T options, including

   ➤ -T geom—Lists the drive geometry (cylinders, heads, and sectors) for all attached drives

   ➤ -T video—Shows the graphic modes that LILO can use, which is important for laptops, specialty displays, and LCD monitors

➤ -u—Followed by the device name (/dev/hda), this option copies the saved boot sector (/boot/boot.NNNN) back to the MBR or first sector. If a device name is not specified, it takes the first bootable device.

LILO is a favorite topic for the first exam, with all sorts of options being tested. Be aware of how to run a command at the next boot, how to back up the MBR, and how to restore it from a boot disk.

LILO Error Codes

When a system boots, that occurs in two stages. The *first stage loader* is a single sector that is read from the BIOS or MBR. The system lets you know it's in the first stage by displaying the letter *L* on the screen, leading eventually to the word *LILO*. When the first stage is done, it prints the letter *I* to the screen and transfers control to the second stage loader.

The second stage loader is called from the first, and it can contain multiple sectors and more information. When the second stage loader receives control, it prints the second *L* in *LILO* to the screen, announcing that it's starting its process. When it has concluded its process, it prints the *O* in *LILO* to the screen, and then any parameters or labels desired can be entered.

If an error occurs, LILO prints a hexadecimal code for the error and attempts the process again. Some important error codes that you might see are shown here:

➤ 01—Invalid disk command

➤ 0A—Bad sector flag

➤ 0B—Bad track flag

➤ 20—Controller failure

➤ 40—Seek failure (BIOS)

➤ 40—Cylinder>1023 (LILO)

➤ 99—Invalid second stage index sector (LILO)

➤ 9A—No second stage loader signature (LILO)

➤ AA—Drive not ready

Grand Unified Boot Loader

Grand Unified Boot Loader (GRUB) is newer than LILO and offers some updated features, such as being able to edit the GRUB menu on-the-fly, rather than having to reparse a file and rewrite the MBR as LILO must.

GRUB's Configuration Files

The GRUB configuration file is the /boot/grub/grub.conf file This file contains several items, including some that are similar to LILO's configuration file.

Listing 1.2 shows a sample grub.conf file.

Listing 1.2   A GRUB Configuration File

```
#
# Sample boot menu configuration file
#
# By default, boot the first entry, if only one entry, it's # the default
default 0
# Boot automatically after 30 secs, remember seconds, not
# deciseconds like LILO!
timeout 30
# Fallback to the second entry.  If there isn't one, it will # just fail.
fallback 1
# To boot Linux
title  Linux
kernel (hd0,0)/vmlinuz root=/dev/hda1
# To boot Windows
title Windows
root (hd0,1)
makeactive
chainloader+1
```

How GRUB Treats Disks

GRUB isn't able to tell the difference between IDE and SCSI disks; it just reads the BIOS entries and goes on from there. To make things more predictable, it detects and uses IDE disks before SCSI disks.

The numbering of disks and partitions is a little different from other boot loaders. The following is a representation of the first hard disk and the first partition on that disk:

```
(hd0,0)
```

GRUB numbers its disks from 0, with 0–3 usually being the IDE disks. The partitions are numbered similarly, with 0–3 being the primary partitions and 4 always being the first logical partition on the disk.

The following is the designator for the first floppy on the systems:

```
(fd0)
```

Multiple partitions aren't possible on a floppy, so no partition designator is necessary.

Setting Up GRUB

Installation consists of running the `grub-install` script with parameters or running `grub` and setting up the boot loader while in GRUB.

Here's an example of installing to the first hard disk:

```
grub-install /dev/hda
```

This simply installs the boot loader into the MBR of the first hard disk.

Here's an example of installing to a /boot directory:

```
grub-install –root-directory=/boot  /dev/hda
```

This is necessary for a system that uses a small /boot partition to hold the boot files and to avoid the 1024-cylinder problem.

Another GRUB Install Option

You don't have to use the `grub-install` script—you can set up GRUB from the `grub>` prompt. In other words, you might be using a different boot loader and decide to install GRUB without knowing some details, such as the location of the GRUB stage loaders.

Example of a Native Install of GRUB

Installing GRUB can be done from within the grub command line itself, as we do here:

```
grub
grub> root (
```

If you're not sure which device holds the grub stage loaders, type **root** (and then press Tab. If presented with several disks and partitions, you can use the following command to find the stage1 loader (the rest of grub's files should be on that disk, too):

```
grub> find /boot/grub/stage1
```

This command finds the stage1 loader and displays which disk it's on. You can then use that to set the root device, like so:

```
grub> root (hd0,1)
grub> setup (hd0)
```

This command sets up GRUB in the MBR of the specified device. If you need to specify that GRUB be set up in the boot sector of a particular partition instead, use the following command string:

```
grub> setup (hd0,1)
grub> boot
```

Next time you boot the system, the GRUB boot menu should show up properly and boot the default without any action on your part.

Even if GRUB is not configured with images and just the grub> prompt shows up, you can easily boot the system, as shown in the next section.

Example of Booting Linux on Unconfigured GRUB

```
grub> root (hd0,1)
grub> kernel /boot/vmlinux-2.4.18-3
```

If necessary, modules can be loaded, such as for a device that is needed for loading the rest of the system. Here's how:

```
grub> module /boot/somemodule
grub> boot
```

Viewing Boot Messages

Viewing your boot messages either because of an observed error or just curiosity is easy using the dmesg command.

Most think that the dmesg command shows all the system boot messages or everything from the first message to right before the login prompt. Not so. The dmesg command shows only the messages that occur before the default runlevel is entered and the streams of messages that end in [OK] or [Failed] start to show up.

Your current distribution might not show the messages and instead display a graphical login and bootup screen. This can normally be disabled easily in the LILO or GRUB configuration files.

The bootup messages are stored in the /var/log/dmesg file and can be viewed in one long screen update by running the command. Or, to show the messages in a more friendly and usable format, you can pipe them to the more and less commands, such as here:

```
dmesg | more
dmesg | less
```

Exam Prep Questions

1. What is the default install mode for Red Hat?

   ○ A. Text
   ○ B. GUI
   ○ C. Headless
   ○ D. Remote

   Answer B is correct because Red Hat Linux defaults to an X11 GUI install. Answer A is incorrect because Text mode must be specified by entering `linux text`. Answer C is incorrect because Headless is not an option for installation. Answer D is incorrect because Remote is not an option for installation.

2. Which command shows currently loaded Kernel modules and their dependencies? (Choose all that apply.)

   ❑ A. `cat /proc/modules`
   ❑ B. `lsdev`
   ❑ C. `cat /proc/kernel/modules`
   ❑ D. `lsmod`
   ❑ E. `kmod --list`

   Answers A and D are correct because they display nearly identical information about the loaded modules and their dependencies. Answer B shows the system's devices, I/O ports, DMA, and IRQs but not modules, so it's incorrect. Answer C is incorrect because that directory and file path do not exist. Answer E is incorrect because there is no such option for the `kmod` daemon.

3. Which of the following LILO command options causes the `cmd1` command to be executed upon reboot of the machine?

   ❑ A. `lilo -b cmd1`
   ❑ B. `lilo -R cmd1`
   ❑ C. `lilo -v cmd1`
   ❑ D. `lilo < cmd1`

   Answer B is correct because the `R` option is designed to run a command upon the next system boot. Answer A is incorrect because the `b` option is for specifying the boot device. Answer C is incorrect because the `v` option specifies verbosity when the command is run. Answer D is incorrect because the `lilo` command doesn't accept input in this fashion.

4. Write in the following line the exact text to cause a default install of Linux to boot directly to `runlevel 2` after system initialization:

   _____

   The correct answer is `linux 2`. There are no alternative answers.

5. You need to create a boot disk on a running Linux system. Which command is used to perform this function?

   ○ A. `rawrite.exe`

   ○ B. `diskcopy`

   ○ C. `makeboot.bat`

   ○ D. `dd`

   Answer D is correct because the `dd` command can write disk images from the installation CD-ROM to a floppy. Answers A, B, and C are incorrect because they run on a DOS/Windows system.

6. During a Red Hat Linux installation, you decide to press Ctrl+Alt+F3. What do you then see?

   ○ A. Installation messages

   ○ B. GUI installation

   ○ C. Miscellaneous messages

   ○ D. Text installation

   Answer A is correct because installation messages are configured to be shown on tty3 or console 3 during an installation. Answer B is incorrect because the GUI installation console is 7. Answer C is incorrect because miscellaneous messages appear on console 5, not 3. Answer D is incorrect because the text installation occurs on console 1.

7. A user is having problems getting X running properly on a machine that has an LCD monitor. Which option in the `/etc/lilo.conf` file should be set to a hexadecimal value other than the default?

   ○ A. mode

   ○ B. vga

   ○ C. linear

   ○ D. boot

   Answer B is correct because laptops and LCD monitors have trouble with the `vga` setting set to normal; it should be set to `vga=2` or another suitable value. Answer A is incorrect because there is no such keyword for the `lilo.conf` file. Answer C is incorrect because the `linear` keyword has to do with supporting smaller disks or SCSI drives. Answer D is incorrect because there is no such keyword used in the `lilo.conf` file.

8. When using the GRUB boot loader, which of the answers describes the first extended partition on the first hard disk in a GRUB configuration?

   ○ A. `/dev/hda4`

   ○ B. `/dev/dsk/c0d0s3`

   ○ C. `(hd0,4)`

   ○ D. `c:8000`

Answer C is correct because GRUB uses a description of (`hdx,y`) where *x* is the disk and *y* is the partition. Answer A is incorrect because it describes a device file, not a GRUB object. Answer B is incorrect because it describes a Solaris Unix device. Answer D is incorrect because it is the debug location for low-level formatting an MFM/RLL disk.

9. Your system's `/etc/lilo.conf` file has been edited to have a value of **50** for the timeout option. What is the effect of this on the system, assuming the `lilo` command was used afterward to update the boot loader location?

   ○ A. The system waits 5 seconds to boot.
   ○ B. The system waits 50 seconds to boot.
   ○ C. The system won't boot; it's incorrect.
   ○ D. The system waits the hex value of 50 to boot.

   Answer A is correct because it will wait 5 seconds to boot the default entry. The timeout option's values are in 1/10ths of a second. Answer B is incorrect because the timeout option's values are in seconds. Answer C is incorrect because the system will boot the default entry. Answer D is incorrect because the timeout option uses 1/10ths of a second for its value.

10. You've upgraded your kernel and kept the name the same as the entry in the `/etc/lilo.conf` file. The system reports an error by putting just the characters **LI** on the screen and refusing to boot. Write in the following line the shortest command to fix this problem:

   _____

   The correct answer is lilo. There are no alternative answers.

Using the Linux Shell

. . . .

Terms you'll need to understand:

✓ Arguments
✓ Command completion
✓ Environment
✓ History
✓ Settings
✓ Shell
✓ Special characters
✓ Variables

Techniques you'll need to master:

✓ Identifying the Linux default shell
✓ Configuring **bash** settings
✓ Understanding login versus non-login shells
✓ Structuring proper commands
✓ Properly completing commands
✓ Using special characters
✓ Executing multiple commands
✓ Configuring prompts
✓ Setting **bash** options
✓ Controlling jobs
✓ Managing processes

Understanding Shells

A *shell* is a program designed to interpret the commands users type, parse for expansions and wildcards, and then produce instructions to the computer to accomplish those tasks.

Unless you change the defaults, the Linux shell is normally the bash shell. Of course, many other shells exist. A partial list is shown in Table 2.1.

Table 2.1 Common Shells						
	Ash	**bash**	**C-shell**	**PD-ksh**	**T-shell**	**Zsh**
Binary	ash	bash	csh	pdksh	tcsh	zsh
Job Control	N	Y	Y	Y	Y	Y
Aliases	N	Y	Y	Y	Y	Y
Functions	Y	Y	N	Y	N	Y
Redirection	Y	Y	Y	Y	Y	Y
History	N	Y	Y	Y	Y	Y
Editing	N	Y	N	Y	Y	Y
Completion	N	Y	Y	Y	Y	Y

Among other pieces of information, the user's default shell is specified in the /etc/passwd entry for that user. If the shell that is specified does not exist, the user gets the bash shell by default.

Special shells can be specified, such as /bin/false (which returns a nonzero error code, effectively blocking access by a user attempting to log in) or /etc/nologin (which is used to block logins for accounts and echo a message that login is denied). The /etc/nologin file should not normally exist on systems.

Global and User Settings

When users log in to the system, either from a remote shell session or via the console, their environment is made up of information from various ASCII text files that are executed or read to make up the user's environment. Different distributions handle these differently, but LPI focuses on the Red Hat and Debian methods, which are outlined next.

A Login Shell Session

A *login shell* is one that is executed when logging in to the system.

The /etc/profile is the global configuration file that affects all users' environments if they use the bash shell. It's sourced (read) every time a user performs a login shell. This file is a script and is executed right before the user's profile script.

The user's ~/.bash_profile script, if it exists, is the next script that's sourced. This file contains variables, code, and settings that directly affect that user's—and only that user's—environment. This script calls, or *sources*, the next script, which is ~/.bashrc.

The **~/.bash_profile** script can also be referred to or named as the **.bash_login** or **.profile** script. If all three exist, the **~/.bash_profile** is sourced alone; otherwise, if it doesn't exist, the **.bash_login** is sourced. Finally, if the first two are nonexistent, the *.profile* script is sourced. This functionality is used almost entirely by Bourne shell users upgrading to a **bash** system as a way to keep their settings in the same **.profile** file.

The ~/.bashrc file is called by the ~/.bash_profile or one of the profile's aliases and is used to set various shell settings and options, set the prompt, and define aliases and functions for command-line execution.

The last script sourced during a user's login session is the .bash_logout file. This file is used to issue the clear command, so text from any previous command is not left on the user's screen after he logs out.

Be careful on the exam because a lot of test-takers do not pick the **.bash_logout** file as part of the user's login session. It's definitely one of the more missed elements in the shell section.

An example of the user's login session might be the following:

1. The user logs in with a username and password.

2. The /etc/profile is sourced.

3. The user's ~/.bash_profile is sourced.

4. The user's ~/.bashrc is sourced from within the ~/.bash_profile.

5. The user conducts his business.

6. The user initiates a logout with the logout or exit command or by pressing Ctrl+D.

7. The user's .bash_logout script is sourced.

A Non-Login Shell Session

Non-login shell sessions are typically the root user using the su command to temporarily become another user or a sysadmin using su to become the root user without loading the entire environment of the root or other user.

When a user executes a non-login session, the only file sourced is the target account's ~/.bashrc file. (On Red Hat machines, the first action in the ~/.bashrc is to source the /etc/bashrc file if it exists.)

Upon exiting that account's login, no logout files or scripts are sourced, nor are the source account's scripts run again.

On a Red Hat machine of the 7.3/AS 2.1 vintage, if the target user's **.bashrc** file is not present, the **/etc/bashrc** file does not automatically get sourced. This can easily be tested if you rename the target user's **.bashrc** file, put a variable in the **/etc/bashrc**, log in as that user, and attempt to echo the variable. Doing this causes the variable to not be there.

Table 2.2 shows each file and when it's sourced.

Table 2.2 Order of Precedence for Configuration Files		
Global	/etc/profile	/etc/bashrc
Local	~/.bash_profile	
	~/.bashrc	
	~/.profile (optional)	
	~/.bash_login (optional)	
	~/.bash_logout	

Using the Command Line

Perhaps one of the most common and important tasks a sysadmin can perform and learn is to be competent with the command line or in the shell. Most of Linux demands good shell skills, and many server implementations don't even load or use the GUI (XFree86) tools, so neglecting the shell is almost criminal negligence.

LPI exams focus heavily on the commands, their options, and how they work together. If you're not familiar or competent with the command line, passing the exams (and being a good sysadmin, for that matter) is virtually impossible. Almost 20 questions of the exam center on the command line/shell and, of those, at least 3–4 will be fill-in-the-blanks, so this is a critical area.

Structuring Commands

For the most part, commands take the following form:

```
command options arguments
```

An example of using a command, an option, and then an argument is the following:

```
ls -R /etc/profiles
```

However, the positions of some of the options are flexible. Often, if you've typed a long command string, having to arrow or hotkey back to a certain position is just too much work, so some options can be tacked onto the end, like so:

```
ls /etc/profiles -R
```

The rule I recommend is to not tack any options that require an argument to the end of the command. Likewise, if the -f option specifies a file, you can't unhook the -f filename pairing and expect it to work.

Breaking Long Command Lines

When constructing a very long command string, it's often useful to break it up onscreen to make it easier to understand or more visually pleasing. The backslash (\) character is used to turn the Enter key into a line feed, not a carriage return. The backslash is for causing special characters to be taken literally.

The following example is confusing because it breaks when it wraps onscreen:

```
rpm -ql package1.1.1.rpm ¦ xargs file ¦ grep -i LSB ¦ nl ¦ pr ¦ tac
```

You could break it like the following and still produce the same results:

```
rpm -ql package-1.1.1.i386.rpm \
>¦ xargs file \
>¦ grep -i LSB \
>¦ nl \
>¦ pr \
>¦ tac
```

Command Completion

The nicest option for the command line by far is the ability to have a <TAB> complete either a portion of a directory/filename or the command if it's in the path.

For example, when you're trying to find out which commands in the /usr/bin directory start with the letters ls, you can use the following:

```
/usr/bin/ls <TAB>
lsattr      lsb_release  lsdev      lsdiff      lskat      lskatproc
➥lspgpot
```

It also works well when changing from one directory to the other. You just need to insert a recognizably unique portion of the next element and press the Tab key to have it complete the directory name:

```
cd /home/rb <TAB>
cd /home/rbrunson/Des <TAB>
cd /home/rbrunson/Desktop/Se <TAB>
cd /home/rbrunson/Desktop/Settings <Enter>
```

Using <TAB> immediately after the rb characters completes the /home/rbrunson directory. Adding a slash (/) to that and typing Des and then <TAB> completes the Desktop directory. Finally, adding /Se to the end and then <TAB> completes the full path for the target directory.

Special Characters in the Shell

There are numerous characters with special meaning to the shell, a smattering of which are defined in Table 2.3.

Table 2.3	Common Special Characters	
Character	**Purpose**	**Example**
~	Shorthand for the current user's home directory	**vi ~/.bashrc**
\	Ignore next character (esc character)	**echo $PRD is \$5**
/	Directory separator	**cd /home/rbrunson**
$	Variable, precedes any var	**echo $VAR**
?	Single-character wildcard	**ls *.t?t**
'	Single (absolute) quotation mark	**echo 'Cost: $100'**
`	Back tick, used for substitution	**echo `date`**
"	Double (soft) quotation marks	**echo "Cost: $VAR"**
*	None-to-many wildcard	**ls dar*.***

(continued)

Table 2.3 Common Special Characters *(continued)*		
Character	**Purpose**	**Example**
&	Background a job in shell	**mozilla &**
&&	If cmd1 exits 0 (Success), then do cmd2	**cmd1 && cmd2**
I	Pipe output to a program	**ls –l I pr**
II	If cmd1 exits 1 (Fails), then do cmd2	**cmd1 II cmd2**
;	Execute multiple commands	**cmd1 ; cmd2**
[]	Ranges of letters/numbers	**ls file[0-9]**
>	Redirect output to a file	**prog1 > file**
<	Redirect input to a program	**prog1 < file**

Controlling Command Execution

When commands are executed, an exit status is always returned. This exit status is not displayed unless a message is echoed to the standard output as a result of the exit status.

Possible Exit Statuses

The following executes a command that's guaranteed to work:

```
ls -a ~
.acrobat   .adobe   .bash_history   .bashrc   .dvipsrc
```

Next, the command is run again with a special character and a special variable to return the exit status:

```
ls -a ~ ; echo $?
.acrobat   .adobe   .bash_history   .bashrc   .dvipsrc
0
```

0 is the exit status of the command, as echoed back by the $? variable.

Now, a command that is fake or you know won't work is run (my favorite is farg). You must suffix it like the previous code with the $? variable; the exit status is something like 1 or 127— anything but 0:

```
farg ; echo $?
-bash: farg: command not found
127
```

To sum this up, either a program executes with no errors (successfully) and returns an exit status of 0 or it has a failure and returns an exit status that is a nonzero value, usually 1 or 127.

Executing Multiple Commands

There are several methods for executing multiple commands with a single Enter key. You can use special characters to just have it execute multiple commands or get fancy with if/then types of multiple-command execution.

Multiple Command Operators

When compiling software, scheduling backup jobs, or doing any other task that requires a particular program's exit status to be a particular value, you need to use these operators:

➤ ;—The semicolon causes all listed commands to be executed independently of each other.

The following example echoes back when a long compile is done:

```
make modules ; echo DO MAKE MODULES_INSTALL NEXT
```

The commands are independently executed and neither command fails or succeeds based on the other's exit status.

➤ &&—The double ampersand causes the second command to be executed if the first command has an exit status of 0 (success). If an exit status of nonzero (fails) is returned, the second command is not attempted.

If you're a sysadmin and want to have a second program do something if the first succeeds, you'd use the double ampersand like this:

```
longcompile && mail root -s "compile complete"
```

This set of commands starts a long compile; if it succeeds, you get an email stating compile complete in the subject line.

➤ ¦¦—The double pipe causes the second command to not be attempted if the first command has an exit status of 0 (success). If the first command has an exit status of nonzero (fails), the second command is attempted.

What if you want to have a second command let you know whether a particular process failed, without having to dig through the log files every morning? You could use the following:

```
tar -czvf /dev/st0 / ¦¦ mail root -s "doh, backup failed"
```

As you can probably guess, this command set attempts a full system backup to a SCSI tape device. Only if it fails does the root user get an email with the subject line indicating it failed.

The Readline Library

This library is used to provide text-editing on the bash command line, with the default set of keystrokes being borrowed from the emacs editor. The editor keymap setting and others can be changed by creating or editing the ~/.inputrc file.

Why is the default mode the emacs keymap set? If you look at both of the editors, vi has mostly single-letter commands that could be mistaken for text to be typed on the command line, whereas emacs has plenty of Ctrl-prefixed keystrokes, making for a more clear and concise set of commands to be used on a command line.

To change the default editor mode from emacs to vi, edit the ~/.inputrc file and add the line:

```
set editing-mode=vi
```

Other variables that can be used to make life easier on the command line are

➤ bell-style—Its values can be none ¦ audible ¦ *visible*.

➤ enable-keypad—Its values can be on ¦ off (it controls the keypad, arrows, and so on).

➤ mark-directories—Its values can be on ¦ off (if it's on, directories are suffixed with a / character, like using ls -F).

Command Substitution

In some instances, you need to take the output of a command and place it into a variable, usually for scripting purposes. Substituting the output of a command for the command itself is accomplished by bracketing the command with the back tick (`) or the unshifted tilde (~) key, like so:

```
`somecmd`
```

An example of this is inserting the output of the date command into a variable, possibly for use in a script, such as in this example:

```
export DATETIME=`date`
echo $DATETIME
Tue Jan 13 17:18:35 PST 2004
```

The export command is used to create a variable named DATETIME that is being populated by the `date` command. When this is executed, the back ticks around the date command cause the output for that command to be inserted into the DATETIME variable as a value.

Another facet of substituting commands is to enclose the command itself between parentheses and declare it as a variable, as in this example:

```
file $(grep -irl crud /usr/src/linux-2.4)
```

The main reason to use a command substitution like this is it allows you to nest commands within commands. Rather than having to use wildcards, you just use the right substitution.

bash's History Feature

The history command shows the stack of previously executed commands.

bash's history function depends on a variable called HISTFILE, normally set to the current user's .bash_history file (located in the user's home directory). When echoed, it returns the full path and name of the user's history file, like so:

```
echo $HISTFILE
/home/rbrunson/.bash_history
```

When a user logs in with either a login or interactive/non-login shell, the user's .bash_history file is opened. Normally, the history stack is *not* written to the .bash_history file until the user logs out of that shell session. In the case of a user logging in and then executing a bash subshell to the login shell, the subshell reads the parent shell's history file and writes to it upon exit. You can see this happen if you do the following steps:

1. Log in to a machine as a user.

2. Execute the following command:

   ```
   echo "this is the main shell history"
   ```

3. Then start a new shell:

   ```
   bash
   ```

4. In the new shell, execute the following:

   ```
   history
   ```

5. Execute these commands:

   ```
   echo "this is the subshell history"
   history
   ```

6. Exit the subshell with the following command:

   ```
   exit
   ```

7. View your history stack with the following:

```
history
```

8. View the last 10 lines of the existing .bash_history file with the following:

```
tail $HISTFILE
```

Important History Variables

Variables are used to control bash's use of history files. The following are common history variables that are initialized when the shell is started:

➤ HISTFILE—Defaults to ~/.bash_history and is set in the environment at login.

➤ HISTCMD—The history or index number of the current command, so echo $HISTCMD shows the number for that command.

➤ HISTCONTROL—If it's set to ignorespace, lines that end in a space are not added to the history file. If it's set to ignoredups, a line that duplicates the previous line is ignored regardless of the times it's repeated.

➤ HISTFILESIZE—The amount of lines used for the history stack when it's written to the history file. If the resulting stack is larger than the size indicated, it is truncated from the front of the file to match the correct size. The default is 500.

The fc Command

The fc command lists portions of the history stack or edits a line or range of lines in your favorite editor.

Just typing the fc command loads the editor and opens the last history line for editing. Try typing the fc command alone and then exiting the vi editor. Remember, fc executes any lines in the buffer upon exit of vi, possibly causing problems.

When you edit a line or range of lines with the **fc** command, anything remaining in the buffer (shown onscreen) in the editor is executed upon exit of the editor. The only way out of executing the commands is to delete all the buffer contents. This can be done in **vi** by first going to the top of the file by pressing the Esc key, followed by **1G** and then deleting the contents by pressing **dG**.

To view a range of commands with `fc -l`, such as the lines 78–85 in the history stack, you would type the following:

```
fc -l 78 85
```

To edit a range of commands with the `fc` command, you specify a command index number to start with, followed by a number to end with. For example, to edit lines 78–85 in the history stack, you would type the following:

```
fc 78 85
```

This loads the specified lines in the default editor, ready to be changed and executed when exiting the editor.

Environment Variables and Settings

The parent process of all processes on a Linux machine is the `init` process, with a process ID (PID) of 1. The `init` process executable is `/sbin/init`, and its environment is inherited by all child processes.

Hard-coded into `init` is a default set of paths that are the basis for all paths that are added by the environment files. This default or set of base paths is shown here:

```
/usr/local/sbin:/sbin:/bin:/usr/sbin:/usr/bin
```

Viewing the system's environment variables in a pure state is difficult because viewing them requires the user to log in and execute the same scripts he is viewing.

To view your environment, use `env` to show environment variables but not shell settings or shell-oriented variables.

The Path

The *path* is a colon-separated list of directories that are searched for executables. It's normally used to locate commands not in the current directory, although Linux does not run a command in the current directory unless that directory is in the path.

You can always refer to an executable in your current directory with one of two methods:

➤ **Absolute pathname**— `/home/ulogin/command`

➤ **Relative pathname**—; `./command`

So, if you see topics on the exam about how a user tried to execute a file in the current directory but couldn't, you know that the directory isn't in the path. The user should refer to the file with the full path from the root (/) or prefix the filename with ./ for the shortest method.

The path is usually set in the /etc/profile for all users or the ~/.bash_profile for an individual user. It's easy to alter the current path and add a directory without disrupting the previous path definitions. The following example shows how:

1. Edit /etc/profile or .bash_profile.

2. Navigate to the bottom of the file with the keystroke G.

3. Open a new line for editing with the keystroke o.

4. Add the following line, replacing *yournewpath* with the path that's correct for your system:

```
export PATH=$PATH:yournewpath
```

Getting $HOME

Some shortcuts and variables point to the user's home directory, and several utilities can take the user there quickly.

The HOME variable is read from the user's home directory entry in the /etc/passwd file. This variable's value is the full path to the current user's home directory:

```
cd $HOME - takes you to /home/username
```

Another method is using the cd command alone. This takes the user back home with the least number of keystrokes.

Finally, you can refer to the user's home directory with the tilde (~) character, so typing cd ~ gets the user home as well.

The exam will test your ability to understand how a user can get home and what certain characters do for you. One of the most missed and misunderstood areas is the use of the **~username** combination. Here's an example:

Your system has a user named **tarfoo**, and you logged in as the root user. There is a directory named **/root/tarfoo** on the system. Running the command **cd ~tarfoo** takes you to the **tarfoo** user's home directory, whereas running the command **cd ~/tarfoo** takes you to the **/root/tarfoo** directory.

Configuring Prompts

Four possible prompts exist on a Linux system, PS1 through PS4. A user usually sees only the PS1 (# or $) prompt, and if he commits a typo or an error in syntax, he might be confronted with the continuation or PS2 (>) prompt.

On a Red Hat machine, the setting for the PS1 prompt is defined in the /etc/bashrc file. In Debian it's defined in both the /etc/bashrc and the /etc/profile. It's good to have a backup, is all I can say!

The PS1 variable constitutes the user's prompt, which is shown every time the user logs in. The PS2 variable normally shows only when lines are continued, such as suffixing a command line with a backslash (\) or if a bracket, parentheses, or quote is left off a command. PS3 and PS4 are rarely used and might as well not exist for the exam's sake. Table 2.4 lists the special characters for the prompt.

Table 2.4	Special Characters for the Prompt
Code	**Will Display**
\a	An ASCII bell character (**07**).
\d	The date in weekday, month, day format (for example, **Tue May 26**).
\e	An ASCII escape character (**033**).
\h	The hostname up to the first ..
\H	The hostname.
\j	The number of jobs currently managed by the shell.
\l	The base name of the shell's terminal device name.
\n	New line.
\r	Carriage return.
\s	The name of the shell.
\t	The current time in 24-hour HH:MM:SS format.
\T	The current time in 12-hour HH:MM:SS format.
\@	The current time in 12-hour a.m./p.m. format.
\A	The current time in 24-hour HH:MM format.
\u	The username of the current user.
\v	The version of bash (for example, **2.00**).
\V	The release of bash, in the format version + patch level (for example, **2.00.0**).
\w	The current working directory.
\W	The base name of the current working directory.

(continued)

Table 2.4 Special Characters for the Prompt *(continued)*	
Code	**Will Display**
\!	The history number of this command.
\#	The command number of this command.
\$	If the effective UID is **0**, it's a **#**; otherwise, it's a **$**.
\nnn	The character corresponding to the octal number *nnn*.
\\	A backslash.
\[	Begin a sequence of nonprinting characters, which could be used to embed a terminal control sequence into the prompt.
\]	End a sequence of nonprinting characters.

Configuring the Prompt Step by Step

Let's change the prompts by editing the various files and causing the prompts to take effect:

1. As the root user, edit the /etc/bashrc file with the following:

```
vi /etc/bashrc
```

2. Press the G key to navigate to the end of the file.

3. Add another line at the bottom of the file by pressing the O key.

4. Enter the following prompt information in your new line:

```
PS1="[\u@\h  global  \W]\\$"
```

5. Press the Esc key to go back to command mode.

6. Save and exit the file by typing :**wq**.

7. Switch to terminal (tty2) number 2 by pressing Alt+F2.

8. Log in as a non-root user. The global test should appear in the prompt.

9. Switch back to tty1 by pressing Alt+F1; then run the following command to reread the /etc/bashrc configuration file for the root user:

```
. /etc/bashrc
```

The command starts with a period and then the full path to the /etc/bashrc file.

10. The settings should be refreshed. You could have also used the following command:

```
source /etc/bashrc
```

Because the /etc/bashrc file affects all users, any user who needs a different configuration must edit her local .bashrc file. Here's how you edit the user's configuration file and zero out the effects of the global configuration file:

1. Switch to the normal user tty by pressing Alt+F2. Then as a non-root user, edit the ~/.bashrc file with this:

   ```
   vi ~/.bashrc
   ```

2. Navigate to the end of the file by pressing the G key.

3. Enter the following line in your new line:

   ```
   PS1="[\u@\h  local  \W]\\$"
   ```

4. Save and exit the file by typing :wq.

5. Source your .bashrc file with the following command:

   ```
   source .bashrc
   ```

6. The prompt should reflect the changes.

Setting Options in **bash**

bash uses the built-in command set to turn on or off options for the shell. New in bash version 2.0 and higher is the shopt command, which encompasses the functionality of the set command. LPI exams focus on the set command:

```
set -o option (sets the option to on)
set +o option (sets the option to off
```

The set command uses a -o option specifier when setting options to on; conversely, it uses a +o specifier to turn options to off.

Important **bash** Options

Bash has a set of options you should know about for the exam, and for use in real life. The most common options are shown in the following list:

➤ emacs or vi—These set the keymap style for editing the command line.

➤ history—This option is on by default. The value of the variable HISTFILE is read to determine the history file.

➤ hashall—On by default, this option enables a hash table of requested commands and their locations for repeated use of the command.

➤ `monitor`—This option causes job control to make background processes run in a separate group and notify the console when they are ended or completed.

➤ `noclobber`—This option is off by default; when it's on, it disallows the overwriting of an existing file by a redirect symbol (>). A syntax error occurs if this is attempted. The use of double redirects (to append the file) is recommended.

➤ `noexec`—A dry run for script files when turned on. Interactive shells ignore it, but a script syntax-checks all commands without executing them.

➤ `notify`—Reports terminated jobs to the console immediately, instead of waiting until the next execution of the `jobs` command.

➤ `verbose`—This option echoes or prints to the screen any commands before they are executed. It's useful for the visually impaired users and as a check of the executed string.

Expect to see questions about how to toggle options with the **set** and **unset** commands. Remember that setting an option is accomplished with the **set –o option** syntax, whereas unsetting or removing an option requires the **set +o option** syntax. Expect to see such options as **noclobber**, **history**, **vi**, and **emacs**.

Job Control

Job control was invented when users had access to only a single terminal and getting more work done usually required another terminal. Job control allows the user to run multiple commands in a background mode while working in the foreground application.

Elements of Job Control

When using the shell, a program can be run, suspended, and then put into the background or the command can be invoked and put into the background in one step. The following steps show how to use job control:

1. Start a task such as an editor.

2. Suspend the program by pressing Ctrl+Z.

3. Execute the `jobs` command to see the status:

```
jobs
[1]+ Stopped              vim
```

4. Send job # 1 to the background by typing **bg** and pressing Enter:

```
bg
[1]+ vim &
```

5. Now start another program such as top in the background with the following:

```
top &
```

6. Run the jobs command to see which jobs are there and how they are numbered:

```
jobs
[1]- Stopped        vim
[2]+ Stopped        top
```

When looking at the jobs command output, there are three designations a job can have:

➤ A plus sign (+) next to it indicates the current job, and any commands such as fg or bg act on that job by default.

➤ A minus sign (-) next to it indicates the previous job or the next-to-last job to be operated on.

➤ Lack of a character indicates it's just a regular job, and no actions are taken on it unless specified by job number.

7. Put the default job into foreground mode with the fg command.

8. The top command should come to the foreground.

9. Quit the top command by pressing Q.

10. Run the jobs command again and notice that the vim job is now the current job again.

11. Kill the vim job by typing its ID with the kill command:

```
kill %1
Vim: Caught deadly signal TERM
Vim: Finished.
```

12. Run the jobs command again; you see the results of your action as reported by the Job Control function. In this case, job # 1 was terminated.

Managing Processes

Managing programs and processes is essential to running a Linux machine. Various utilities can help you manage those processes. Let's begin with viewing processes and then move on to removing processes. Finally, we'll affect process priorities.

When you need to see what's running on your machine, regardless of any GUI tools or programs, you can use the ps command. The ps command is used to display process information and has switches to format the output.

For example, to show a single user's processes, just type the ps command, like so:

```
ps
 PID TTY          TIME CMD
19856 pts/0    00:00:00 bash
20057 pts/0    00:00:00 ps
```

This is the simplest view of your system's processes, but it leaves out a lot of backgrounded or nonterminal-associated processes. Use the following to show progressively more information:

```
ps -a
 PID TTY          TIME CMD
 1497 tty1     00:00:00 startx
 1510 tty1     00:00:00 xinit
 1523 tty1     00:00:00 gnome-session
 1528 tty1     00:00:00 xinitrc <defunct>
15075 pts/1    00:00:00 ps
```

Obviously, you got more information because the a switch is used for showing all processes that are terminal-bound. That means if another user was on the system, you could see her processes listed, too.

Now type the following:

```
ps -a ¦ wc -l
     66
```

The important number is the one reported by the wc command: It's the number of lines in the output. Each one represents a running process. This machine has 66 processes found by the ps command.

More ps command switches to know are as follows:

➤ a—Shows all processes for all users

➤ u—Shows user information for processes

➤ x—Shows processes without a controlling tty

Use the `pstree` command to show the hierarchical nature of the processes on the system, such as the following example:

```
init-+-apmd
     |-atd
     |-bdflush
     |-bonobo-activati
     |-crond
     |-cupsd
     |-dhcpcd
     |-evolution-alarm
     |-gconfd-2
     |-gnome-cups-mana
     |-gnome-name-serv
     |-gnome-panel
     |-gnome-settings-
     |-gnome-smproxy
     |-gnome-terminal-+-bash
     |               `-mgt-pty-helper
```

Attention, older or seasoned Unix users: There will likely be questions that test how well you know the **ps** command, including what Linux uses as the equivalent of the command:

```
ps -ef
```

Verify how similar **ps -ef** is to **ps aux** with the following:

```
ps -ef > psef
ps -aux > psaux
vimdiff psef psaux
```

You'll find a number of similarities between the two output streams. The **ps aux** command is from Linux, whereas **ps -ef** is from Unix.

Sending Signals to Processes

The normal method for stopping a process is to use either the `kill` or the `killall` utility to send a polite kill to it. When you encounter a process that can't be removed from memory, because it's not receiving signals or perhaps due to sheer orneriness, you need to `kill` the process and remove it from memory.

Remember, the `kill` and `killall` commands simply send a signal to the process—they don't actually remove the processes themselves. Approximately 60 signals exist. The following list contains the important and useful signals and their number equivalents:

```
SIGTERM = 15
```

The default killing signal is numbered 15, and the signal name is SIGTERM. This politely requests the process to end, allowing it to clean up its memory.

If you type the `kill` command and the process ID (`PID`) of a program, the 15 or `SIGTERM` signal is sent to that program.

```
SIGHUP = 1
```

The `SIGHUP`, `HUP`, or 1 signal is a special case. It's what we could call a *bounce* signal, where the process isn't just killed but instead is signaled to end itself and then restart itself. The most frequently used reason for doing this is to have a process such as a server daemon stop, reread its configuration files, and then start back up.

```
SIGKILL = 9
```

The `SIGKILL` or 9 signal is the ultimate kill signal. Even if a process is a zombie (can't be killed by any other means), a `kill -9 PID` command usually kills the process and removes it from memory. The process being `SIGKILL`ed has no opportunity to save data or do anything else.

Here are a couple of examples of usage:

```
kill PID (Politely kills the process, allows saves)
kill -9 PID or kill -KILL PID (puts a bullet in the process, no saves)
kill -1 PID or kill -HUP PID(bounces or restarts processes)
```

Managing Process Priorities

Linux uses a combination of priority and scheduling to run multiple processes in what appears to be multitasking on a single processor. On multiple processors, this makes for actual multitasking.

Strangely enough, the process priorities are backward like a lot of other things, and they stretch from the highest (20) to the lowest (19) (see Figure 2.1).

Figure 2.1   Linux process priorities.

A process's default priority is normally 0 when started, unless the programmer has a need to set the starting priority higher. Although users can lower (from 0 to 19) a process's priority, only the root user can take a process to a higher (0 to -20) priority.

Many a sysadmin has discovered too late what it means to have multiple programs running at too high a priority. Too many processes with high priorities can slow a machine drastically, and even cause crashes.

There are two main methods to alter a processes priority, at program start and while it's running.

To start a program with a lower priority, use the `nice` command, such as follows:

```
nice kitty.scr
```

This causes the `kitty.scr` script to run at a priority of `10`. The `nice` utility makes programs play nice with others, relieving some of the stress of running multiple processor or I/O-intensive programs.

To change a process's priority while it's running, you use the `renice` program, such as shown here:

```
ps aux ¦ grep mybigcompile
rbrunson 14729 19.2 0.6 1656 524/pts/0 R 01:30 mybigcompile
renice +5 14729
```

This command string causes the process `mybigcompile` (process ID 14729) to run at an altered priority of +5. When using the `renice` utility, there isn't a default priority—one must be specified.

The other option for altering a running program's priority is a feature of the `top` command. The `top` command shows a refreshing screen of processes with the highest CPU usage, configurable to show only active processes or a specific number of processes (see Figure 2.2).

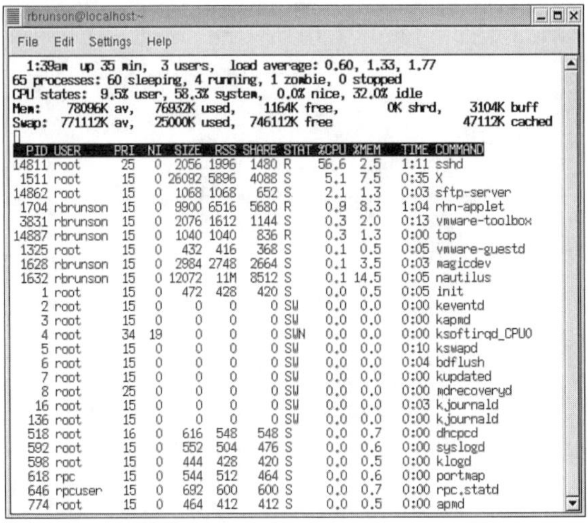

Figure 2.2 The **top** command.

`top` reads its configuration from `/etc/toprc` or `.toprc`, where it can be restricted for use by users, removing some of the dangerous features. `top` runs interactively by default, refreshing every 5 seconds.

To make `top` do some fun things, try these:

```
top d 1 (runs and refreshes every 1 secs.)
top i (shows only active processes, toggleable)
```

Some of the interactive (inside `top`) options you can use are

➤ `space`—Updates the display immediately

➤ `h`—Provides help for `top`

➤ `k`—Kills a process; a prompt appears for the PID

➤ `i`—Either displays or ignores zombie/idle processes

➤ `n`—Is prompted for the number of processes to display

➤ `r`—Prompts for the PID to affect and then the new priority

Exam Prep Questions

1. On a default Linux system, if a new user is created with user-related commands, what is the default shell?

   ○ A. `vsh`
   ○ B. `ksh`
   ○ C. `bash`
   ○ D. `sh`

   Answer C is correct because `bash` is the default Linux shell. Answer A is incorrect because there isn't a `vsh` command. Answer B is incorrect because `ksh` is not a Linux shell, although `pd-ksh` is. Answer D is incorrect because `sh` is the Bourne shell, ostensibly the first, but not the default.

2. Which file if present is sourced from the user's `~/.bash_profile` file during a normal default user's login session?

   ❏ A. `/etc/profile`
   ❏ B. `~/.bashrc`
   ❏ C. `/etc/bashrc`
   ❏ D. `~/.bash_logout`
   ❏ E. `~/.exrc`

   Answer B is correct because it's sourced from the user's `~/.bash_profile` file. Answer A is incorrect because it's the system's profile file. Answer C is incorrect because it's the system's `bash` configuration file and is sourced from the `~/.bashrc` file if needed. Answer D is incorrect because it's the last file that gets run as the user exits the system. Answer E is incorrect because it's the configuration file for the `vi` editor.

3. Which of the following command structures executes on the command line? (Choose all that apply.)

   ❏ A. Command option argument
   ❏ B. Option argument command
   ❏ C. Command argument option
   ❏ D. Argument option command

   Answers A and C are correct because most commands accept options both immediately after the command or at the end of the structure. Answers B and D are incorrect because their improper orders won't allow execution.

4. You are curious as to the name of the file **bash** uses for storing the commands you've previously typed. To echo the name of this file screen, which variable name would you use? (Type just the variable name as it would be used with the **echo** command [no **$**].)

   The correct answer is **HIST_FILE**.

5. What is the name of the library that provides editing functions to commands, such as the **bash** shell's capability to edit the commands before you execute them?

   ○ A. **history.c**

   ○ B. **.bash_lib**

   ○ C. **libedit.so.2**

   ○ D. **readline**

   Answer D is correct because the **readline** library is used to provide editing support for command lines in programs. All other answers are incorrect because they don't exist as files on the system.

6. You want a particular variable that was just declared to be available to all subshells. Which command would you use to ensure this?

   ○ A. **set**

   ○ B. **export**

   ○ C. **bash**

   ○ D. **source**

   Answer B is correct because running **export VARNAME** makes that variable available for all subshells. Answer A is incorrect because it is used to set **bash** shell options, not to export variables. Answer C is incorrect because it is the **bash** shell executable. Answer D is incorrect because the **source** command is used to reexecute configuration scripts, not export variables.

7. You've executed a number of consecutive commands and want to make a script out of them. Which command would you use to cause lines 78–85 of the **history** command stack to be editable and executable immediately thereafter?

   ○ A. **fc -l 78 85**

   ○ B. **fc 78-85**

   ○ C. **fc 78 85**

   ○ D. **history > fc ¦ grep "78 85"**

   Answer C is correct because it loads lines 78–85 in the **fc** editor (a specialized **vi** session) and executes the remainder of the buffer on exit. Answer A is incorrect because it only lists lines 78–85 from the **history** stack. Answer B is incorrect because there should not be a dash between the beginning and ending numbers. Answer D is incorrect because the command string sends the output of the **history** command to a file named **fc** and does not pipe it to the **fc** command.

8. You are in the current user's home diretory, which is not in the system's path. You want to run an executable named **tarfoo** in the current directory. It won't run when you type just the command. Which of the following executes the program? (Choose all that apply.)

- ❏ A. `../.tarfoo`
- ❏ B. `./tarfoo`
- ❏ C. `~tarfoo`
- ❏ D. `/home/user1/tarfoo`

Answers B and D are correct because commands not in the path can be specified either via the full path or by prefixing them with `./`. Answer A is incorrect because it attempts to execute a file in the `/home` directory named `.tarfoo`. Answer C is incorrect because that string would attempt to execute the home directory for the user **tarfoo**.

9. You are the sysadmin for a mid-sized company and have a particular user who consistently overwrites important files with meaningless content. The files cannot be set read-only because they are written to by the shell and its functions. Which of the following options, when used with the **set** command, fixes this problem?

- ◯ A. `append-only`
- ◯ B. `noclobber`
- ◯ C. `hashall`
- ◯ D. `monitor`

Answer B is correct because the **noclobber** option allows the user to only append to files, not overwrite their contents. Answer A is incorrect because it doesn't exist as an option in **bash**. Answer C is incorrect because the **hashall** option builds a table of recently used commands. Answer D is incorrect because the **monitor** option has to do with job control and notification of process statuses.

10. You've just started four jobs in the background with the following:

```
Cmd1 &
Cmd2 &
Cmd3 &
Cmd4 &
```

When you view the jobs menu by typing the **jobs** command, they are numbered from 1 to 4 from the top. If you stop jobs number 1 and 3 and then start a new job, what number will be assigned to it?

- ◯ A. 1
- ◯ B. 3
- ◯ C. 4
- ◯ D. 5

Answer D is correct because the jobs menu is numbered statically until all the current jobs have been ended. Answers A, B, and C are incorrect because job #4 existed and all new jobs will start with #5 and higher.

Basic vi Skills

Terms you'll need to understand:

✓ Command mode
✓ Insert mode
✓ LastLine mode
✓ Message line
✓ Named buffers
✓ The Unnamed buffer

Techniques you'll need to master:

✓ Opening a file for editing
✓ Saving and exiting files
✓ Searching for text, including ranges and regular expressions
✓ Navigating within a file, including using the H, J, K, and L keys
✓ Searching and replacing text using different methods
✓ Setting, unsetting, and displaying options for vi
✓ Executing commands within vi
✓ Performing advanced editing functions

Editors

The LPI exams focus on vi as the default editor for Linux. No matter how much you think emacs rocks, or that pico/nano is much easier to use with the onscreen menus, it's essential that you have basic vi skills.

Modes in vi

One of the most confusing things about vi is the presence of *modes*, or states, in the editor. The three modes are

➤ Command

➤ Insert

➤ LastLine

Editing in vi

vi always starts in Command mode. True editing takes place in what's known as Insert mode. The keys you commonly use to invoke Insert mode from Command mode are

➤ **i**—The most common method of moving into Insert mode is to press the i key, leaving the cursor at the current position. All typing from that point pushes existing text to the right.

➤ **I**—The uppercase I key moves to the beginning of the current line and from there acts like the i key.

➤ **a**—The second most common method is to press the a key, moving the cursor one character to the right, essentially behaving like an i key after that.

➤ **A**—The uppercase A moves to the end of the current line and from there acts like an a key.

➤ **o**—Use this key to open a new line under the present line. For example, if you're on line 3 in Command mode, pressing o drops line 4 down to become 5 and opens a new line 4 that's empty.

➤ **O**—The uppercase O opens a new line at the current line. For example, if you're on line 3, pressing O drops line 3 down to become line 4 and opens a new empty line 3 for editing.

If you press one of the previously mentioned Insert mode keys, in the bottom left of the vi screen (the left end of the Message Line) the following text appears:

```
-- INSERT -
```

Getting back to Command mode is easy: Press the Esc key at least once, although many people double-press it just to make sure they're really there. At any time you can return to Command mode from Insert mode by pressing the Escape key (Esc).

The Message Line

The bottom of the vi screen should contain a number of pieces of information that can help you, varying to suit the situation and actions just completed. This section details some of the messages that can appear.

If you've just entered vi file1, when the editor opens the file, the message line should contain something similar to the following:

```
"/home/rbrunson/file1" 57L, 1756C              18,1  Top
```

The numbers 18,1 on the right side of the message line are the current line and column numbers, and the Top text is the current position of the cursor. This changes to be Bot if you entered the last half of the file. The other value possible is All, which simply means that all the contents of the file are currently on the screen.

A new file (one invoked with vi file1) would show the line:

```
"file1" [New File]                       0,0   All
```

Opening a File for Editing

To create a new file in the current subdirectory, you type the following:

```
vi filename
```

To create a new file in a particular directory, use the full path as follows:

```
vi /full/path/to/file
```

Sometimes you will want vi to open a file with a search string and put the cursor on the first found instance of that string. To accomplish this you'd enter

```
vi +/string filename
```

Other times you'll want to edit a file and have the cursor jump to a particular line when the file is opened, such as the `initdefault` line in the `/etc/inittab`. You'd enter this:

```
vi +18 /etc/inittab
```

Expect questions about opening files with particular options, searching a file upon opening it, and other ways to start the vi editor.

Navigating Within a File

The vi editor uses the following keystrokes to move left, right, up, and down, but if you have cursor keys, you can use them, too. Here are some useful keystrokes:

➤ **H**—This is the left arrow; it's easy to remember because it's the leftmost key in the four-key set.

➤ **J**—Use this for the down arrow.

➤ **K**—Use this for the up arrow.

➤ **L**—Use this for the right arrow.

Figure 3.1 illustrates how these keys work.

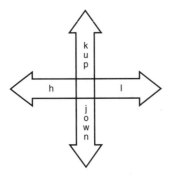

Figure 3.1 Cursor key directions.

As you can see in Figure 3.1, one of the ways to remember the keyboard cursor keys is to just look down at the home row and remember that H is the leftmost, J goes *jown* (down), K goes *kup* (up), and L is on the right. Makes perfect sense, right?

You'll see questions about the movement keys on the exam. The arrow keys are a favorite topic, whereas the Ctrl keys don't get much love. Know those arrow movement keys!

Other keystrokes move you around in vi using the Ctrl key and a letter:

➤ **Ctrl+F**—Moves forward a page

➤ **Ctrl+B**—Moves backward a page

➤ **Ctrl+D**—Moves forward a half-page

➤ **Ctrl+U**—Moves backward a half-page

Force Multipliers

Just about any keystroke or action can be done X number of times by prefixing it with a number.

For example, to move the cursor to line 5, you would press 5G. Moving 12 words to the right is accomplished with 12w.

A lot of editing, inserting, and escaping back can sometimes leave the message line without some pertinent information showing, such as the name of the file being edited. When you get confused as to where you are or under which filename you saved this iteration of the file, pressing ctrl+G shows the filename, total number of lines, and current position expressed as a percentage of the total lines in the file.

Undo Operations

A useful and largely unknown set of options are the undo operations. You press U in Command mode to undo a single operation or the latest in a series of changes. If you opened a file, made 30 changes, and then pressed the U key 30 times, you'd end up with the exact same file you had opened.

Don't bother trying U to undo all changes—that's not what it's for. Instead, use the :+E+! keystroke combination in Command mode to undo all changes since the last disk write to the file.

Quitting Files

When you've made changes to the buffer, vi won't let you quit normally, such as with :q. One of the toughest situations every vi user faces is the dreaded

`E37: no write since last change (add ! to override)` message. This error can be fixed only by using the correct additional ! character. To exit a file that is read-only or that you don't want to save the changes to, you must use the keystrokes :q!. This is known as *qbang* or *quit dammit*.

Saving Files

The most straightforward way to save a file in vi is to enter :w in Command mode. You save the file and can continue to edit it.

Saving and quitting a given file is pretty simple, too. In Command mode you enter :wq. If you find yourself as the root user being unable to write to a configuration file, entering :wq! forces the file to be written, as long as the only barrier is a missing write permission.

Two additional methods of saving and quitting a file are available. The first entails entering :x to save and exit. The second is to press Shift+ZZ (hold down the Shift key and press the Z key twice); this is my personal favorite and is easy to remember.

Read questions carefully when asked about saving and/or exiting the vi editor. Many test-takers have mentioned that the question's syntax is critical to getting it right. For example, the question, "Which of the following saves *and* exits a file in **vi**?" is very different from the question, "Which of the following can be used to save *or* exit a file in **vi**?"

Command Mode Editing

In this section we use a sample text file to perform some editing functions. The system must have been installed with the Kernel Development section if it's a Red Hat distribution, or the equivalent packages from a Debian distribution:

`/usr/src/linux-2.4/Documentation/watchdog.txt`

The following is a suitable file for practicing editing commands:
/usr/src/linux-2.4/Documentation/watchdog.txt

Inserting and Adding Text

One of the most common tasks in a vi session is making changes to the text in a file. This involves using one of the following keys to change from Command mode to Insert mode:

➤ **i**—Inserts text to the left of the cursor

➤ **I**—Inserts text at the beginning of the text in that line, not the beginning column of the vi screen

➤ **a**—Appends to the right of the cursor

➤ **A**—Appends at the end of the current line

➤ **o**—Begins a new line below the current line

➤ **O**—Drops the current line and begins a new one in its place

Changing or Replacing Text

The following are incredibly useful when you're altering an existing file and need to change a character, a line, a sentence, or just a word:

➤ cw—Changes a single word from the current cursor position. To change a whole word, you put the cursor on the first character of it.

➤ c$—Changes the current line but doesn't extend to change the rest of a wrapped sentence on the screen.

➤ r—Replaces the character under the cursor.

➤ R—Replaces text on the same line until Esc is pressed, but it doesn't change text on the next line. Instead, it pushes it ahead of the current changes.

NOTE   Remember to use the force multipliers in the appropriate places. You can easily change multiple words by using **5cw** or replace 10 characters with **10r**.

Deleting Text and Lines

A more advanced use of vi is to remove or delete characters, words, or even lines. Be careful to check your deletions and changes, or press the u key to get things back to normal and try it again.

➤ **x**—Deletes a single character under the cursor

➤ **X**—Deletes a single character before the cursor

➤ **dw**—Deletes a single word that's currently under the cursor, from the cursor position onward

➤ **dd**—Deletes the current line entirely, regardless of the cursor position in the line

➤ **D**—Deletes all text from the current cursor position to the end of the line

➤ **dL**—Deletes all text from the cursor to the end of the screen

➤ **dG**—Deletes all text from the cursor to the EOF

➤ **d^**—Deletes all text from the beginning of the line to the cursor

In the lexicon of computer software verbiage, *delete* in **vi** stores the cut or deleted string of text in the unnamed buffer for future use. This buffer's contents will be over-written by any further cuts or deletions.

How you delete is important on the exam. If asked to delete from the current position to the end of the line, don't pick or type the keys that delete the whole line—there are no partial credits on the exam!

The Cut, Copy, and Paste Commands

The process of moving text around in vi is a little complex, so practice on a scratch file first. The following keystrokes are used to cut, copy, and paste text in a vi session:

➤ **yy**—Copies a line of text to the unnamed buffer

➤ **3yy**—Copies three lines of text to the unnamed buffer

➤ **yw**—Copies a word (under the cursor) to the unnamed buffer

➤ **3yw**—Copies three words to the unnamed buffer

➤ **p**—Pastes the contents of the unnamed buffer to the right of the cursor

➤ **P**—Pastes the contents of the unnamed buffer to the left of the cursor

Yanking (or copying) lines (the y key) and pasting (the p key) them back in are done on a whole-line basis, whereas yanking a word or several words is done solely on a word basis. Pasting data back in happens to the right of the current cursor position, so take care to put the cursor directly to the left of the desired insertion point. Pasting puts lines as a new entry directly below the current cursor line.

> NOTE
>
> A common use of the cut, copy, and paste commands is in the **/etc/fstab** file when you've added another file system or disk. Open the file, find a line similar to the desired new one, and press yy; then move the cursor to the line above the position you desire for the line, then press yy. The yanked line will appear under the current cursor line.

Named and Unnamed Buffers

The vi editor has a total of 27 buffers: 26 named buffers (a–z) and 1 unnamed buffer that is overwritten by each new operation.

Unless you have specified a named buffer, all operations use the unnamed buffer, and two operations right after each other have the second operation overwrite the data from the first operation.

Named buffer operations are always preceded by the double quotation mark ("), which tells the machine that a named buffer operation is to follow.

When you perform named buffer operations, the buffers must be referred to in the command as either a lowercase or uppercase letter of the alphabet (which is part of the command, and not sent to the buffer):

➤ **Lowercase buffer letter**—Overwrites the buffer

➤ **Uppercase buffer letter**—Appends to buffer

For example, the following string, when entered in Command mode with the cursor in column 1, causes line 1 to copy the next four lines to the named buffer (a), overwriting any contents of that named buffer:

```
"a3yy
```

The Message Line echoes the number of lines and the operation, such as

```
3 lines yanked
```

The syntax for the editing commands remains the same; just remember to precede the operation with a double quotation mark, a lower- or uppercase character, and then whatever operation you want to perform with that named buffer.

Other examples include

➤ "ayy—Yanks a line to the named buffer (a), overwriting the current contents

➤ "Ayy—Appends the current line to the a buffer

➤ "A3yy—Yanks three lines from the current cursor position and appends the lines to the A buffer

➤ "ap—Pastes the a buffer to the right of the cursor (the case of the buffer letter is meaningless in paste operations)

NOTE Performing single-line operations with named buffers usually doesn't echo anything to the Message Line, but anything involving more than one line of data echoes the number of lines affected. Word operations are usually not noted in the Message Line either.

Searching in vi

Searching for text in Linux utilities typically follows a common convention. In the less, more, and vi commands, a forward slash followed by a search term/string searches forward in the file from the current cursor position or the top of the file, highlighting found strings. Initiating a backward search from the cursor position is done with a question mark followed by the string to search for, such as ?string.

NOTE Searches are performed only in Command mode, so remember to press the Esc key to get back there.

Finding the next occurrence (whether a forward or backward search) is usually accomplished by pressing the unshifted N key to search forward. You press Shift+N for a backward search.

Searching and Replacing

Searching a document for a given string or character to replace it is commonly performed either in vi while editing a given file or by the sed command on a large set of data. Both vi and the sed command share a common search-and-replace syntax, with small differences that won't confuse you if you use both. Indeed, learning to search and replace in one will teach you how to use it in the other.

The search-and-replace syntax is as follows:

```
action/tofind/replacewith/modifier
```

For example, the following string in vi replaces just the first instance of the string bob in the current line with the string BOB:

```
:s/bob/BOB/
```

To replace all instances of the string bob with BOB in the current line, you would use this line:

```
:s/bob/BOB/g
```

The g stands for global or doing the action on every found instance of the string.

To replace all instances of bob with BOB in the entire file, no matter how many exist or how many changes are made to each line, you would use this:

```
:%s/bob/BOB/g
```

 It's critical that you read the exam question and all its answers (except for a fill-in-the-blank) to see exactly what is being asked for. A percent symbol (%) in front of the search-and-replace string is the *only* way to cause **vi** to search the entire file, and not just the current line.

Fuzzy Searches

Finding matches for fuzzy searches in vi is a good thing to know about. In a *fuzzy* search, you find something you only know a part of.

For example, if you wanted to find all the instances of the word *The* at the beginning of a line, you could use this search:

```
/^The
```

To find all the instances of the word *kernel* at the end of a line, you could use this search:

```
/kernel$
```

In some instances, you'll need to find what's called a *metacharacter*. For example, say you wanted to find the instances in a file of the asterisk (*) character because it stands for many characters. You could use something like this:

```
/The \* character
```

Another example might be finding the text *kernel.*, with the period being treated only as a period. Otherwise, you'd find *kernels*, *kernel?*, *kernel!*, and so on. To find just *kernel.*, you'd use the following:

```
/kernel\.
```

Finally, matching a range of characters is helpful, such as trying to find all instances of the version number string v2.1 through v2.9. You either have to perform several searches or use something like this:

```
/v2.[1-9]
```

The square brackets denote a single character, stretching from the first character to the one after the dash. If you wanted instead to find all versions of the word *the*, including *THE*, *THe*, and *tHE*, you would use the following:

```
/[tT][hH][eE]
```

Options in vi

You have three methods of specifying options with the vi editor. All have their place, but if you find yourself frequently having to set options manually, try putting them in the ~/.exrc file. An example is shown here:

```
set number
set tabstop=5
set nohlsearch
```

The previous code should be placed in the .exrc file, one option per line, the file being a simple text file in the user's home directory.

If you want all users to have the exact same vi options, edit the **/etc/exrc** file to set the options.

Having this in the user's home directory or having a customized one in a folder you specify uses the file found in the local directory (if any) as the active configuration file when you start a vi session. If there isn't one in the current directory, the user's ~/.exrc is used if it exists; otherwise, the defaulting system /etc/exrc file is used if it is configured.

To set options on-the-fly, enter them at the : prompt, such as :set number, :set noerrorbell, and set tabstop=5. These last only for the current session and have to be repeatedly reset in future sessions.

Your final option for setting an option with vi is on the command line that started vi. For example, to start vi with nonprinting line numbers onscreen, you would use

```
vi +"set number" file1
```

The reason for the double quotation marks is the space between set and number; otherwise, it would give you a syntax error.

More than 60 options are available in the vi editor. You can view them easily by typing :set all in the editor, or to see which options are currently set for your session, type :set while in the editor. Finally, you can type :set optionname? to find out about that particular option's status.

For some reason, LPI really wants you to know the options for setting numbers, including the shortcuts for how options are set. Examples of how you could set the numbers option on and off include

➤ :set number—Turns on line numbers (screen only).

➤ :set nonumber—Turns the number option off.

➤ :se nu—This is the shortest string that turns this option on, and putting no in front of the option turns that option off.

Advanced **vi**

Several tasks are part of vi that don't fit in any other section. Most of these are quite advanced, such as running external commands, joining lines, and splitting windows. This section covers these in detail.

Running External Commands in **vi**

A frequent question on the exams is how to run an external command inside vi, such as seeing an ls -l listing of the current directory so you can remember a filename:

```
:! ls -l
```

In this, the command ls -l executes, with the command's output displaying onscreen, and you need only press Enter or enter a command to return to the vi session. If the output scrolls more than one screen, it's piped to the more command and all the normal movement keystrokes will apply.

Joining Lines

It's quite irritating in vi to be at the front of a line and want to use the Backspace key to move that line to the end of the previous line. The Backspace key works only on the current line. If you need a line to be joined to the previous line, you can position the cursor in either line and press Shift+J to cause the second to be appended to the end of the first line.

Say you have a file named `file1` that contains the following text:

```
This is line 1
This is a longer line 2
This is an even longer line 3
```

You want to join line 1 and line 2, so you position your cursor somewhere on line 1 and press the J key. The file then looks like the following:

```
This is line 1 This is a longer line 2
This is an even longer line 3
```

Putting the cursor on line 2 and pressing J joins line 2 and line 3 in a similar fashion.

Split Windows

Last, but not least, is splitting windows in vi, specifically the vim version of vi. When you're editing a particular file and want to see either another section of that same file or even another file altogether, you can use the following:

➤ `:split`—This splits the window horizontally, with the same file and lines shown in both windows.

➤ `:vsplit`—This splits the window on the same file vertically, with the same document shown in both the left and right panes.

Moving between the panes is somewhat counterintuitive because you must press Ctrl+W twice to move between the windows.

To edit a completely different file, you should edit the first one in vi; then to split the screen horizontally with the other file loaded in the second pane, you can enter

```
:split file2
```

To set the height of the newly split window from the split, you could enter the following:

```
:10split /etc/fstab
```

This command splits the top 10 lines of the screen and displays the contents of the `/etc/fstab` file therein.

If you wanted to close the split window, you would focus on it by pressing Ctrl+W and then entering

```
:close
```

Better yet, after comparing something or getting a filename straight, you can close all the other split windows and just have the current window open by entering the following:

`:only`

Many times I've opened a couple of split windows to see the difference between two files or used the **diff** command. The easiest way to compare two files and make edits to them is to use the **vimdiff** command, such as

:vimdiff file1 file2

This loads the two files into a vertically split **vim** session and uses color and other symbols to show you what is similar or different between the two files. This is useful for comparing a log file before and after a problem or two configuration files to see why one doesn't work.

Exam Prep Questions

1. What is the default editor for Linux systems?

   ○ A. emacs

   ○ B. joe

   ○ C. vi

   ○ D. pico

   Answer C is correct because vi is in nearly every distribution of Linux that exists. Answer A is incorrect because, even though emacs is very well known, it's considered an add-on to Linux. Answer B is incorrect because joe is a specialized editor and not normally included in a distribution by default. Answer D is incorrect because pico is used only for document-style text editing, and is not the default editor.

2. Which of the following saves and exits a file you are editing in vi? (Choose all that apply.)

   ❏ A. `:x`

   ❏ B. `:q!`

   ❏ C. Shift+ZZ

   ❏ D. `zz`

   ❏ E. `:wq`

   Answers A, C, and E are correct because they save and exit a given file in `vi`. Answer B is incorrect because it forces a nonsaving exit to a modified buffer or file. Answer D is incorrect because only a shifted pair of `z` characters saves and exits a file properly.

3. After opening a file with `vi`, you want to navigate to the end of the file as quickly as possible. Which of the following, when performed in Command mode, accomplishes this?

   ○ A. Ctrl+PgDn

   ○ B. Shift+G

   ○ C. Meta+End

   ○ D. Shift+End

   Answer B is correct because it takes the cursor to the end of the file. Answer A is incorrect because Ctrl+PgDn does nothing in `vi`. Answer C is incorrect because it moves to the end of the current line. Answer D is incorrect because it does nothing in `vi`.

4. On the line below, enter the **vi** command that would open the file **mytestfile.txt** and cause nonprinting line numbers to appear to the left of all file contents:

The answer is **vi +"set number" mytestfile.txt.**

Alternative possible correct answers are

```
vi mytestfile.txt +"set number"
vi mytestfile.txt "+set number"
```

5. While editing a file with **vi**, you press Esc to enter Command mode and then use the keystrokes 3+J+4+L. What is the result?
   - ○ A. Three columns left and four lines down
   - ○ B. Three columns right and four lines up
   - ○ C. Three lines up and four columns left
   - ○ D. Three lines down and four columns right

   Answer D is correct because the J key denotes the down arrow and the L character denotes the right arrow. Answers A, B, and C are incorrect because they don't use the correct keystrokes.

6. Which of the following commands opens a file named **file1.txt** with nonprinting line numbers displayed in **vi**?
   - ○ A. **vi /set number file1.txt**
   - ○ B. **vi +"set number" file1.txt**
   - ○ C. **vi < .exrc file1.txt**
   - ○ D. **vi "se nu" file1.txt**

   Answer B is correct because it turns on the line numbering. Answer A is incorrect because it has a slash (/) instead of a plus symbol (+). Answer C is incorrect because it either produces a syntax error or just edits the **.exrc** file. Answer D is incorrect because it's missing the necessary plus symbol (+).

7. You want to edit a file with **vi** and have the word **string1** highlighted if found. Which of the following accomplishes this in one command?
   - ○ A. **vi +/"string1" file**
   - ○ B. **vi /string1 file**
   - ○ C. **vi +/string1 file**
   - ○ D. **vi --find string1 file**

   Answer C is correct because it searches for and highlights the string **string1** properly. Answer A is incorrect because it has added quotation marks around the search string. Answer B is incorrect because it's missing the necessary plus symbol. Answer D is incorrect because there is no **--find** option for **vi**.

8. While editing a file in **vi**, you need to display the permissions for the normal files in the current directory. Which command accomplishes this from Command mode?

○ A. `:x "ls -l"`
○ B. `:e! ls -l`
○ C. `Shift+L+S+-+L`
○ D. `:! ls -l`

Answer D is correct because it starts a subshell and displays the normal files in the current directory. Answer A is incorrect because it exits the file and ignores the `ls` command. Answer B is incorrect because it attempts to edit all the files returned by the `ls` command and errors out. Answer C is incorrect because it just starts displaying the text on the screen in **vi**.

9. You'll be editing the files in **/project1** by executing **vi** from that location. You want a set of options to always be set for this project, and not other **vi** sessions. Which of the following files would you edit to best accomplish this?

○ A. `/project1/.exrc`
○ B. `~/.vimrc`
○ C. `.virc`
○ D. `/etc/editorrc`

Answer A is correct because it configures **vi** with the necessary options only if executed from the **/project1** directory. Answer B is incorrect because the `.vimrc` file in question is located in the current user's home directory, not the **project1** directory. Answer C is incorrect because the file named is a fake. Answer D is incorrect because no such file as `/etc/editorrc` exists.

10. While in **vi**, you need to search and replace all instances of the string **snark** with **FARKLE** in the current file. Write the answer on the line below, including everything necessary to accomplish this from Command mode:

The answer is `:%s/snark/FARKLE/g`. There are no alternative correct answers.

Hardware

Terms you'll need to understand:

✓ Driver
✓ I/O ports
✓ Interrupts
✓ Network interface card
✓ Plug and Play
✓ Point to Point

Techniques you'll need to master:

✓ Memorizing IRQ associations
✓ Troubleshooting hardware conflicts
✓ Viewing SCSI information
✓ Configuring Ethernet devices
✓ Setting IPs manually
✓ Configuring PPP sessions
✓ Configuring system time
✓ Viewing and setting USB configurations

Hardware

The LPI objectives include several hardware-specific items. You must be familiar with the topics in this chapter to be a good sysadmin.

IRQs and Ports

IRQs are numbered from 0 to 15. Some constants in the numbering are the system timer (0), keyboard (1), and floppy controller (6). Table 4.1 shows common IRQ assignments.

Table 4.1	Typical IRQ Assignments
IRQ	**Device**
0	System timer
1	Keyboard
2	Cascade from IRQs 8–15
3	COM2 or COM4
4	COM1 or COM3
5	Some sound cards or a second LPT
6	Floppy disk controller
7	First LPT
8	Real-time clock (in CMOS)
9	Varies
10	Varies
11	Varies
12	PS/2 mouse
13	Math coprocessor
14	Primary ATAPI controller
15	Secondary ATAPI controller

LPI focuses mostly on what happens if a conflict occurs from a secondary or new card, such as the conflict that can occur when a machine has two printer ports and a sound card is placed in the machine. Knowing the open or available IRQs and what a particular card type likely uses is invaluable on the exam.

Another important set of information is the layout of communication or serials ports for the system. Whereas Windows uses com and lpt to denote the serial and parallel ports, Linux uses ttyS and lp to represent them. Table 4.2 is arranged to help make the connections between what Windows uses to identify these and what Linux refers to them as, along with the IRQ and I/O addresses assigned them normally.

Table 4.2	Typical Assignment Combinations		
Win	Linux	IRQ	I/O Address
COM 1	/dev/ttyS0	4	03f8
COM 2	/dev/ttyS1	3	02f8
COM 3	/dev/ttyS2	4	03e8
COM 4	/dev/ttyS3	3	02e8

What Windows calls COM ports, Linux calls a *tty or serial* port. These are typically numbered from ttyS0 to ttyS3. For example, the full path and filename of the second serial port on the system would be

/dev/ttyS1

Remembering the ports and their names can be easy, but the IRQ associations can be difficult sometimes. What works for me is to remember that COM 1 and COM 3 share the sum of their numbers, IRQ 4. COM 2 and COM 4 share the number in between their numbers, IRQ 3. Once you've got that, remembering that Linux does 0 through 3 is not hard. As for the I/O addresses, I use 32f and 32e to recall their order and numbers.

Printer Ports

Although most PCs have one physical printer port, some servers and other machines have two parallel or printer ports. When referring to Linux parallel ports, the letters *lp* are typically used. When a single lp is present, IRQ 7 is typically assigned to it. If a second lp is present, it's normally assigned IRQ 5.

 A common hardware question involves adding cards to the system and what might make the new card or old card not work directly afterward. Bonus points if you said a conflict between an **lp** port and a sound card!

The IRQs and I/O addresses for parallel ports are as shown in Table 4.3.

Table 4.3	Typical Parallel Port Addressing		
Win	**Linux**	**IRQ**	**I/O Address**
LPT 1	/dev/lp0	7	0378
LPT 2	/dev/lp1	5	0278

Modems

Modems on Linux machines are /dev/ttySx device files that have been sym-linked to appear as if they were actually mapped to /dev/modem. On a system that has only one modem, it's logical to map it in this way.

Modem devices are initialized during system startup. The common method of doing this is to call the /etc/rc.local/rc.serial script. More than four modems might require custom initialization scripts and definitely some shuffling of IRQs.

LPI focuses on a standard modem setup, with one or two modems being the maximum we've seen on the exam.

UARTs

A universal asynchronous receiver/transmitter (UART) is used on the sending modem to take complete bytes and send them in a sequential method to the receiving modem, which reassembles them properly into the complete bytes again.

Any session conducted over a modem is affected by the quality or the level of the UART. The 8250-class UART is capable of a maximum of only 9,600bps. Many sources lump the 16450 UART in this class, leaving only the more modern 16550 or 16550A UARTs capable of high-speed communications, all the way up to 115,200bps.

Expect to see a question or two about the UARTs on the exam, with the main focus being which UARTs are capable of which speeds. Just remember that the 16550 and higher are capable of speeds over 9600.

Using the **setserial** Command

The `setserial` command is used to view and modify settings for the serial ports on the system. Let's be clear: Most sysadmins don't configure modems on a daily basis, but it's a very important skill, particularly for mobile users.

The exam will ask you how to set options, view information, and determine settings for your local modems. Be aware also that WinModems—those modems that depend on the Windows OS for proper functions—are incompatible with Linux. The exam will emphasize this point.

The following example of `setserial` demonstrates how to get device information for the first serial port on the system:

```
setserial /dev/ttyS0
```

The output would be as follows:

```
/dev/ttyS0, UART: 16550A, Port: 0x03f8, IRQ: 4
```

The command shows the basic information about the specified port including the UART type, interrupts, and IO address.

Getting information on all your serial ports is slightly confusing, but you won't have more than four in most cases.

```
setserial -g /dev/ttyS[0-3]
```

The output would be as follows:

```
/dev/ttyS0, UART: 16550A, Port: 0x03f8, IRQ: 4
/dev/ttyS1, UART: 16550A, Port: 0x02f8, IRQ: 3
/dev/ttyS2, UART: 16550A, Port: 0x03e8, IRQ: 4
```

If you display all the serial device files, they'll be out of order (1, 11, 12, 13, and so on) and need sorting. Besides, the first four are the likely candidates.

Let's say you need to configure a port with settings other than the defaults. First, you need to show detailed information about that port, like this:

```
setserial /dev/ttyS0 -a
```

The output would be as follows:

```
/dev/ttyS0, Line 0, UART: 16550A, Port: 0x03f8, IRQ: 4
        Baud_base: 115200, close_delay: 50, divisor: 0
        closing_wait: 3000
        Flags: spd_normal skip_test
```

Setting the baud rate for a modem is a common question. This is accomplished with some variation on the following command:

```
setserial /dev/ttyS0 baud_base 57600
```

This command sets the serial ports base rate to be 57,600bps, with the default being 115,200bps.

Ethernet/NIC Devices

On a Linux machine that doesn't have a physical network interface card (NIC) installed, there is only one network device—/dev/lo, which is the loopback device. The loopback device has an IP of 127.0.0.1 and an entry in the /etc/hosts file line that sets the hostname to localhost.

This device is mapped to IP 127.0.0.1, which is part of the reserved 127.0.0.0 subnet and has no meaning outside the local machine.

If a machine has an embedded NIC on the motherboard, that device typically is read as the /dev/eth0 device.

The first installed network device is mapped to the device file /dev/eth0. On a Red Hat machine, the configuration file for this device (where the IP and others are set) is /etc/sysconfig/network-scripts/ifcfg-eth0. An example of this file is shown in Listing 4.1.

Listing 4.1   Typical Network Device Configuration

```
DEVICE=eth0
ONBOOT=yes
BOOTPROTO=static
IPADDR=192.168.1.200
NETMASK=255.255.255.0
GATEWAY=192.168.1.1
```

Explanations of ifcfg file settings:

➤ DEVICE—The value is the device /dev file that the interface uses, set by the system.

➤ ONBOOT—When set to yes, the device is initialized when the system is booted.

➤ BOOTPROTO—The value is either static or dhcp. This governs how the device gets an IP.

➤ IPADDR—If the BOOTPROTO is set to static, this setting is present, with the IP set to the value that follows the = sign.

➤ NETMASK—This is present only if BOOTPROTO is set to static, and it is the subnet mask for the IP that's set.

➤ GATEWAY—Another BOOTPROTO=static-related entry, this sets the primary default gateway, which should also be reflected in the routing table.

Configuring NICs

The ifconfig command sets addressing information for the network interface devices. The following is an example of its typical use:

```
ifconfig eth0 10.1.1.1 netmask 255.255.255.0 up
```

This configures the eth0 interface with the 10.1.1.1 IP, sets a subnet mask of 255.255.255.0, and starts the interface.

To query the interfaces, type either **ifconfig** or **ifconfig -a**, which is the default. This displays all the configured/started interfaces and their IP-related information.

> The exam will ask you things about this area that will test whether you have ever set an IP statically, whether you're familiar with the output of the **ifconfig** command, and whether you know the difference between the **/dev/lo** interface and others.

A useful companion command is the arp command. It's used to view and set the ARP cache for the machine. The ARP cache is populated every time you ping another machine by name or IP and get a successful return, storing the resolved IP and the MAC address of the remote machine (or gateway to its network) for a period of around 10 minutes.

The ARP Cache

The ARP cache is a pairing of the MAC address for a machine and its present IP. Because MAC addresses don't usually change but IPs can and frequently do, the ARP cache times out its entries periodically, forcing a rediscovery of the paired addresses.

A good example of viewing the ARP cache information is

```
arp -a
```

Here is the output:

```
(192.168.1.2) at 00:40:CA:38:DB:0B [ether] on eth0
(192.168.1.1) at 00:04:5A:D0:C5:CD [ether] on eth0
(192.168.1.103) at 00:08:74:E3:E5:9D [ether] on eth0
```

In the previous example, the IP is shown because it's included in the packets on the network, but it can be shown as the remote host's name if it's resolvable either through the /etc/hosts or DNS or NIS sources. This is automatically done if DNS is configured properly for the hosts involved.

The at 00:... section shows the MAC of the remote host, followed by the type ([ether]) and the actual interface (eth0) used.

 If the remote host is not on the same logical subnet or network, the entries shown might not match what you think you've pinged or connected to. For example, if a remote host is reached through a gateway and you look at the ARP table, you'll see only the gateway address listed, not the remote address.

Finally, if you need to, a static entry that will never time out can be set in the ARP cache. This might be a good idea for the default gateway or a server that is accessed constantly and is not going to change its IP or NIC device anytime soon.

For example, say your ARP cache entry for a gateway device presently shows the following:

```
(192.168.1.1) at 00:04:5A:D0:C5:CD [ether] on eth0
```

You can therefore set that device to always be in the ARP cache with that exact match between the IP and MAC addresses with this command:

```
arp -s 192.168.1.1 00:04:5A:D0:C5:CD
```

Check the entry again with this command:

```
arp -a 192.168.1.1
```

Typical output would be

```
(192.168.1.1) at 00:04:5A:D0:C5:CD [ether] PERM on eth0
```

The entry is in the ARP cache until it's unconfigured with this command:

```
arp -d 192.168.1.1
```

The entry remains in the cache, listed as incomplete, until the next time the host is queried for its ARP information.

Point to Point Protocol

The Point to Point Protocol (PPP) daemon and its related files exist so you can establish networking sessions over serial point-to-point links, usually with a modem as the device.

Using Chat to Connect

Contrary to popular belief, the daemon pppd doesn't make the connections with the remote device; it relies on the chat program to perform this function.

Chat is typically script-driven—nobody wants to type those strings over and over again. A typical chat script might look like the following:

```
chat " " ATZ OK ATDT5558080 CONNECT " " login: username word: password
```

This script is broken up into call/response pairs (client does something and the server replies), so the whole transaction is conducted in these steps:

1. Chat starts with an empty string that just lets the modem know it's being woken up.

2. Chat sends an ATZ reset command (the call) to the modem to reset its state and waits for the OK string to come back indicating it's ready to roll (the response).

3. Chat sends a dial command (ATDT Number) (a call) and waits for the CONNECT string to be returned from the modem (the response).

4. Then Chat sends an empty string to wake up the remote computer (the call) so it will send the login: prompt (the response) back.

5. The username is sent to the remote machine (the call), and it sends back the password: prompt (the response).

6. Finally, the password is sent, and upon acceptance the chat program is killed, leaving the line open.

The PPP Daemon

After the connection is made, you can have pppd govern the connection. Just having chat establish a link doesn't establish an IP or set up networking. It's just an open connection to be used by the protocols and pppd.

To have pppd set up networking with the remote host, you run the following command:

```
pppd /dev/cua1 57600 crtscts defaultroute
```

This command has pppd change over the /dev/cua1 interface to a PPP connection type and set up networking with the remote computer. The expected speed is set to 57,600bps, with the crtscts option present to turn on hardware handshaking. Finally, the defaultroute option is used to have the local machine see the default gateway as being the remote machine's IP, rather than the local gateway, if present.

Additionally, you can use pppd to call the chat command to make a connection all in one command. The chat command in turn calls a script that contains all the call/response pairs from the previous steps. This would look similar to the following:

```
pppd connect "chat -f chatscript" /dev/cua1 57600 crtscts modem defaultroute
```

We've looked at everything except the modem keyword, which simply tells pppd to monitor the modem for dropped lines.

An additional option that might be applied in some situations is demand, which essentially establishes connections when traffic attempts to contact the remote network or host.

A complementary option to demand is holdoff. If a link is set to be established on demand, it times out if traffic is not continuously streaming to the remote host. The holdoff timer is set to ensure that a dropped or interrupted connection doesn't attempt to reconnect immediately, possibly while the remote is still on-hook. Not setting a holdoff=5 or similar value causes an endless loop condition in some instances because the remote responds to the next attempted connection, only to have it repeatedly dropped.

 Expect questions about options for **pppd**, particularly the **crtscts** and **holdoff** options.

Setting **pppd** Options

The /etc/ppp/options file is used to set options that govern pppd. The package ships with a template file, named options.tpl, but Red Hat and others don't include it. The /etc/ppp/options file shown in Listing 4.2 will do for most purposes.

Listing 4.2   The pppd **Options File**

```
# /etc/ppp/options
#
# Prevent pppd from forking into the background
-detach
#
# use the modem control lines
modem
# use uucp style locks to ensure exclusive access to the serial device
lock
# use hardware flow control
crtscts
# create a default route for this connection in the routing table
defaultroute
# do NOT set up any "escaped" control sequences
asyncmap 0
# use a maximum transmission packet size of 552 bytes
mtu 552
# use a maximum receive packet size of 552 bytes
mru 552
#
# force pppd to use your ISP user name as your 'host name' during the
# authentication process
name username
#
# If you are using ENCRYPTED secrets in the /etc/ppp/pap-secrets
# file, then uncomment the following line.
#+papcrypt
```

The exam doesn't make much of the contents of this file, focusing more on the steps needed to make a connection.

Authentication Options

PPP doesn't restrict who can connect from a client to a server because it's not designed to. Without authentication mechanisms such as PAP and CHAP, getting access to a machine over PPP is easy.

Linux supports the following protocols for authentication:

➤ **Password Authentication Protocol (PAP)**—This protocol provides clear text authentication.

➤ **Challenge Handshake Authentication Protocol (CHAP)**—With this protocol, passwords are never sent unencrypted.

➤ **Microsoft Challenge Handshake Authentication Protocol (MSCHAP)**—This is the Microsoft-specific CHAP version.

Both PAP and CHAP use *secrets* files to secure their logins, with differing degrees of effectiveness. PAP uses a procedure similar to the username and password pair for logging on to a machine, sending the information across the communications link.

CHAP uses a random string and the hostname to send an authentication request to the server, where it's compared and a similar set of data is sent back to the client. CHAP doesn't just authenticate at the initialization of the link, but at random times for the duration of the session, making it much more secure.

The `/etc/ppp/pap-secrets` and `/etc/ppp/chap-secrets` files contain four fields that are delimited by spaces, an example of which is shown here. This `/etc/chap-secrets` file is on the host `blue`:

```
# Secrets for authentication using CHAP
# client  server  secret
  blue     red     fuschia
  red      blue    magenta
```

On the `red` host the `/etc/ppp/chap-secrets` file would contain the following:

```
# Secrets for authentication using CHAP
# client  server  secret
  red      blue    fuschia
  blue     red     magenta
```

When `blue` is initiating a session to `red`, it looks for the line that lists `blue` as the client and `red` as a server and uses that secret string to build the authentication message. This means that when `blue` encrypts a message asking `red` to authenticate itself, `red` sends the message back encrypted with `fuschia`.

When the `red` host is initiating the connection, it looks for its own hostname in the client field and the `blue` hostname in the server field and sends a message built with the `magenta` string.

Both the **/etc/ppp/pap-secrets** and **/etc/ppp/chap-secrets** must be owned by the root user and root group with the permissions set to 740.

In addition, you can use the **minicom terminal adapter** application as a quick test of the modem's connectivity.

Plug and Play

When Plug and Play (PnP) is used, a device usually configures itself when plugged into the system bus. Plug and Play helps match drivers and devices with the correct communication mechanisms.

Linux isn't truly a Plug and Play OS, but the kernel does read the registers for the devices on the system, many of which can be easily recognized and made available to the device drivers via a table managed by the kernel.

The kernel does provide programmatic help to drivers in the form of programs and code that do PnP, and typically that's enough to get the device working. The kernel also assists in keeping resource conflicts from occurring by restricting bus resources to a single device. The 2.2 kernel provided this only for the IRQ and DMA resources, but the 2.4 kernel now provides this support for I/O addresses as well.

Most BIOSs are PnP-compatible, and if the BIOS reads the device and then the kernel can see it from there, it's not really PnP, but it works.

PnP Tools

The main utility for configuring devices under Linux is the `isapnp` program. Part of the isapnptools suite, it's run at startup on many Linux distributions to discover the resources located on the ISA bus using software. (Remember that the PCI bus typically discovers devices using hardware and then makes those devices available to Linux.)

`isapnp` is configured with the `/etc/isapnp.conf` file, consisting of a custom mapping of which devices are going to use which resources on the system.

pnpdump reads the devices on the ISA bus and dumps that information out to the console by default. You can use pnpdump to view the configuration of a device and then edit `isapnp.conf` to add a similar device to the system, particularly if that device was not recognized properly.

Thankfully, LPI doesn't think that we should be delving into the **isapnp.conf** file or the gory details of PnP outside of the concept, needed files, and commands we have covered here.

Configuring Sound and Time

If you're lucky enough to have a sound card that works with Linux already, you'll hear the welcome sounds in KDE or be able to play CDs and sound files in X or the command line.

If the sound card on the system doesn't currently work with Linux, the first thing to run is the sndconfig program. This exists on Red Hat Systems and plays a sound clip of Linus Torvalds pronouncing *Leenux*.

> The primary cause of a recently added sound card not functioning is a conflict with a secondary parallel port because both are using IRQ 5. The exam will test your knowledge of the IRQs and conflicts. Anytime you see a new card being inserted and something not working, an IRQ or I/O address conflict is somewhere in the answer.

Local System Time

Being able to set system time properly is important for the accurate date and time on emails, synchronization of databases, and anything else that requires a reasonably accurate system clock.

Two clocks affect a system's time: the hardware clock, which runs even when the system is off, and the system clock, which is a function of the kernel and an interrupt on the system. System time is a value derived by the time elapsed since January 1, 1970, or the number of seconds since 1969 ended.

The hardware clock exists to supply time to the booting Linux kernel and is ignored thereafter until the system is booted again.

The date Command

The date command affects the system clock or time. To set your system time manually, use the date. The program offers a couple of ways to accomplish this, one for exquisite setting of the time, such as in a script, and the other for quick fixes in a shell session.

To set the system time to July 1 (0701), 4 a.m. (0400), 1995 (95), you'd use the following:

```
date 0701040095
Sat Jul  1 04:00:00 PDT 1995
```

To set the system time with a quickie update, you'd use the date command's normal time formatting, like so:

```
date
Sat Jul  1 04:01:39 PDT 1995
date -s "Sat Jul  1 04:01:39 PDT 1999"
```

Just cut and paste the output from the date command to the new command line by selecting the output while holding down the left mouse button, positioning the cursor, and pressing the middle mouse button to paste it. Alter the time to suit and press Enter.

If you don't have a middle mouse button, you can try to *chord* the left and right mouse buttons by pressing them both at the same time to paste the information. You're actually better off typing it in, based on my experience.

To display the date in an alternative format, use the +FORMAT style. Instead of outputting the date and time with the normal formatting, you can cause it to meet certain character restrictions such as for naming files. For example, to display the date in yyyy-dd-mm format, you'd use the following:

```
date +%Y-%d-%m
```

This shows the following output:

```
2004-09-09
```

Naming a new file at the same time as it was created is simple if you know the previous code. To create a new directory named backup and prefix it with the current date (so it will sort nicely), you would use

```
mkdir `date +%Y-%d-%m`_backup
```

Be sure to use the back tick character (`` ` ``), not the apostrophe ('). The back tick is normally found on the same key as the tilde character (~).

The hwclock Command

hwclock affects the hardware clock, not the system clock or time. If you've spent a few cycles getting the system clock to the precise time, you'll need to ensure that those time values are stored to the hardware clock properly.

Most shutdown routines include a synchronization of the system time to the hardware clock, but just in case, follow the examples here to set it properly.

```
hwclock -r
hwclock --systohc
hwclock --hctosys
```

The first example reads the hardware clock values and displays them on the console.

The second example takes the system time and commits it to the hardware clock.

The third example reads the hardware clock time and sets the system clock to that time.

USB Devices

Most universal serial bus (USB) devices were supported in the 2.2 version of the kernel, with ever-expanding support in the 2.4 and 2.6 kernels.

USB devices are on a hierarchical tree, with a controller and a root hub. All device communications occur through the USB bus, with devices incapable of directly accessing other devices.

The USB 1.0 specification allows for 127 connected devices, with any other hubs plugged in to the main hub taking up 1 device. USB 2.0 might appear on the exam, but not questions about the specification or features. You'll just see questions about USB devices and so on.

Controller Types

There are two main USB controller types: the universal host controller interface and the open host controller interface.

The universal host controller interface (UHCI) is an Intel specification, with a simpler function and more software and processor cycles needed.

The open host controller interface (OHCI) is a Compaq specification that is slightly less dependent on the software and processor.

USB Devices and Linux

To use the USB devices under Linux, the necessary drivers are

➤ usbcore.o

➤ usb-uhci.o, uhci.o, or usb-ohci.o

If the USB core and proper specification driver aren't running, you might have to insert the proper spec driver with insmod or modprobe to get it running.

A quick way to see whether the USB drivers are loaded properly is to run **lsmod** and see whether they show up in the output. If they are present, and other devices are dependent on them, this is shown in the rightmost column.

Linux and USB have a different relationship from other operating systems and USB. For example, every object on a Linux system is a file and everything is organized under a single path hierarchy. This leads to the next point, that USB devices are organized under a USB device file system that appears under the /proc abstracted file system.

The USB device file system is usually mounted at system initialization on /proc/bus/usb. This directory always contains two subdirectories called /drivers and /devices. When a device is attached to the file system, the first device is numbered 001, then 002, and so on.

USB and Storage Devices

USB storage devices (such as detachable hard disk enclosures) show up as SCSI devices in the configuration for the system because they could be any type of device and the SCSI drivers present the most flexible set of options.

Run the mount command string to search the output for the characters usb:

```
mount ¦ grep usb
```

This shows the following output:

```
usbdevfs on /proc/bus/usb  type usbdevfs (rw)
```

The output shows the USB device file system mounted at the expected location. Other commands you can use to view USB devices include scsi_info, which is designed to enumerate both SCSI and USB devices. For example, if a mass storage device such as a disk is located on /dev/sda, you would use the following command:

```
scsi_info /dev/sda
```

In addition, if the device were a storage device, you could use fdisk -l to see which /dev file it was mapped to. Then you can either map it manually or insert it as an entry in the /etc/fstab file.

Finally, for the graphically oriented crowd, you can use the usbview command, which shows the USB devices and configuration in a two-paned view.

Using usbmgr

The usbmgr command loads or unloads necessary kernel modules and executes various scripts to set up USB devices. The kernel configuration must have the USB Support option selected and compiled in. Depending on the distribution, you should edit the /etc/rc.config or rc.sysinit script to configure the START_HOTPLUG setting to true.

usbmgr configuration files consist of the following:

➤ usbmgr.conf—Includes data for load/unload modules

➤ preload.conf—Includes kernel modules to load at startup

However, if, during a kernel reconfiguration, you do compile in all USB drivers, the usbmgr command has nothing to do and is unnecessary. If you'll be using USB devices frequently, compile everything in the kernel to make things load more quickly and result in fewer dependencies.

USB Devices and Drivers

The drivers file contains a list of loaded drivers, which vary depending on what's attached or loaded for each system. To see a listing of this file, execute this sample command:

```
more /proc/bus/usb/drivers
```

This produces the following output:

```
hid
printer
hub
```

The *devices* file is much more verbose, showing attached device information in a series of lines per device:

```
cat /proc/bus/usb/devices
```

This produces the following output:

```
T:  Bus=01 Lev=00 Prnt=00 (Topology)
B:  Alloc=  0/900 us ( 0%), #Int=  0, #Iso=  0
D:  Ver= 1.00 Cls=09(hub  ) (Device Descriptor)
P:  Vendor=0000 ProdID=0000 (Continuation of D:)
S:  Product=USB UHCI Root Hub (Strings returned from device)
S:  SerialNumber=1060 (Continuation of S:)
```

USB coverage on the exam is mostly a matter of knowing what relationship USB has to the system, (it's a device file system) and how it's constructed (as a hierarchy of devices under the root hub). Be sure to view all files mentioned and read the man pages for **/etc/hotplug** and **usbmgr**.

Setting Up SCSI

LPI assumes that you'll have some server systems with Linux on them, with SCSI being the storage device of choice on high-capacity and throughput-intensive systems.

When taking the exam, remember that the SCSI bus type determines the density of devices (8 or 16), such as

➤ **8-bit SCSI**—Eight devices (0–7)

➤ **16-bit SCSI**—Sixteen devices (0–15)

Each device is associated with a number that determines the priority in accessing the SCSI bus.

SCSI ID 7 is normally reserved for the controller. This dates back to when there were only 8 IDs to choose from and the controller could be put on either end; ID 7 was therefore chosen. Now that you have 16 IDs from which to choose, you can make the controller ID 15. However, for consistency's sake, ID 7 is still used by most sysadmins.

In part because of ID 7 historically being the controller, the priority order for SCSI devices is as follows:

7, 6, 5, 4, 3, 2, 1, 0, 15, 14, 13, 12, 10, 9, 8

Typically, the host adapter should have the highest priority, which is another reason to keep the controller at ID 7.

Linux uses the device designator sd followed by a number or two to define each SCSI logical unit number (LUN) or device. For example, the first SCSI device on a system should be mapped to /dev/sda. You can determine the upper limit of possible devices/LUNs on your system with the following command:

```
ls -1 /dev/sd* ¦ wc -l
```

This produces the following output:

```
2048
```

The /proc file system is where the SCSI device information is kept, in the /proc/scsi/scsi directory. You can view the devices and other information with the following command:

```
cat /proc/scsi/scsi
```

This produces the following output:

```
Attached devices:
Host: scsi0 Channel: 00 Id: 00 Lun: 00
  Vendor: VMware,  Model: VMware Virtual S Rev: 1.0
Type:   Direct-Access           ANSI SCSI revision: 02
```

Here are a few final exam tips for the hardware section: Know the port device names, interrupts, and I/O addresses. Know how to modify serial port configurations and how to set an IP and other IP information manually for a NIC. Also, know which files and procedures are used for a PPP connection.

Exam Prep Questions

1. You are configuring a dial-up connection for a Linux desktop user. What is the actual device filename for the modem that is using I/O address `02e8h`? (Choose two.)

   ❏   A. `/dev/ttys1`
   ❏   B. `/dev/ttyS3`
   ❏   C. `/dev/modem`
   ❏   D. `/dev/cua3`

   Answers B and D are correct because the device is using IRQ 3 and I/O address `03e8h`; therefore, `setserial /dev/ttyS3` and `setserial /dev/cua3` confirm this. Answer A is incorrect because there must be a capital *S* in the device filename and it points to the wrong port. Answer C is incorrect because `/dev/modem` is most often a link to an actual device filename, such as `/dev/ttyS1`.

2. A user complains that after using the `setserial` command to configure his modem, it can no longer communicate at a rate faster than 9600kbps. What are the most likely settings that would cause this problem? (Choose two.)

   ❏   A. UART
   ❏   B. `line`
   ❏   C. `spd_normal`
   ❏   D. `Baud_base`
   ❏   E. IRQ

   Answers A and D are correct because `Baud_base` is the setting that reflects the speed of the connection and the UART setting is the type of controller, which, if set to 8250 or lower than 16550, keeps the speed at 9600kbps or less. Answer B is incorrect because the `line` setting has no bearing on the speed of the connection. Answer C is incorrect because `spd_normal` is used to set a requested speed as the actual speed. Answer E is incorrect because an incorrectly set IRQ would keep the connection from occurring altogether.

3. You are configuring a NIC to communicate with the network. Your network administrator assigned you an IP of 192.168.33.104, the netmask is the default for that class, and your interface is the first Ethernet device on the machine. Which of the following sets up this device so a ping to another device will work?

   ○   A. `netconfig -ip=192.168.33.104 -mask=C`
   ○   B. `ifconfig eth0 192.168.33.104 netmask 255.255.255.0 up`
   ○   C. `netstat -a 192.168.33.104/255.255.255.0 on`
   ○   D. `route add IP 192.168.33.104 255.255.255.0`

Answer B is correct because it correctly sets the IP and netmask for `eth0` and then turns on the interface. Answer A is incorrect because `netconfig` is not a command that can be used in this fashion; it's menu-oriented. Answer C is incorrect because `netstat` doesn't set IPs; it shows connections to and from the machine. Answer D is incorrect because the `route` command is for manipulating the routing table, not setting IP information for interfaces.

4. You want to place a static mapping for your gateway IP in the ARP cache. The IP is 192.168.33.1 and the MAC address is 00:04:5A:D0:C9:C9. In the blank below, write the command that accomplishes the static mapping:

The correct answer is `arp -s 192.168.1.1 00:04:5A:D0:C9:C9`. There are no alternative correct answers.

5. Which of the following options affects how long an interrupted PPP connection is idle before a reconnection is attempted?
   - ○ A. `demand`
   - ○ B. `hold_down`
   - ○ C. `idle_time`
   - ○ D. `holdoff`

Answer D is correct because the `holdoff` option sets how long a connection that has been dropped remains idle until a reconnection is attempted. Answer A is incorrect because the `demand` option causes the connection to be initiated upon receipt of traffic but does not specifically reconnect dropped connections. Answer B is incorrect because the `hold_down` option doesn't exist in this situation. Answer C is incorrect because there isn't an `idle_time` option in this situation.

6. Which of the following protocols is supported for a Linux PPP machine to connect to a dial-up server such as an ISP? (Choose all that apply.)
   - ❏ A. PAP
   - ❏ B. SPAP
   - ❏ C. CHAP
   - ❏ D. MSCHAP
   - ❏ E. EAP

Answers A, C, and D are correct because they are supported protocols on a Linux machine for use with a PPP connection. Answer B is incorrect because SPAP is not a supported protocol for PPP connections. Answer E is incorrect because EAP is not a supported protocol for PPP connections.

7. After system bootup is completed, what is the most common component of the PC's BIOS that is accessed by Linux?

   ○ A. PCI configuration
   ○ B. Onboard VGA BIOS
   ○ C. Hardware clock
   ○ D. ACPI

   Answer C is correct because Linux typically doesn't use anything but the hardware clock after bootup. Answers A, B, and D exist in the BIOS but are not accessed by a default Linux installation after the system is booted.

8. Which of the following is involved in setting up an unrecognized ISA device to be Plug and Play for your Linux system? (Choose all that apply.)

   ❑ A. `isapnp`
   ❑ B. `/etc/pcipnp.conf`
   ❑ C. `pnpdump`
   ❑ D. `/etc/isapnp.conf`
   ❑ E. All of the above

   Answers A, C, and D are correct because these files are elements of the Plug and Play configuration for a Linux machine. Answer B is incorrect because no such file exists for a Linux system. Answer E is incorrect because not all of the choices are correct.

9. How many storage devices can be addressed on a 16-bit SCSI controller interface? (Choose the best answer.)

   ○ A. 7
   ○ B. 8
   ○ C. 15
   ○ D. 16

   Answer C is correct because a 16-bit SCSI controller requires a single ID for the controller itself, leaving 15 for storage and other devices. Answer A is incorrect because it references the number of devices, other than the controller, possible on an 8-bit SCSI controller. Answer B is incorrect because it references the total number of IDs on an 8-bit SCSI controller interface. Answer D is incorrect because it references the total number of IDs on a 16-bit SCSI controller interface, not the total number of possible IDs for the device.

10. Where can you find SCSI device definitions for a running system? Write the full path and filename for the object in the blank below:

   _____

   The correct answer is `/proc/scsi/scsi`. There are no alternative correct answers.

Partitioning and File Systems

Terms you'll need to understand:

✓ Device file
✓ Disk utilization
✓ File system
✓ Inode
✓ Mounting/unmounting
✓ Primary, logical, and extended partitions
✓ Superblock

Techniques you'll need to master:

✓ Identifying device types
✓ Identifying file system types
✓ Partitioning a disk
✓ Creating a file system
✓ Mounting a file system
✓ Unmounting a file system
✓ Checking a file system
✓ Tuning and debugging a file system
✓ Identifying disk usage

Overview

Devices on a Linux system are not available to users unless the root user makes them so by setting their access and options in the appropriate configuration files.

The order in which to make a device usable for storing data (and having users access it) is as follows:

1. Install the device.

2. Partition it.

3. Make a file system on the partition(s).

4. Make or choose a mount point (directory).

5. Mount the file system (or put it in /etc/fstab).

6. Change the ownership.

7. Set the permissions.

Linux devices are linked with a device file in the /dev directory (which is where devices are associated with device or dev files). There are many pre-existing files in this directory.

Linux devices are identified with a two- or three-letter device designator and typically use a progression of numerals or letters to denote the actual device of that type. An example of this would be the first IDE drive on the system being labeled /dev/hda. The following table explains the Linux device types and designators:

Major Type	Description
hd	IDE hard drive partitions
sd	SCSI hard drive partitions
scd	SCSI CD-ROM drives
st	SCSI tape drives
ht	IDE tape drives
fd	Floppy drives
lp	Parallel ports
tty	Terminals or console ports
pty	Remote (network) terminals
ttyS	Serial ports
modem	Link to the first modem
cua	Communication ports

Device prefixes combine with a number to indicate an exact partition on a given drive. Some device media don't allow or support partitions such as CD-ROM or floppy devices. The IDE devices on a system are arranged to fit the number of IDE channels and connections on a standard PC. The following lists the four standard IDE connectors and their device designations:

➤ hda—Master drive on the primary IDE channel

➤ hdb—Slave drive on the primary IDE channel

➤ hdc—Master drive on the secondary IDE channel

➤ hdd—Slave drive on the secondary IDE channel

The CD-ROM on an IDE system is normally in the /dev/hdc or secondary master position and is typically linked to the /dev/cdrom device file. This convention lets the sysadmin easily find and mount or work with the CD drive.

Partitions

Disks on PCs can have up to four primary partitions per disk, and in cases when you need more than four, one of the primary partition slots can be exchanged for an extended partition.

There is allowance for only one extended partition per disk. The extended partition can hold an unlimited number of partitions, although warnings abound to hold the number down to 12 or so.

The logical partitions inside an extended partition are virtually identical to a primary partition; they just happen to live only inside an extended partition. No perceivable difference exists between a primary and extended partition except in the numbering, position on disk, and the fact that the boot files for a Linux machine should exist on a primary partition.

NOTE

The need for the boot files to be on a primary partition leads many experienced sysadmins to create a small (200MB or so) **/boot** partition and then declare the rest of the disk as an extended partition with all other partitions as logicals therein.

Swap

Swap files and swap partitions are necessary for performance. Even a system with plenty of extra RAM will use swap space for storing bits and pieces of programs and code.

Swap is normally configured as a separate partition on Linux systems. Swap files can be created on demand to satisfy a momentary need, but they suffer from the twin disadvantages of being slower than raw partition access due to file systems and such and taking up extra space.

 Windows uses a **pagefile.sys** file that can be equal to and often one and a half times the size of RAM. If three versions of Windows exist on the same machine, each needs its own **pagefile.sys**. Linux, on the other hand, can have many different versions on the same machine, all using the exact same swap partition(s) when that version is running.

How much swap space should you have? Until the 2.2 version of the kernel, it was recommended that you have 2x the size of physical RAM up to 128MB of swap space. Now with the 2.4 and higher kernel, you need from 1.5x to 2x the size of RAM, up to about 1GB at the most.

You can have up to 8 swap partitions or files (32 are possible after kernel version 2.4.10), and you should have swap space broken up into several equal pieces if multiple physical drives are in the system. For example, if you have two 40GB drives on the system, one primarily for the system (/ and such) and the other for user data, the swap space for the system should be split into two pieces, one on each drive. The /home tree and some swap commonly appear on the second disk, which reduces contention for the system drive's swap and isolates users' data.

 Many sysadmins believe that keeping the most frequently used files on the outer tracks of the disk improves sequential reads because reads happen faster on the outer edges of the disk. This might get you a few milliseconds per hour, but most sysadmins have a lot more to do than try to micro-manage that closely. If I don't get a significant increase in performance (5% or more), I don't usually bother with such machinations.

Drive Partitioning Schemes

Partitioning depends on what the system will be used for, with workstations usually having fewer partitions and servers having the most. For example, a common workstation partitioning scheme is shown in Figure 5.1.

With such a simple partition structure, hda1 could only be the root of the system, which leaves hda2 to be a swap partition for the system.

With a server, the converse is true: There are more partitions, and they're there for a variety of reasons, not the least of which is to keep something (or someone) from filling up the system partition with files.

hda1	hda2
Primary	Primary

Figure 5.1 Workstation partitions.

For example, a server might have the partitions laid out as shown in Figure 5.2.

hda1	hda2	hda3	hda5	hda6	hda7
Primary	Pri	Primary	logical	logical	logical

Figure 5.2 Server partitions.

You will notice that this server partitioning layout has three primary partitions and then uses an extended partition to lay out a few more. In this case, the extended partition (hda4) takes up no actual space and contains only the logical partitions hda5, hda6, and hda7.

 Logical partitions always start with the number 5. In the scheme of partitioning, 1–4 are slots for primary partitions, or one of them can be traded for an extended partition. The system always begins the logical partitions with 5 to allow for flexibility in the use of the primary partitions.

Disk Partitioning Tools

The lingua franca of partitioning tools is the fdisk utility. Nearly every system has a copy of fdisk that can be used to create or alter the partition table. Having said that, various other tools can be used, and distribution vendors have come up with others that make the partitioning stage easier and clearer. The three tools that must be discussed are

➤ **fdisk**—Included on nearly every system that runs Linux.

➤ **DiskDruid**—Red Hat's graphical tool is used only on Red Hat.

➤ **cfdisk**—Debian and derivatives use it, and others might.

fdisk

In the case of Red Hat, fdisk is used to set the initial partition tables, but the DiskDruid tool must be used as well to set the labels and partition paths, such as when you set /dev/hda1 to map to the /boot partition. This leads most second-time installers to just use DiskDruid for the whole routine.

 Red Hat's latest versions (such as Red Hat 9) don't allow the use of fdisk or other partitioning tools, defaulting to DiskDruid only. Use fdisk from a boot disk or rescue CD-ROM to partition with it instead of using DiskDruid.

fdisk's interface is line-based and has constantly disappearing lines of screen output, making it sometimes hard to remember where you are or what happened.

Starting the fdisk tool to partition a drive is easy—just remember to specify the device file that contains the partition table you want to edit, such as

```
fdisk /dev/hda
```

The following steps show you how to create a quick layout of three partitions with fdisk, including setting the swap and viewing your handiwork afterward:

1. Start the fdisk program with the following command:

   ```
   fdisk /dev/hda
   ```

   When you see the message about how your disk is larger than 1024 cylinders, ignore it.

2. Press the P key to view the current (if any) partitions on the system.

3. If there are partitions, clear them by pressing the D key and work back from the highest-numbered partition to the lowest, pressing the D key and the next number that represents the partition.

4. When you're finished, confirm that the partition table is empty by pressing P.

5. Create a new partition by pressing the N key and then the P key to create a new primary partition.

6. Choose the first partition by typing 1 and then pressing Enter.

7. Leave the default cylinder start value (1) as is by pressing Enter.

8. Specify a 200MB boot partition by typing +200M and pressing Enter. Leave the default cylinder value alone and press Enter.

9. Press P to verify that the partition was created.

10. Now create a 4GB root partition by typing **n, p** for primary, and **2** for the partition number.

11. Specify a 4GB partition by typing **+4000M** and pressing Enter.

12. Check the new partition's presence by pressing P.

13. Finally, create a swap partition by typing n for a new partition, **p** for primary, and **3** for the partition number. Then press Enter. Leave the default cylinder value alone and press Enter.

14. Specify a 750MB swap partition by typing **+750M** and pressing Enter. Leave the default cylinder value alone and press Enter.

15. Press the P key again to verify that partitions 1–3 exist.

Now change the third partition to the swap type by typing **t** for the type, **3** for the partition to change, **L** to list the possible values, and then **82**. Press Enter to set the partition to the correct type.

16. Note the third partition is changed to be a swap partition.

17. Write your changes by pressing the W key and Enter.

This works only on a machine that you are destructively partitioning for an installation.

Confirming that you've correctly partitioned the disk layout after a system is running or viewing the partition tables is easy. You can run the following command:

```
fdisk -l
```

The exams test your basic knowledge about fdisk, which letter commands are used to accomplish which tasks, the types of partitions that are used by default, and so on.

For the real world, mail a copy of this output to your sysadmin's account with this command:

```
# fdisk -l ¦ mail root -s "Fdisk params for server X"
```

This sends an email to your root account with the subject shown in quotation marks, so you can find it if you mess up the partition table of the system.

DiskDruid

Restricted to Red Hat machines only, this tool is the final setup step for partitioning on Red Hat machines. As of late, this tool is the only supported option during the installation of the systems, either in TUI (Text-based User Interface) or GUI mode.

The advanced features of the tool make it a nice one-stop-shop for partitioning and assigning the label/path of the various partitions on the system.

For example, even after using fdisk or cfdisk to partition a system, when installing Red Hat on it you have to assign the partition's paths to the physical partition in DiskDruid. For the most part, this is simple: You just highlight the partition to be altered and click the Edit button to assign the path and choose the formatting options. See Figure 5.3 for an example of the /boot partition being set.

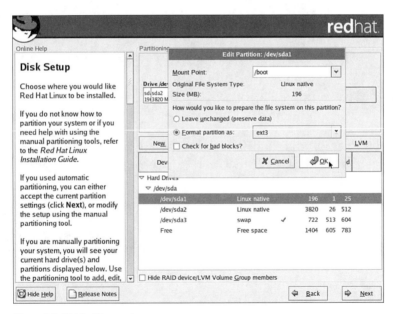

Figure 5.3 DiskDruid example.

DiskDruid isn't featured much on the exam, most likely because it's a small part of the installation mechanism and exists strictly on Red Hat machines.

Interestingly enough, DiskDruid is not available after the installation process—only fdisk is. It seems odd that the tool would be so heavily used in the installation routine but not invokable afterward.

Lastly, DiskDruid offers several options that aren't possible in either cfdisk or fdisk, namely choosing the formatting and making software raid sets, all in the interface.

cfdisk

The cfdisk tool is used mainly on Debian and its derivative distributions. However, it can be used on any system with the appropriate distribution boot disks or rescue CDs.

Many regard cfdisk as the most stable and competent of the partitioning tools, even to the extent of slagging it in the man pages for the different formatting commands.

The main reason to use cfdisk is the screen-based nature of its interface. All the interactions with cfdisk take place on the screen in full view; nothing scrolls by or disappears unless you exit the tool. The cfdisk menus are interactive and context-sensitive, including presenting options for a group of free space blocks that are different from the options displayed for a selected partition.

The cfdisk tool isn't featured much on the exams, so just knowing its features and how to work it will suffice. Doing an install of Knoppix or any other Debian distribution will teach you as much as you need to know about the exam's treatment of cfdisk.

An excellent way to gain cfdisk experience is to install Knoppix 3.3 or later to a hard disk because it uses cfdisk and the entire bootup and installation can be completed in about 40 minutes on a gigahertz or higher processor machine.

Overview of File Systems

A *file system* is an organizing construct that acts like a database or hierarchical structure that contains directories and files in a partition.

Think of everything on a Linux system as a file, starting with the file system itself. A *directory* on the file system is a special type of file that contains links from the file's name to the inode that represents the file on the file system itself.

To illustrate this, open the /etc directory in the vi editor and navigate from link to link, proving that the directory is a file that links from one place to another. Try it as shown here:

1. Open a shell session as a normal user.

2. Edit the /etc directory in vi with the following command:

```
vi /etc
```

You'll see something like the following:

```
" Press ? for keyboard shortcuts
" Sorted by name (.bak,",.o,.h,.info,.swp,.obj at end of list)
"= /etc/
../
CORBA/
X11/
aep/
alchemist/
alternatives/
amanda/
atalk/
bonobo-activation/
cipe/
cron.d/
cron.daily/
```

3. Place the cursor on the X11/ line and press the Enter key.

Notice that the directory changes to reflect your being in the /etc/X11/ directory.

| If you navigate to a regular file and press Enter, you load that file and are unable to return to the higher directories. Doing this simply edits the file, just as if you had invoked the vi editor with that file as an argument.

4. Navigate back to the /etc directory by pressing the Enter key while the cursor is on the ../ entry.

5. For curiosity sake, when back in the /etc directory, choose the ../ entry and notice that you're now in the root of the system.

It's interesting to note that you can navigate the entire tree of the file system as one big file if you choose to.

6. Exit the vi editor by typing :q! to ensure you didn't make any changes.

Now you can see that the entire file system is like a big file that contains entries that point to other directory files or regular files.

Superblocks

The *superblock* is stored in the first sector of the file system and contains the file system size, location, number of inodes, and cylinder and disk block usage for the file system. The superblock contents are replicated multiple times, making it much easier to recover from errors. The first available backup superblock copy is usually the 8,193rd block.

The space taken up by duplicate superblocks isn't hard to calculate. They occupy about 36 bytes and occur every 8,192 blocks, so a file system that contains 1.5 million blocks might have 176 superblock copies, each taking up 36 bytes, or about 63K total.

It's not really the space usage of the superblock copies; it's the time needed to write all the duplicate information that can be consuming resources.

Inodes and Files

The relationship between files as expressed in the file system directory files and the data on disk is a construct called an *inode*. An inode, or index node, represents the ability to associate a file with blocks on the disk. Only one inode is assigned to a file at its creation. That inode and its information are viewable with the stat command, as shown in this example:

```
stat /etc
  File: "/etc"
  Size: 8192      Blocks: 16    IO Block: -4611693096533487616 Directory
Device: 803h/2051d     Inode: 224449      Links: 88
Access: (0755/drwxr-xr-x)  Uid: (   0/   root)  Gid: (   0/   root)
Access: Sun Feb  8 03:25:21 2004
Modify: Sun Feb  8 03:04:24 2004
Change: Sun Feb  8 03:04:24 2004
```

On the exam it's important to know that everything descriptive about the file except the actual filename is stored in the inode. The file's data is kept in the IO block, which is shown in the inode's **stat** output. The total amount of inodes is set only at the file system creation, and their number cannot be changed without re-creating the file system.

Inodes are pointers to disk constructs called *disk blocks*. Disk blocks are grouped in sets of eight; each group is called a *block group*. Each inode is by default assocaiated with a disk block that is at the front of its block group, and that block group is initially reserved for that file only. This gives the file room to grow without being fragmented.

Inodes and Disk Space

Inode amounts are set at file system creation, with only three sizes being available for all needs:

➤ 1024KB—The smallest size used is best for news/html.

➤ 2048KB—The default is used for most purposes.

➤ 4096KB—The largest size is best for larger data sets, databases, and so on.

If a file system is to contain a lot of little files, such as Usenet messages or HTML files, it should be formatted to contain many inodes, each representing a certain set of blocks of information. This is done using the smallest block size available, effectively creating more inodes to handle the possible number of files.

The real danger of having a large block size and relatively few inodes (such as for a database server) is that you might run out of available inodes and still have disk space left over. A system can run completely out of inodes and still have available disk space, a situation that often requires extensive troubleshooting and work to remedy.

The best way to fix this problem is to use the `type` option of the mkfs program when creating the file system. The syntax of this is as follows:

```
mkfs -t ext3 /dev/hdb1 -T largefile
```

The values for the `-T` option are as follows:

➤ `news`—Makes one inode per 4KB block

➤ `largefile`—Makes one inode per 1MB of blocks

➤ `largefile4`—Makes one inode per 4MB of blocks

The block size at file system creation sets a particular number of inodes, and you can override the amount of space each inode is associated with by specifying one of the previous options. Some file systems that contain large files need to dedicate more space to data rather than to inodes that won't be accessed or used. The `largefile` options allow up to 4MB of data to be associated with a single inode by default, rather than the measly 32KB that a 4,096-byte block gives you.

File System Types

Linux uses a large set of file systems on its storage devices, including

➤ ext2—The default Linux file system.

➤ ext3—Essentially ext2 with journaling (logging).

➤ iso9660—The CD-ROM file system.

➤ udf—The DVD file system.

➤ minix—Obsolete; it's not present on all systems.

➤ vfat—A 32-bit file system (Windows FAT32).

➤ msdos—A 12- or 16-bit FAT file system.

➤ umsdos—An extended Linux version of msdos file system.

➤ proc—A virtualized file system that represents the kernel's processes and structures.

➤ hpfs—Nearly obsolete; it's the OS/2 file system.

➤ sysv—System V file system that incorporates support for multiple Unix file systems.

➤ nfs—The Network File System by Sun Microsystems, which is the default network file sharing protocol for all of Unix/Linux.

➤ smb—The Samba file system is Microsoft's default file sharing protocol for network shares. It's otherwise known as CIFS (Common Internet File System).

For a more extensive description of all the file systems available under Linux, use the **man 5 fs** command.

Very little mention is made of ReiserFS, JFS, and XFS on the exams. The only questions about these file systems seem to be to determine which file system is the easiest to upgrade to from an **ext2** file system—that being **ext3**, without a doubt.

Creating File Systems

When a proper partition exists for the file system to reside on, creating the file system takes a relatively short time, although the options available are extensive.

The **mkfs** Command

The mkfs command is somewhat unique: It's the front end for many programs for creating file systems on Linux. The mkfs command, when used with the -t fstyp option, calls the mkfs.fstyp program to make the actual file system. Here's an example:

```
mkfs -t ext2 /dev/sda5
```

This command executes the mkfs program, supplying the type of ext2, which in turn executes the mkfs.ext2 program against the target partition, creating an Ext2 file system.

The long commands, (called *file system builders*) can be invoked directly, saving some time and confusion, as shown here:

```
mkfs.ext2 /dev/sda5
```

Specifying options works with whichever method you choose, so let's focus on the shortcuts that exist for the various mkfs-specific programs:

Command	FS Builder	Shortcut
mkfs	mkfs.ext2	mke2fs
	mkfs.ext3	mke2fs
	mkfs.jfs	(no shortcut)
	mkfs.reiserfs	(no shortcut)
	mkfs.msdos	mkdosfs
	mkfs.vfat	mkdosfs
	mkfs.cramfs	mkcramfs

Other file system creation mk tools are available on the system. Here is a sample list of the important ones:

➤ mkisofs—Creates ISO file systems and is used for CD creation

➤ mknod—Creates special files (dev files, named pipes, and so on)

➤ mkraid—Creates raid sets from separate disks

➤ mkswap—Makes a partition or file into swap space for use as part of virtual memory

File System Creation Options

Creating file systems can either be quick and default or take some time and involve a good number of options. Several examples of quick and default were given in the previous section, so let's dive into the long and involved ones.

Creating a specific file system such as ext3 is accomplished with one of three methods:

➤ mkfs -t ext3 device

➤ mkfs.ext3 device

➤ mke2fs -j device

Setting other options for the file system is accomplished with either a specific option or the general-purpose -o option (which allows you to specify multiple options after -o).

For example, the following command creates an ext3 file system on the /dev/sdb5 logical partition with a 4,096 block size, a reserved block percentage of 2%, a volume label of data, and the sparse_super option for less superblock copies for the disk:

```
mkfs.ext3 -b 4096 -m 2 -L data -O sparse_super /dev/sdb5
```

The file system parameters can be checked with the dumpe2fs command, such as

```
dumpe2fs -h /dev/sdb5
```

The output looks like this:

```
dumpe2fs 1.32 (09-Nov-2002)
Filesystem volume name:   <none>
Last mounted on:          <not available>
Filesystem UUID:          ba53d447-2e60-4dfa-8ce5-208a32bd4a0b
Filesystem magic number:  0xEF53
Filesystem revision #:    1 (dynamic)
Filesystem features:      filetype sparse_super
Default mount options:    (none)
Filesystem state:         clean
Errors behavior:          Continue
Filesystem OS type:       Linux
Inode count:              125696
Block count:              250999
Reserved block count:     12549
Free blocks:              247040
Free inodes:              125685
First block:              0
Block size:               4096
Fragment size:            4096
Blocks per group:         32768
Fragments per group:      32768
Inodes per group:         15712
Inode blocks per group:   491
Filesystem created:       Fri Jan 23 05:10:51 2112
Last mount time:          n/a
```

```
Last write time:          Fri Jan 23 05:10:51 2112
Mount count:              0
Maximum mount count:      24
Last checked:             Fri Jan 23 05:10:51 2112
Check interval:           15552000 (6 months)
Next check after:         Wed Jul 21 06:10:51 2112
Reserved blocks uid:      0 (user root)
Reserved blocks gid:      0 (group root)
First inode:              11
Inode size:               128
```

The use of the -h option keeps the group information from showing up, which is usually unnecessary unless an error occurs on the file system.

On the exam, you'll need to know exactly what the options do and how to format them properly. The previous examples should serve as a firm foundation. Practice making all the various types of file systems with the more common options.

Advanced File System Commands

The file systems on your machines are relatively robust but need some care and attention now and then. Different tools can be used to check the file systems, configure settings that affect their performance, and debug their operations.

File System Checker

When a file system is broken or has errors, an fsck (file system check) is in order. The mount count and maximum mount count are how the system knows when to check the file system structure and data health (see the section "Tuning File Systems" for more on mount counts and using tune2fs). On a file system such as ext2, this is important because a periodic check can save you hours of heartache and troubleshooting (repairing the file system after a crash) when the data is most needed.

Shortcut commands for the fsck command include

➤ e2fsck—Shortcut for checking the ext2/3 file system

➤ dosfsck—Used for all varieties of the DOS/FAT file system

➤ reiserfsck—Used for the ReiserFS file system

The fsck tool uses the /etc/fstab file to automatically check file systems at system start. If a file system is marked unclean for reasons that include a power outage, unexpected system stoppage, or other event that didn't let the system finish writing to disk properly, a lengthy check of the file system is probably required.

The worst scenario is file system damage, usually noticed when restarting a downed system. The system attempts to run a quick fsck session on the file systems noted in /etc/fstab, beginning with those that have a 1 in the sixth column, and continuing on numerically until finished. The fsck program skips any that have a 0 (zero) in the sixth column.

All file systems that have a 1 in the column are checked first in parallel, then any that have a 2 in the column in parallel, and so on.

If the damage is too great to fix automatically, the system presents you with a message stating Ctrl-d to continue, otherwise enter the root password to perform a file system check. Entering the root password displays the shell prompt and prints a helpful message that tells you the file system that needs checking.

fsck options that can help the busy sysadmin include

➤ -A—Moves through /etc/fstab checking all file systems in one long pass

➤ -c—Percentage or hash mark progress bars for any operations that support their display

➤ -N—Performs a dry run (makes no changes), showing what would be done; don't change anything (good for seeing how bad it is)

➤ -V—Produces verbose output for everything, including commands that are being executed by fsck

➤ -a—Doesn't ask questions and noninteractively repairs the file system

fsck makes five passes or types of changes to the file system, shown here:

➤ **Pass 1**—Checking inodes, blocks, and sizes

➤ **Pass 2**—Checking directory structure

➤ **Pass 3**—Checking directory connectivity

➤ **Pass 4**—Checking reference counts

➤ **Pass 5**—Checking group summary information

When fsck finds serious errors such as blocks claimed by multiple files (cross-linked), blocks claimed outside of the file system, too few link counts (the number of directories linked to an inode), or unaccounted blocks or directories that correspond to unallocated inodes, it displays an error message and asks to be run manually.

 Always, always run **fsck** on unmounted or read-only mounted file systems. This is mandatory; otherwise, an fsck and a user write might occur, causing corruption. If it's the root file system, you should either do it in single user mode or use the rescue CD-ROM to ensure that the root is mounted read-only.

The following is an example of a simple check of a file system that was mounted on the /fun directory and resides on /dev/hdb1:

```
umount /fun
fsck.ext2 -v /dev/hdb1
```

Here is the output from fsck:

```
e2fsck 1.18, 11-Nov-1999 for EXT2 FS 0.5b, 95/08/09
/dev/hdb1: clean, 9692/1237888 files, 1754206/2474002 blocks
```

The following is an example of a verbose (without all the yes answers) forced check on the same file system that is currently unmounted:

```
fsck.ext2 -v -f /dev/hdb1
```

Here is the output:

```
e2fsck 1.18, 11-Nov-1999 for EXT2 FS 0.5b, 95/08/09
Pass 1: Checking inodes, blocks, and sizes
Pass 2: Checking directory structure
Pass 3: Checking directory connectivity
Pass 4: Checking reference counts
Pass 5: Checking group summary information
9692 inodes used (0%)
157 non-contiguous inodes (1.6%)
# of inodes with ind/dind/tind blocks: 1194/205/0
1754206 blocks used (70%)
0 bad blocks
```

Tuning File Systems

The tune2fs command is used to set parameters, such as the maximum mount count, after the file system is created. This number is set to 20 by default, unless you set it at file system creation or change it afterward with tune2fs. An example of setting the mount count to 0 (zero) for an ext3 journaling file system is shown here:

```
tune2fs -c 0 /dev/hda1
```

This causes the system to completely ignore the mount count and never initiates a file system check routinely. This is desired on an ext3 file system, which never marks the file system as dirty or corrupted because the journal is where the state of the file system is stored.

In addition to the mount count, error checking can be altered so the system will do one of three things when an error is detected by the kernel for the file system:

➤ continue—Continues normally

➤ remount-ro—Remounts the file system read-only, ready to fsck

➤ panic—Causes the kernel to panic, which stops the system (not recommended unless you're a system tester)

The reserved percentage (space available only to the root user) associated with the root user can also be associated with a system group with the -g option, such as

```
tune2fs -g admins /dev/sdb5
```

Debugging File Systems

The debugfs command is useful for debugging and fiddling with the file systems on your machine. It's also extremely easy to delete or corrupt a portion or all of the file system, so extreme caution is recommended.

In fact, you'll have to read the man page for **debugfs** to even see how to damage the file system. It's not mounted read-write by default, probably due to the fact that users can find the command. You've been warned.

The debugfs tool is interactive, with a command-line shell environment you can get help with by typing ? and pressing Enter.

For example, you can enter the tool simply by typing

```
debugfs /dev/sdb5
```

Then type ? and press Enter to see a menu of commands available to you. Interesting and informative commands include

➤ open—Opens a file system for debugging

➤ features—Shows the file system's feature set

➤ stats—Shows the statistics for the file system and is similar to the dumpe2fs -h output

➤ ls—Shows the directory, which by default is the root (/)

➤ pwd—Shows the working directory

➤ undelete—Undeletes a file (used immediately after the deletion in successful cases)

➤ logdump—Shows the contents of the journal (if in a journal-led file system)

➤ quit—Quits the tool

Mounting and Unmounting

In the final section of this chapter, we will discuss mounting and unmounting file systems, the options available, and how this subject is used for the exam.

The File System Table

For a file system to be used by normal users, that file system must either be mounted by the root user or be put in the /etc/fstab file with the correct options that allow users that privilege. When a proper entry exists in the /etc/fstab, a user only needs to issue the mount command with the full path of a mount point or device to accomplish the mount.

File systems should be set up in /etc/fstab, one per line. Entries that are mounted are reflected in /etc/mtab, which is maintained by the system as a description of the mounted file systems. This information (or most of it) is also in the /proc/mounts file.

Type the mount command to see the current list of file systems. Here's an example:

```
mount
/dev/sda2 on / type ext3 (rw)
none on /proc type proc (rw)
usbdevfs on /proc/bus/usb type usbdevfs (rw)
/dev/sda1 on /boot type ext3 (rw)
none on /dev/pts type devpts (rw,gid=5,mode=620)
none on /dev/shm type tmpfs (rw)
/dev/sdb8 on /home/data type ext3 (rw)
```

This output can be compared with the output from the /proc/mounts file:

```
cat /proc/mounts
rootfs / rootfs rw 0 0
/dev/root / ext3 rw 0 0
/proc /proc proc rw 0 0
usbdevfs /proc/bus/usb usbdevfs rw 0 0
/dev/sda1 /boot ext3 rw 0 0
none /dev/pts devpts rw 0 0
none /dev/shm tmpfs rw 0 0
/dev/sdb8 /home/data ext3 rw 0 0
```

Either command works, but the mount command includes options and other useful information.

The file system table (/etc/fstab) should consist of one line per file system, with a device, a mount point, a file system type, options, and dump/check orders. This file (WHR) should be modifiable only by the root user; otherwise, any user could put a removable device or disk in the system and mount it, potentially copying data to a rogue device.

Here's an example of a live /etc/fstab file:

```
LABEL=/         /             ext3    defaults        1 1
LABEL=/boot     /boot         ext3    defaults        1 2
LABEL=/data     /data         ext3    defaults        1 2
none            /proc         proc    defaults        0 0
none            /dev/shm      tmpfs   defaults        0 0
/dev/hdc1       /cdroms       ext2    defaults        0 0
/dev/hda3       swap          swap    defaults        0 0
/dev/fd0        /mnt/floppy   auto    noauto,user     0 0
/dev/cdrom      /mnt/cdrom    iso9660 noauto,users,ro 0 0
```

The column contents (from left to right) are as follows:

➤ **Device**—This is any device; local dev files, NFS shares, or partition labels

➤ **Mount point**—This is any directory, empty or otherwise.

➤ **File system type**—This is a valid file system type.

➤ **Options**—Options are separated by a comma. The defaults option is made up of rw, suid, dev, exec, auto, nouser, and async.

➤ **Dump**—If this value is 0 (zero), the dump command doesn't act on it; otherwise, a 1 indicates that the file system should be dumped on demand.

➤ **fsck**—This causes the file system with a 1 to be checked first and then those with a 2 and so on to be checked next.

The auto option in the file system column for the floppy probes the superblock for the device to attempt identification of the file system type. This works for nearly any other file system type, including ext2, ext3, iso9660, udf, and ntfs to name a few.

Notice also the mutually exclusive user and users options in the floppy and CD-ROM entries' options column. These enable either exclusive or nonexclusive mounting for users on that device.

For example, if the user option is present for the system's CD-ROM and the daytime user Sally mounts her favorite Spice Girls release into the drive and plays it, only user Sally (and the root user) can unmount that CD-ROM.

This is unacceptable to Steven the night shift operator, who simply must have his Tenacious D CD-ROM to help the night pass. Steven should request that the root user switch that option with the users option, which allows any user to mount the device and any other user to unmount it.

Manually Mounting File Systems

If a file system isn't configured in the /etc/fstab file, it can be mounted manually following this convention:

```
mount -t type -o option device mountpoint
```

The following example of a manual mount includes the type, the option, the device, and a mount point:

```
mount -t iso9660 -o exec /dev/cdrom /mnt/cdrom
```

With this mount command, the system's CD-ROM is mounted, allowing user access.

Mounting options that are important include

➤ -a—Mounts all file systems listed in /etc/fstab

➤ -f—Fakes the mounting of file systems

➤ -r—Mounts the file system read-only

➤ -w—Mounts the file system in write mode

➤ -n—Mounts without updating /etc/mtab

➤ -L—Mounts a file system with a given label, instead of using the device filename

Automatically Mounting File Systems

All file systems that are in the /etc/fstab and don't have the noauto option set are mounted when the system is booted. This is equivalent to issuing a mount -a command as the root user.

The **noauto** option is necessary for floppies and CD-ROMs because access errors would occur if an empty removable media drive were to be affected by the mount system call. This option is also useful for rarely needed or user-specific file systems, allowing a script or user to invoke the mount as desired.

Unmounting File Systems

The unmounting command name is umount, and it works similarly to the mount command, acting on the label, mount point, or device that's listed in the /etc/fstab entry.

For example, to unmount the /mnt/cdrom, use either of the following:

```
umount /mnt/cdrom
umount /dev/cdrom
```

The most important fact about the umount command is that it doesn't let you unmount any device currently in use, including a device that has a user accessing it via a file manager, a shell session, or a file in use on that device.

Space Utilization

There are several methods of determining the space used by data on your system. It's important to know when to use which command because each acts differently and displays different information.

The LPI exams test whether you can parse the question and whether you know what the various utilities produce as output. If you've not used the options for the **du** and **df** commands, some questions (particularly fill-in-the-blank ones) will be unanswerable.

Using du

To see the space used by a set of files or a file tree, you use the du command. This command is configurable to show file and directory sizes, including summarization and human-readable output (KB, MB, and GB).

To restrict the output to just the regular files in the current directory, use the following command:

```
du *
4     anaconda-ks.cfg
20     install.log
4     install.log.syslog
```

To see the current directory and all below with KB/MB/GB human-readable output, use the following command:

```
du -h
24K     ./.gconfd
8.0K     ./.gstreamer
8.0K     ./.gconf/desktop/gnome/applications/window_manager
12K     ./.gconf/desktop/gnome/applications
8.0K     ./.gconf/desktop/gnome/file_views
24K     ./.gconf/desktop/gnome
28K     ./.gconf/desktop
... Output removed
```

To view the space used by all files on a given directory tree, such as the /home user's tree, use this command:

```
du -sh /home
```

Typical output would look like this:

```
404 MB     /home
```

It's very important when using du to not traverse NFS systems across the network, causing extra traffic and annoying router users. To restrict your query to the local system only, use the following:

```
du -shx /home
22M     /home
```

Without the x option, (which restricts du to the local system) a remotely mounted user's home directory or attached separate disk drive is shown in the output. Therefore, you should know from which drive and system the data is shown.

Using df

The df command is different from the du command: It can't show a set of files disk usage, unless that set of files is an entire mounted file system.

The df command displays used and available disk space for all mounted file systems, on a per–file system basis (shown here with the -h human readable output option) such as

```
df -h
Filesystem        Size  Used Avail Use% Mounted on
/dev/sda2         5.5G  1.8G  3.5G  34% /
/dev/sda1          99M  9.3M   85M  10% /boot
none               62M     0   62M   0% /dev/shm
/dev/sdb8         966M   38M  909M   4% /data
```

Notice that `df` works only on mounted file systems, and that the output includes

➤ The size of the partition

➤ The size used in MB or GB

➤ The size available in MB or GB

➤ The percent used

➤ Where the device is mounted

To view disk-free statistics on local-only file systems, (excluding NFS and other remote mounts) use the following command:

```
df -l
```

To see the disk utilization statistics expressed in KB, use this command:

```
df -k
Filesystem       1K-blocks      Used Available Use% Mounted on
/dev/sda2          5708320   1794004   3624344  34% /
/dev/sda1           101089      9426     86444  10% /boot
none                 62996         0     62996   0% /dev/shm
/dev/sdb8           988212     38180    929952   4% /home/data
```

Finally, to see the amount of the disk's free and used inodes expressed in disk utilization statistics, use the following command:

```
df -i
Filesystem        Inodes   IUsed   IFree IUse% Mounted on
/dev/sda2         725760  104049  621711   15% /
/dev/sda1          26104      41   26063    1% /boot
none               15749       1   15748    1% /dev/shm
/dev/sdb8         125696     889  124807    1% /home/data
```

Notice that the number of inodes total, used, free, and percent used is shown on a file system–by–file system basis. This option is incredibly useful for busy sysadmins who are worried about running out of space or inodes.

The **du** and **df** commands are prominently featured on the exams, particularly questions about the output of each and what is shown for various options. Expect to see questions that have the keywords *disk utilization* and *amount of free space* or words to that effect.

Exam Prep Questions

1. You are configuring your `/etc/fstab` file and want to have a file system mountable by non-root users. Which option in which column would you use to accomplish this?

   ○ A. `owner` in the third column

   ○ B. `owner` in the fifth column

   ○ C. `noauto` in the fourth column

   ○ D. `user` in the fourth column

   Answer D is correct because the fourth column is the options column and the `user` option is the proper one to use. Answers A and B include valid options but are in the wrong column. Answer C is the wrong option in the right column.

2. You are troubleshooting your Linux machine after an unexplained crash. The automated file system check fails with a message to perform a check manually. What's the most important thing to make certain of for the affected file system before initiating the manual check?

   ○ A. It should be unmounted.

   ○ B. It should be mounted read-write.

   ○ C. It should be in noauto mode.

   ○ D. The `user=root` option should be set.

   Answer A is correct because the file system should be unmounted if possible, mounted read-only if not. Answer B is incorrect because mounting it read-write would cause errors in the fsck process. Answer C is incorrect because there isn't a noauto mode, although there is a `noauto` option. Answer D is incorrect because the user being set to something in options doesn't affect the fsck process.

3. You are installing a Linux server that will primarily hold users' data. If you could place two directory trees on a separate drive, which would be the most effective choice? (Choose two.)

   ❑ A. `/tmp`

   ❑ B. `/var`

   ❑ C. `/home`

   ❑ D. `/data`

   Answers B and C are correct because the highest traffic partitions in the choices are `/home` (users data) and `/var` (log files, print spools, Web, and FTP). Answer A is incorrect because on a user file server, `/tmp` isn't as heavily used as it would be on a developer station. Answer D is incorrect because anything at all could be in a directory tree named `/data`, whereas the `/home` directory tree is almost certainly user data.

4. You require your system to check a particular file system every 50 times the file system is mounted. Which command would you use to make this change?

○ A. `debugfs`
○ B. `dumpe2fs`
○ C. `tune2fs`
○ D. `setfs`

Answer C is correct because the maximum mount count option can be set with the `tune2fs` command. Answer A is incorrect because the `debugfs` command manipulates the file system inodes and contents but not the needed parameter. Answer B is incorrect because the `dumpe2fs` command shows only parameters for the file system. Answer D is incorrect because the `setfs` command doesn't exist.

5. A user reports that one of his fellow users is hogging all the disk space on their shared server. Which command would you use to show that system's disk statistics for its mounted file systems?

○ A. `dir`
○ B. `df`
○ C. `du`
○ D. `ls`

Answer B is correct because the `df` command shows the disk statistics for mounted file sytems. Answer A is incorrect because `dir` is only an alias for the `ls` command. Answer C is incorrect because the `du` command can show the space used by files, but not disk statistics like `df` can. Answer D is incorrect because the `ls` command can show file sizes but not disk statistics.

6. What is the device name of the third SCSI device on a Linux system? Fill in the blank with the full path and filename of the device:

_____

The correct answer is /dev/sdc. There are no alternative answers.

7. Which portion of a file's information is not stored in the `inode` or `data blocks`?

○ A. Link count
○ B. Link permissions
○ C. Filename
○ D. Owner

Answer C is correct because the filename is not stored with the `inode` or in the data location for the file; it occurs only in the directory file that contains the filename entry. Answer A is incorrect because the link count affects only hard links and is shown by the `stat` command. Answer B is incorrect because link permissions affect only a symbolic link, and the symbolic link permissions are kept in the links inode. Answer D is incorrect because the ownership information is kept in the inode for the file.

8. Which command is used to alter the maximum mount count so an `ext3` file system isn't checked every 20 mounts by default?

   ○ A. `fsck`
   ○ B. `mkfs.ext3`
   ○ C. `hdparm`
   ○ D. `tune2fs`

   Answer D is correct because the `tune2fs -c 0` command changes a file system's maximum mount count to not have it checked automatically. Answer A is incorrect because the `fsck` command can't change the maximum mount count. Answer B is incorrect because the `mkfs.*` tools are for creating file systems, and even though they can set the maximum mount count at file system creation, using these tools on existing file systems would destroy the file system. Answer C is incorrect because, although `hdparm` is good for changing parameters, the `tune2fs` command is the best choice for this task.

9. When upgrading a system that has multiple data partitions of the `ext2` file system type, which of the following would represent the least disruptive journaling file system to upgrade them with?

   ○ A. `ext3`
   ○ B. `ReiserFS`
   ○ C. `JFS`
   ○ D. `XFS`

   Answer A is correct because the `ext3` file system type does not require any reformatting to upgrade an `ext2` file system. Answers B, C, and D are incorrect because they require backing up the file system data, formatting with the new advanced file system, and restoring the data.

10. Which utility on your system can display the number of free and used inodes as a total and percentage?

    ○ A. `ls -li`
    ○ B. `du -sh`
    ○ C. `df -i`
    ○ D. `find -inum`

    Answer C is correct because the `df` command has an option to query the number and percentage of inodes used and free for all mounted file systems. Answer A is incorrect because the `ls -li` command shows only groups of file object inode information, not totals. Answer B is incorrect because the `du -sh` command doesn't show inode percentages, just object sizes and size totals. Answer D is incorrect because `find -inum` searches for a specific inode but does not show totals or percentages.

File Systems and Commands

Terms you'll need to understand:

✓ Attributes
✓ File System Heirarchy Standard
✓ Hidden files
✓ Inode
✓ Recursive
✓ Root / directory
✓ Special bits

Techniques you'll need to master:

✓ Understanding file system structure
✓ Navigating a file system
✓ Viewing and identifying file objects
✓ Moving, copying, and managing file objects
✓ Creating, removing, and managing directory objects
✓ Creating boot disks
✓ Searching for objects
✓ Using hard and symbolic links
✓ Changing and modifying permissions and ownership
✓ Configuring quotas

File System Overview

The file system's structure starts with the root of the file system, which is denoted by the forward slash character (/). Every item on the file system is accessible by a single unique path from the root of the system.

LPI bases the exam questions about the directory structure from the FHS 2.2 (File System Hierarchy Standard). The FHS isn't really a standard but a firm set of suggestions that most, but not all, distribution vendors obey. A good number of questions on the exams reference the FHS.

What Belongs Where

The exams make somewhat of a big deal about what the proper directories and locations are for Linux files, but few things are more vexing than to be asked what should positively be in the root (/) directory, or what can be elsewhere.

The Root of the System

Starting in the root (/) directory, the following table lists common top-level directories and includes a short explanation for each:

Directory	Description
bin	Binaries for all users
boot	Kernel, system map, boot files
dev	Device files
etc	Configuration files for the host
home	Home directories for users
lib	Necessary shared libraries/modules
lost+found	Storage directory for unlinked files (found with **fsck**)
mnt	Mount point for detachable media
opt	Third-party application software
proc	Kernel and process information
root	The root user's home directory
sbin	System binaries (not for non-root)
tmp	Temporary data
usr	Shareable, read-only data and programs, no host-specific data
var	Variable data, logs, Web, FTP, and so on

The exam makes a big deal out of what's optional and required in the **root** (/) directory. If you read the FHS 2.2 (highly recommended), you'll see that the word *optional* appears next to the **/root** and **/home** directories. This is key because you'll be asked questions about which directories are optional in the root file system.

Oddities in the FHS

Because of the way the FHS is laid out, with the root file system being section 3 and then /usr being 4 and /var being 5, it's easy to misunderstand what is really supposed to be in the root of the system.

The relationship between /usr and /var is that the data presently in /var used to be a part of /usr (long ago in Unix times) and can be as long as the /usr section is local-only and not a remote NFS mount. With the increased use of networking and remote NFS mounts of the /usr section, /var was created to hold the variable portions of the data.

The FHS documentation states, "The contents of the root file system must be adequate to boot, recover and/or repair the system. This leads to the recommendation that the **/usr**, **/opt** and **/var** sections may be located on other partitions or file systems on the machine, or on the network."

Mix this with the previous exam alert to prepare for questions about what should be present on the root of the system or what can be located elsewhere.

Where Programs Live

The FHS does not allow programs to create their individual named directories in the /usr section. The subdirectories allowed to exist directly under the /usr directory are

➤ bin—Contains user commands

➤ include—Contains header files for C programs

➤ lib—Contains libraries

➤ local—Contains local/sharable programs

➤ sbin—Contains nonessential system binaries

➤ share—Contains data/programs for multiple architectures

The /usr section has a location for programs named /usr/local. This is for the sysadmin to locally install software for this machine. Programs in the /usr/local path are also allowed for sharing amongst groups of hosts but aren't kept in /usr.

For example, say your developers have come up with the perfect amortization program and you want to install it on the workgroup server for other systems to remotely mount and use. Because this is a third-party or custom application, the logical place for it is in /usr/local/appname, possibly with a link to the program binary in the /usr/local/bin directory (because that's in the path).

If given a choice between putting the software package **BIGPROG** in the **/usr/local/BIGPROG** section and the **/opt/BIGPROG** section, it's hard to choose. Read any relevant exam question closely—the main difference being that the **/opt** section is not considered to be sharable, whereas the **/usr** section is often shared and mounted by client systems.

File Management Commands

A major section of the 101 exam is dedicated to how to run commands properly with the right options and arguments. As a good sysadmin, you'll be expected to know how to create, delete, edit, set permissions on, display, move, copy, and determine the type of files and programs.

You must be able to pick proper and working commands out of lists of possibilities, type in appropriate strings in fill-in-the-blank boxes, and in general show that you've run the programs and utilities in question.

Tips for Working with Linux Files

Because most users and sysadmins come from a Windows or other OS background, a quick set of recommendations for the less-experienced can be of help here:

➤ **Hidden files aren't really hidden**—They just begin with a ., such as the .bashrc and .bash_profile files. These are not viewable by normal users with conventional commands and switches and aren't deleted by commands such as rm -f *.*.

➤ **Filenames can contain multiple periods or no period characters**— The filenames this.is.a.long.file and thisisalongfile are perfectly reasonable and possible.

➤ **Spaces in filenames look nice, but are a pain to type**—Use an _ or a - instead of spaces because it's neater and easier than prefixing all spaces with a \. (To display a space in a filename, the system shows a space prefixed with a backslash.)

> **Filenames can begin with numbers**—Unlike DNS, where numbers aren't used much and can break things, use them as you need, particularly for sorting by dates.

> **File extensions aren't mandatory**—But they are useful for sorting, selection, and copy/move/delete commands, as well as for quickly identifying a file's type.

Basic Navigation

The cd command is used frequently, and knowing how to move around the file system is a main focus of the exams.

 It's common and recommended to use the full path of commands and in operations that move or copy files to and from directories on the file system. Continuously changing directories is a needless typing task when the entire system can be referred to with absolute path and filenames.

By itself, the cd command takes you back to your user's home directory, wherever you happen to be. Other uses of the cd command include single-level moves.

The following command simply moves you from wherever you are to the /etc directory. This type of move uses absolute pathnames and can be used from any directory to any other:

```
cd /etc
```

Moving relatively from the current directory to a subdirectory is quick and easy, such as if you are in the /etc/ directory and want to change into the /etc/samba directory. Here's how:

```
cd samba
```

This is referred to as a *relative path* because the ability to get to the /etc/samba directory with the previous command requires you to be in the /etc directory because the location of the samba subdirectory is relative to its location in the /etc/ directory.

If you get confused as to where you currently are, use the pwd command to print the working (current) directory:

```
pwd
/etc/samba
```

Other methods of accomplishing a move to the user's home directory are using the ~ shortcut to the current user's home directory (**cd ~**) and the **$HOME** variable (**cd $HOME**) to reach your home directory. The nice thing about these two shortcuts are they can be used in scripts, whereas the **cd** command by itself is limited in its appeal for scripting.

Advanced Navigation

It's good to get experience with some complex relative path situations. For example, if you were in the directory /home1/user1 and wanted to move into the directory /home2/user2, which command could be used?

```
/
|-- home1
|    `-- user1
`-- home2
     `-- user2
```

Remember, you aren't using absolute pathnames, just relative pathnames.

Answer:

```
# cd ../../home2/user2
```

Each of the .. pairs takes you up one level, and then it's absolute pathnames from that point on. Practice this method, and remember that going up one level in this exercise only got you to the /home1 directory.

Listing Files and Directories

The ls command is used for listing directories or files, or both.

If you use the ls command to see a multicolumn output of the current directory, only the file or directory names are shown, not other details about the file:

```
ls
file1   file2   file3   file4
```

Use the -l long listing option to see all the details of a particular object or set of objects in a single column, like so:

```
ls -l
total 0
-rw-r--r--    1 root     root            0 Jan 24 18:55 file1
-rw-r--r--    1 root     root            0 Jan 24 18:55 file2
-rw-r--r--    1 root     root            0 Jan 24 18:55 file3
-rw-r--r--    1 root     root            0 Jan 24 18:55 file4
```

The **–l** long listing style is the only way to use the **ls** command and see the permissions, ownership, and link counts for objects. The only other command that can give such information is the **stat** command, which shows a single file system object at a time.

Other examples of using the ls command include

➤ ls /home/user—Shows a plain listing of that directory

➤ ls -a—Lists all files, including hidden . files

➤ ls -d—Lists just the current directory name, not the contents

➤ ls -i—Lists the inode information for the targetfile or directory

➤ ls -l—Shows permissions; links; and date, group, and owner information

➤ ls -lh—Shows human-readable output, in KB, MB, and GB, along with file details

Chaining the options together produces useful results. For example, if you needed to see all the files (including hidden ones) in the current directory, their permissions, and their inode numbers, you'd use the following command:

```
ls -lai
290305 drwxr-x---  13 root    root       4096 Jan 24 18:55 .
     2 drwxr-xr-x  20 root    root       4096 Jan 24 17:56 ..
292606 -rw-r--r--   1 root    root       1354 Jan 21 00:23
[ic:ccc]anaconda-ks.cfg
292748 -rw-------   1 root    root       3470 Jan 24 18:16
[ic:ccc].bash_history
290485 -rw-r--r--   1 root    root         24 Jun 10  2000
[ic:ccc].bash_logout
290486 -rw-r--r--   1 root    root        234 Jul  5  2001
[ic:ccc].bash_profile
290487 -rw-r--r--   1 root    root        176 Aug 23  1995 .bashrc
290488 -rw-r--r--   1 root    root        210 Jun 10  2000 .cshrc
```

Determining File Types

With no requirement for extensions on Linux files, a tool for easily determining file types is essential. The file command can be used to read the file's headers and match that data against a known set of types.

The file command uses several possible sources, including the stat system call, the magic number file (/usr/share/magic), and a table of character sets including ASCII and EBCDIC. Finally, if the file is text and contains recognizable strings from a given programming or other language, it is used to identify the file.

The output can be used, manipulated, and filtered to show you very useful things.

For example, simply using the `file` command on a given file shows the type:

```
file file1
file1: ASCII text
```

Running the `file` command against a known binary shows various elements, usually ELF and 32-bit, such as shown here:

```
file /bin/ls
/bin/ls: ELF 32-bit LSB executable, Intel 80386, version 1 (SYSV),
 [ic:ccc]for GNU/Linux 2.2.5, dynamically linked (uses shared libs),
stripped
```

Notice that the file is correctly identified as an Intel 386–compatible (or higher) executable. Query RPM files before you install them to ensure the architecture matches, as shown here with the `i386` portion of the filename showing the architecture:

```
file tree*.rpm
tree-1.2-7.i386.rpm: RPM v3 bin i386 tree-1.2-7
```

Running the `file` command against a directory full of files is useful for viewing the possible types, but the real gold lies in filtering the output:

```
file /etc/* ¦ grep empty
/etc/dumpdates:                          empty
/etc/exports:                            empty
/etc/fstab.REVOKE:                       empty
/etc/motd:                               empty
/etc/printconf.local:                    empty
```

I use the previous command to find all the empty (zero byte) files in the `/etc/` directory of a new machine, usually for verifying NFS mounts that aren't configured.

Touching Files

There are various reasons to use the `touch` command, such as creating a new blank log file or updating a group of files to a common date before distributing them to others.

To create a new file, you can use the relative pathname for creating one in the current directory:

```
touch filename
```

Or, you can use absolute pathname to create the file, such as shown here:

```
touch /home/rossb/filename
```

Expect to see **touch** on the exams for log file creation, along with using a reference file after a backup and so on. In other words, if a log file is created from a successful backup, that file can be used as a date and time reference file because it occurred at a desirable time.

When you use `touch` on an existing file, the default action is to update all three of the file's times:

➤ `access`—The last time a file was written/read from

➤ `change`—Altering the permissions, name, owner, and so on

➤ `modify`—Altering the contents of the file

Changing the time or altering the permissions, name, and owner is not affected by **touch**.

A programmer preparing a new release of a software package would use the `touch` command to ensure that all files have the exact same date and times. Therefore, the release could be referred to by the file date, given multiple revisions.

Setting a file's date is relatively easy; the following command sets `file1`'s date to a particular date and time:

```
touch -t 200212010830 file1
```

The time format used is represented by yyyymmddhhmm, or a four-digit year, two-digit month, two-digit day, two-digit hour, and two-digit minutes.

Reference files are useful, particularly when you just want to have a file or set of files updated to a particular date/time, not the current one. You could use

```
touch -r reffile file2update
```

The `reffile` date and time are pasted onto the `file2update` file date and time.

Copying Files and Directories

One of the aspects of copying an object is that the act creates a new file with a separate inode.

When you create an object in a file system, it doesn't retain the original object's permissions by default. This can be done, but it requires the use of the **-p** option to preserve the permissions and ownership.

A normal copy is simple to perform. You're essentially causing the file to be replicated to the new location:

```
cp file1 /dir1/file2
```

A few options that make life easier for copying files include

➤ -d—Doesn't follow links; copies the link instead

➤ -f—Doesn't ask to overwrite existing files

➤ -i—Interactively asks before overwriting

➤ -l—Creates a hard link to the source file

➤ -r or -R—Recursively traverses directories (copying everything)

➤ -s—Creates a symlink to the source file

➤ -u—Only copies when the source is newer than the target or the target doesn't exist

➤ -x—Doesn't traverse to other file systems

Copying an existing directory to a new one is simple:

```
# cp -r dir1 dir2
```

The -r option is necessary because the cp command doesn't process directories by default. As long as the target directory does *not* exist, the previous command makes an identical copy of the source and all subordinate files and directories in the target directory.

Copying a source directory to an existing target directory doesn't attempt an overwrite; it makes the source directory into a new subdirectory of the target.

For example, if you are in the /test directory and have the structure shown in the following, you might assume that issuing a cp -r dir1 dir2 would overwrite dir2, or at least prompt you to see whether you wanted to:

```
|-- dir1
|   |-- file1
|   `-- subdir1
`-- dir2
```

When you issue the cp -r dir1 dir2 command, the file system (along with the cp command) notices the existing dir2 entry and automatically drops the source directory into dir2 as a subdirectory, like this:

```
|-- dir1
|   |-- file1
|   `-- subdir1
`-- dir2
```

```
`-- dir1
    |-- file1
    `-- subdir1
```

The correct way to copy the contents of dir1 into dir2, thereby mirroring dir1 exactly, is to focus on the word *contents*. By suffixing the source (dir1) with a forward slash and an asterisk (dir1/*), you tell the cp command to ignore the directory entry and act only on the contents of that directory.

With the same initial setup, if you issue the command cp -r dir1/* dir2, you'll get the correct results:

```
|-- dir1
|   |-- file1
|   `-- subdir1
`-- dir2
    |-- file1
    `-- subdir1
```

 The inability to properly copy a directory or its contents will come back to haunt you on the exam. In addition, if you see a source directory with only a trailing forward slash (**dir1/**) but no asterisk, it's identical to using (**dir1**). In other words, to copy just the contents of a directory, you have to address them specifically with the forward slash and asterisk (**dir1/***).

Another interesting use of the path and the single and double dot (. and ..) characters in each directory is to copy something from an existing directory or set of files to your current location.

For example, if you are currently in the /home/rossb directory and want to copy a set of files from the /home/lukec directory, you can avoid typing the full path of the current directory with the (.) character. Both of these commands perform the same action:

```
cp /home/lukec/*.mp3 .
cp /home/lukec/*.mp3 /home/rossb
```

Moving Objects

Where the cp command copies a file and creates a new file system entry, inode, and data, the mv command simply changes which directory file contains the file or directory entry or alters the entry in the file if it stays in the same directory.

Create a file named file1; then run the stat command on it to check the details, like so:

```
touch file1
stat file1
  File: `file1'
```

```
  Size: 0               Blocks: 0          IO Block: 4096    Regular File
Device: 802h/2050d      Inode: 17404       Links: 1
Access: (0644/-rw-r--r--) Uid: (   0/    root)  Gid: (   0/    root)
Access: 2004-01-25 12:53:56.000000000 -0800
Modify: 2004-01-25 12:53:56.000000000 -0800
Change: 2004-01-25 12:53:56.000000000 -0800
```

Now move the file to a new name with the following command:

```
mv file1 file2
stat file2
  File: `file2'
  Size: 0               Blocks: 0          IO Block: 4096    Regular File
Device: 802h/2050d      Inode: 17404       Links: 1
Access: (0644/-rw-r--r--) Uid: (   0/    root)  Gid: (   0/    root)
Access: 2004-01-25 12:53:56.000000000 -0800
Modify: 2004-01-25 12:53:56.000000000 -0800
Change: 2004-01-25 12:54:22.000000000 -0800
```

As you can see, the file is identical to the original, except the change time has been updated to the time it was written to the new filename.

When you move a file, the mv command first checks the target to see whether it exists. If it does, the default action is to ask whether you want to overwrite the target. This can be avoided for large sets of objects with the -f force option.

Another quirk of the command is the lack of a -r, or recursive, option. I like to explain that mv itself *is* recursive because it acts equally upon files and directories that you want to move.

You can avoid the overwriting of newer target files or directories with the -u option, preserving the latest copy of an object.

Examples of moving files and directories include moving a single directory to another directory name, as shown here:

```
mv -f dir1 dir2
```

This merely changes the directory entry dir1 to the new name dir2. It also removes the "are-you-sure" prompt with the -f option.

As the **root** user, you'll notice that when you use the **cp**, **mv**, and **rm** commands, you see a prompt that doesn't appear to normal users. This is because you have (by default) some aliases that affect the **root** user. If any account should be prompted by default, it's the **root** user. Remember that **root** can remove large portions of the file system by accident.

Just like the cp command, moving directory contents requires a correctly formed command; otherwise, you'll move a directory not to the new name, but to a subdirectory of the existing directory.

For example, consider the /test directory again, with its structure similar to the following:

```
|-- dir1
|    |-- file1
|    `-- subdir1
`-- dir2
```

If you were a Windows administrator, it would make sense to run the following command to move dir1 to dir2:

```
mv dir1 dir2
```

If you run the tree command, you see the following output:

```
`-- dir2
    `-- dir1
        |-- file1
        `-- subdir1
```

To properly move the contents of the source dir1 to the target dir2, you don't need to use the nonexistent -r option (exam trick). You can just use a forward slash and an asterisk, like this:

```
mv dir1/* dir2
```

If you run the tree command, you see the following output:

```
|-- dir1
`-- dir2
    |-- file1
    `-- subdir1
```

Finally, when you're using the mv command to move directories around on the system, the exam might say you are in a given directory and want to move the *contents* of /dir1 to the current directory. You'll then be asked the shortest way to accomplish this. This answer is

```
mv /dir1/* .
```

Transforming Data Formats

The dd command is useful for a variety of tasks, not the least of which is creating ISO files from CD-ROMs you want to copy. The two main formats dd interacts with are the raw device file and the full path of a file or object on the system.

For example, when creating a new boot disk, the .img binary file is read block by block from the CD-ROM (as a file) and written to the floppy raw device as a set of blocks:

```
dd if=/mnt/cdrom/images/boot.img of=/dev/fd0
```

Creating an image of a floppy involves reading the raw floppy device block by block and creating a file on the file system that contains all those blocks:

```
dd if=/dev/fd0 of=/root/floppy.img
```

To duplicate a disk from the first disk drive to the second, the command is

```
dd if=/dev/fd0 of=/dev/fd1
```

 The **if** keyword means input file and the **of** keyword means output file. The exact order is unimportant, but as you can imagine, mixing these up can cause you to do terrible things such as writing a floppy over the first 1,440 blocks of a production hard drive.

The dd command is also often used to duplicate a drive or partition of a drive to another like object.

For example, to copy the first partition from the /dev/hda disk to the same location on the second IDE drive on the system, you'd use the following command:

```
dd if=/dev/hda1 of=/dev/hdb1
```

You can also copy an entire disk device to another on the system by leaving off the partition numbers:

```
dd if=/dev/hda of=/dev/hdb
```

This works only if the second device is as large as or larger than the first; otherwise, you get truncated and worthless partitions on the second one.

Backing up the MBR is another trick that dd does well. To create a disk file that contains only the first 512 bytes of the first IDE drive in the system, use this command:

```
dd if=/dev/hda of=/root/MBR.img count=1 bs=512
```

The count keyword sets the number of reads from the input file you want to retrieve, and the bs keyword sets the block size.

 If you don't set the count and block size on this command to back up the MBR, you'll be copying the entire device's blocks to the file system—a snake-eating-its-own-tail operation that is guaranteed to fill up the partition quickly and crash the system.

Creating and Removing Directories

A basic task of file management is to be able to create and remove directories, sometimes creating/removing whole trees at once.

To create a directory named dir1, you use

```
mkdir dir1
```

To create a directory named `subdir1` in the `dir1` directory, you use the following:

```
mkdir dir1/subdir1
```

Always think of the last segment of any directory path as the object being created or removed, and think of the rest as supporting or parent objects. The `mkdir` and `rmdir` commands are similar in features and options, including the capability of `mkdir` to create a deep subdirectory tree from scratch in a single command:

```
mkdir -p /dir1/dir2/dir3/dir4
```

One of the quirks about the `rmdir` command is its inability to remove anything but an empty directory. For example, the last directory of the chain `/dir1/dir2/dir3/dir4` is the real target for this command, and only if that directory is empty (no regular or directory files) can it be removed.

```
rmdir -p /dir1/dir2/dir3/dir4
```

 One option to the **rmdir** command does allow it to remove directories that have files and so on in them. It's called **ignore-fail-on-non-empty** and is the longest option I know of in Linux. I'd rather type **rm –rf targetdir** 20 times than this beast.

Removing Objects

It follows that you'll want to remove objects after creating or copying them, and this is done with the `rm` command for most objects. `rmdir` can also be used.

Deleting files with the `rm` command is a matter of choosing the target to be removed and the options that will work best.

If you want to remove a particular file and never be prompted by confirmation messages, the command is

```
rm -f target
```

To remove a directory and all its contents, and never get a confirmation message, the command is

```
rm -rf /full/path/to/target
```

The following command does *not* remove the entire directory structure, but it does fail when it has removed the library the `rm` command needs (effectively disabling the system):

```
rm -rf / 2> /dev/null
```

Where Are Those Files?

Having a mechanism for finding or locating files on a Linux system is essential because the sheer amount of directories and files makes searching manually a nearly impossible task.

There are two methods for accomplishing this task—quick and dirty or slow and methodical. Most people try the quick `locate` command before resorting to the plodding `find` command.

Locating Files with **locate**

The quickest way to find a file or set of files is to use the `locate` command. It's fast, database-driven, and secure, but because it's a static database, the command is always playing catch-up with the actual contents of the disk.

`locate` has a quirky way of showing results. You'd probably expect that using `locate` for a file named `readme` would locate only files named `readme`, but that's not quite true. It finds anything that has a filename of `readme`, including regular files and any part of the path.

For example, while attempting to locate the `readme` file, you run the following command:

```
locate readme
```

This find both of the following entries, one with the string `readme` as a part of the filename and the other being a directory:

```
/readme
/usr/src/linux-2.4.20-8/drivers/net/wan/8253x/readme.txt
```

Running the `find` command on the string `readme` finds only the `/readme` directory.

Use the `locate` command to find items you know are on the disk, or that you know existed before the last `locate` database update. (The `locate` database is updated on demand or scheduled in the `crontab`.) If you don't have permissions to the object, it isn't shown in the `locate` output.

Using `locate` to find any version of a given string is accomplished with the `-i` option, for case-insensitivity:

```
locate -i string
```

The secure nature of `locate` can be turned off to further increase the speed of returned results, like so:

```
locate -l 0 string
```

The `locate` database might need to be updated regularly to ensure good results, which can be put into a `cron` job or otherwise run manually. Nothing is more irritating than having to run the update solely so you can find something right now.

The update commands must be run as `root`, and either one will do the job:

```
updatedb
slocate -u
```

Sometimes you'll want to exclude files or directories from the `locate` database because they either are inappropriate or simply take too long to index without any apparent benefit. This is configurable in the `/etc/updatedb.conf` file. This file is read and the variables are used by the updating commands.

The two main methods of excluding objects in the configuration file are either by file system type or path. The following output is an example of a working `/etc/updatedb.conf` file:

```
PRUNEFS="devpts NFS nfs afs sfs proc smbfs autofs auto iso9660"
PRUNEPATHS="/tmp /usr/tmp /var/tmp /afs /net /sfs"
export PRUNEFS
export PRUNEPATHS
```

The `PRUNEFS` keyword is for file system types you want excluded from the `locate` database update; as you might expect, the `PRUNEPATHS` keyword is for directory trees you want excluded. Notice that most of the paths are temporary data locations or automount and exotic file locations.

 Remember for the exam that **locate** returns results for the search string in any portion of the path or filename it finds the string in. There will be questions that **locate** is right for, and some that really want the **whereis** command.

Finding Files

The `find` command is the most accurate but time-consuming method for searching the system for file objects. The command consists of several (sometimes confusing) sections. But, if it's learned properly, it can be a powerhouse for the busy sysadmin.

The structure of a `find` command is

```
find startpath -options arguments
```

To make sense of this jumble of sections, let's take a look at a useful `find` command and match up the sections:

```
find /home -iname *.mp3/home/snuffy/g3 - red house.mp3
```

The previous command sets the start path to the `/home` directory and then looks for any instance of the string `mp3` as a file extension, or after the last . in the filename. It found a file in the user `snuffy`'s home directory and returned the full path for that file.

Operators for `find` include

➤ `group`—Based on files belonging to the specified group

➤ `newer`—Based on files more recent than the specified file

➤ `name`—Based on files with names matching a case-sensitive string

➤ `iname`—Based on files with names matching a non-case-sensitive string

➤ `user`—Searches for files belonging to the specified user

➤ `mtime`—The modify time; it's used for finding files x days old

➤ `atime`—Based on the number of days since last accessed

➤ `ctime`—Based on the number of days since the directory entry was last changed

A useful feature of the `find` command is its capability to execute another command or script on each and every entry that is normally returned to standard output.

For example, to find all MP3 files in the user's home directories and archive a copy into the root user's home directory, you could use this command:

```
find /home -iname *.mp3 -exec cp -f {} .\;
```

This command uses the `-exec` option, which accepts every line returned to standard output one by one and inserts the full path and filename between the curly brackets (`{}`). When each line of output is parsed and the command is executed, it reaches the `\;` at the end of the line and goes back to standard input for the next line. The last line of output is the last one with a command executed on it; it doesn't just keep going and error out.

Running multiple operators in a single command is possible, too. Just be sure not to get the values for one operator mixed up in the next. You could look for all MP3 files that were owned by a given user with the following command:

```
find /home -iname *.mp3 -user snuffy/home/snuffy/bls - all for you.mp3
```

The `find` command is pretty complex, and rather than bore you with more possible options, I've worked out a number of examples of how to use `find`:

To find a file and execute `cat` on it, you'd use

```
find /etc -iname fstab -exec cat {} \;
```

To delete all `core` files older than seven days, the following can be used:

```
find /home -mtime +7 -iname core -exec rm -f {} \;
```

To find all files on the system owned by `bob` and change the ownership to `root`, you'd use

```
find / -user bob -exec chown root {} \;
```

To find all files by user `smedley` and change his group, you'd use this command:

```
find /data -user smedley -exec chown .users {} \;
```

To find all inodes related to a hard link, you'd use this command:

```
find / -inum 123456
```

 The **find** command's operators and the capability to execute commands on the search results will be covered on the exam. Practice all the examples you see here and get inventive with the possibilities. Particularly watch out for the use of **-mtime** and its cousins: **-atime** and **-ctime**.

Which Command Will Run?

With the plethora of commands and executable scripts offered on a Linux machine, you need to know which of the possible commands will run when you type the name of it on the command line. This all depends on the contents of the PATH variable. This variable's contents are used as a sequentially read set of locations to search for executable objects.

The `which` command is used to determine the full path of commands that are queried from the PATH variable. To determine which command will indeed be executed just by typing the name, run the following command:

```
which ls
alias ls='ls --color=tty'
        /bin/ls
```

As you can see, two entries were found that contain the `ls` command. The first is an alias, one that sets some color functions to the `ls` command; the other is the real command binary in `/bin/ls`.

 When you execute a command, it finds the first available match, which might not be the one you wanted, as is the case with the **ls** command. To make it execute a physical binary and ignore any aliases that have been set, preface the command with a backslash (\), like so:

\ls

Try it again on a command that has two executables on the system, the gawk command:

```
which gawk
/bin/gawk
```

This returns a single entry, but there are multiple gawk commands on a Linux box. The first matching command found is returned by default, and only if you use the proper switch does it find all possibilities:

```
which gawk
/bin/gawk
/usr/bin/gawk
```

Researching a Command

When you need more information about a command than just which one will execute, try whereis. This command shows up to three possible bits of information, including its binary files, the man page path, and any source files that exist for it. Here's its syntax:

```
whereis ls
ls: /bin/ls /usr/man/man1/ls.1.gz
```

Options for whereis include

➤ -b—Searches for binaries

➤ -m—Searches for manual entries

➤ -s—Searches for sources

➤ -u—Finds unusual or improperly documented entries

 To find a file by name but not get all the entries that contain the name in the path, use the **whereis** command—not the **locate** command—because it finds the string in all elements of the path.

Linking Files

Links come in two varieties: symbolic and hard. (Symbolic links are often known as *soft* links.) Each has its own set of advantages and disadvantages. Sysadmins use links for a multitude of purposes; chief amongst them is the need to make shortcuts on the system for users to access data without having to navigate multiple directory levels.

If you have users on your Linux systems, you'll need to have a single mount point that's accessible to multiple users. The options include having users navigate to the /mnt/somemount directory to save data or putting a link to that mount point in their home directories. You're much better off using a link for this task.

Symbolic Links

Symbolic links are used primarily to make a shortcut from one object to another. A *symbolic link* creates a tiny file with its own inode and set of data that points to the linked file. Symlinks can span across file systems and drives, primarily because a symlink has its own inode. Figure 6.1 shows the relationship between a symlink and the target file.

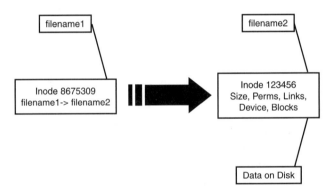

Figure 6.1   Symbolic link detail.

For example, you might mount a remote NFS share on the /mnt/projdata mount point and want each user be able to access that remote share from her own home directory. You simply have to issue the following command in each user's home directory to accomplish this:

```
ln -s /mnt/projdata projdata
ls -l projdata
lrwxrwxrwx    1 root    root     13 Jan 26 12:09 projdata -> /mnt/projdata
```

Notice that the listing for the new symlink shows exactly where the link points, and the permissions are set to the maximum so as to not interfere with the permissions on the target object.

 Don't try to change the permissions on a symlink; the **chmod** command isn't equipped to change their permissions. You should leave the link permissions alone, and take care to set the target file permissions to the appropriate levels.

Hard Links

A *hard link* is normally used to create a backup or an anchor of an important file to which users must have read-write access. A hard link is simply an additional name in a directory file that points to the exact same inode and shares every aspect of the original file except the actual name. Figure 6.2 shows the relationship between a hard link and the target file.

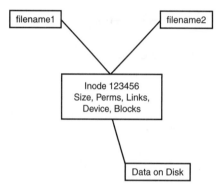

Figure 6.2 Hard link detail.

For an example of using a hard link, consider the need to ensure that a frequently deleted file is easily restorable for a given user. The user, Jaime, travels a lot, but when he's in the office he seems to delete things a lot or claims the system has eaten his files. When Jaime is flying, you don't have any issues, so the problem must be the user's actions.

To anchor or back up an important file such as the company contact list in Jaime's home directory, you first must create a backup directory, something like /backup.

Then, you create a hard link from Jaime's ccontactlist.txt file to a file in the /backup directory, like so:

```
cd ~jaime
ln ccontactlist.txt /backup/home_jaime_ccontactlist.txt
ls -l ccontactlist.txt
-rw-r--r--   2 jaime    users    0 Jan 26 13:08 ccontactlist.txt
```

Notice that the file appears normal, but the number 2 for the link count lets you know that another name entry for this file exists somewhere.

Also notice that the listing for the new hard link doesn't show the target file, or seem to refer to it in any way. Running the stat command on this file won't show you the other filename or seem to be aware of it outside of the higher link count.

The name of a file is the only thing about the file not stored in the inode. This appears on the exam in questions for this set of objectives.

Hard links can't be created if the target is on another file system, disk, or remote object. The need to hook multiple names to the same inode makes this impossible.

Be careful when changing the permissions and ownership on the hard-linked files because all name entries point to exactly the same inode. Thus, any changes are instantly made to what would appear to be multiple files but what, in reality, are only filenames.

To delete a file that has multiple hard links requires the removal of every hard link or the multiple names. To find all the links for a file, run the following command:

```
ls -i ccontactlist.txt
17392 ccontactlist.txt
find / -inum 17392
/home/jaime/ccontactlist.txt
/backup/home_jaime_ccontactlist.txt
```

On the exam, remember that a symlink is another actual file with its own inode. A large amount of symlinks can therefore cause a problem for a file system, such as one that contains users' home directories. Too many inodes used can restrict you from using the storage space that's available. Run the **df –i** command to see what the statistics are.

Working with Permissions

Permissions determine how users can access resources on the system. System security is configured by the user's UID (User ID), her GIDs (Group ID), (both primary and secondary), and the permissions on the object she is attempting to access.

Permission Trio Bits

Figure 6.3 shows the 10 positions (1 type bit and 3 trios of permission bits) that make up the permissions section of a file.

Type	User			Group			Other		
	r	w	x	r	w	x	r	w	x
	4	2	1	4	2	1	4	2	1

Figure 6.3 Permission trios.

The first bit of the 10 shown is the type of object:

➤ -—Used for normal files

➤ l—Used for symlinks that point to other objects

➤ b—Used for block device files

➤ c—Used for character devices

➤ d—Used for directory

The next nine bits are what I call the permission trios. Each of the trios affects a certain set of users with its permissions. To determine which permissions a user has to a given object, begin from the left and as soon as a match is made, that trio alone is the permissions that are in effect for that user and object. Here are the three trios:

➤ user—If the user is the user owner, this is the permission trio in effect.

➤ group—If the user's primary or secondary groups are this group, but only if that user is not the user owner, this is the permission trio in effect.

➤ other—If the user is neither the user owner nor a member of the group owner, this is the permission trio in effect.

Do not mix up the Windows environment and Linux in your mind. There is no such thing as effective permissions for a Linux object; that is entirely a Windows concept. For example, a user who matches the user owner and is also a member of the group owner does not have the greater permissions of the two trios slapped together; he is restricted only to the user owner trio's permissions.

The trios are made up of 3 bits (4, 2, 1) and work similarly to bits in an IP. If on, the value counts; if off, the value doesn't count. The bits work like light switches: The bit is not counted unless on, and the addition of the bits turned on equals a value. That value is used with the chmod and other commands.

The bit values equate to the following permissions:

➤ **4**—Read, which is the ability to view the file's contents.

➤ **2**—Write, which is the ability to change the file's contents, permissions, ownership, and so on.

➤ **1**—Execute; the file can be executed. (Read is needed for a script, but binaries can execute with only the Execute permission.)

If you do an ls -l of an object and its permission trios are 666, the only way that number could be arrived at with the possible bit values is for the 4 and

2 bits to be on, or rw (read and write). If you see a file that is set to 666, that equates to all three trios having the same permissions—read and write.

Watch for questions that try to trick you with a user who's both the user owner and a member of the group owner, but the correct permissions for executing or changing the file aren't in a single trio. You can't mix the trios, even if your profile encompasses several of the trios.

For example, say a user named fred is the user owner of the file object /home/fred/22AcaciaAvenue.mp3 and is also a member of the group owner of that object. The file's listing has the following permissions set:

```
-rw-r-xr-x   2 fred    users   0 Jan 26 13:08 22AcaciaAvenue.mp3
```

fred's permissions might seem to span the various trios, but because fred is the user owner, he matched the first trio and stopped there.

Manipulating Permissions

chmod is the command to use when modifying or altering an object's permission trio bits. Only the root and object owners can alter permissions.

The two modes of manipulating the permissions for an object are numeric and symbolic. Both modes have their place, and if there were only one mode, someone would have to invent the other, just for variety.

Numeric Mode

Numeric permissions are the most often used, and they appear on the exam with greater frequency than the symbolic style. As a rule, I recommend using the numeric mode to *set* or force permissions on an object. For example, if you are told that the current permissions for an object are 644 and you are asked to ensure that all users have read and write access to that object, you can assume that the numeric style is correct, as shown here:

```
chmod 666 file1
```

The chmod command works great on groups of files, too:

```
chmod 644 /home/lukec/*.txt
```

It even works on directories and their contents. For example, say the user bertrandr has a home directory he inherited from someone else and a few files are not set properly to be readable only by him. He asks you to set all the files in his home directory to 640 for security's sake and to give him read/write access to them. You might use the command:

```
chmod -R 640 /home/bertrandr/*
```

Take a moment to understand why this command works the way it does. The chmod command has an -R recursive option that affects the object named and all its child objects. However, bertrandr didn't ask you to change his home directory and all the contents, but just the contents, which is why the slash and asterisk characters are on the end of the target. This command acts on the entire *contents* of bertrandr's home directory but leaves the directory alone.

The chmod command has surprisingly few options:

➤ -c—Reports only changed files

➤ -v—Reports all files

➤ -h—Changes symbolic links, not the original file

➤ -f—Suppresses error messages

➤ -R—Operates recursively through directories

The **chmod** command's recursive option is an uppercase *R*, not a lowercase *r* as in some other commands. Familiarize yourself with the case of the various command options, and you will be fine.

Symbolic Mode

When using chmod with symbolic values, keep in mind that you can force the permissions like the numeric mode, but a much longer command results. The primary reason to use symbolic mode is to affect, or alter, permissions rather than to set or overwrite them.

The symbolic mode uses a letter to identify the trios (user = u; group = g; other = o; and all = a), a qualifier (+, -, or =), and then the permissions being altered or set (r = read; w = write; and x = execute).

To use the symbolic values to set permissions, you can do them all at once, like so:

```
chmod a=rwx file
```

This produces permission trios that are set to -rwxrwxrwx.

Or you can use each one of the identifiers with its qualifier and permissions separated by commas:

```
chmod u=rw,g=rx,a=
```

This produces a file that has its permissions set to -rw-r-x---.

This method of using the symbolic mode is viewed as unwieldy and somewhat inelegant for constant use. Use symbolic mode when you want to tune up the permissions, not set them initially.

To change just the user owner's permissions to rwx, you would use the following command:

```
chmod u=rwx mystuff
```

To change the group owner's permissions to r-x, you would use the command shown here:

```
chmod g=rx mystuff
```

To change the other or everyone permissions to r, you would use this command:

```
chmod o=r mystuff
```

On the exam the idea is to get the question answered, so if it's a multiple-choice question and you're sure something will work on the command line, that's probably the answer. Watch out for the fill-in-the-blank answers because you don't get any partial credit. What's typed is checked against a table of possible correct answers, but it must be executable on the command line and work to be right.

Setting a file to be executable, without knowing its other permissions, can be done several ways.

For example, if you know a file exists but don't know the permissions and you are told to make sure it's executable by all permission trios, you would use the following command:

```
chmod a+x file1
```

Alternatively, you can leave the a off and get all the trios by default:

```
chmod +x file1
```

User and Group Ownership

To set the stage for the chown and chgrp commands, let's review how users and groups are set to function on a Linux machine. Changing user owner and group owner for objects can be frustrating unless you understand some ground rules about how Linux sets the ownership for objects:

➤ A user has two types of groups associated with her: The primary group is the one whose GID appears in the user's /etc/passwd entry.

➤ Users can be members of other groups via entries in the /etc/group file. These group memberships are called *secondary groups*.

➤ If a user has a group set as her primary group, she doesn't have to be physically listed as a group member in the /etc/group file. The primary group setting acts as a full membership option, too.

➤ When a user creates an object, her primary group GID/name is set as the group owner by default.

➤ Changing a user's primary group doesn't automatically update any of the owned objects and can cause problems if that user isn't a member of the new group owner for the object.

Changing Ownership

The chown command is used to set the user owner, group owner, or a combination of the two with one command.

The format for the chown command is

```
chown -options user:group object
```

The chown command accepts both of the following commands as valid:

```
chown snuffy:users file1
chown snuffy.users file1
```

In addition, you can use the following syntax with chown:

➤ owner—Changes only the owner

➤ owner:group—Changes both the owner and group

➤ owner:—Changes the owner and sets the group to the login or primary group of the user

➤ :group—Changes only the group and leaves the owner unaffected

Let's say that the user snuffy has the primary group of users and a secondary group membership of accounting. By default, every object snuffy creates on the system will have snuffy as the user owner and users as the group owner. This can cause problems in shared directories, and it often does. (Later in the chapter, we'll discuss the SUID or SGID, which can make shared directories more palatable.)

If snuffy visits a shared directory whose ownership is set to root/accounting and creates a file named snuffysexpenses.txt, that file will be inaccessible to any of the other users who share that directory unless they are also members of the group users. Say the user martha does expenses and needs to have ownership of the file.

To change the file snuffy created to be owned by martha/accounting, you would use this command:

```
chown snuffy:accounting snuffysexpenses.txt
```

Let's say that now the file needs to be owned by another user who cuts the checks, fluchre, so you can just change the user owner without having to bother with the group, which will be unaffected:

```
chown fluchre snuffysexpenses.txt
```

If, for some reason, you decide that an entire directory tree of files needs to have its ownership changed, you can do so at one time with the following command:

```
chown -R root:accounting /accounting
```

Changing Group Ownership

When just the group owner needs to be changed, the simplest method is to use the chgrp command. The syntax of the command is very straightforward:

```
chgrp newgrp file1
```

Changing a large set of files to another group owner requires the use of the -R recursive option:

```
chgrp -R newgrp /data/*
```

The previous command changes just the contents of the /data directory to the group owner newgrp but leaves the user owner alone.

Options for the chgrp command include

➤ -c—Shows a line of output only for changed objects

➤ -h—Changes symbolic links, not the original file

➤ -R—Recursively affects the target and all children

➤ -v—Shows a line of output for every object, regardless of the actions performed on the object

Special File Permissions

Several facts about how the Linux and Unix file systems are constructed can cause problems for administrators. The first interesting factoid is that because only a single group can be the group owner for a given object, whoever wants access to that object has to be a member of the owning group.

 Yes, there are now access control lists (ACLs) on some Linux systems and in a few distributions, but not on the exam, so be very careful when considering special bit and group ownership questions.

Trying to configure many groups and users to have access to the right files can be difficult. Every user has a primary group and secondary groups, and you must make sure that every user who shares data in a given directory has the same primary group. That's nearly impossible beyond 10 or so users.

There's a way out of this situation: You can set an additional or special bit on the shared directory, which causes all users who have access to inherit the group owner of the directory on all their created objects.

Secondly, although Linux has a limited set of permissions, in some situations special bits must be used to allow users who aren't any kind of owner of an object to access that object. (If this sounds like a security risk, it is, but stay tuned and I'll explain this.)

Special Bit Permissions

The following special bits are available for Linux file system use:

➤ **SUID**—The Set User ID allows users to run a program as if they were the owner, be it another user or root (numeric = 4000).

➤ **SGID**—The Set Group ID allows you to apply group permissions to a set of files, making shared directories and data possible (numeric = 2000).

➤ **Sticky bit**—Save Text mode used to be for keeping programs in memory to speed access, but now it's used to keep nonowners from deleting files in a common directory (numeric = 1000).

Remember that these bits are used when necessary, which isn't often, and they are a security risk, even when properly used. Additionally, any user who can copy a file can change that file, but the SUID and SGID bits are stripped off any copied file for security.

Special bits can be set either of two ways—numeric or symbolic, much like setting other permissions with chmod.

The use of the characters **XXX** in the following examples indicates that permissions exist and need to be included but removes the focus from the permissions. I have substituted the **XXX** characters. Focus on the special bits instead.

The first way is to use the numeric mode, which you use when you are setting the permissions. All permissions must be overwritten when using numeric mode:

```
chmod 4XXX /some/program
```

Several bits can be changed or set simultaneously:

```
chmod 6XXX /some/program
```

This sets both the SUID and SGID bits for the program.

The second way is to use the symbolic mode when you aren't sure of the existing permissions or just know you want to add or subtract a special bit permission:

```
chmod +s /some/program
```

Again, you can set several special bits at once even with the symbolic mode, although it's a little more complex in the syntax:

```
chmod u+s,g+s /some/program
```

Be careful removing special bit permissions because reversing the **+** to a **-** in the previous command does not set the file back to the original permissions. Be sure to note the initial permissions before removing special bits.

Setting the SUID Bit

A good example of when to set the SUID bit is when you need to have a normal user back up your system, such as someone trusted but who you're not about to give the `root` password to. The `dump` command is a good example of a command that performs only a small set of tasks.

To set the `dump` command to be executable by a normal user, you'd use the following:

```
chmod +s /sbin/dump
```

This allows a normal user to run the program as the root user, but only that program and only for the duration of the program's execution.

Setting the SGID Bit

The first and easiest scenario in which to use the SGID bit is when you need to make a program executable by anyone who is in a certain group that is the owner of the program in question:

```
chmod +g /sbin/dump
```

This makes the dump program executable by anyone who is a member (primary or secondary) of the owning group, usually the root group. Change the group owner to the target group to make it executable by users in that group.

The second and more complex way to use the SGID bit is for a shared directory. Having users share a common directory for files means that they all must at least be members of the group owner of that directory. For example, say you have the following users on your system (note the primary and secondary memberships):

User	Primary	Secondary
snuffy	users	accounts snuffy
billybob	billybob	users accounts
ursula1	accounts	users ursula1

These users all share at least one group (users), and that's the one that should be set as the group owner on the /data directory:

```
chgrp users /data
ls -ld /data
drwxr-xr-x   2  root users    4096  Feb 17 12:10  /data
```

Now, you have to set the directory to be writable so the users can make changes to the file (add files, remove files, and so on) with the following command:

```
chmod g+w /data
ls -ld /data
drwxrwxr-x   2  root users    4096  Feb 17 12:10  /data
```

At this point, you'd think the users could just go nuts making files and directories, sharing data, and so on. Not so—or not so in a sane manner. Here's what would happen if all three of the users executed the touch file1.username command in the shared directory:

```
ls -l /data
-rw-rw-r--   1 billybob billybob    0 Feb 17 12:22 file1.billybob
-rw-r--r--   1 snuffy   users       0 Feb 17 12:22 file1.snuffy
-rw-r--r--   1 ursula1  accounts    0 Feb 17 12:24 file1.ursula1
```

Would this be a problem? Absolutely. Because each user, by default, creates objects that inherit the user's primary group, this directory is already in trouble. As it's set, only `billybob` has access to his file, while he and both the other users can access `snuffy`'s and `ursula1`'s files. Here's the solution: Before letting the users into the shared directory, set the SGID bit on the directory itself:

```
chmod g+s /data
ls -ld /data
drwxrwsr-x  2 root      users        4096 Feb 17 12:24 /data
```

Make believe that the users haven't made any files yet and, if you let them into the directory and all three make files, the ownership is now

```
ls -l /data
-rw-rw-r--   1 billybob users           0 Feb 17 12:31 file1.billybob
-rw-r--r--   1 snuffy   users           0 Feb 17 12:31 file1.snuffy
-rw-r--r--   1 ursula1  users           0 Feb 17 12:31 file1.ursula1
```

The problem is solved, at least for group ownership. If you have users who don't have a common primary group and who need to have access to all the files in a shared directory, set the SGID bit to cause group owner inheritance for all created objects.

 You must understand the SGID directory scenario. Try it several times with at least two or three users. This scenario will appear on the exam.

Setting the Sticky Bit

Perhaps the most oddly named part of Linux and Unix, the *sticky bit* was created to keep programs in nonswappable memory, so they'd execute that much faster. The sticky bit is used mostly for ensuring that users in a shared directory can't delete anyone else's files.

Taking the previous example of our /data directory, everything is configured properly for it but the users can still delete any other user's files. You therefore must set the sticky bit with this command:

```
chmod +t /data
ls -ld /data
drwxrwsr-t  2 root      users        4096 Feb 17 12:31 /data
```

Now, if one of your users issues an `rm *` or similar command in the shared directory, only the files of which he is listed as user owner are deleted, even though it might ask whether the user wants to delete files that don't have a write permission in the group trio.

You'll notice that **billybob**'s file has a write permission in the group trio and the other files don't. The **billybob** account is the only one that has its primary group set to the user's own group, **billybob**.

Finding Files by Permission

Attackers attempting to breach your system often attempt to set certain files to have the SUID or SGID bit set, allowing their otherwise normal account to perform all sorts of unauthorized tasks.

The find command has an operator that makes finding your vulnerable files easy. The -perm operator is usually followed by a three- or four-digit set of permissions, such as the example shown here:

```
find /usr/bin -perm 777
```

This extreme example searches for any object in the /usr/bin directory and below that has the exact permissions of rwxrwxrwx. This is fine, but it doesn't help find security risks that are caused by the SUID and SGID bits. This next command does, however:

```
find / -perm +6000
```

At first glance, this might look as if we're searching for all files that have the SUID/SGID bits and then blank permissions from that point on. It really searches the entire system for all files that have either the SUID or the SGID bit set, regardless of the other permissions.

The -perm operator uses several additional qualifiers for the permissions:

➤ No prefix finds those exact permissions.

➤ - finds the exact combination of special bits the next number adds up to (-6000 finds SUID and SGID).

➤ + finds files with any of the special bits that make up the next number (+7000 finds SUID, SGID, and sticky bit).

You should install the system and then run a find command that reports any file that has a special bit set, like so:

```
find /usr/bin -perm +7000 -exec ls -l {} \;
-rwsr-xr-x   1 root     root        35484 Nov 13 07:10 /usr/bin/chage
-rwsr-xr-x   1 root     root        36308 Nov 13 07:10 /usr/bin/gpasswd
-r-xr-sr-x   1 root     tty          7420 Jun 25  2003 /usr/bin/wall
-rws--x--x   1 root     root        14140 Sep 25 06:10 /usr/bin/chfn
```

Redirect this output to a file and keep that file on a disk or in some safe place off the system. Every so often, you should run the same `find` command and then compare the results to the original with the `diff` command, such as

```
diff /root/latestfindperm /mnt/floppy/findperm.orig
> -rwxr-xr-t    1 root      root        700108 Aug 25 21:17 /usr/bin/align
```

If you ran the previous command and got the output shown, that would mean that something or someone had set the `align` command to have the sticky bit set. Use your imagination, improvise, adapt, script!

You also need to understand the files the various `-perm` operators bring back. Make a new directory named `/root/test`; then change to that directory. Create a set of four files with the following permissions:

```
-rwsrwxrwx 1 root  root   0 Dec  8 08:30 file1
-rwxrwsrwx 1 root  root   0 Dec  8 21:14 file2
-rwxrwxrwt 1 root  root   0 Dec  8 21:16 file3
-rwsrwsrwx 1 root  root   0 Dec  8 21:19 file4
```

Run the following queries and see what you get:

```
find /dir -perm  4000  FILES:_____
find /dir -perm -4000  FILES:_____
find /dir -perm +6000  FILES:_____
find /dir -perm +1000  FILES:_____
```

Answers:

```
Query 4000  FILES: No Files Found
Query -4000 FILES: file1 file4
Query +6000 FILES: file1 file2 file4
Query -1000 FILES: file3
```

Default Permissions

If your system is a default Linux system, a single value is set in the `/etc/bashrc` or `~/.bashrc` file for users and governs the permissions any created object has. This value is known as the `umask`, and there is only one for both directories and files.

The default permissions for directories and files are different. The default permissions with no `umask` set are

➤ `rw-rw-rw-` `666`—Used for files

➤ `rwxrwxrwx` `777`—Used for directories

Check the `umask` on the system you have handy with the following command:

```
umask
0022
```

This just means that of the four possible positions to mask out, the last two have the write permission masked out, or not used.

If you create a file in the /root/test directory with the umask set to 0022, the file's permissions are as follows:

```
-rw-r--r--    1 root    root        881 Feb 17 09:11 file1
```

If you create a directory in the same directory with the same umask set, the directory's permissions are as follows:

```
drwxr-xr-x    2 root    root       4096 Feb 17 14:47 dir1
```

You can change the umask value to a more restrictive one with the command:

```
umask 027
```

Now, you can create another file and the permissions should be

```
-rw-r-----    1 root    root        881 Feb 17 09:22 file2
```

Create another directory and the permissions should be

```
drwxr-x---    2 root    root       4096 Feb 17 14:48 dir2
```

As you can see, the umask value changes the default permissions of a created object to match the following formula:

Default value – umask value = create value

Notice that the umask has a value greater than the default value of the file being created. The umask values go from 000 to 777 because a directory object has a default value of 777, whereas files have 666. The umask must encompass both sets of possible values, so if you have a 7 in a umask, files just stop at 0 (zero) and don't go into negative numbers.

umask will show up on the exam, with questions about which **umask** value would cause the listed files to have these permissions, and the other way around.

Using Disk Quotas

Most sysadmins have had a server system partition fill up due to one thing or another, usually followed closely by a system crash or kernel panic (and sysadmin panic). A package on nearly every Unix/Linux system, called quota, lets you limit disk usage on a per-user and per-file-system basis.

If you see situations in which two directory trees (**/home** and **/var/www**, for example) need to have conflicting or different quotas, these directory trees must be on separate file systems, which essentially means separate partitions. This scenario will appear on the exam, so be ready for it.

Quota Commands and Files

The quota system is designed to limit users to a certain amount of disk space per file system. The `quota` command allows a user to view the quotas that are in place for her account.

The commands and files that are used for quotas are as follows:

➤ `quotaon`—Turns on quotas

➤ `quotaoff`—Turns off quotas

➤ `quotacheck`—Updates the `aquota.*` files

➤ `edquota`—Used for editing the user's quota amounts

➤ `quota`—Used by users to see quota limits/space

➤ `aquota.user`—The binary file that contains user quota information

➤ `aquota.group`—The binary file that contains group quota information

➤ `usrquota`—The `/etc/fstab` option for user quotas

➤ `grpquota`—The `/etc/fstab` option for group quotas

Quota Concepts

The following are terms you need to understand to configure quotas:

➤ **Soft limit**—This is a limit that can be exceeded, with resulting warnings up until the grace period is met.

➤ **Hard limit**—This is usually set higher than the soft limit and cannot be exceeded.

➤ **Grace period**—The soft limit can be exceeded up to the hard limit until the grace period value is met. Then, to save more data, the amount used must be brought below the soft limit.

Configuring Quotas

To set up quotas, you need to choose a file system. It's not recommended to set quotas on the root (`/`) file system, but instead to set quotas on the file systems that have the most active sets of users and data.

For example, this next exercise was done on a system that has a partition on the device /sdb5 mounted to the mount point /data. An entry in the /etc/fstab mounts this partition on system boot. The permissions for the /data file system allow users who are in the users group to create objects in it. There are already files from various users in that directory.

To set up quotas on the /data file system, do the following:

1. Ensure the /data partition is mounted by issuing the mount command and inspecting the output.

2. Create the files aquota.user and aquota.group in the root of the /data file system, and set their permissions properly with the following commands:

```
touch /data/aquota.user ; touch /data/aquota.group
chmod 660 /data/aquota.*
```

3. Edit the /etc/fstab file and add usrquota and grpquot, as shown here, to enable both user and group quotas:

```
/dev/sdb5  /mnt/data  ext3  defaults,usrquota,grpquota  0 0
```

4. Remount the /home file system with the following command:

```
mount -o remount,rw /data
```

5. Check that it has the correct options (shows usrquota and grpquota) with this command:

```
mount ¦ grep usrquota
/dev/sdb5 on /mnt/data type ext3 (rw,noexec,nosuid,nodev,usrquota,
➡grpquota)
```

6. Add a normal user to test quotas with the following:

```
useradd -m quotaboy
passwd quotaboy
usermod -G 100 quotaboy
```

7. Now update the aquota.* files with the following command:

```
quotacheck -avug
quotacheck: WARNING -  Quotafile /data/aquota.user was probably
➡truncated. Can't save quota settings...quotacheck: WARNING -
Quotafile /data/aquota.group was probably
➡truncated. Can't save quota settings...
quotacheck: Scanning /dev/sdb5 [/data] done
quotacheck: Checked 155 directories and 422 files
```

 The errors you see are just the **quotacheck** command letting you know the quota files don't contain data yet, but it will update them with the right information.

8. Edit the quota settings for this user with this command:

```
edquota -u quotaboy
```

9. You'll see the user's quota information in vi, so you can edit the amounts, like so:

```
Disk quotas for user quotaboy (uid 500):
Filesystem   blocks    soft    hard    inodes    soft      hard
/dev/sdb5         0       0       0         0       0         0
```

10. Set quotaboy's block quotas to match the following:

```
Filesystem   blocks    soft    hard    inodes    soft      hard
/dev/sdb5         0    5000    6000         0       0         0
```

11. Save and exit the file; it will be loaded properly by the quota system.

No user should access the **/data** file system during the configuration of its quotas. If you can, either take the network down using the **service network stop** command or disable logins by creating the **/etc/nologin** file with the **touch** command.

12. Sign on as, or use the su - command to become, quotaboy:

```
su - quotaboy
```

13. Create a new file in the /data directory as quotaboy:

```
touch /data/file1.quotaboy
```

14. Exit as quotaboy and, as the root user, run the quotacheck command again:

```
quotacheck -avug
quotacheck: Scanning /dev/sdb5 [/data] done
quotacheck: Checked X directories and XXX files
```

Sometimes you have to run several **quotacheck** commands to get a user to show up in the quota output. Use the **repquota -a** command to show all users' quotas and statuses.

15. As the root user, check to see that quotaboy has a quota listed:

```
quota quotaboy
Filesystem  blocks   quota   limit  grace   files  quota  limit   grace
/dev/sdb5        0    5000    6000              1      0      0
```

16. Turn on the quota system for the /data file system:

```
quotaon /data
```

17. Log in as `quotaboy` or `su` over to his account:

```
su - quotaboy
```

18. Run the `quota` command to see what `quotaboy`'s usage is presently:

```
quota
Disk quotas for user quotaboy (uid 501):
Filesystem blocks   quota   limit grace  files   quota limit grace
 /dev/sdb5      0    5000    6000             0       0     0
```

19. As the `quotaboy` user, copy all the regular files in the `/etc` directory to the `/data` directory:

```
# cp /etc/* /data
```

20. Run the `quota` command to see how many blocks are used and free:

```
Disk quotas for user quotaboy (uid 502):
Filesystem blocks   quota   limit  grace files   quota limit grace
 /dev/sdb5   2524    5000    6000          152       0     0
```

21. Fill up your quota by copying the entire `/etc/` tree to the `/data` directory, observing the multiple errors about the disk quota being exceeded:

```
cp -r /etc /data
```

22. Be sure to clean up the mess on your test system and try it again until you're comfortable with configuring quotas.

 To ensure quotas are always on when users are on the system, add the **quotaon** and **quotacheck** commands to a script and have the **/etc/rc.d/rc.sysinit** or similar script call them after the file systems are mounted.

Hard and Soft Limits

Dissecting the `edquota -u quotaboy` editor session is important because there are several items that will be on the exam. Let's look at each section of the output:

```
Filesystem  blocks   soft   hard   inodes   soft    hard
/dev/sdb5       0      0      0        0      0       0
```

The sections are described here:

➤ `Filesystem`—This is the file system on which the user has a quota.

➤ `blocks`—This is the number of blocks presently used by the user on the file system in question.

➤ soft—This is the soft limit, which can be exceeded for the grace period.

➤ hard—This is the hard limit, which cannot be exceeded.

➤ inodes—This is the number of inodes presently in use.

➤ soft—If set, this is the number of inodes for which you want to set a soft limit (if you can't think why, don't use it).

➤ hard—This is the hard limit for inodes, which, if met, keeps the user from creating more files.

The editable fields are the soft and hard settings for both blocks and inodes. Editing any of the other values does not do anything.

Setting the Grace Period

Use edquota -t to set the grace period for users; it's configurable in days, hours, minutes, or seconds. You're a pretty tough sysadmin if you configure a grace period that's less than a day. Here's the syntax for it:

```
edquota -t
```

To establish a grace period before enforcing soft limits for users, use the following command, where time units can be days, hours, minutes, or seconds:

```
Filesystem          Block grace period      Inode grace period
/dev/sdb5                 7days                   7days
```

Getting Quota Information

Run the quota command as a normal user to get just that user's quota information (as seen in the previous exercise). If there are no quotas for that user, the output states there are none.

The root user has the ability to get quota statistical data on all users, like so:

```
repquota -a
*** Report for user quotas on device /dev/sdb5
Block grace time: 7days; Inode grace time: 7days
                        Block limits               File limits
User            used    soft    hard  grace    used  soft  hard  grace
--------------------------------------------------------------------
root       --   32844      0       0              5     0     0
snuffy     --       0      0       0              1     0     0
quotaboy   +-    6000   5000    6000  6days    1464     0     0
```

File Attributes

Many sysadmins think there aren't any special or hidden attributes for files on a Linux file system, but there are a few that can help make life easier and speed your system up, if not enhance its security.

Special attributes for file objects are set with the chattr command and viewed with the lsattr command. The attributes are

➤ A—Don't update access time on modify.

➤ a—Append only for writing.

➤ c—Compressed; the file is compressed from its natural state.

➤ d—No dump; when the dump command is executed, exclude files with this attribute set.

➤ i—Immutable; no changes are possible to the file, it cannot be altered.

➤ s—Secure deletion; contents are zeroed on deletion.

➤ u—Undeletable; the file cannot be deleted unless the attribute is reset.

➤ s—Synchronous updates are performed.

The three qualifiers for the options are +, which adds or sets the option; -, which removes the option; and = followed by several options. Using the = operator overwrites the current attributes with the new ones.

As an example of setting a useful attribute, let's imagine you have a user who is up to no good but who either does not use her bash shell to do her misdeeds or erases the entries in the .bash_history file afterward.

You can set the user's .bash_history file to be only appendable with the following command:

```
chattr +a /home/baduser/.bash_history
```

I worked at a company where this was used to find an administrator who was altering important databases, for personal enrichment. The appendable-only option doesn't even let the user delete the offending file. The user can't overwrite it or do much except type as many commands as possible in the hopes of pushing the incriminating lines out of the 1000-line long history buffer.

Exam Prep Questions

1. You are installing a customized server and need to strip the root file system down to the essentials only. According to the FHS 2.2, which of the following are considered optional on the **root** (/) file system? (Choose two.)

   ❑   A. `/root`
   ❑   B. `/usr`
   ❑   C. `/tmp`
   ❑   D. `/home`

   Answers A and D are correct because the FHS states that the `/root` and `/home` partitions are optional. Answers B and C are incorrect because the FHS doesn't list them as optional for the root file system.

2. One of your programmers has produced an order entry system that will be shared among your users from a central file server. What is the appropriate directory to place this program and its associated files in?

   ◯   A. `/usr/local/bin`
   ◯   B. `/usr/local`
   ◯   C. `/usr/share`
   ◯   D. `/opt`

   Answer B is correct because the FHS states that shareable programs should be in `/usr/local/appname`. Answer A is incorrect because the `/usr/local/bin` directory is for single binaries and is often just a link to some application in `/usr/local/appname/bin`. Answer C is incorrect because the `/usr/share` directory contains files for multiple architectures and the question does not state that multiple architectures are involved. Answer D is incorrect because the `/opt` directory is for locally installed programs only and is not to be shared out for multiple system usage.

3. Which of the following is a true statement about files on a default Linux system? (Choose all that apply.)

   ❑   A. Filenames can start with a numeral.
   ❑   B. Filenames can contain multiple periods.
   ❑   C. Filenames can contain spaces.
   ❑   D. Filenames can contain ampersands (`&`).
   ❑   E. Filenames can contain backslashes (\).

   Answers A, B, and C are correct because they are true statements about files on a default (**ext2**) file system. Answer D is incorrect because the ampersand character is a special character that is used to send a job to the background. Answer E is incorrect because the backslash character is the exception character and cannot be used in a filename.

4. You find a string in a shell script that contains the following command:

```
cp /data/*.doc ~tarfoo
```

What is the meaning of the characters `~tarfoo`?

○ A. A special function named `tarfoo`

○ B. A directory named `tarfoo` in your home directory

○ C. The `tarfoo` user's home directory

○ D. The `/data/tarfoo` directory

Answer C is correct because the use of a ~ character in front of a string parses the `/etc/passwd` file for a username of that string. Answer A is incorrect because functions begin with a left parentheses mark and contain commands. Answer B is incorrect because, for that string to denote a directory named `tarfoo` in your home directory, it would need to be `~/tarfoo`. Answer D is incorrect because the `/data` directory is nonstandard and does not normally contain a user's home directory.

5. You are currently in the directory `/home1/user1/subdir1` and need to navigate to the directory `/home12/user3`. Which of the following commands will accomplish this?

○ A. `cd home12/user3`

○ B. `cd ~/user3`

○ C. `cd ../../home12/user3`

○ D. `cd ../../../home12/user3`

Answer D is correct because the series of `..` and forward slashes that precede the `/home12/user3` string correctly navigate to that directory. Answer A is incorrect because the path is not absolute; it's relative and would work only from the root of the system. Answer B is incorrect because the `~/user3` string denotes a subdirectory of the current user's home directory named `user3` and would have to be changed to `~user3` to work. Answer C is incorrect because the string does not go back to the root of the system; it only goes back up to the `/home1` directory.

6. You have a directory named `/dir1` that contains subdirectories and regular files. You want to replicate this directory structure exactly into an existing directory named `/dir2`. Which of the following commands will accomplish this? (Choose all that apply.)

❏ A. `cp --contents dir1/ /dir2`

❏ B. `cp -r /dir1/* /dir2`

❏ C. `xcopy /dir1 /dir2`

❏ D. `cp -r /dir1 /dir2`

Answer B is correct because, to copy the contents of a directory, the source must end with a `/*`; otherwise, the directory itself is copied as a subdirectory of the target. Answer A is incorrect because there isn't a

`--contents` option to the `cp` command. Answer C is incorrect because
the `xcopy` command is offered only on DOS and Windows machines.
Answer D is incorrect because the source directory doesn't include a `/*`
suffix and therefore copies the source into the target as a subdirectory.

7. You are currently in the `/bbb` directory and want to move the contents
from the `/ccc` directory to this one. What is the shortest command that
will accomplish this?

   ○ A. `mv /ccc/*.* .`
   ○ B. `mv ../ccc/*.* .`
   ○ C. `mv /ccc/* .`
   ○ D. `mv /ccc/ /bbb`

Answer C is correct because this command moves the contents from
the source to the target and is the shortest command. Answer A is
incorrect because this command doesn't work for copying the
contents—`*.*` is incorrect syntax for the command. Answer B is incorrect because the same condition exists—the string `*.*` doesn't stat any
files or directories. Answer D is incorrect because it moves the `/ccc`
directory to be a subdirectory of the `/bbb` subdirectory.

8. Which option to the `mkdir` and `rmdir` commands allows you to create a
nested subdirectory tree?

   Example:
   `/dir1/dir2/dir3/dir4`

   ○ A. `-c`
   ○ B. `-n`
   ○ C. `-d`
   ○ D. `-p`

Answer D is correct because the `-p` option allows `mkdir` and `rmdir` to
create and remove parent directories. Answers A, B, and C are incorrect: These options are not available to the `mkdir` and `rmdir` commands.

9. You are the sysadmin of a busy server and need to save space on your
`/home` partition. You need to remove all files named `core` that are older
than seven days in the users' home directories, without receiving any
prompts.

   Write the exact command that will accomplish this in the blank below:

   _____

The correct answer is `find /home -mtime +7 -name core -exec rm -f {}`
`\;`. There are no alternative correct answers.

10. You are configuring your server after a system crash due to a full disk. When configuring a user quota for the /**home** directory of 60MB and a user quota for the /**var**/**ftp** directory of 20MB, what must be true about those directory trees for quotas to work?

   ○ A. They can exist only on an **ext2** file system.

   ○ B. They must have the **sparse_super** option set.

   ○ C. They must be mounted with the **usrquota** option.

   ○ D. They must exist on different partitions or drives.

Answer D is correct because quotas are configurable only on a per-file-system basis. In this case, one or both must be off the root (/) file system to have a different quota assigned. Answer A is incorrect because the **ext3** file system and others support user quotas. Answer B is incorrect because the **sparse_super** option is used only for creating fewer superblock backups for a file system. Answer C is incorrect because these are directories, not file systems, and the **usrquota** option is entered in the /**etc**/**fstab** entry for a file system, not a directory tree.

XFree86 Configuration and Troubleshooting

Terms you'll need to understand:

✓ Client/server
✓ Desktop
✓ Display manager
✓ Virtual terminal
✓ Window manager

Techniques you'll need to master:

✓ Understanding X Window System concepts
✓ Configuring X
✓ Customizing X
✓ Choosing a window manager
✓ Choosing a desktop
✓ Customizing display parameters
✓ Configuring fonts
✓ Identifying defaults for X
✓ Using virtual terminals
✓ Troubleshooting configuration files

Quick Overview of X

The Linux XFree86 project is a completely free and GPL-friendly port of the X Window System that has become the default version of X to be included with most distributions. (We'll call XFree86 by the shortcut "X" from this point on.)

X provides a desktop metaphor to the system; users typically interact with the graphic representation of the programs and files with a mouse or other pointing device.

Most sysadmins use the X system to open multiple **xterms** (shell prompts in a window) so they can switch easily from one to the other.

How X Works

The X system uses a client/server model, with one important change: Each system has an X server that interacts with and handles access to the system's hardware. The X server makes it possible for an X client (some program) to display data or graphics on the screen. The X client requests an action, and the X server performs the action.

Server, in this case, is defined as the computer that provides needed functionality for clients requesting services.

Another interesting feature of this model is the capability for an X server to handle X clients from either local or remote sources. In short, an X client executed from the local system displays along with X clients that have been invoked and run on a remote system and displays locally. Figure 7.1 shows the local workstation displaying both local and remote applications.

This flexibility opens up immense opportunities for centralizing your application code on a single server or set of servers and having clients attach and run the applications. Disadvantages include network bandwidth usage and troubleshooting the connections.

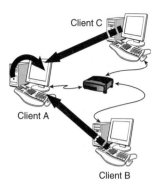

Figure 7.1 Displaying remote and local X clients.

Window Managers

It might seem odd to mention and work with window managers before desktops such as KDE and GNOME, but you need a window manager, while a desktop is not mandatory.

X window managers have one main purpose: When the X server draws a window on the screen, the window manager puts the scrollbars, minimize and maximize buttons, and all the garnish on that X client window. Some window managers are more full-featured than others and can provide the previous features plus virtual desktops, toolbars, wallpaper options, menus, and so on.

The least-featured of all window managers is the Tab Window Manager, or twm. Just like having an old car is better than having no car at all, having twm is better than not having any control over the look and feel.

Popular window managers include

➤ Afterstep

➤ Blackbox

➤ Enlightenment

➤ FVWM/FVWM2

➤ ICEWM

➤ SawFish

The window manager is typically invoked from the /usr/lib/X11/xinit/ xinitrc file, but it can be changed or invoked from other files during the X initialization process. The window manager can be invoked from any of the following files, in order (if the user doesn't configure the order, a failover mechanism chooses either the FVWM2 or twm window manager):

```
~/.Xclients -> /etc/X11/xinit/Xclients -> /usr/lib/X11/xinit/xinitrc
```

If a desktop is installed, the choice of which window manager is used is normally made by the desktop, with a preferred window manager being configured by default. However, you can choose another window manager in the Control Center or Control Panel applet.

 Watch out for questions that ask you for valid window managers on the exam. The previous list is by no means all-inclusive, but it is a solid set of likely candidates.

Linux Desktops

KDE was the first Linux desktop environment, and GNOME was primarily invented because its author wasn't happy with the licensing of the libraries used for the KDE desktop.

It doesn't really matter which one you use, but KDE is more aesthetically pleasing whereas GNOME does things from an architecturally correct perspective. Both get the job done. I recommend KDE for most user situations and GNOME for power users.

A desktop environment can be defined by the following common criteria (to name a few):

➤ File manager

➤ Control Panel/Center

➤ Window manager

➤ Common look and feel

➤ Integrated Office suite

➤ Media players

 Another desktop that is coming into prominence is called XFCE, but it won't be on the exam, or be the default in most distributions, for a while yet.

The XFree86 System

Although the X Window System was developed at MIT, the Linux version of X is a freely redistributable open-source version of the original and is maintained by the XFree86 Project, Inc.

The XFree86 implementation of the X Window System is similar in function to the original and provides an abstraction layer that allows applications to be either run and displayed locally or run remotely and displayed locally.

Installing XFree86

X can be installed in two manners, either when the system is installed or as an add-on to a running system. If you like 1,000-piece jigsaw puzzles, the latter is for you, but most sysadmins install X from the outset.

If you have a Red Hat system, you can get the Red Hat Network to install X from a single command; however, this is definitely not easy. The best option is to either use the APT-RPM tool from Conectiva's excellent programmers or do an upgrade to the existing installation, selecting Custom and then selecting the XFree86 files.

Debian has a huge advantage in this regard, with X installation being as easy as issuing a couple of commands:

```
apt-get update
apt-get install x-window-system
```

With a few questions and a lot of downloading, you'll have X on the Debian system.

XFree86 Versions

There has been a recent change from XFree86 versions 3.x to XFree86 versions 4.x. The main benefits of this change are increased speed, increased stability, support for advanced features, and 3D video cards. Another side benefit is the now smaller and less-complex xF86Config-4 file.

The exam will test you on the versions of the XFree86 configuration file, with version 3 being **XF86Config** and the new version 4 being **XF86Config-4**. They neatly avoid confusing you with questions that mix the two versions.

The newer X version 4 video driver and X server model are easier to configure and more modular, making updates and changes smoother.

The XFree86 Configuration File

Although you'll probably never have to construct an X configuration file by hand, you do need to know the overall structure, sections, and some of the entries for the exam.

Whatever version it is, the configuration file sets up the server, drivers, input devices, paths for fonts, and other modules. Then it sets up the display parameters, refresh rates, modes, and resolutions.

The older XF86Config format is a lot longer and includes many entries that don't change much, if ever. Part of the reorganization was to simplify the overly complex file format. The newer format is much easier to understand and configure manually.

The older XF86Config file's sections are listed here with short descriptions:

➤ Files—Font paths and color database location

➤ ServerFlags—Customization of the X server

➤ Keyboard—Keyboard configuration

➤ Pointer—Mouse or pointing device configuration

➤ Monitor—Monitors and modes configured

➤ Device—Video devices (cards)

➤ Screen—The resulting combination of a device and the monitor

In contrast, the XF86Config version 4 from Red Hat's Enterprise Linux line contains fewer sections and is representative of the new format. Version 4's sections are listed here, with a short description of each:

➤ ServerLayout—This identifies components of the server.

➤ Files—This is where you get fonts from, local or remote.

➤ InputDevice—Usually two, a keyboard definition and a mouse definition, are included. Others might be included, depending on your hardware.

➤ Monitor—This is the horizontal sync, vertical refresh, model name, and so on.

➤ Device—This is the video card driver name and RAM amount.

➤ Screen—This is the color depth and resolutions for that screen.

You will see questions about the format and sections of the **XF86Config** file, regardless of the version. If asked which section configures the pointing device, and the keyword **InputDevice** is not present, it's asking about the older file, and **Pointer** is correct. LPI exams always give you just enough information to answer the question, no more.

Important **XF86Config** Sections

Some sections are more likely to be configured or to cause certain effects to happen, so we'll take them one by one to ensure you understand how they work and can be configured.

Here's the `Files` section:

```
# Lots of comments removed...
        RgbPath      "/usr/X11R6/lib/X11/rgb"
        FontPath     "unix/:7100"
```

The entries of importance in the `Files` section are

➤ `RgbPath`—The database of colors and aliases (names) that applications will use

➤ `FontPath`—Can be a local path (`unix/:7100`), a remote system (`tcp/some.domain.com:7100`), or an X font server path (in a later section)

It's important to know the entries for a local path and how to denote a remote path. References to remote systems are typically pointing to a font server, and are used by multiple machines to enforce common fonts in an application.

The `InputDevice` section is as follows:

```
Section "InputDevice"
        Identifier   "Mouse0"
        Driver       "mouse"
        Option       "Protocol" "IMPS/2"
        Option       "Device" "/dev/psaux"
        Option       "ZAxisMapping" "4 5"
        Option       "Emulate3Buttons" "no"
EndSection
```

The entries of importance in the `InputDevice` section are

➤ `Driver`—This is the actual driver for the mouse. It's loaded and, if it's not the right one, the mouse won't function.

➤ `Protocol`—This is the communication method used to interpret the mouse movements (if the scroll wheel doesn't work, try `IMPS` rather than `PS/2`). USB mouse devices might need the `Auto` protocol.

➤ `Device`—This is the actual device file entry that represents the system's mouse, usually `/dev/psaux` or `/dev/mouse`.

➤ `ZAxisMapping`—This is for enabling scroll wheel mouse devices and should be followed by either `4 5` or `4 5 6"`. The ZAxis numbers allow the scroll wheel movements to be recognized by the system.

If your mouse malfunctions when X is run, what could be wrong? If you have the wrong protocol, the mouse might not work right because the system might not be properly recognizing the motions of the mouse.

Configuring xf86config

Adventurers might configure X by hand, but it's recommended that you use one of the fine tools provided in most distributions. The tools that are likely to be on the exam or in your distributions are as follows:

➤ **xf86config**—This older, text-based program requires detailed knowledge to configure X. It might be out of date on some distributions.

➤ **XF86Setup**—This program is graphical and fairly easy to use. This tool is ancient and might not support your X version.

➤ **xf86cfg**—Part of the XFree86 suite of programs, it shares similarities with the XF86Setup tool's menu choices and graphical setup options.

➤ **Xconfigurator**—Red Hat's X tool, this has an expert mode, is fully menu-based, and always supports Red Hat's distributions. (Check out the expert mode for more choices in video drivers.)

Other tools, such as SuSE's SaX and Mandrake's DrakeX, won't be on the exam but are extremely easy to use. Knowing the previous tools and the listed descriptions is more than enough information for the exam.

Starting X

Starting the X environment is usually done by running the `startx` command. `startx` is an executable script that is a more user-friendly front-end for the `xinit` command.

The X startup process is as shown in Figure 7.2.

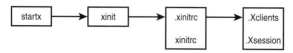

Figure 7.2   Startup path.

The X startup process can encompass many files, but at its base elements, the following steps are performed:

1. The user types startx.

2. startx invokes xinit.

3. xinit looks for any of two files in this order: 1) ~/.xinitrc 2) /usr/X11/xinit/xinitrc. Only the first file found is executed.

4. xinit launches the X system, typically looking for the following files:

> ➤ .Xclients or /etc/X11/xinit/Xclients

> ➤ .Xsession or /etc/X11/xdm/Xsession

 Starting X is almost always done with the **startx** script, which calls the xinit program. After **startx** calls **xinit**, any other combination is possible, but the next step is usually to look for a configuration file (**xinitrc**), and finally to invoke user programs. Read any questions about this topic very carefully.

X Customization Files

X uses a plethora of customization files, with the main ones being

> ➤ .xinitrc or xinitrc—Either a local file for the user or a system default file, this contains commands and options that set up the X environment.

> ➤ .Xclients or Xclients—This tries to start the preferred desktop or window manager; if that fails, it starts twm.

> ➤ .Xsession or Xsession—This sets up the user's X session, programs to run at startup, desktop/window manager preference, and so on.

> ➤ .Xresources or Xresources—This is used by the window manager at initialization for program defaults and customizations.

> ➤ .Xdefaults or Xdefaults—This is used by the window manager during sessions and can be interchangeable with the .Xresources or Xresources files.

The exam requires you know the right file for the right task, such as program customizations in the **.Xdefaults** files and so on. Details of the files are beyond the scope of the exams.

Fonts in X

X comes complete with a set of fonts that are referenced in the XF86Config file's Files section, under FontPath. On machines that don't use the X font server xfs, the font path is configured either as a set of directories and remote paths or as an entry that indicates a local path. The following entries for the FontPath are parsed and in memory and put together to form a single font path for the system:

```
FontPath "/usr/X11R6/lib/X11/fonts/100dpi"
FontPath "/usr/X11R6/lib/X11/fonts/75dpi"
FontPath "tcp/somepc.example.com:7100"
```

The fonts found in the local and remote paths are treated as one set of fonts to which the applications on the system have access.

If you want to use TrueType fonts, you need the X font server, or xfs. An advantage of xfs is speed when rendering fonts because large sets of complex fonts can make the system freeze up while rendering. xfs is multithreaded, so it can handle simultaneous requests, whereas the X server doesn't handle multiple requests well.

 If you choose to use the X font server, you'll have to start it before running X or have it started in the system runlevels; otherwise, X won't start.

Using the xfs server (locally, pointing to local files) requires the following line in the XF86Config:

```
FontPath "unix/:7100" [or "unix/:-1")
```

The xfs configuration file is capable of providing user limits, alternative font servers for clients to try if the current one is busy or unavailable, and the catalog of available fonts. The default xfs configuration file is

```
/usr/X11R6/lib/X11/fs/config
```

Adding fonts to the font directories requires running the mkfontdir command with a directory argument(s) to create or update the fonts.dir file. The fonts.dir file first lists the number of fonts found and then each font filename followed by the name of the font.

The fonts.alias file is manually edited to map missing fonts to an acceptable alternative.

Finally, to add to the existing FontPath without restarting the X font server or X itself, you can use the following command:

```
xset fp+ /usr/local/newfontdir
```

To remove a portion of an existing font path, use the xset -fp *portion* format. You can add a portion of a font path with the command xset +fp newsection. The xset fp rehash command should be run after adding fonts to a directory and re-creating the fonts.dir file with mkfontdir.

X Display Manager

The X Display Manager (XDM) is for managing logins and sessions on an X server. Its design is such that remote and local logins are handled equally well. The user enters her username and password; then the session is started, transferring control from the XDM to the user's session manager.

XDM's configuration file is /etc/X11/xdm/xdm-config. Some customizations require additional configuration files that are kept in the same directory, such as

➤ Xservers—Entries that represent X servers to manage with XDM

➤ Xaccess—For controlling which X clients can request access to your X server

➤ Xresources—Described earlier

➤ Xsession—Described earlier

The XDM is run by your system when you want to boot it into the graphical login mode. If you look at the last couple of lines of the /etc/inittab file, you'll see a line that causes the XDM to be started after system initialization, respawns the XDM process whenever you log out, and manages the users' logins.

When the system is set to runlevel 5, a particular line in the /etc/inttab file causes the XDM to be loaded and a graphical login screen to be shown to the user:

```
# Run xdm in runlevel 5
x:5:respawn:/etc/X11/prefdm -nodaemon
```

When the `prefdm` script is executed, as shown in the code, it looks (on Red Hat) at the `/etc/sysconfig/desktop` file for a preferred display manager. If that file is not found or configured, it tries in succession `gdm`, `kdm`, and `xdm` to try to load a display manager.

All the display managers get the login screen setup information from the `/etc/X11/xdm/Xsetup_0` file, which also calls the `Xresources` file for other setup information.

 If you want to customize the login screen to include font choices, login prompt size, colors, welcome messages, and background graphics, these settings are made in the **/etc/X11/xdm/Xresources** file.

Tuning X

Several programs exist to help you get the most out of your display and monitor with X. These are typically included with X or are a package that's closely related to X.

For example, some monitors don't display the screen correctly, with part of the output being cut off, or off-center. To fix some of these problems, you can use the `xvidtune` command. Running `xvidtune` from within X shows the interface in Figure 7.3.

Figure 7.3 The **xvidtune** program.

This program comes with some dire warnings, and with good reason. You can damage your monitor and when the tube goes, you will see (and smell) the "magic blue smoke" from the ruined tube. The best thing about the `xvidtune` program is that it tells you the display resolution and lets you adjust the image on your monitor to stretch properly from edge to edge and be centered properly.

Another interesting program is the xwininfo tool for querying a window and getting a listing of its geometry and, particularly, the color depth.

Running the xwininfo command causes very little to happen onscreen; the mouse pointer changes into a plus sign (+) and a message tells you to select the window you want to get information about.

The output shown here is typical of the tool:

```
xwininfo: Window id: 0x1600011 "rbrunson@localhost:~"
  Absolute upper-left X:  6
  Absolute upper-left Y:  21
  Relative upper-left X:  6
  Relative upper-left Y:  21
  Width: 657
  Height: 412
  Depth: 24
  Visual Class: TrueColor
  Border width: 0
  Class: InputOutput
  Colormap: 0x20 (installed)
  Bit Gravity State: NorthWestGravity
  Window Gravity State: NorthWestGravity
  Backing Store State: NotUseful
  Save Under State: no
  Map State: IsViewable
  Override Redirect State: no
  Corners:  +6+21   -361+21   -361-335   +6-335
  -geometry 80x24+0+0
```

The exam tests your knowledge of particular tools, such as what shows the current color depth, what can be used to adjust a screen's video image, and so on.

Into and Out of X

One of the topics that crops up now and then on the exam, and often enough in real life, is how to fix a frozen X display or do anything if X freezes up.

Let's review: Linux configures, by default, the keys F1–F6 as virtual consoles, mapped to /dev/tty1 through /dev/tty6. You can switch back and forth amongst these virtual consoles using the Alt and F keys, each one being an entirely different login session.

Sometimes you'll need to get from X into text mode. The Alt and F keys are mapped inside X, so an additional keystroke is required to escape the surly bonds of a broken X environment. For example, if you're in X, you would press Ctrl+Alt+F2 to reach a login screen that would drop you to the shell prompt in /dev/tty2.

After you're out of X, you can use the Alt+F key combinations to switch to any configured virtual console. Most sysadmins just save energy by using the Ctrl key all the time when switching virtual consoles—it doesn't hurt anything.

Let's say you've fixed the problem, killed a program, and freed up X. To get back into X, you press Alt+F7 or Ctrl+Alt+F7 to return to /dev/tty7, which is configured for X by default.

Remember that, while you're in text mode

➤ Alt+F1–F6 switch text terminals.

➤ Alt+F7 switches to X if running.

While you're in an X session

➤ Ctrl+Alt+F1–F6 switches to that session.

➤ Alt+F7 or Ctrl+Alt+F7 switches back to X.

Changing video resolution while in X is possible if you've configured multiple resolutions in your color depth. For example, in the Xconfigurator tool, you can choose multiple resolutions in 8-bit, 16-bit, or 24-bit, so changing from one resolution to another is a matter of using the following keystro kes in X:

➤ For higher Resolution, you use Ctrl+Alt+<keypad +>

➤ For lower resolution, you use Ctrl+Alt+<keypad ->

This might not always work because some laptops don't have the right keyboard to allow this, some machines don't allow resizing the display, and some computers change the resolution, but the screen then pans or scrolls around. You then must change the mode/resolution and restart X.

Remote Clients

Remotely displaying X client applications is a strength of X, making a centralized application server with multiple thin or slim clients a possibility. If all the client machine does is boot and connect to run applications, it can be replaced in very short order, reducing user downtime significantly.

Allowing remote machines to connect to your X server indiscriminately isn't a good security plan, so configuring the hosts access is accomplished with the xhost command.

The xhost command has three modes:

➤ xhost—Shows the current state

➤ xhost ---Enables security; only those that are authorized can connect

➤ xhost +—Disables security; anyone can connect

First, run the xhost command to determine the state of the security mechanism, like so:

```
xhost
access control enabled, only authorized hosts can connect
```

You now know the machine isn't accepting connections from just anyone, but you have a decision to make; do you want to block everyone and allow a few, or do you want to allow everyone and block just a few?

To leave the system in a secure state and allow just two hosts to connect and run applications, run the following command:

```
xhost +host1 host2
host1 being added to the access control list
host2 being added to the access control list
```

Now these hosts can connect via Telnet (unsecure) or ssh (secure). When they execute an X client, the display output will be sent over the network to the client machine's X display.

Say another system doesn't have much on it, but you don't want to spend time messing with the security. Your users are technically literate and it's not a problem to have an open X server, so you run the command shown here:

```
xhost +
access control disabled, clients can connect from any host
```

The machine is wide open, but users still must sign on to an account and get authenticated to run anything from this machine.

If, at this point, you discover a couple of users who are being ridiculous with the open system, you can block just their systems with this command:

```
xhost -host3 host4
```

The exam will focus on scenarios for X security, including how to disable, enable, and display the status, and how to configure the access list.

Displaying X Clients

Now that we've covered how to keep hosts more secure, it's time to discuss how a client system can display an X client application running on a remote system locally.

There are two primary methods to have remote applications display locally, via Telnet or ssh.

If you use Telnet to connect to the remote machine, you'll have to sign on and then decide to export either your entire display or just the application. If you are going to be interacting with the desktop of the remote machine and otherwise enjoying the full experience, use this command:

```
export DISPLAY=192.168.1.100:0.0
```

The export command sets the remote session's $DISPLAY variable to your machine's hostname or IP address. The 0.0 means display.screen.

Anything X-related that you start from that Telnet session displays on the local client's machine.

If you use ssh to connect from the client to the X server remote host, there is less to configure or troubleshoot because ssh is set up by default to display any X-related applications on your local host display. You have only to sign on and run the application to have it back-hauled across the network to your system.

Multimonitor displays bring out another feature of X that's similar to the exporting of your display. If you want to run or display the Mozilla browser on your machine's second monitor (0.1), you would issue this command:

```
mozilla --display yourhost:0.1
```

This shows just that client application on the specified screen, and you can continue with the other programs and tasks in that shell or on the remote machine.

Exam Prep Questions

1. You have installed a new default Linux workstation, and the mouse works in text mode. When X is started, the mouse won't work. Which of the following could be the problem? (Choose all that apply.)
   - ❏   A.   Protocol
   - ❏   B.   Mode
   - ❏   C.   Device
   - ❏   D.   Mapping
   - ❏   E.   Emulation

   Answers A and C are correct because the wrong protocol or device configuration in the `/etc/X11/XF86Config` can cause a mouse to malfunction. Answer B is incorrect because mouse configuration for X doesn't use a mouse mode. Answer D is incorrect because the mapping for a mouse is specific to the buttons on the mouse. Answer E is incorrect because the emulation for a mouse is related to whether a two-button mouse can emulate a three-button mouse.

2. You need to configure a custom resolution for the graphical desktop of your Linux system. Which of the following files would you edit to accomplish this?
   - ○   A.   `xf86config`
   - ○   B.   `XF86Setup`
   - ○   C.   `XF86Config`
   - ○   D.   `Xconfiguration`

   Answer C is correct because the `XF86Config` file contains the resolution modes and configuration for the X system. Answer A is incorrect because the `xf86config` program is used to configure X on some distributions but isn't a file to edit to make the changes. Answer B is incorrect because it, too, is a configuration program, not an editable file. Answer D is incorrect because there is no such file as the Xconfiguration file on a default Linux system.

3. After adding fonts to the proper directory for your X server to utilize, which command must be run to ensure that the system will recognize those fonts?
   - ○   A.   `killall -1 X`
   - ○   B.   `xreconfig --fonts`
   - ○   C.   `xsetfp --reindex`
   - ○   D.   `mkfontdir`

   Answer D is correct because the `mkfontdir` program is needed to re-create or update the `fonts.dir` file in that directory so the system can use the fonts. Answer A is incorrect because issuing a `SIGHUP` against X only restarts X and does not index the new fonts. Answer B is incorrect because there isn't an xreconfig program. Answer C is incorrect because there isn't an xsetfp program.

4. When updating an older X system, you decide to install and use the **xfs** X font server. Which of the following entries should be included in the **Files** section of the **XF86Config** file to have X use **xfs**?

   ○ A. `Fontpath "/usr/X11R6/bin/xfs"`
   ○ B. `FontPath "unix/:7100"`
   ○ C. `FontServer "xfs"`
   ○ D. `export FSERVER=/usr/sbin/xfs`

   Answer B is correct because this entry enables the **xfs** X font server if it has been installed. Answer A is incorrect because the **FontPath** entry doesn't allow an executable as an argument. Answer C is incorrect because there isn't a **FontServer** entry in the **XF86Config** file. Answer D is incorrect because there isn't an FSERVER variable that affects the font server selection.

5. You want to sign on to a remote system via Telnet to have an application execute on the remote machine and be shown on your local system's screen. Which environment variable should be configured on the remote system to accomplish this?

   ○ A. **XSESSION**
   ○ B. **DISPLAY**
   ○ C. **SCREEN**
   ○ D. **XSERVER**

   Answer B is correct because the variable **DISPLAY** should be set on the remote system to send the display information to the local client's screen. Answers A, C, and D are incorrect because those variables are not valid on a Linux system.

6. There is a program that provides scrollbars, widgets, menus, background wallpaper, and virtual desktops for the X environment. Which phrase best describes this program?

   ○ A. Desktop
   ○ B. X server
   ○ C. Window manager
   ○ D. X client

   Answer C is correct because the window manager is capable of providing scrollbars, widgets, and so on for the X environment. Answer A is incorrect because a desktop typically has the mentioned features but is better known for providing an integrated environmental look and feel along with an Office suite and other utilities. Answer B is incorrect because the X server just manages the display and paints the output on the screen. Answer D is incorrect because an X client depends on the window manager to provide the mentioned options.

7. The _____ command controls access to the local X server's resources. Fill in the blank with just the program name:

_____

The correct answer is `xhost`.

8. A power user complains that he can't get a particular application to display the second physical monitor of his Linux graphical desktop. Which of the following would display the application `someapp` in the location requested?

   - ○ A. `someapp -geometry +10+10`
   - ○ B. `xset DISPLAY:1.1=`someapp``
   - ○ C. `export DISPLAY=localhost:1.1`
   - ○ D. `someapp -display localhost:0.1`

   Answer D is correct because the `-display localhost:0.1` parameter displays the application on the second physical monitor where `0.1` equals display.screen. Answer A is incorrect because `-geometry` refers to the position of the application on the current or default screen, not another screen. Answer B is incorrect because it's a completely bogus distracter. Answer C is incorrect because it exports the entire display, not just the application, and in addition, it targets the second display's second physical monitor.

9. The _____ switch or option to the `startx` script is used to set the foreground color in X. Fill in the blank:

_____

The correct answer is `fg`.

10. You are tasked with constructing a custom login screen with a particular background color, fonts, and company logo for all your X workstations. Which file would you customize to make these changes?

    - ○ A. `startx`
    - ○ B. `Xresources`
    - ○ C. `.Xsession`
    - ○ D. `xdm-config`

    Answer B is correct because the `/etc/X11/xdm/Xresources` file is used to configure custom login screens. Answer A is incorrect because the `startx` script is used as a front end for the `xinit` program. Answer C is incorrect because the `.Xsession` file is used to set up the user's session and affects only a single user. Answer D is incorrect because the `xdm-config` file is used to configure the XDM, but the `Xresources` file is for customizing login screens.

8

Text Processing

. . . .

Terms you'll need to understand:

✓ Filters
✓ Pipes
✓ Redirection
✓ Regular expressions
✓ Standard error
✓ Standard input
✓ Standard output

Techniques you'll need to master:

✓ Understanding data flow
✓ Redirecting data flow
✓ Using pipes
✓ Identifying command actions
✓ Parsing command strings
✓ Understanding **sed**
✓ Using regular expressions
✓ Finding text with grep

Unix/Linux Toolset Mentality

In this chapter we focus on the concepts and practice of getting a lot done on the shell command line. Chief among the skills you will gain from this chapter is the ability to choose commands and chain them together properly, and sometimes interestingly, to get your work done.

Unix and Linux have a toolset mentality that needs to be cultivated, and it must be learned to be successful in your sysadmin/programming work and on the exams.

Everything in the Linux command arena needs to do three things:

➤ It should do one thing very well.

➤ It should accept standard input.

➤ It should produce standard output.

With these commands and the shell's constructs that help connect things together (pipes, redirection, and so on), it becomes possible to accomplish many things with just one command string of connected commands.

Working with I/O Streams

Linux supports separate streams to handle data on the shell command line. These are called *file descriptors* and are used primarily to send data to and from programs and files and to handle errors.

The three file descriptors and their associated files are

Name	fd Number	Associated File
/dev/stdin	0	/proc/self/fd/0
/dev/stdout	1	/proc/self/fd/1
/dev/stderr	2	/proc/self/fd/2

Standard in, or stdin, is what all programs accept, or it's assumed they will accept. Most programs accept stdin either from a redirected file argument or using the file as an argument to the program:

```
program < file
```

or

```
program file
```

For most programs, these examples are identical. We'll cover several commands that don't handle arguments properly, such as the tr command.

Standard out, or stdout, is the text or data that's produced by a command and shows up on the screen or console. By default, all text-mode commands produce stdout and send it to the console unless it's redirected. To understand this, run the following command:

```
cat /etc/fstab
```

The text shown onscreen is a perfect example of the stdout stream. It's considered elegant to run commands first to see what they produce before redirecting the output to a file, particularly because you might get errors.

Standard error, or stderr, is a parallel stream to the sdtout, and by default it shows up mixed into the stdout stream as the errors occur. It's hard to produce errors on purpose; however, we can always use the find command to produce some access denied or permission errors for us to experiment with.

As a normal user, run the following command:

```
find / -iname *.txt ¦ more
```

Right away you see errors that indicate the user can't access certain directory trees to find certain items. Notice that useful output (stdout) is mixed directly with error messages (stderr), making it hard to use the good data for anything else.

The life of a sysadmin is defined by the search for producing good data and properly discarding or storing the errors produced. Good data can be sent on to another program, while errors are usually dumped at the earliest possible moment to use the processor and resources to produce good data more efficiently.

To clean up the good data and get rid of the bad data, we need to use redirection operators. To see this work, use the up arrow and rerun the previous command, as shown here:

```
find / -iname *.txt 2> /dev/null ¦ more
```

This produces output similar to

```
./.kde/share/apps/kdeprint/printerdb_cups.txt
./1.txt
./2.txt
./3.txt
```

Notice that you get only good data (stdout) after using a > redirection symbol to dump the bad data (stderr) to the system's black hole, or garbage disposal—in other words, a pseudo-device designed to be a place to discard data securely.

Redirection of Streams

In the quest for good data, being able to redirect or change the destination of stdout and stderr, and to some degree stdin, is essential to your tasks.

Redirection symbols include

➤ <—Redirects a file's contents into a command's stdin stream. The file descriptor for the < input redirection symbol is 0.

➤ >—Redirects the stdout stream to the file target to the right of the symbol. The file descriptor for the > output redirection character is 1, which is implied, except in certain instances.

➤ >>—Redirects stdout to a file, appending the current stream to the end of the file, rather than overwriting the file contents. This is a modifier of the > output redirection descriptor.

 If using the > redirection symbol to write to a file, that fill is overwritten unless the **noclobber** bash shell option is set. With that option set, you cannot overwrite the file; it will produce an error and file. The only way to get data into that file is to use the >> redirection append symbols.

Redirecting Standard Input

Redirecting stdin consists of sending a file's contents to a program's stdin stream. An example of this is

```
sort < file1
```

Although it might seem odd to have a couple of ways to do the same thing, the previous command is essentially the same as the following command:

```
cat file1 ¦ sort
```

Redirecting Standard Output

Redirecting stdout consists of either a single redirection symbol (>) or two (>>) for appending. The main difference is that the use of a single redirection descriptor overwrites a file whereas using double redirection descriptors appends to the end of a file, like so:

```
cat file1 > file2
```

This overwrites the contents of `file2` or, if it doesn't exist, creates it.

The following command appends the data from `file1` to `file2` or, if it doesn't exist, creates `file2`:

```
cat file1 >> file2
```

As an alternative example, say you run the `find` command and it produces errors and found files to the screen. You can capture the good data to a file and let the errors show on the console with the command shown here:

```
find / -iname *.txt > foundfiles
```

When you are redirecting `stdout`, the numeral or file descriptor `1` doesn't need to be used for most cases. Redirection of `stdout` is so common that a single > symbol suffices.

Redirecting Standard Error

Redirecting `stderr` consists of understanding that, by default, `stderr` shows up on the same target as the `stdout`, mixed right in but separable.

To continue the previous example but capture the `stderr` and let the good data show on the default target (console), you would change the command to

```
find / -iname *.txt 2> errors
```

The `2> errors` section of the command redirects the `stderr` and puts it into the file `errors`, leaving the `stdout` stream free to show on the default target (console) or even get written to another file.

The key to understanding what happens when using `stdout` and `stderr` is to visualize them as shown in Figure 8.1.

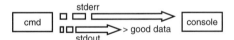

Figure 8.1   Path of data streams.

As you can see, the > character grabs the `stdout` stream and puts that data into the file `gooddata`, whereas the `stderr` stream is unaffected and is sent to the console for display.

Grabbing both streams and putting them into different files is as simple as adding a redirection symbol preceded with the `stderr` numeral:

```
find / -iname *.txt > gooddata 2> baddata
```

This grabs both streams and puts them into their proper files, with nothing displayed to the console.

Redirection Redux

Sometimes all the possible output from a particular command must be trapped because it will cause problems, such as when a command is run as a background job and you're using vi or some other console-based program. Having stderr show up onscreen during an editing session is disconcerting at the least, and if you're configuring important files, it's downright dangerous.

To trap all output from a command and send it to the /dev/null or black hole of the system, you'd use the following:

```
find / -iname *.txt > /dev/null 2>&1
```

 You will see items like the previous as exam topics, and it's very important that you've done the task yourself, multiple times if possible. Take a few minutes to experiment with the examples shown in this text. Getting this set of symbols right in a fill-in-the-blank question is difficult if you've not typed it a number of times.

Pipes

A pipe (¦) is used for chaining two or more programs' output together, typically filtering and changing the output with each successive program the data is sent through. For example, to print a code sample with numbered lines and printer formatting, you use the following command string:

```
cat codesamp.c ¦ nl ¦ pr ¦ lpr
```

It's essential that you know the difference between a redirection symbol and a pipe. Say you are shown a command such as

```
cat file1 ¦ nl > pr
```

This command produces a file in the current directory named pr, not output that has been filtered through both nl and pr.

 Ross's Rule: Redirection always comes from or goes to a file, whereas piping always comes from or goes to a program.

Good examples of using pipes to produce usable data include

```
sort < names ¦ nl
```

This sorts and then numbers `names`.

Another example is

```
who ¦ wc -l
```

This counts the users attached to the system and shows just the total number.

Here's one more example:

```
lsof /mnt/cdrom ¦ mail root -s"CD-ROM Users"
```

The previous command is designed to show you who is currently accessing or has opened files on the CD-ROM of the server, so you know who to tell to log off when it's needed.

Two commands that work well with and complement the use of pipes are the `tee` and `xargs` commands.

The `tee` command is designed to accept a single `stdin` stream and produce two completely identical and usable `sdtout`/`stderr` stream pairs.

You might use `tee` when running a program that must produce output to a file and you want to monitor its progress onscreen at the same time, such as the `find` command. To redirect all output to a single file and also see the same output on the screen, use

```
find / -iname *.txt ¦ tee findit.out
```

This command is designed to log the output of a stream to a file and pass another complete stream out to the console. Financial institutions that have to log and simultaneously process data find `tee` very useful.

The `xargs` command is another useful command. It takes a list of returned results from another program and parses them one by one for use by another simpler or less-capable command.

A good example of this is your wanting to have all readme files on the entire system in one large file called `mongofile.txt` in your home directory. This would enable you to search the documentation with a single `less mongofile.txt` command.

To do this, we'll use the `locate` command to find the full path and filename of the readme; then we'll use the `cat` command to take the contents and redirect the results to our target file:

```
locate -i readme ¦ cat > mongofile.txt
```

Then we can use the `less mongofile.txt` command to see what went wrong. We didn't get the output we wanted—the `cat` command isn't smart enough to determine that the output from the `locate` command is actually discrete lines that can be used individually. It just echoes the output as it was given it.

Run the command again with the `xargs` command acting as a buffer for the `cat` command. It reads all the output and feeds `cat` a single line as an argument until there are no more lines to feed to `cat`, like so:

```
locate -i readme ¦ xargs cat > mongofile.txt
```

Now use the `less mongofile.txt` command to verify that it worked as we originally intended. We now see that all the files have been enumerated to make one large file.

Filters

A *filter* is a command that accepts `stdin` as input and performs an action, alteration, or other process on the input, producing `stdout` and `stderr` from it.

Sorting

The `sort` command is a typical filter. It takes a command as an argument or can have `stdin` sent to it; then it either performs a default sort or accepts a large number of options. A good example of how `sort` can help is to take a file (`file1`) that has the following lines in it:

```
Ross Brunson
Peabody McGillicuddy
Ursula Login
Snuffy Jones
```

Sorting this file with the default sort options produces the following output:

```
sort file1
Peabody McGillicuddy
Ross Brunson
Snuffy Jones
Ursula Login
```

The `sort` command uses fields to sort by, and the default field is 0, or starting at the first column and ending at the first blank space. The typical field separator or delimiter is a space character. However, the delimiter can be set to be any non-blank character. This particular file was sorted by the first name of the listed people.

To sort by the last names, use the following command and options:

```
sort +1 file1
Ross Brunson
Snuffy Jones
Ursula Login
Peabody McGillicuddy
```

Another useful option with sort is the -n (numeric sort) option. If a file contains numbered lines that start with 1 and go to 30, the standard sort would sort them as

```
sort numbers
1
11
12
13
```

To tell sort to read the longest number and pad the lower numbers with leading zeroes internally during the sorting process, you use the command shown here:

```
sort -n numbers
1
2
3
4
```

Numbering Lines

The nl command is useful for numbering either every line in a file or stream of input, or just the lines with data on them. This is helpful when trying to troubleshoot source code or producing a list of numbered items automatically.

To number only the lines in a file that contain data, use this command:

```
nl file1
```

To number every line in a file, regardless of the line having data in it, use this:

```
nl -ba file1
```

Expect to see the **nl** command used with commands such as **pr** and **tac**, chained or piped together to produce a particular output.

Order matters, so be sure to notice whether the question wants to number all lines or just nonempty lines.

Counting

In many situations, being able to determine the number of lines or words in a particular file or output is useful. The wc command shows items in any of three counts:

➤ -l—Lines of output

➤ -w—Words of output

➤ -c—Characters (or bytes) of output

For example, a great way to see how many users are on the system at a given time is to use wc to count the lines of output from the who or w commands:

```
who | wc -l
34
w | wc -l
36
```

Both of these commands were done on the same system, one right after the other, with the same number of users. The **w** command has two header lines that are counted by the **wc** program, whereas **who** just outputs a line for each user. Be careful when using **wc** to count items without first viewing the raw output; otherwise, you'll misreport or represent inaccurate information.

Tabs

Handling the placement of columnar data is tough sometimes. When output is formatted for the screen, a tab-delimited file can display with oddly placed columns due to the length of the data in each field. The expand command helps change tabs to a set number of spaces.

Consider a file contains the following lines (the line numbers are just for reference sake):

```
1: steve        johnson
2: guillermo    villalobos
3: ed           denzler
4: lawrence     aribacus
5: marge        innovera
```

If tabs were used to separate the data fields, lines 1, 3, and 5 would have two tabs between fields 1 and 2, so the columns would line up. Lines 2 and 4 would have only one tab, due to the length of the first field. expand converts the tabs to a set number of spaces, making the data display right in most cases.

Cutting Columns

Although the objectives of the Level 1 of LPI's exams don't include the `awk` command (the king of columnar data), they do test you on the `cut` command, which is great at chopping data off between two columns:

```
cut -c 20-40 /etc/passwd | tail -n 5
ar/spool/postfix:/bin
hare/pvm3:/bin/bash
ross brunson:/home/rb
home/snuffy:/bin/bash
:/home/quotaboy:/bin/
```

This displays only from column 20 to column 40 of `file1`, excluding all other data on each line.

It can also grab certain fields from a file, such as the `/etc/passwd` file. To grab the username, description, and home directory fields for each user, use the following command:

```
cut -d: -f 1,5,6 /etc/passwd | tail -n 5
postfix::/var/spool/postfix
pvm::/usr/share/pvm3
rbrunson:ross brunson:/home/rbrunson
snuffy::/home/snuffy
quotaboy::/home/quotaboy
```

The `-d` option sets the delimiter, which in this case is the : character. By default, `cut` uses tabs for a delimiter.

Pasting and Joining

Two commands that are similar in function are `paste` and `join`. `paste` doesn't remove any data from the output, but `join` removes redundant key fields from the data.

For example, say you have the following files:

```
file1:

Line one of file1
Line two of file1
```

```
file2:

Line one of file2
Line two of file2
```

Using "paste" on these two files produces the output:

```
Line one of file1       Line one of file2
Line two of file1       Line two of file2
```

Notice that nothing is lost from the files. All the data is there, but this can be redundant in the extreme if you want to produce a joint file from two or more files.

The join command is more of a database join style than a catenation style. It takes a file as the first argument and by default treats the first field of that file as a key field. The second and subsequent files are treated in the same fashion. The output is each matching line of the files in order, minus the redundant key fields from any but the first file.

For example, say you have the following files, users and location:

users:

```
rbrunson:500:
snuffy:501:
quotaboy:502:
```

location:

```
rbrunson       123 anystreet   anytown ID    83858
snuffy         123 circle loop chicago IL    88888
quotaboy       123 some lane    anyburg MT    59023
```

As you can see, the output of these includes only the unique information from each file, leaving out the location key field:

```
join users location
rbrunson:500:    rbrunson    123 anystreet   anytown ID    83858
snuffy:501:      snuffy      123 circle loop chicago IL    88888
quotaboy:502:    quotaboy    123 some lane   anyburg MT    59023
```

Unique Data

When you consolidate servers, one of the tasks to accomplish is merging the /etc/passwd files. As long as all the users have the same UID/GID settings in each file, merging the files still makes an output file that contains multiple entries for various users.

For example, if you've copied all the /etc/passwd files from three servers into a single file, running the following command outputs only the unique lines from the entire file:

```
uniq -u /etc/bigpasswd
rbrunson:x:500:500::/home/rbrunson:/bin/bash
snuffy:x:501:501::/home/snuffy:/bin/bash
quotaboy:x:502:502::/home/quotaboy:/bin/bash
```

The -u option causes only the unique lines from the file to be output, so the command shown here could be used to redirect the output to a new /etc/passwd file by just adding a redirection symbol and the new filename:

```
uniq -u /etc/bigpasswd > /etc/newpasswd
```

To print a single example of each line that is a duplicate in a file, use the following command:

```
uniq -d bigpasswd
```

To print every instance of each repeated line, use this command:

```
uniq -D bigpasswd
```

Heads or Tails?

The head command is used primarily (and by default) to see the first 10 lines of a given text file by default. head can be made to show a particular number of lines, starting at the top of the file. The -n parameter followed by the number of lines that are to be shown starting from the beginning of the file is used to show more than the default. This parameter is used in the following manner:

```
head -n 5 /etc/fstab
LABEL=/                 /                        ext3    defaults          1 1
none                    /dev/pts                 devpts  gid=5,mode=620    0 0
none                    /proc                    proc    defaults          0 0
none                    /dev/shm                 tmpfs   defaults          0 0
/dev/hda6               swap                     swap    defaults          0 0
```

The head command can't display ranges of lines, only from the beginning of the file.

The tail command is the exact opposite of the head command: It displays the last 10 lines of a given file by default and can be configured to show less or more lines, but only from the end of the file. It can't show ranges. Here's an example:

```
tail -n 5 /etc/passwd
netdump:x:34:34:Network Crash Dump user:/var/crash:/bin/bash
quagga:x:92:92:Quagga routing suite:/var/run/quagga:/sbin/nologin
radvd:x:75:75:radvd user:/:/sbin/nologin
rbrunson:x:500:500::/home/rbrunson:/bin/bash
snuffy:x:501:501::/home/snuffy:/bin/bash
```

The tail command is also useful for following log files, such as the /var/log/messages file to see the latest attempts to log on to the system:

```
tail -f /var/log/messages
```

This returns output similar to what's shown here:

```
Feb 23 21:00:01 localhost sshd(pam_unix)[29358]:
➥session closed for user root
Feb 23 21:00:04 localhost sshd(pam_unix)[29501]:
➥session opened for user root by (uid=0)
Feb 23 21:00:13 localhost sshd(pam_unix)[29501]:
➥session closed for user root
Feb 23 21:00:16 localhost sshd(pam_unix)[29549]:
➥session opened for user root by (uid=0)
```

It's when you combine the two commands that truly interesting things become possible. For example, say you wanted to view lines 31–40 of a 50-line file. Remember that you can't display ranges with either of the commands, but by putting them together, you can display a range of lines from the file 50linefile with the following command:

```
head -n 40 50linefile ¦ tail
31
32  Both software and hardware watchdog drivers are available in the
➥standard
33  kernel. If you are using the software watchdog, you probably also want
34  to use "panic=60" as a boot argument as well.
35
36  The wdt card cannot be safely probed for. Instead you need to pass
37  wdt=ioaddr,irq as a boot parameter - eg "wdt=0x240,11".
38
39  The SA1100 watchdog module can be configured with the "sa1100_margin"
40  commandline argument which specifies timeout value in seconds.
```

 Watch for the **head** and **tail** commands on the exam—particularly the **-f** option for following a log file's latest entries.

Splitting Files

The split command is useful for taking a large number of records and splitting them into multiple individual files that contain a certain amount of data.

The split command's options include (the # character represents a number of prefix characters)

➤ -a #—Uses a suffix a specified number of characters long (the default is xaa).

➤ -b #—Output files will contain the specified number of bytes of data.

➤ -c #—Output files will contain the specified number of lines of bytes of data.

➤ -l #—Output files will contain the specified number of lines of data.

The # value can be b (which is 512 bytes), k (which is 1024 bytes), or m (which is 1024 kilobytes). For example, if you need to split an 8.8MB text file into 1.44MB chunks, you can use this command:

```
split -b1440000 bigtextfile.txt
ls -l x??
-rw-r--r--    1 root      root      1440000 Feb 23 09:25 xaa
-rw-r--r--    1 root      root      1440000 Feb 23 09:25 xab
-rw-r--r--    1 root      root      1440000 Feb 23 09:25 xac
-rw-r--r--    1 root      root      1440000 Feb 23 09:25 xad
-rw-r--r--    1 root      root      1440000 Feb 23 09:25 xae
-rw-r--r--    1 root      root      1440000 Feb 23 09:25 xaf
-rw-r--r--    1 root      root       249587 Feb 23 09:25 xag
```

When cat Goes Backward

In some cases you will want to display a file backward or in reverse order, which is where the tac command comes in. You can use it like so:

```
cat file1
```

This produces output similar to the following:

```
1     Watchdog Timer Interfaces For The Linux Operating
2
3     Alan Cox <alan@lxorguk.ukuu.org.uk>
4
5     Custom Linux Driver And Program Development
```

Using tac on this file produces the following output:

```
tac file1
```

This produces output similar to

```
5     Custom Linux Driver And Program Development
4
3     Alan Cox <alan@lxorguk.ukuu.org.uk>
2
1     Watchdog Timer Interfaces For The Linux Operating
```

Viewing Binary Files Safely

The od command is used to view binary or non-ASCII files safely; otherwise, the display will likely become garbled and the system will beep plaintively.

od is capable of displaying files in different methods, including

➤ -a—Named

➤ -o—Octal

➤ -d—Decimal

➤ -x—Hexadecimal

➤ -f—Floating point

Most of these formats aren't of daily use, with only the hexadecimal and octal formats displaying output of much interest.

Watch out for questions about how to view binary files. The **od** command is just about the only possibility for such viewing.

If you do have a problem with a garbled console after accidentally viewing a binary file, use the `reset` command. It reinitializes the terminal and makes it readable again.

Formatting Commands

The `pr` and `fmt` commands are used to do line wrapping and formatting for the printing of text streams or files.

The `pr` command is useful in formatting source code and other text files for printing. It adds a date and time block, the filename (if it exists), and page numbers to only the top of each formatted 66-line page, like so:

```
pr 50linefile
```

This produces output similar to what's shown here:

```
2112-02-23 21:19                    50linefile                    Page 1

    1           Watchdog Timer Interfaces For The Linux Operating System
    2
    3                   Alan Cox <alan@lxorguk.ukuu.org.uk>
    4
    5               Custom Linux Driver And Program Development
```

The `pr` command can display columns of data, cutting the columns to fit the number per page, like so:

```
pr --columns=2 50linefile
2004-02-23 21:02                    50linefile                    Page 1

    1        Watchdog Timer Inte     26  and some Berkshire cards. T
    2                                27  internal temperature in deg
    3                Alan Cox <a     28  giving the temperature.
    4                                29
    5            Custom Linux D      30  The third interface logs ke
```

The `fmt` command is useful for formatting text files, too, but it's limited to wrapping long lines to fit on smaller pages or within columns that `pr` has set.

The previous example of `pr` columns chops the data off at the columns, losing data on the page. This can be fixed by mixing the commands, as shown here:

```
[root@localhost root]# fmt -35 50linefile ¦ pr --column=2
2004-02-23 21:49                         50linefile
                       Page 1


    1           Watchdog              temperature.  29 30  The third
Timer Interfaces For The              interface logs kernel messages
Linux Operating System 2              on additional alert events.
    3               Alan Cox          31 32  Both software and
```

Translating Files

The `tr` command is for changing characters in files or streams, but not whole words or phrases—that's for `sed` to do.

For example, if you have a file that contains a lot of commands from a sample in a book, but some of the commands are dysfunctional because the editor capitalized the first characters of the lines, you can translate the file's uppercase letters to lowercase with the following command:

```
tr 'A-Z' 'a-z' < commands.txt
```

The `tr` command isn't capable of feeding itself. The `<` operator is therefore mandatory; otherwise, the command won't work. The following command can be used to accomplish the same results:

```
tr [:upper:] [:lower:] < commands.txt
```

Remember that **tr** is incapable of feeding itself, so the < redirection symbol is needed to send the input file to the command. Anything else is a broken command and will produce a syntax error.

He **sed**, She **sed**

The `sed`, or stream editor, command is used to process and perform actions on streams of text, such as the lines found in a text file. `sed` is amazingly powerful, which is a way of saying it can be quite difficult to use.

One of **sed**'s most-used operations is searching and replacing text, including words and complete phrases. Whereas **tr** works only on characters and numerals as individuals, **sed** is capable of very complex functions, including multiple operations per line.

sed uses the following syntax for commands:

```
sed -option action/regexp/replacement/flag filename
```

Rather than struggle through an explanation of what happens when certain options are entered, let's see what sed does when we use those options. Using sed properly includes being able to, ahem, "reuse" sed commands from other sysadmins.

To replace the first instance of bob with BOB on each line in a given file, you'd use this command:

```
sed s/bob/BOB/ file1
```

To replace all instances of bob with BOB on each line in a given file, you'd use this command:

```
sed s/bob/BOB/g file1
```

sed allows for multiple operations on a given stream's lines, all of which are performed before going on to the next line.

To search for and replace bob with BOB and then search for BOB and replace it with snuffy for every line and every instance for a given file, you'd use this:

```
sed 's/bob/BOB/g ; s/BOB/snuffy/g' file1
```

The use of a semicolon character is similar to bash's ability to run several commands independently of each other. However, this whole operation, from the first single quotation mark (') to the last single quotation mark is all performed inside of sed, not as part of bash.

When sed is used for multiple commands, you can either use a semicolon to separate the commands or use multiple instances of -e to show the multiple commands:

```
sed -e s/bob/BOB/g -e s/BOB/snuffy/g file1
```

On the exam, and whenever you might use **sed** with spaces in your patterns, bracket the whole pattern/procedure in single quotation marks, such as
sed 's/is not/is too/g' file1

This keeps you from getting syntax errors due to the spaces in the strings.

Sooner or later, you'll get tired of typing the same operations for sed and want to use a script or some method of automating a recurring task. sed has the capability to use a simple script file that contains a set of procedures. An example of the previous set of procedures in a sed script file is shown here:

```
s/bob/BOB/g
s/BOB/snuffy/g
```

This script file is used in the following manner:

```
sed -f scriptfile targetfile
```

Many multiple procedures can be performed on a single stream, with the whole set of procedures being performed on each successive line.

Obviously, doing a large number of procedures on a given text stream can take time, but it is usually worth it because you only need to verify that it worked correctly when it's done. It sure beats doing it all by hand in vi!

Another neat feature of sed is its capability to suppress or not have displayed any line that didn't have changes made to it.

For example, if you wanted to replace machine with MACHINE on all lines in a given file but display only the changed lines, you'd use the following command with the -n option to make the command suppress normal output:

```
sed -n 's/machine/MACHINE/pg' watchdog.txt
```

The pg string at the end prints the matched or changed lines and globally replaces for all instances per line, rather than just the first instance per line.

To do search and replace on a range of lines, prefix the s/ string with either a line number or a range separated by a comma, such as

```
sed -n '1,5s/server/SERVER/pg' sedfile
The X SERVER uses this directory to store the compiled version of the
current keymap and/or any scratch keymaps used by clients.  The X SERVER
time.  The default keymap for any SERVER is usually stored in:
```

 On the exam, the **sed** questions are all about what will find and replace strings, with particular attention on global versus single replaces.

Getting a **grep**

One of the more fun text-processing commands is grep. Properly used, it can find almost any string or phrase in a single file, a stream of text via stdin, or an entire directory of files (such as the kernel source hierarchy).

grep (global regular expression print) uses the following syntax for its commands:

```
grep -options pattern file
```

The grep command has a lot of useful options, including

➤ -c—This option shows only a numeric count of the matches found, no output of filenames or matches.

➤ -c #—This option surrounds the matched string with X number of lines of context.

➤ -H—This option prints the filename for each match; it's useful when you want to then edit that file.

➤ -h—This option suppresses the filename display for each file.

➤ -i—This option searches for the pattern with no case-sensitivity; all matches are shown.

➤ -l—This option shows only the filename of the matching file; no lines of matching output are shown.

➤ -L—This option displays the filename of files that don't have a match for the string.

➤ -w—This option selects only lines that have the string as a whole word, not part of another word.

➤ -r—This option reads and processes all the directories specified, along with all the files in them.

➤ -x—This option causes only exact line matches to be returned; every character on the line must match.

➤ -v—This option shows all the lines in a file that don't match the string; this is the exact opposite of the default behavior.

Examples of Using grep

grep can either use files and directories as the target argument or be fed stdout for parsing. An example of using grep to parse output follows:

```
who ¦ grep ross
```

This command parses the who command's stdout for the name ross and prints that line if found.

A more complex example of `grep` being used is to combine it with another command, such as `find`:

```
find / -name readme -exec grep -iw kernel {} \;
```

The previous command finds all the files on the system named `readme` and then executes the `grep` command on each file, searching for any instance of the whole word `kernel` regardless of case. A whole word search finds the string `kernel` but not `kernels`.

An innovative use of the `grep` command's options for finding strings is to have it show you lines that don't match the string. For example, you might want to check the `/etc/passwd` group periodically for a user that doesn't have a shadowed password:

```
grep -v :x: /etc/passwd
snuffy:$1$30238jrk$WcT15uH7V0EgxdtFTlxkK1:501:501:::/home/snuffy:/bin/bash
```

It looks like `snuffy` has an encrypted password in the `/etc/passwd` file. You should therefore run the `pwconv` command to fix this and make `snuffy` change his password immediately.

In classes, we usually spend a reasonable amount of time in the kernel source code looking at examples. After a while, students usually notice the incidence of certain words, such as *darn*, *heck*, and *shoot* in the code we're viewing. I always take the time to show everyone how to find some fairly amusing and instructive terms in the code, and everyone ends up learning a lot about the use of `grep` and perhaps a few new ways to use its options.

Every attempt has been made to use this section as a learning tool by having the reader use **grep** to search for certain terms, the least disturbing having been chosen carefully. The ability to use **grep** and its options is essential to the exam.

To search for the word `idiot` in the kernel source, use the following command:

```
grep -ir idiot /usr/src/linux-2.4 ¦ tail
```

This produces the following output:

```
/usr/src/linux-2.4/Documentation/cdrom/sbpcd:a complete idiot needs to
➥understand your hassle already with your first
/usr/src/linux-2.4/abi/svr4/xti.c:                /* Idiot check... */
/usr/src/linux-2.4/drivers/media/video/margi/dvb_filter.c:
➥ printk("NULL POINTER IDIOT\n");
/usr/src/linux-2.4/drivers/net/3c59x.c: if (vp->cb_fn_base)
➥        /* The PCMCIA people are idiots. */
/usr/src/linux-2.4/drivers/net/3c59x.c:          if (vp->cb_fn_base)
➥           /* The PCMCIA people are idiots. */
```

```
/usr/src/linux-2.4/drivers/net/aironet4500.h://darn idiot PCMCIA stuff
/usr/src/linux-2.4/drivers/scsi/ChangeLog:    * scsi_ioctl.c: Make
➥ioctl_probe function more idiot-proof.  If
/usr/src/linux-2.4/fs/jffs/jffs_fm.c:
➥
the shore like an idiot...  */
/usr/src/linux-2.4/net/ipv4/ip_gre.c:   what the heck these idiots
➥break standards established
```

Notice that you got matches with the pattern idiot as a whole word and as part of things like idiots. To tighten this up to just show you the pattern, add the -w option:

```
grep -irw idiot /usr/src/linux-2.4 ¦ tail
```

This produces the following output:

```
/usr/src/linux-2.4/Documentation/cdrom/sbpcd:a complete idiot needs to
➥understand your hassle already with your first
/usr/src/linux-2.4/abi/svr4/xti.c:                   /* Idiot check... */
/usr/src/linux-2.4/drivers/media/video/margi/dvb_filter.c:
➥ printk("NULL POINTER IDIOT\n");
/usr/src/linux-2.4/drivers/net/aironet4500.h://darn idiot PCMCIA stuff
/usr/src/linux-2.4/drivers/scsi/ChangeLog:    * scsi_ioctl.c:
➥Make ioctl_probe function more idiot-proof.  If
/usr/src/linux-2.4/fs/jffs/jffs_fm.c:
➥the shore like an idiot...  */
```

As you can see, the output is different—only the lines that match the pattern as a whole word are shown now.

Using Regular Expressions and **grep**

Using grep to find particular words and phrases can be difficult unless you use regular expressions. A *regular expression* has the ability to search for something that you don't know exactly, either through partial strings or using the following special characters:

➤ .—A period matches any single character and enforces that the character must exist (a.v is a three-letter regular expression).

➤ ?—A question mark matches an optional item and is matched only once.

➤ *—An asterisk matches from zero to many characters (a*v finds av, a2v, andv, and so on).

➤ +—A plus sign means that the item must be matched once and can be matched many times.

➤ {n}—A curly-bracketed number means that the item will be matched n times.

➤ {n,}—A curly-bracketed number followed by a comma character will be matched *n* or more times.

➤ {n,m}—A curly-bracketed pair of numbers separated by a comma will be matched from *n* to *m* times.

What's the use for all of this? Try finding just the word *kernel* in the source tree with the following command:

```
grep -rl Kernel /usr/src/linux-2.4 ¦ wc -l
   331
```

The command finds 331 files that contain at least one match for `Kernel`. Now try finding just the word *Kernel* as a whole word with this command:

```
grep -rlw Kernel /usr/src/linux-2.4 ¦ wc -l
   322
```

Now try the same command again, but modify it so that the word *Kernel* is searched for, but only followed by a period:

```
grep -rwl Kernel\. /usr/src/linux-2.4 ¦ wc -l
   44
```

Now, let's search for the word `idiots` as the search pattern:

```
grep -rwl idiots /usr/src/linux-2.4 ¦ wc -l
   2
```

Run the command again with the context number set to three lines to see what was being commented on:

```
grep -rw idiots /usr/src/linux-2.4
/usr/src/linux-2.4/drivers/net/3c59x.c: if (vp->cb_fn_base)
➡        /* The PCMCIA people are idiots.  */
/usr/src/linux-2.4/drivers/net/3c59x.c:          if (vp->cb_fn_base)
➡            /* The PCMCIA people are idiots.  */
/usr/src/linux-2.4/net/ipv4/ip_gre.c:   what the heck these
➡idiots break standards established
```

You'll need to be familiar with how to use regular expressions on the exam, particularly how to find strings that start and end with a particular letter or letters but contain other text in between.

Another example of regular expressions in action is searching for a particular phrase or word, but not another that is very similar.

The following file is `watch.txt` and contains the following lines:

```
01 The first sentence contains broad
02 The second contains bring
```

```
03 The third contains brush
04 The fourth has BRIDGE as the last word: bridge
broad 05 The fifth begins with BROAD
06 The sixth contains none of the four
07 This contains bringing, broadened, brushed
```

To find all the words that begin with *br* but exclude any that have the third letter as *i*, you'd use the following command:

```
grep "\<br[^i]" watch.txt
01 The first sentence contains broad
03 The third contains brush
broad 05 The fifth begins with BROAD
```

The \< string just means that the word begins with those letters. The use of the [^i} characters is to find all but the letter *i* in that position. If you used a ^ in front of a search term inside a program such as vi, it would search at the front of a line, but using the ^ symbol inside a set of square brackets is to exclude that character from being found.

To find a set of words that ends with a certain set, use this command:

```
grep "ad\>" watch.txt
01 The first sentence contains broad
broad 05 The fifth begins with BROAD
```

As with the previous example, using the \> characters on the end of a search looks for words that end in that string.

Search strings that grep allows include

➤ broad—Searches for exactly *broad*, but as part of other words (such as *broadway* or *broadening*) unless you use -w to cause *broad* to be searched for as a standalone word

➤ ^broad—Searches for the word *broad* at the beginning of any line

➤ broad$—Searches for the word *broad* at the end of the line

➤ [bB]road—Searches for the words *broad* and *Broad*

➤ br[iou]ng—Searches for *bring*, *brong*, and *brung*

➤ br[^i]ng—Searches for and returns all but *bring*

➤ ^......$—Searches for any line that contains exactly six characters

➤ [bB][rR]in[gG]—Searches for *Bring*, *BRing*, *BRinG*, or any combination thereof

Exam Prep Questions

1. Which of the following allows a file to be written to from `stdout` without overwriting the file's current contents?

   O A. `>`

   O B. `<`

   O C. `>>`

   O D. `<<`

   O E. `2>&1`

   Answer C is correct because the double redirection symbols allow for appending data to a file. Answer A is incorrect because it overwrites the file's contents. Answer B is incorrect because it is used to send a file's contents to a program. Answer D is incorrect because it sends input to a program until a particular string is matched. Answer E is incorrect because it appends both `stderr` and `stdout` to the same source.

2. Your boss wants to have the file `codesamp` to have all its lines numbered, regardless of content, and then have the filename, date, and page numbers added to it. Finally, she wants to send this file to the default printer. Write the command to accomplish this in the blank below:

   _____

   The correct answer is `nl -ba codesamp ¦ pr ¦ lpr`. There are no alternative correct answers.

3. Which command produces two separate but identical output streams when presented with standard input?

   O A. `pipe`

   O B. `redirect`

   O C. `xargs`

   O D. `tee`

   Answer D is correct because the `tee` command produces two identical streams, normally sending one to a log file, with the other being displayed on the console by default. Answer A is incorrect because `pipe` is an email program that has nothing to do with this scenario, and it's also the name for the ¦ symbol. Answer B is incorrect because a `redirect` is the action caused by the > symbol, and it is used to write output to a file. Answer C is incorrect because the `xargs` command is used to take multiple lines of full path and filename output and feed them to limited array programs.

4. Write the command that is used to convert tabs in a file to a set number of spaces:

   _____

   The correct answer is `expand`. There are no alternative correct answers.

5. In what order does the `wc` command produce its output?

   ○ A. Words, lines, bytes
   ○ B. Lines, words, bytes
   ○ C. Bytes, lines, words
   ○ D. Words, bytes, lines

   Answer B is correct because the `wc` command outputs counts in lines, words, and then bytes. Answers A, C, and D are incorrect because their orders are wrong.

6. Which of the following commands correctly outputs the user's name, GID, and home directory from the `/etc/passwd` file?

   ○ A. `awk -f {printf:1,3,7] /etc/passwd`
   ○ B. `grep -f=1,3,5 /etc/passwd`
   ○ C. `cut -d: -f 1,3,6 /etc/passwd`
   ○ D. `crop -f 1,3,4 /etc/passwd`

   Answer C is correct because the command properly outputs the fields needed. The key is the `-d:` string, which sets the delimiter to a `:`. Answer A is incorrect because `awk` can do this operation but not with the command shown; as it is here, it produces a syntax error. Answer B is incorrect because `grep` can pull lines out of a file but not fields out of a line. Answer D is incorrect because there is no such command as `crop` on a default Linux system.

7. You need to strip out lines 21–40 from a 50-line file named `file1` and write those lines to another file named `file2`. Enter the commands, with options, to accomplish this:

   _____

   The correct answer is `head -n 40 file1 ¦ tail -n 20`. There are no alternative correct answers.

8. If you use the following `split` command on a 10,000-line file, what is the result?

   `split -a 5 10000linefile`

   ○ A. Two thousand 5-line files
   ○ B. A syntax error
   ○ C. `xaaaaa` through `xaaaaj`
   ○ D. Five 2000-line files

   Answer C is correct because the command uses a 5-digit prefix with the `-a` option, producing ten 1000-line files named `xaaaaa` through `xaaaaj`. Answer A is incorrect because it doesn't match the option in the command; it would have to be `split -l 5 10000linefile`. Answer B is incorrect because the command isn't a valid command. Answer D is incorrect because the command to produce this answer would be `split -l 2000 1000linefile`.

9. Your boss wants all instances of an executive's name replaced with her title in a document. You've tried counting the instances and find you need to replace more than 500 of them. In the blank below, fill in just the name of the command that accomplishes this in a single command sequence:

_____

The correct answer is **sed**. There are no alternative correct answers.

10. You want to search a set of files for a given string but know only that the string begins with the characters **theo**, with a variety of endings. Which of the following, when used with **grep**, finds all the instances of text you want? (Choose all that apply.)

- ❏ A. `\<theo`
- ❏ B. `theo*`
- ❏ C. `^theo`
- ❏ D. `theo.*`

Answers A, B, and D are correct because these strings bring back a result for the text, with some notable differences in the output; however, they all work. Answer C is incorrect because the string `^theo` finds only the text at the beginning of a line in the files.

Software Installation

Terms you'll need to understand:

✓ Build
✓ Header
✓ Package
✓ Query
✓ Source
✓ Tarball

Techniques you'll need to master:

✓ Installing software from the source
✓ Identifying makefile sections
✓ Repairing library links
✓ Determining necessary libraries
✓ Installing software from packages
✓ Removing software from the RPM Database
✓ Querying software details
✓ Rebuilding the RPM Database

Important Exam Information

LPI has broken the 101 exam into two separate exams, 117-101-RPM and 117-101-DPKG. This means you can either focus on the RPM package method or the DEB package method. You must specify the exam desired at scheduling, and to both VUE and Prometric's credit, the customer reps are trained to query you about the desired exam.

 The 101 exams are identical in every way, except for the package management questions. You cannot safely ignore Debian entirely; topics such as the **/etc/passwd** and **/etc/shadow** permissions are tested on the 101 RPM exam.

It's the author's strenuous recommendation that unless you are a) really into Debian b) getting paid to learn and run Debian systems or c) masochistic, you should take the RPM exam. Before the protests of Debian Penguinistas fill my inbox and that of Que, let me be clear: The Debian package format is in many ways superior to the RPM method. It's mostly due to market share that I make this recommendation.

Methods of Managing Software Installation

Software is installed either via source code (compiling and installing) or via packages. We'll discuss both options, their advantages and disadvantages, how to perform most functions, and troubleshooting.

Installing Software from Source

Source code is the heart of all computing, with access to that source being the linchpin of Linux and open source software. Without access to the source, you can't inspect the code for bugs, security issues, or other flaws.

When programmers produce source code, they typically *tar* it up or create a compressed archive of it, called a *tarball*. Tarballs are typically created with the tar command and some switches; then the software is made available on the Net so users can try it and report bugs.

The advantages of installing programs via source code include

➤ It allows inspecting code for flaws, bugs, and security issues.

➤ It's available earlier than binary packages.

➤ Compiling optimizes the resulting program for the current system.

➤ It feeds that cutting-edge need (beta-testing can be fun!).

Typically, you won't see a program that's under heavy development in any other format than a source tarball. It's time-consuming and unwieldy to make a package out of the source code until it's at least of release or late beta stability.

After you've installed a program from source, you'll be more comfortable with the process, so start with small programs and work your way up. For example, you might download and install rdesktop (http://www.rdesktop.org) and see the whole process in a couple of minutes, including compile time. The other end of the scale would be installing Apache or Samba from source, which is a much longer and complex process.

The disadvantages of installing programs via source code include

➤ It requires a more complex installation.

➤ The necessary dependencies might not exist or might be very difficult to resolve.

➤ It's often poorly documented, sometimes with only a readme or install file available.

➤ Uninstalling source packages can be difficult, particularly if the package's makefile doesn't have an uninstall routine, requiring you to manually discover and remove the package files.

When installing from source, a number of conflicts and dependency problems can occur. Until a package is released by the various distribution vendors as a part of their products, it's typically not for the faint of heart. If your goal is stability, wait for the eventual release; otherwise, you might spend hours searching for missing libraries and other needed files.

You should use source code installs when needed for performance and security.

Components of a Source Code Install

Source code tarballs typically include the following:

➤ **Configure script**—This checks the system out and configures the makefile.

➤ **Makefile**—This file governs the installation location, parameters, and other variables.

➤ **Source files**—These are the actual directories of the source files.

➤ **Readme**—This readme file contains important information about the installation process.

➤ **Install**—Typically, this contains the actual installation instructions; it's not present in all source installs.

➤ **Install script**—Often a single script, if run, performs the installation.

The Makefile

A makefile is the set of instructions and compiling parameters that makes the installation possible. After it's updated by the configure script, typically the `make` command and then the `make install` command are run to compile and install the software.

To quote the man page for `make`:

The purpose of the `make` utility is to determine automatically which pieces of a large program need to be recompiled, and issue the commands to recompile them.

A makefile typically contains the following sections:

➤ **Platform**—The platform of the system

➤ **Debug**—How to handle errors

➤ **Optimize**—Items that are customized by `.configure`

➤ **Source**—Where the source files are found

➤ **Targets**—All, install, clean, dist, and so on

Targets of the makefile deserve a little attention because some confusion exists about what they consist of. The `make` command by itself usually compiles the source code but does not do anything else. Running the `make` command with the `clean` target usually removes any temporary files from a previous attempt to compile the code. If you run the `make` command with the `install` target, it puts the compiled code into the right directories in the path and so on.

Expect to be asked about the typical targets of the makefile on the exam. The targets in a makefile vary, but typically they are the keywords mentioned here, along with anything the developer wants to have in addition.

The typical makefile has the following paths and variables (again, this can vary program from program):

➤ `install-prefix   = .`

➤ `bin_dir   = $(install-prefix)/bin`

➤ `uparm_dir   = $(install-prefix)/lib/uparm`

➤ `include_dir   = $(install-prefix)/include`

These tell the installation and other targets where to put the various pieces of the program, with the `$(install-prefix)` indicating that, upon compiling, the software is stored in the subdirectories of the current directory—for instance, `./bin`, `./lib/parm`, and `./include`.

Example of a Compilation of Source Code

In this example, a simple program is compiled and installed on a default Linux system. (You must have the `gcc` compiler and related development tools and libraries installed to compile source code.) Here's how you do it:

1. Open a browser and go to `http://www.rdesktop.org`.

2. Click the Download link.

3. Click the latest stable version.

4. Choose the closest location to you in the list of download links, and then click the small page icon under the Download column at the right of the page.

5. When prompted, put the source code in your user's home directory. Usually all you have to do is click the Save button in the browser you're using.

6. Open a shell session or xterm client.

7. Navigate to the directory that contains the `rdesktop-1.3.1.tar.gz` file (or whatever the version is currently).

8. Unpack the archive file with the following command:

```
tar -xzvf rdesktop-1.3.1.tar.gz
```

9. After the scrolling stops, change to the source directory:

```
cd rdesktop-1.3.1
```

10. Run an `ls` command and notice the files present.

11. Run the `configure` script with the following command:

```
./configure
```

12. When done, run the `make` command to compile the software.

13. When finished compiling, install the program with the `make install` command.

 If you get a message about not being able to install the target directory, you need to become the root user with the command **su** and enter the root user password. This is necessary in some cases so that the compiled software can be written to directories such as **/usr/local/bin** that are not write-enabled for normal users.

14. Rerun the `make install` command if you had to become the root user.

15. Make sure you're running X and have a Windows machine to connect to via Terminal Services or Remote Desktop Connection; then type the following:

```
rdesktop -g 1024x768 IPADDRESS
```

16. Substitute your TS or RDP machine's IP address for *IPADDRESS*. You should be able to sign on to that machine with full color and even set the client to full screen with a little reading of the help screen for rdesktop.

Shared Libraries

Libraries provide access to common functions, with shared libraries providing common functions for many different programs on Linux systems.

Programs link libraries in one of two ways:

➤ **Statically**—Has a larger file size and less dependencies

➤ **Dynamically**—Has a smaller file size and won't work if missing

A good example of shared libraries is the use of system calls to open a file, get a file's information from the `inode` with the `stat` call, and many other very common functions.

The system's main shared libraries are stored in the following:

➤ `/lib`—Main shared libraries

➤ `/usr/lib/`—Supplemental libraries

➤ `/usr/X11R6/lib`—X Window shared libraries

In those directories, you might find two types of shared libraries, some named with the following convention:

```
libraryname-major-minor-patch.so (libc.2.2.4.so)
```

You also might find others named with the following convention:

```
libraryname.so.major-minor-patch (libc.so.6)
```

You'll notice that, for example, doing an `ls -1 /lib/libc.so.6` yields the link from `libc.so.6` to `libc.2.2.4.so`. Consider the following:

```
ls -1 /lib/libc.so.6
```

This displays the output shown here:

```
lrwxrwxrwx    1 root     root     13 Feb 26 10:04 /lib/libc.so.6 ->
➥libc-2.2.4.so
```

Programs that expect the presence of a library version (and filename) can be accommodated by creating a link with that filename to the proper and newer library that contains that functionality.

The suffix so means shared object, and the various naming conventions support both new and legacy library names.

Using links to libraries allows for updates and replacing a library with a newer version, with all the programs that expect the older version using the named symbolic link to access the actual library that satisfies that request.

Determining Required Libraries

When you find a program and want to know whether the libraries it relies on are present, either run it and see what breaks (the unsafe way) or query the program for the necessary libraries with the `ldd` command:

```
ldd /bin/ls
```

This returns the following output:

```
        libtermcap.so.2 => /lib/libtermcap.so.2 (0x40033000)
        libc.so.6 => /lib/i686/libc.so.6 (0x40037000)
        /lib/ld-linux.so.2 => /lib/ld-linux.so.2 (0x40000000)
```

Those libraries must be accessible to the program and be either in the trusted library paths (`/lib` and `/usr/lib`) or set in a variable called `LD_LIBRARY_PATH`, which contains the library path(s) separated by colons (:).

To set this variable, you can declare it on the command line, like so:

```
export LD_LIBRARY_PATH=/some/path/name
```

Or, you can edit the /etc/profile or ~/.bash_profile file and export it from there.

 Although this must be known for the exam, the **LD_LIBRARY_PATH** is considered to be a security risk because it might allow unauthorized programs access to system libraries accidentally or otherwise expose system library paths to unauthorized users.

Some library files might not have enough header or internal information to be correctly identified by the ldconfig program when it builds the links in the library directories.

The ldconfig program reads the headers of all the libraries in the /lib and /usr/lib directories and any directories noted in the /etc/ld.so.conf file. From those headers and the filenames of the libraries, ldconfig makes the proper links to the libraries, particularly for the legacy programs that expect older libraries to exist.

The ldconfig program also builds the /etc/ld.so.cache file, a binary file that is an ordered list of the libraries on the system. This file is not readable as text but is used as a quick reference by the system linker ld.so.

Installing Software with Packages

A typical Linux installation has more than 2,000 packages, with many multiple files per package. A *package* is a container file that holds applications, configuration files, and anything else that a particular program or set of programs needs to function.

Two types of packages are tested on the LPI exams:

➤ Red Hat Package Manager (RPM)

➤ Debian Package Manager (DPKG)

 This chapter focuses on the majority player, RPM, with the Debian package management information covered in Appendix A, "Debian Package Management."

Red Hat Package Management

RPM refers not only to the package format, but the rpm command and the RPM Database. The components of the RPM package management style are

➤ **The RPM Database**—A collection of files that manages the RPMs on a system

➤ **Package files**—The packages in RPM format that are distributed with the .rpm extension

➤ **The rpm command**—Used for all package installation, removal, and query tasks

A quick word is needed about graphical package management tools such as gnorpm or the RPM-handling routines built in to the various file managers (Nautilus and Konqueror). These are typically just a front end to the text-mode **rpm** command and provide a friendly interface for installing packages.

Although the 101-RPM exam usually has only about 14 questions that cover both installation and package management, it'll seem like most of the exam is about RPM, particularly if you're not adequately prepared. Study the RPM sections in this text thoroughly, read the man pages for man (8) and the extra documentation in **/usr/share/doc/rpm-4.0.4**, and (most importantly) try the commands and options shown previously.

The RPM Database

The RPM Database is a collection of Berkeley database files that together make up a database of the packages and the files that were installed by those packages on the system.

The RPM Database is located in the /var/lib/rpm directory, with each file in that directory being part of the database as a whole. Thankfully, you don't need to know all the files and their purposes, just that they are there and exist in an uncorrupted state.

The RPM Database is mostly restricted to the root user, except for querying and ver- ification, which can be run by any user.

Like any database, the RPM Database can become outdated or corrupted with heavy usage and need to be rebuilt. To rebuild the database from the installed package's headers, you use the following command:

```
rpm --rebuilddb
```

This command does not produce any output unless errors are found, and even then the errors are purely informational and not of much use for fixing the problem.

The RPM Database is locked during most operations, such as an installation or removal. Thus, any attempt to run additional commands results in this message:

```
error: cannot get exclusive lock on /var/lib/rpm/Packages
error: cannot open Packages index using db3 - Operation not permitted (1)
error: cannot open /var/lib/rpm/packages.rpm
```

This message simply conveys that the database is in use and cannot be locked for additional tasks at this time. This keeps multiple sysadmins from causing corruption by performing incompatible tasks simultaneously.

RPM Package Files

RPM packages come in two types: source and binary. A *source* RPM file is a collection of the source files needed for installing the package, plus some instructions for building the binary RPM from the source. A *binary* RPM file is a discrete package that, when installed, copies the compiled binary files, other associated files such as documentation, and any other files needed to run that package to the specified locations.

An important distinction must be made between *installed* packages and *uninstalled* package files. Information about an installed package comes from the RPM database, whereas information about an uninstalled package comes from the RPM file itself. After an RPM file has been installed, the original RPM is no longer required.

RPM packages contain a set of files and configuration scripts that comprise a software program or application in most instances. Notable exceptions are packages that are strictly for placing text configuration files, such as files that are in the /etc directory. RPM packages should contain at least the following:

➤ Compressed binary application files

➤ The name and version of the package's software

➤ The build date and host on which it was built

➤ A description of the package and its purpose

➤ The checksums and dependencies required

Package Name Conventions

Installed packages are known by a short name, although some operations require the long names be used. Typically, long package names are needed for deletions when multiple packages whose short names match exist.

Here's an example of a short package name:

```
ethereal
```

Here's an example of a long package name:

```
ethereal-0.8.9-1.i386
```

An example of two packages installed with different versions of the same software is as follows:

```
rpm -q tree
```

This returns the output:

```
tree-1.2-17
tree-1.2-7
```

This makes viewing a particular package's information difficult if you use the -l and -i options for file listings and info pages. This is fine if you want to compare the differences, but it's maddening when you really need to see just the latest version's information. You need to use the long name (tree-1.2.17) to get just that package's information.

The instances of multiple packages with the same short names appear in the package removal questions, with the **--allmatches** option being necessary to remove multiple packages with the same short names. You can find more on this in the next section.

The rpm Command

The text-mode .rpm package tool is used to perform all operations on packages on the system, either installed and in the RPM Database, or uninstalled and on disk.

Common operations that use the rpm command include

➤ Installing packages

➤ Upgrading packages

➤ Removing and uninstalling packages

➤ Querying the RPM database for information

➤ Verifying the package file

➤ Checking installed files

➤ Building a binary package from the source

The `rpm` command keywords and options come in several formats. The common options are short and use a single letter—for example, `-i` is the installation option. There are almost always long options that match, and some options occur only in the long format.

On the exam you might see long options in several locations, either right after a short option or on the end of the entire command. The important thing is to have tried the long options and to know that you can tack them on the end, as long as something else doesn't depend on that option's placement.

Validation of Packages

It's important that you validate or check the signatures of packages that are downloaded from any source other than the distribution vendor's site.

Validating packages typically takes place when the package is accessed or installed, although it can be triggered explicitly. To check the md5 checksum and gpg signatures for the `gentoo` file manager, you would use the following command:

```
rpm -K gentoo-0.11.39-1.fr.i386.rpm
```

This returns the following output:

```
gentoo-0.11.39-1.fr.i386.rpm: (SHA1) DSA sha1 md5 (GPG) NOT OK
➥(MISSING KEYS: GPG#e42d547b)
```

If the package has a gpg signature, that file might need to be downloaded and imported into the RPM Database with the `--import` option.

Knowing that signatures come in md5 and gpg varieties, plus the **--checksig** and **–K** options, is plenty for the exam. The key is to be sure that the package you have is the original from the maintainer, not one full of Trojan horses and rootkits.

Installation of Packages

Installing software via packages requires root access, the `rpm` command, and a package(s). Installation causes the `rpm` command to check the following:

➤ That enough free disk space exists for the package

➤ That existing files will not be overwritten

➤ That all dependencies listed in the package are met

You install packages with at least the -i option, (and the --install long option), often including other options that improve the experience. To install the gentoo package, get a progress bar (consisting of hash marks printed onscreen) and verbose messages on the installation; then use the command:

```
rpm -ivh gentoo-0.11.39-1.fr.i386.rpm
Preparing...                       ################################## [100%]
   1:gentoo                         ################################## [100%]
```

These options work well for installing groups of packages, too. Instead of specifying a singular package as shown previously, specify a file glob instead:

```
rpm -ivh *.rpm
```

Wildcards can be used for installing upgrading but not removing packages because a misapplied *.* could wipe out the system and cause numerous dependency issues.

Additional Installation Options

Whenever you install RPM packages, keep in mind that there will be exten-uating circumstances such as files that exist on the system that RPM doesn't know about but that will be overwritten by a package's contents.

These can be handled with the replacefiles or force option. (These options are identical.) For example, if you try to install a package named tarfoo-1. 2-3.i386.rpm and it finds a file on the system that will be overwritten by a file in the package, you get an error message stating so and the installation fails:

```
rpm -ivh tarfoo-1.2-3.i386.rpm
tarfoo    /etc/tarfoo.conf conflicts with file from snafu-1.1
```

The key is to check the offending file and either remove it if it's unnecessary or use this command to force it:

```
rpm -ivh --force tarfoo-1.2-3.i386.rpm
```

This returns the output shown here:

```
Preparing...                       ################################## [100%]
   1:tarfoo                         ################################## [100%]
```

If the package won't install due to unresolved dependencies, you can (some-what foolishly!) use the --nodeps option to have the rpm command ignore dependencies. Using --nodeps without a clear fix in mind or a documented recommendation from the package vendor will almost certainly cause more dependency issues.

For example, if you try to install the pebkac package and it has dependency issues, it might look like this:

```
rpm -ivh pebkac.rpm --nodeps
```

This returns output such as

```
error: failed dependencies:
        libc.so.6(GLIBC_2.3) is needed by pebkac-7.23-20031119.5
        libpthread.so.0(GLIBC_2.3.2) is needed by pebkac-7.23-20031119.5
        libstdc++.so.5(CXXABI_1.2) is needed by pebkac-7.23-20031119.5
        libstdc++.so.5(GLIBCPP_3.2) is needed by pebkac-7.23-20031119.5
```

You have the possibility of seriously munging your system if you use the **--nodeps** option outside of a recommendation from the distribution vendor or a support professional. You might so severely damage things that a reinstall is the only option.

Verifying a Package's Integrity

After you've installed a package, you should periodically check that the package is working properly and that all packages are okay.

The verification mechanism uses nine characters to the extreme left of the returned output to indicate what's going on with a package:

➤ S—The file size differs.

➤ M—The mode differs (permissions or type of file).

➤ 5—The MD5 sum differs; this is also seen by --checksig.

➤ D—The device's major/minor number doesn't match.

➤ L—A readLink(2) path problem exists.

➤ U—The user ownership was altered.

➤ G—The group ownership was altered.

➤ T—The mTime is different from the original.

➤ c—A configuration file has changed.

To verify the state of a single package on the system, you use the -V option (or --verify) with the package short name, like so:

```
rpm -V setup
```

This displays the following output:

```
S.5....T c /etc/printcap
```

The output shown indicates that the setup package contains a file named /etc/printcap that has been altered since the original build of the package or after it was installed on this system.

To verify the state of all the packages on the system, you use the -v option, as such:

```
rpm -Va
```

This displays output similar to

```
S.5....T c /etc/sysconfig/rhn/rhn-applet
S.5....T c /etc/pam.d/system-auth
S.5....T c /usr/share/a2ps/afm/fonts.map
.M......   /dev/shm
missing    /var/lib/dav/lockdb.dir
missing    /var/lib/dav/lockdb.pag
```

The a in the options for the previous command indicates that all packages should be checked. As you can see, the changed files span the different types, with some altered configuration files, the /dev/shm shared memory device file, and some missing lock files that were initially installed and likely were deleted by the closing of a program.

If you want to log the state of your configuration files for comparison against a future date, you can check the condition of every configuration file on the system and write it to a file with this command:

```
rpm -Vac > /root/somelog.txt
```

Freshening Versus Upgrading

The daily maintenance of your newly installed system will likely involve updates and fixes downloaded as .rpm files. Properly applying these to the system takes some finesse, particularly when you have a system that must stay as stable as possible or not have new software added to it without strict testing.

The -U and --upgrade options are designed to install or upgrade versions of packages to the latest version. An interesting side effect of these options is the removal of all other versions of the targeted package, leaving just the latest version installed.

As an example, the following command upgrades the system to the latest version of the RPMs in a particular directory of patches and fixes downloaded from the distribution vendor:

```
rpm -U *.rpm
```

Remember that the **–U** and **--upgrade** options both upgrade and install. Therefore, if a package isn't on the system and you invoke it with these options, it is installed, whereas an existing package is upgraded.

Freshening your system is different in one important aspect: If a package is installed and a new package is invoked with the -F or --freshen option, it is upgraded to the latest version. If that package does not currently exist on the system, it is not upgraded or installed.

As an example, you'd use the following to apply a directory full of .rpm files that contains security patches and fixes to a firewall or other security server:

```
rpm -Fvh *.rpm
```

This feature is useful for local package cache updates, where you've downloaded the latest patches and fixes to a local network resource and want to run scripts on your machines to update them to the latest security releases.

Removing Packages

Removing a package or set of packages consists of using the -e or --erase option and requires root access. Removal of packages can be even more fraught with dependency problems than installation because a package can be deeply buried in a tree of dependencies over time.

Removing a package without dependencies is easy. To remove the tarfoo package, you would use the following command:

```
rpm -e tarfoo
```

There's usually no output, the package is removed, and the system returns to the prompt.

The trouble begins when you have multiple packages that all have the same short name, such as tree. With two versions of the tree package on a system, querying the database for the package tree as shown here returns both packages' long format names:

```
rpm -q tree
```

The output is as follows:

```
tree-1.2-17
tree-1.2-7
```

If you attempt to remove the package tree, you get this error:

```
rpm -e tree
```

The output is as follows:

```
error: "tree" specifies multiple packages
```

To remove both packages with one command, you use

```
rpm -e tree --allmatches
```

No output is returned if all is successful; you just get a return to the prompt. If you don't want to remove both of the packages, the only choice is to specify the long package name of the package you want to remove.

Other Removal Options

At times you will need to force the removal of a package or remove one regardless of the broken dependencies. A good example of this is fixing a broken package by forcibly removing it and reinstalling it to refresh the files and links that were broken. This usually takes place on the recommendation of support professionals, not some guy on Usenet!

To remove a package that has dependencies, you use the following command:

```
rpm -e foobar --nodeps
```

Be careful removing packages you can't replace or don't have the original package file to reinstall from. You should repackage these while they are working to ensure you can get it back after some reconfiguration. You must repackage the package as it's removed.

To remove and repackage a package and place the resulting package file in the /var/spool/up2date directory (on a Red Hat 7.x machine), you use this command:

```
rpm -e ark-3.0.0-4 --repackage
```

The package file is identical to the package on the system and can be installed back onto the system.

Removing packages can also leave behind altered or customized configuration files. For example, if you've altered a package's main .conf file and then remove the package, the configuration file is saved with its original name suffixed with .rpmsave. This configuration file can be archived for future use or, if the package is to be upgraded with the -U option, a complex set of algorithms goes into play to ensure the configuration is properly applied.

Querying Packages

Querying for package data is only one of the steps that takes place when you manage packages, although it has arguably the most options of all the tasks RPM performs.

It's very important that you understand the difference between packages installed on the system (that appear in the RPM Database) and packages that exist simply as files on the disk or other resource. The chief difference in the rpm command's usage is the addition of the -p option to specify that the package being acted on is a file on disk.

The most basic of all queries is to return output that a particular package is or is not on the system:

```
rpm -q krbafs
```

This returns the output shown here:

```
krbafs-1.1.1-1
```

Simply by adding a few modifier characters to this query, you can gather much more information about any package. The first modifier I usually recommend is to get information on the package:

```
rpm -qi krbafs
```

This returns the following output:

```
Name       : krbafs                    Relocations: (not relocateable)
Version    : 1.1.1                          Vendor: Red Hat, Inc.
Release    : 1
➥Build Date: Tue 05 Mar 2002 05:08:20 PM EST
Install date: Wed 13 Aug 2003 10:30:50 AM EDT
➥Build Host: porky.devel.redhat.com
Group      : System Environment/Libraries
➥Source RPM: krbafs-1.1.1-1.src.rpm
Size       : 46832
➥License: Freely Distributable
Packager   : Red Hat, Inc. <http://bugzilla.redhat.com/bugzilla>
Summary    : A Kerberos to AFS bridging library, built against Kerberos 5.
Description :
This package contains the krbafs shared library, which allows programs
to obtain AFS network filesystem tokens using Kerberos IV credentials,
without having to link with official AFS libraries which may not be
available for a given platform.
```

To get information about a package's files, use the both the -q (query) option and the -l (file listing) option:

```
rpm -l krbafs
```

This returns

```
/etc/krb.conf
/etc/krb.realms
/usr/kerberos/lib/libkrbafs.so.0.0.0
/usr/share/doc/krbafs-1.1.1
/usr/share/doc/krbafs-1.1.1/COPYRIGHT
/usr/share/doc/krbafs-1.1.1/ChangeLog
```

When you get questions about listing package files or information, remember the difference between listing the contents of a package in the database and doing the same for a package on disk:

➤ rpm -qil package_name—Used for installed packages

➤ rpm -qilp package_name—Used for uninstalled packages

In addition, remember that you can specify these options in any order, as long as they are all there. In effect, **rpm -qipl**, **rpm -qlip**, and **rpm -pliq** all work.

To see a revision history or changelog for the package, use this command:

```
rpm -q --changelog krbafs
```

This returns the following output (truncated for readability):

```
* Fri Mar 01 2002 Nalin Dahyabhai <nalin@redhat.com> 1.1.1-1

- update to 1.1.1
- build shared only, and use a map file to only export symbols from the
  shared library which are declared in the header

* Fri Feb 22 2002 Nalin Dahyabhai <nalin@redhat.com> 1.1-4

- rebuild
```

This output is similar to the CHANGELOG, REVISIONS, or RELEASES files found in most software package source code repositories describing the history of the package's changes.

This is the sort of thing that LPI loves to put on the exam. If you've never used **rpm** to this level, the questions will get the best of you. Don't forget that you must use the **-q** and **--changelog** options together; otherwise, you'll get a syntax error.

To find all the configuration files for a package, you use the query and config options like so:

```
rpm -qc sendmail
```

This returns

```
/etc/aliases
/etc/mail/Makefile
/etc/mail/access
/etc/mail/domaintable
/etc/mail/helpfile
/etc/mail/local-host-names
/etc/mail/mailertable
/etc/mail/sendmail.mc
/etc/mail/statistics
/etc/mail/trusted-users
/etc/mail/virtusertable
/etc/rc.d/init.d/sendmail
/etc/sendmail.cf
/etc/sysconfig/sendmail
/usr/lib/sasl/Sendmail.conf
```

Remember, this shows only the configuration files, not the rest of the package contents—the contents are displayed by the **-ql** option.

To see which other capabilities or packages a given package requires, you use the `--requires` or `-R` option (remember it's a package on disk, so use `-p`), like so:

```
rpm -qRp tree-1.2-7.i386.rpm
```

This returns the output shown here:

```
ld-linux.so.2
libc.so.6
libc.so.6(GLIBC_2.0)
```

If the system doesn't provide these capabilities, you'll probably be in for a downloading and dependency-resolving session. Check out **http://www.rpmfind.net** and **http://freshrpms.net** for search engines and help.

What if you can't remember a package's name? Use the output from the `rpm` command and grep to filter out what you don't need, like so:

```
rpm -qa | grep string
```

What about the problem of finding the package from which a particular file was installed? For example, if the `/etc/krb.conf` file were somehow damaged, you could find the package it came from with this command:

```
rpm -qf /etc/krb.conf
```

This returns the following output:

```
krbafs-1.1.1-1
```

 The use of the **-f** option requires the full path and filename of the queried file. That's how it's listed in the package information queried from the database. Failure to include the full path for a queried file when answering a fill-in-the-blank question causes it to be marked wrong.

Building RPMs

For the process of the exam, building RPMs simply requires a set of steps to understand. The actual process of building RPMs can be much more complex than you see here.

Sysadmins use source RPMs and build custom RPMs for better performance, a guarantee of what's in the RPM files, security of their environment, the integrity of machines, and many other reasons.

A tree of directories makes up the build environment and can be found in the /usr/src/redhat directory as subdirectories. These include

➤ BUILD—This is where the source for the package is uncompressed to and the software is built.

➤ RPMS—Binary package files that are created by the build process are written to this directory.

➤ SOURCES—This contains the source packages, any patches, and fixes.

➤ SPECS—This is where .spec files (essentially a glorified makefile) are kept and the build is initiated from.

➤ SRPMS—This is where any source packages generated by the build process are stored.

What Happens in a Build?

The first step is to download the source .rpm or the tarball of compressed code. The steps are the same for both, except a .spec file must be built for the tarball of source code, whereas a source .rpm has all that included.

If it's a source .rpm, you install the .rpm file (rpm -i source_pkg.rpm), which places the source files in the /usr/src/redhat/SOURCES directory and the spec file in the /usr/src/redhat/SPECS directory.

Then you edit the `/usr/src/redhat/SPECS/somepkg.spec` file to make any changes you require. The `.spec` file consists of a set of information and macros, paths to the files to include, and the installation instructions for the package when it's installed as an `.rpm` file.

Here's an example of a `.spec` file:

```
# Preamble of spec file
Summary: a special program to do something.
Name: blah-woof
Version: 0.99
Release: 33
Copyright: GPL
Group: Applications/Special
Source: ftp://ftp.brunson.org/blahwoof.tar.gz
BuildRoot: /var/tmp/blahwoof-root
%description
Blah-woof is the greatest program it does everything and nothing
%prep
rm -rf $RPM_BUILD_DIR/blah-woof-1.0
tar zxf $RPM_SOURCE_DIR/blah-woof-1.0.tar.gz
%build
make
%install
rm -rf $RPM_BUILD_ROOT
mkdir -p $RPM_BUILD_ROOT/usr/{bin,man/man1}
make DESTDIR=$RPM_BUILD_ROOT install
%clean
rm -rf $RPM_BUILD_ROOT
%files
%doc README
/usr/bin/blah-woof
/usr/bin/blah.inc
/usr/man/man1/blah-woof
%changelog
* Wed 10th of Nov. Some developer some@guy.int
- fixed tendency to crash unexpectedly
```

For the file to be used to install a package, it must contain the following sections:

➤ `Preamble`—The summary and other information that shows up in a query of the info page for the package.

➤ `%description`—This is just a description.

➤ `%prep`—This is where the source tarballs are unpacked and processed into the BUILD directory (including any patches that were applied).

➤ `%build`—This is where the actual software is built, usually with a `make` command, just like regular software.

➤ `%install`—The instructions that constitute the installation for the source files, usually a `make` install.

➤ `%clean`—This section cleans up after the file is built, removing all the temporary files created in the `make` process.

➤ `%files`—This is the complete list of files that are in or are to be included in the package. If it's not in this list by its full path and filename, it won't be in the package.

➤ `%doc`—Files marked with this section header are places in the `/usr/share/doc` directory with a name set to the package name, such as `/usr/share/doc/blah-woof-1.0`.

➤ `%changelog`—This is a listing in reverse chronological order of the changes to the package, including convention date, name of the maintainer, and what happened.

Next, you change directories to the `/usr/src/redhat/SPECS` directory and issue this command:

```
rpm -ba blah-woof-1.0.spec
```

This command produces output that's too voluminous to show here. Suffice it to say it's similar to running **make** on a source tarball.

This builds the package and places a copy of it in the `/usr/src/redhat/RPMS/i386` directory as the `blah-woof-1.0-33.i386.rpm` package file.

A source package is also built (that contains the spec file and all files considered necessary to rebuild this package) and places it in the `/usr/src/redhat/SRPMS` directory with the name `blah-woof-1.0-33.src.rpm`.

Take heed: You will see questions about the steps of the RPM build process on the exam. I recommend that you look closely at Chapters 10 and 11 of the book *Maximum RPM* (information on where to find this book is included in the "Need to Know More" file on the CD-ROM included with this book).

Exam Prep Questions

1. Which of the following steps is most likely to require a user to be the root when installing software from a source tarball? (Choose the best answer.)

   ○ A. `make dep`
   ○ B. `make clean`
   ○ C. `make install`
   ○ D. `make mrproper`

   Answer C is correct because the `make install` operation typically attempts to write software to directories writable only by the root user. Answers A, B, and D are correct steps of compiling software but access only the local directories and can be performed by any user.

2. In the blank below, enter the full path of the directory in which a package is placed when it has been built with the `rpm -b` process on a default Red Hat Linux machine:

   _____

   The correct answer is `/usr/src/redhat/RPMS/i386`. There are no alternative answers.

3. Which of the following commands shows the revision history for a software application from the package file on disk?

   ○ A. `rpm --revision tree-1.2-7.i386.rpm`
   ○ B. `rpm -qp tree-1.2-7.i386.rpm --changelog`
   ○ C. `rpm -qc tree-1.2-7.i386.rpm`
   ○ D. `rpm -qlp tree-1.2-7.i386.rpm --showrev`

   Answer B is correct because the combination of the `-qp` and `--changelog` options shows the changelog or revision history for a package that's on disk. Answer A is incorrect because there is no such thing as a `--revision` option for the `rpm` command. Answer C is incorrect because there isn't a `-p` option to query the package on disk, nor does `-qc` show the required information. Answer D is incorrect because the `-qlp` option shows the files in the package, not the revision history and there isn't a `--showrev` option to the `rpm` command.

4. In the blank below, enter the full path and filename to the file that's produced by the ldconfig program after it's run and has processed all the library files on the machine:

   _____

   The correct answer is `/etc/ld.so.cache`. There are no alternative answers.

5. What is the purpose of running the ldd program?

   ○ A. Rebuilding links to library files

   ○ B. Creating a link to a library file

   ○ C. Displaying a program's required libraries

   ○ D. Reading a program's library capabilities

   Answer C is correct because the ldd program, when used with a program name as the argument, shows the necessary libraries for the program's functionality. Answer A is incorrect because ldconfig is used to rebuild links to library files, not ldd. Answer B is incorrect because creating a link to a library file is done by the `ldconfig` or `ln` command, not `ldd`. Answer D is incorrect because the `ldd` command does not read a program's library capabilities; instead it reads its dependencies.

6. Which variable is used to provide additional library support and is also considered to be a security risk? Please enter the variable name only in the blank below:

   _____

   The correct answer is `LD_LIBRARY_PATH`. There are no alternative answers.

7. Which of the following is a valid cause to receive the error message `error: cannot get exclusive lock on /var/lib/rpm/Packages`? (Choose all that apply.)

   ❏ A. Attempting an `rpm` install command as non-root

   ❏ B. Performing multiple remove commands simultaneously

   ❏ C. Performing multiple verification commands simultaneously

   ❏ D. Performing multiple install commands simultaneously

   Answers A, B, and D are correct because they cannot be performed in any way except singly at any given time because the database is locked or because normal users cannot perform the action. Answer C is incorrect because multiple verification commands can be performed simultaneously because the operation is a read, not a read-write.

8. You need to remove all instances of the package woohoo, regardless of the version, with a single command. Which of the following accomplishes this task? (Choose all that apply.)

   ❏ A. `rpm -e woohoo*`

   ❏ B. `rpm -ea woohoo`

   ❏ C. `rpm -a woohoo --remove`

   ❏ D. `rpm -e woohoo --allmatches`

   Answer D is correct because the command is the only one that removes all instances of the package woohoo with a single command. Answer A is incorrect because asterisks do not invoke multiple removals and can be used only in installation situations for multiple packages on disk. Answer B is incorrect because the `-ea` option does not allow for multiple removals and works only in queries. Answer C is incorrect because there is no `--remove` option for the `rpm` command.

9. You are the system administrator of two firewalls and want to apply updates from a set of packages in the current directory, but you don't want to install any new packages on the systems. In the blank below, enter the exact command with any options and arguments to accomplish this:

The correct answer is `rpm -F *.rpm`. An alternative answer is `rpm --freshen *.rpm`.

10. To view the list of required capabilities that a package needs to function properly, which command and options display this for an installed package? Enter only the command and options in the blank below:

The correct answer is `rpm -qR`. An alternative answer is `rpm -q --requires`.

PART II
LPIC Exam 102

Linux Boot Process and Runlevels

Terms you'll need to understand:

✓ Boot process
✓ Master boot record
✓ Runlevel
✓ Sector
✓ Signal
✓ System initialization

Techniques you'll need to master:

✓ Understanding the boot process
✓ Booting into various runlevels
✓ Understanding runlevels
✓ Configuring runlevels
✓ Shutting down a system
✓ Making a boot disk

This is the formal beginning of the material for Exam 117-102.

In this chapter we'll discuss the Linux boot process, the runlevels, and how to configure your system to boot the correct level with the correct services running.

The Linux Boot Process

The Linux system's boot steps are similar across distributions, except maybe for Slackware and the BSD variants. In the following list I walk you through the boot steps and give some exam tips you can use during this process:

1. Turn on the system power.

2. The basic input/output system (BIOS) code loads and looks for a valid boot sector.

3. The BIOS loads the boot sector from a floppy disk, HD, or CD-ROM according to the seek order.

4. The master boot record (MBR) is read; it's contained in the first 512 bytes of the first sector of the first or active hard disk.

5. Any boot loader code found is executed.

6. If using LILO (Linux Loader), the menu code (usually in /boot/boot.b) is shown. The prompt for LILO is either LILO: in text mode or a graphical menu of choices.

7. The user selects or types in a choice, or the boot loader times out and begins to load the default entry.

8. If you select a Linux image, the path to load the Linux kernel is read and the compressed kernel is executed.

If another image type is selected, such as a dual-boot to Windows, the first 512 bytes of that partition are read for the NTLDR or whatever that OS uses to initiate the system.

9. When the Linux kernel is loading, it initializes the devices, loads any necessary modules, looks for the initial RAM disk (initrd), and loads

that if necessary. Then it mounts the root filesystem, as defined by the root=/dev/*xxx* information in the entry.

10. The /sbin/init program is loaded and becomes PID 1, the grandfather of all other processes on the system.

11. The init process then reads the /etc/inittab file and runs the /etc/init.d/rcS script for Debian systems and the /etc/rc.d/init.d/ rc.sysinit script for Red Hat systems.

12. The system initialization script loads the necessary modules, checks the root file system, mounts the local file systems, starts the network devices, and then mounts the remote file systems (if configured to do so).

13. The init process reads the /etc/inittab again and changes the system to the default runlevel by executing the scripts in the appropriate directory.

14. The runlevel scripts are executed, with the Sxxservice scripts in the default runlevel directory being run in standard numeric sorting order (this is easy to see in most boot situations because a load of [OK] notations appear in green on the right of the system's screen indicating the service loaded properly).

When discussing the startup scripts being executed, it's important to note that Debian uses links in **/etc/rc0.d** through **/etc/rc6.d** that point back to the **/etc/init.d** directory and the service executables. Red Hat, on the other hand, uses links in **/etc/rc.d/rc0.d** through **/etc/rc.d/rc6.d** and points to the service executables in the **/etc/rc.d/init.d** directory.

15. The mingetty sessions laid out in /etc/inittab are loaded and the system (and login) shows the login prompt and waits for the user to log in.

Differences exist between various distributions, but all basically follow the steps outlined here. Expect questions about what comes after certain steps on the exam or, if a problem occurs, what is next or can be fixed to get past that error.

Note that starting the system within a maintenance runlevel will likely show up on the exam, too. This is covered later in the text.

Understanding Runlevels and init

A *runlevel* is a definition of the state of the system, where the number (by default) represents a set of services and some applications that are run.

Every distribution supports the presence of runlevels 0–6. There are nine runlevels total, but no Linux distribution that I am aware of uses more than six. The rest are of historical note only.

For something that appears on every Linux system, you'd think that runlevels would be standardized, but they're not. Most Red Hat derivatives use the following runlevel layout:

➤ **0**—System Halt. It's not powered off, but no processes running.

➤ **1**—Single User/Maintenance mode. There are no attached users, just the system and a shell plus a few tools.

➤ **2**—Undefined by default on Red Hat systems, it's user configurable.

➤ **3**—Full multiple user; this has full networking capability text login mode.

➤ **4**—Undefined by default on Red Hat systems, this is user configurable.

➤ **5**—Full multiple user; this has full networking, GUI login, and X running by default.

➤ **6**—Reboot; the system shuts down and reboots.

 Remember that a system goes straight from the **sysinit** script to the default runlevel, instead of marching up the runlevels like some traditional Unix systems do.

On a currently running system, you can determine the runlevel with the `runlevel` command:

```
runlevel
```

This produces the following output:

```
N 3
```

The first character represents the previous runlevel. An `N` in this position indicates that this system was booted and went directly to the default runlevel, represented by the second character—in this case, `3`. If the system had been in any previous runlevel, the first character would reflect that runlevel.

Modifying the system's runlevel from the shell involves the `init` command, or the `telinit` command, which is a symlink to the `init` command and exists for legacy compatibility.

To take the system to runlevel 3, you'd use the following:

```
init 3
```

The system displays messages consistent with the leaving of the current runlevel and the entering of the new runlevel.

The following takes the system to the GUI login mode represented by runlevel 5:

```
init 5
```

You should see the appropriate messages, culminating in a GUI login screen.

 Don't mistake the running of X with the setting of runlevel 5. X is just an application that is run by default in runlevel 5, and it can be run in most other runlevels, too.

If you get paid for system uptime or for keeping the system in a power-on condition, don't reboot; just take the system to the maintenance runlevel and back up to a functional runlevel. It then cleans out most error service conditions and makes the system clean. It's much better than a full reboot and saves time.

To perform a runlevel bounce, you'd use this command:

```
init 1 ; init 3
```

Shutting Down a System

To shut down the system, you can either use the `init` command to bring the system to a halted condition and then power it off or use the `shutdown` command.

The following shows the format of the `shutdown` command syntax:

```
shutdown -t # -options time message
```

Important options for the `shutdown` command include

➤ h—Halts the system when all the processes have been shut down (runlevel 0, not 1).

➤ r—Reboots the system after shutting it down.

➤ t#—Where # is the time in seconds to wait before signaling the processes or entering another runlevel.

➤ f—This doesn't force fsck on reboot.

➤ F—This forces fsck on reboot.

➤ c—This cancels a running shutdown process.

➤ a—This uses the /etc/shutdown.allow file.

Using the shutdown command can be easy or complex. The easiest method of using it is to simply shut down the system right away with the command shown here:

```
shutdown now
```

This shuts down the system immediately, sending the SIGTERM signal to all running processes and invoking the init process to bring the system to single user maintenance mode by default. (This is functionally identical to using init 1.)

To turn off a compatible system after shutting off all the running process, you can use the -h option to halt the system, like so:

```
shutdown -h now
```

To reboot the system after shutting it down, use this command:

```
shutdown -r now
```

To signal all users that the system is going down at 5 p.m. and perform that shutdown, you use

```
shutdown -h 17:00 "System going down at 5PM"
```

You can specify the time in absolute terms (17:30) or in a number of minutes in the future (+10). Using shutdown with a delay causes the system to create the /etc/nologin file, which disallows user logins. This file is removed right before the runlevel changes are made.

The /etc/shutdown.allow file is designed to have usernames placed in it to allow them to shut down the system as a non-root user. This file allows a maximum of 32 user entries and is consulted only when you invoke the shutdown command with the -a option.

Watch for questions about how to shut down a system at a specific time or the number of minutes/hours in the future and how to cancel a shutdown command after it has been invoked with a delay.

Other commands to halt or power down the system include the halt command and two commands that are symlinks to the halt command: poweroff and reboot.

The halt command is directly used only in runlevels 0 and 6; otherwise, it simply calls the shutdown command with the appropriate action of reboot or halt. This can be overridden by the use of halt -f to force a system halt rather than just calling shutdown.

You can power down the system after halting is done with the poweroff command, which is a symlink to the halt command. On compatible systems, this halts the system and powers the computer off.

The reboot command is another symlink to the halt command, which calls the shutdown command with the -r parameter to effect a reboot of the system.

 You need to know that the **poweroff** and **reboot** commands are symlinks to the **halt** command and that they all use the **shutdown** command in the stated s ituations.

The init Process

When executed, the /sbin/init program becomes the first or parent process and is assigned PID 1. All other processes are children of init and inherit the environment and attributes of the init process by default.

The init process is configured by the /etc/inittab file and refers to this file at various times in its operations.

The /etc/inittab File

The system and, in particular the init process, refers to this file; it's responsible for the runlevels, how many programs function and respond to stimulus, and how the system is initialized.

Entries in the /etc/inittab file consist of the following sections:

```
id:runlevels:action:process
```

For example, the system's virtual terminals (tty1 through tty6 by default) mingetty processes are configured by the following lines in the /etc/ inittab file:

```
# Run gettys in standard runlevels
1:2345:respawn:/sbin/mingetty tty1
2:2345:respawn:/sbin/mingetty tty2
3:2345:respawn:/sbin/mingetty tty3
4:2345:respawn:/sbin/mingetty tty4
5:2345:respawn:/sbin/mingetty tty5
6:2345:respawn:/sbin/mingetty tty6
```

The first column is the ID—in this case, it should be the numeral associated with the tty being configured for system accounting purposes, but it could be almost any number.

The second column is the runlevels in which this command or service is allowed to run or for which the program should take action in.

The third column is the action that should be taken for this entry; the possibilities are shown in the section following this one.

The fourth column is the command or service to be affected or run, along with any options and arguments needed.

Important values for the action column are

➤ respawn—This restarts the process when it's terminated; it's used mostly for X and login mingettys or gettys.

➤ sysinit—This is run before the default runlevel is entered.

➤ initdefault—This one sets the default runlevel.

➤ ondemand—Entries with this action can be invoked with an init command and options a, b, or c. No runlevel change happens—just the invoking of the configured program.

➤ once—This causes entries to be invoked only one time when the noted runlevels are entered.

➤ wait—This action is for processes that must be completed before anything else can happen, usually at the beginning of the entry into the runlevel. Then init continues.

The system's default system runlevel entry lets the system know to which runlevel you want it to jump when the sysinit scripts are finished. This entry is important because the system defaults to this runlevel anytime the system is booted or rebooted. Any entry to have the system boot by default into a mode that features full multiple-user and networking capabilities but that presents a text-mode login would be as follows:

```
id:3:initdefault:
```

The system initialization entry sets the script or program that is run upon system initialization and before the default runlevel is reached. Notice there are no runlevels for this entry; they occur later:

```
si::sysinit:/etc/rc.d/rc.sysinit
```

Trapping Ctrl+Alt+Delete

An entry in the /etc/inttab file takes a particular action by default when the keystrokes Ctrl+Alt+Delete are pressed, normally to initiate a shutdown -h. You can alter this line to make it impossible for anyone to press those keystrokes and take your production systems down precipitously.

For example, on a Red Hat machine, your /etc/inittab file has the following line to configure what happens when you press Ctrl+Alt+Delete:

```
ca::ctrlaltdel:/sbin/shutdown -t3 -r now
```

This line watches for Ctrl+Alt+Delete to be pressed, initiates a shutdown, and reboots with a 3-second delay before the processes are signaled; however, it starts the shutdown immediately. This can be a catastrophe on a production server and must be secured during the initial configuration of most machines.

To fix this problem, alter the line to echo some warning or comment like the following:

```
ca::ctrlaltdel:echo "Your sabotage attempt has been recorded
➥on video and sent to HR"
```

The init process does not read /etc/inittab unless the system is restarted or is told to. If you have made changes to the /etc/inittab file, the following command causes the init process to reread the /etc/inittab file:

```
init q
```

 You do not have to restart a machine to have **/etc/inittab** changes take effect. You just need to update it with the **q** option. No - (dash) is needed with this option.

If some perpetrator does press the magic keys, this message shows onscreen and the system does not reboot.

 Exam questions about the **init** and **/etc/inittab** processes will occur, so be aware of how to configure **init** and the contents of the **inittab** file. A good read of this chapter and the man pages for **init**, **shutdown**, and **/etc/inittab** will give you more than enough information to correctly answer the questions posed.

The Runlevel Directories

The two main system startup variations are the BSD/Slackware method, which is comprised of relatively few and longer startup scripts, and the SysV method, which involves the sysinit script and a set of directories that contain links to the system's services, each representing a runlevel.

Red Hat and Debian use a similar structure for these directories, with one main difference. Red Hat's tree structure is shown on the left, with Debian on the right:

Red Hat   Debian

```
/etc/rc.d                        /etc/
      |-- init.d                       |-- init.d
      |-- rc0.d                        |-- rc0.d
      |-- rc1.d                        |-- rc1.d
      |-- rc2.d                        |-- rc2.d
      |-- rc3.d                        |-- rc3.d
      |-- rc4.d                        |-- rc4.d
      |-- rc5.d                        |-- rc5.d
      `-- rc6.d                        `-- rc6.d
```

The init.d directory in each case contains all the configured daemon executables. These are linked to from the runlevel directories by two types of scripts—start and kill scripts. Both scripts are symlinks to the daemon executables in the init.d directory.

Start scripts look like S24pcmcia, where the presence of the capital S signals the daemon to start itself, the numerals force a particular start order, and the name of the service is the last piece of the link name as a mnemonic.

Kill scripts use the same naming convention, with a capital K instead of an S. The presence of the capital K signals the daemon to gracefully turn itself off.

After the system initialization is finished, the init process reads the /etc/inittab file and finds the line that sets the default runlevel value. After that value is obtained, the init process finds the appropriate runlevel directory and, upon entering it, runs the start scripts in number order (0–99).

When the runlevel is changed, the system takes note of the state of the current runlevel's daemons, inspects the target runlevel's scripts, and leaves those that are defined with an S symlink running. If no S symlink exists in the target runlevel for a daemon, it's considered *undefined* and the K script to terminate that daemon is run before the runlevel is changed.

NOTE   The use of **.pid** files in the **/var/run** or **/var/lock/subsys** directories helps the system determine what's running and the state of those daemons. This is not particularly relevant to the exam, but a good sysadmin should read more about it, starting with the **init man** pages.

Configuring the Runlevels

There are several methods of altering or configuring the runlevel's start and kill scripts:

➤ **Manually**—This involves using the rm, ln, and mv commands to manipulate the links that point to the init.d daemons.

➤ **Scriptable**—This involves using chkconfig, update-rc.d, and other noninteractive tools that facilitate scripting.

➤ **GUI**—This involves using ntsysv, SysVConfig, tksysv, and other tools that run in GUI mode.

Red Hat includes both ntsysv and chkconfig, whereas Debian uses a tool called update-rc.d. In the next section, we'll look at the ntsysv and chkconfig tools because they will appear on the exam.

Using the ntsysv tool for service configuration is quick and easy; by default it edits the current runlevel. After invoking ntsysv, you see a list of daemons that can be turned on or off. Press the spacebar to toggle an asterisk in the square brackets ([*]) to set a daemon to run in the current runlevel, or you can clear the brackets ([ ]) to turn off a daemon in the current runlevel. You must leave the current runlevel to have the changes take effect.

To configure a runlevel different from the current, use this command:

```
ntsysv --level 5
```

To configure several runlevels at once, specify all the runlevels after the --level option (the following command affects both runlevels 1 and 6):

```
ntsysv --level 016
```

Using **ntsysv** on the exam is usually to affect the current runlevel, but there might be situations that test your knowledge of the syntax for multiple runlevel configurations.

One of the most useful utilities for configuring the runlevels is chkconfig. It doesn't have any menus and is noninteractive and scriptable. However, you can write a short script that you can run on multiple machines to configure them identically as far as the daemons go.

Using chkconfig to list the present configuration of the runlevel daemons is insightful. The following is a truncated set of output:

```
chkconfig --list
```

This produces the output shown here:

```
keytable        0:off   1:on    2:on    3:on    4:on    5:on    6:off
atd             0:off   1:off   2:off   3:on    4:on    5:on    6:off
syslog          0:off   1:off   2:on    3:on    4:on    5:on    6:off
gpm             0:off   1:off   2:on    3:on    4:on    5:on    6:off
sendmail        0:off   1:off   2:on    3:on    4:on    5:on    6:off
kudzu           0:off   1:off   2:off   3:on    4:on    5:on    6:off
microcode_ctl   0:off   1:off   2:off   3:off   4:off   5:off   6:off
netfs           0:off   1:off   2:off   3:on    4:on    5:on    6:off
```

As you can see, this is a useful command because it shows you the state of the daemon (on the left) in each of the runlevels. All you have to do is decide whether you want them on or off in various runlevels.

To set a particular service to be on in a set of runlevels, use this command:

```
chkconfig --levels 345 smb on
```

Be aware that using the **--levels** option affects only the specified runlevels. If you have a daemon configured in runlevel 2, the previous command does not affect it.

This turns on the smb (Samba) daemon in runlevels 3, 4, and 5, which can be verified with this command:

```
chkconfig --list ¦ grep smb
```

This produces the following output:

```
smb             0:off   1:off   2:off   3:on    4:on    5:on    6:off
```

If you want to add a particular daemon to be managed by chkconfig, use the --add option, like so:

```
chkconfig --add tarfoo
```

This sets the service tarfoo to have either a start or a kill entry in particular runlevels (set in the daemon or service itself and read by chkconfig) making it fully configurable by chkconfig.

You should note that the last displayed set of daemons are the ones governed by the inetd or xinetd daemon.

Single User Mode

Sometimes going into maintenance or single user mode is necessary, even desirable, for a sysadmin. If you have a disk that needs fsck'ing, you'll most likely want to either be in runlevel 1 or have the system disconnected from the network.

There is some confusion about the differences between runlevels s, s, and 1. The s and s runlevels are the same and exist primarily to run the scripts associated with runlevel 1 before completing the transfer to runlevel 1.

A situation that often confronts sysadmins is a system that won't properly enter the default runlevel or, in the case of runlevel 5, won't start X properly.

Let's say you are a sysadmin with a machine that's configured with a default runlevel of 5, so it's supposed to settle down to a GUI login screen. However, the system experiences a failure when it tries to start X, and you have to fix it. You would likely reboot the system and, if using LILO, you'd enter linux 1 or whatever the correct label is and the number 1 for the maintenance mode. In the example shown here, you would type the bold text:

```
LILO: linux 1
```

An emergency mode is additionally available to you and is reached by typing the following at the LILO or other prompt:

```
LILO: linux emergency
```

You have to enter the root password to fully enter emergency mode, which is a basic system that has no /proc mounted.

 TIP Please refer to Chapter 1, "Linux Installation," for a refresher on GRUB. The boot loaders appear on both exams.

Making Boot/Rescue Disks

I often tell customers who ask if I have a boot disk that they should make one during the installation—it's easier and faster, but there are situations where you may need to make one from a running machine.

To create a boot/rescue disk on a Red Hat machine, place a disk in the floppy drive and run the following command, substituting your kernel version for 2.4.18-3:

```
mkbootdisk --device /dev/fd0 2.4.18-3
```

This prompts you with the following:

```
Insert a disk in /dev/fd0. Any information on the disk will be lost.
Press <Enter> to continue or ^C to abort:
```

To find out your kernel version, either run the `uname -a` command or do an `ls` on the `/lib/modules` directory to see what the listed versions are.

If you need to make one from the images on the Red Hat CD-ROM, use the `dd` command as previously noted to create one from either the `/mnt/cdrom/images/boot.img` file or the `/mnt/cdrom/images/rescue.img` file. Your distribution version might have slightly different files, but it will have images to use.

On a Debian system, you can make a boot/rescue disk with a slightly different set of steps. First, put a disk in the floppy drive and then run this command:

```
mkboot /boot/vmlinuz
```

This prompts you with the following output:

```
Insert a floppy diskette into your boot drive and press <Return>.
```

The `/boot/vmlinuz` file is usually a link to the real kernel, or you can specify the real kernel file.

Exam Prep Questions

1. What does the line in the `/etc/inittab` file that configures the default runlevel contain? Fill in the blank below with exactly the contents to configure a system to boot in runlevel 3:

   The correct answer is `id:3:initdefault:`. There are no alternative answers.

2. One of your junior sysadmins calls in a panic. He was supposed to set the system to shut down at 6 p.m.; instead, he has set it to shut down in 60 seconds. Which of the following commands will stop the pending `shutdown` command?

   - ○ A. `shutdown --stop`
   - ○ B. `shutdown -x`
   - ○ C. `shutdown -k`
   - ○ D. `shutdown -c`

   Answer D is correct because the `shutdown -c` command stops a pending `shutdown` command. Answer A is incorrect because there is no such thing as a `--stop` option for the `shutdown` command. Answer B is incorrect because there isn't a `-x option` for the `shutdown` command. Answer C is incorrect because the `-k` option only sends a message and does not cancel a pending shutdown.

3. You have a system that fails to enter X when booted with a default runlevel of 5 and freezes up. When you reboot and get to a `LILO:` prompt, which of the following can you enter to repair the system? (Choose all that apply.)

   - ❏ A. `linux 1`
   - ❏ B. `linux S`
   - ❏ C. `linux s`
   - ❏ D. `linux 4`

   Answers A, B, and C are correct because they all point to the same maintenance runlevel in which you can edit the `/etc/inittab` file or fix X. Answer D is incorrect because runlevel 4 is not used by default.

4. What is the full path and filename of the system initialization script on a default Red Hat system? Enter the full path and filename in the blank below:

   The correct answer is `/etc/rc.d/rc.sysinit`. There are no alternative answers.

5. Which of the following is a valid configured runlevel on a default Red Hat system? (Choose all that apply.)

❏ A. 1

❏ B. 2

❏ C. 3

❏ D. 4

❏ E. 5

Answers A, C, and E are correct because they are all valid and configured runlevels on a default Red Hat system. Answer B is incorrect because it's undefined by default on a Red Hat system. Answer D is incorrect because runlevel 4 is not used by default.

6. You are the sysadmin of a default Red Hat Linux machine and want to use a script to configure your system's daemons so that some start on boot and others don't. In the blank below, enter the name of the command that makes the most sense to use in this script:

_____

The correct answer is `chkconfig`. There are no alternative answers.

7. Where can you interactively specify to which runlevel the system will boot? (Choose all that apply.)

❏ A. `Boot:`

❏ B. `Sysinit`

❏ C. `LILO:`

❏ D. `ROOT:`

❏ E. `grub>`

Answers A, C, and E are correct because the system can be using LILO or GRUB. With LILO, both the `LILO:` and `Boot:` prompt are correct and, with GRUB, the `grub>` prompt is correct. Answer B is incorrect because there is no Sysinit prompt. Answer D is incorrect because there is no ROOT: prompt.

8. Where can LILO install its boot menu information? (Choose two.)

❏ A. bootblk

❏ B. MBR

❏ C. The first sector

❏ D. FAT

Answers B and C are correct because LILO can use the MBR (master boot record) and the first sector of the Linux partition to store the boot loader code. Answer A is incorrect because bootblk is a Solaris construct. Answer D is incorrect because FAT is a DOS/Windows construct.

9. On a Debian system, which of the following would build a boot disk?

   ○ A. `mkboot /dev/floppy`

   ○ B. `makeboot --device /dev/fd0 2.4.18-12`

   ○ C. `mkbootdisk --device /dev/fd0 2.4.18-12`

   ○ D. `mkboot /boot/vmlinuz`

Answer D is correct because it's the only one that contains all the right elements to create a Debian boot disk: `mkboot` and the full path of the link to the compressed kernel. Answer A is incorrect because the `mkboot` command doesn't use the raw floppy device for an argument. Answer B is incorrect because the `makeboot` command is a Windows command. Answer C is incorrect because the `mkbootdisk` command is a Red Hat command.

10. After mapping more `mingetty` to `tty` connections in the `/etc/inittab` file, you want the system to recognize the new configuration but not experience any downtime. In the blank below, enter the exact command with any needed options to accomplish this:

_____

The correct answer is `init q`. There are no alternative answers.

Using Linux and GNU Documentation

Terms you'll need to understand:

✓ Internet resources
✓ Locate
✓ **man** page
✓ Newsgroups
✓ Search

Techniques you'll need to master:

✓ Memorizing **man** page sections
✓ Finding documentation on items
✓ Finding source, binary, and **man** pages
✓ Searching **man** pages
✓ Identifying Internet resources
✓ Using additional system documentation

One of the shortest objectives in the LPI certifications is documentation. This is deceptive because there will be a fair number of questions on the exam about finding help, using the man pages, and using other system commands to get more information on just about any object on the system.

The man Pages

One of the most informative and useful items on Linux systems is the set of man pages and associated utilities that allow you to search and glean information from the man pages.

The man Page Sections

The Linux man pages are broken up into sections and shown to searchers in a particular order. The man page sections are as follows:

➤ **1**—Executable programs or shell commands

➤ **2**—System calls

➤ **3**—Library calls

➤ **4**—Special files

➤ **5**—File formats and conventions

➤ **6**—Games

➤ **7**—Miscellaneous

➤ **8**—System administration commands

➤ **9**—Kernel routines

What's in a man Page

Individual man pages are made up of various sections or headers including, but not limited to, the following:

➤ NAME—The name and a short description of the object.

➤ SYNOPSIS—A list of all the acceptable command-line options.

➤ DESCRIPTION—Anywhere from a short description to a long dissertation explaining the object. This can include examples.

➤ OPTIONS—A more detailed explanation of the options supported by the object if it's a command or service.

➤ EXAMPLES—An optional section listing specific examples of usage.

➤ FILES—Any files that are associated with the object.

➤ SEE ALSO—A list of other man pages to use for more information.

➤ BUGS—Any bugs that haven't been fixed or that are part of the design of the object.

➤ AUTHOR—The author(s) of the object or references to a governing body that regulates the object.

Where man Pages Live

The man pages are located (according to the FHS) in /usr/share/man, with the actual directories that contain the man page sections 1–9 corresponding to the following sections:

```
man
|-- man1
|-- man2
|-- man3
|-- man4
|-- man5
|-- man6
|-- man7
|-- man8
`-- man9
```

Using the man Command

When you are stumped or need more information about a command or file on your Linux system, the man pages are the first place you should look.

If it were that simple, though, life would be easier. The man pages are hard to tame, but once mastered, you'll find information much more quickly. What follows is a crash course in using the man command not only in real life, but also on the exam.

man Configuration and Path

Several variables affect the man pages, indirectly or directly. Configuring these and other settings will make your experience richer and more fulfilling.

The MANPATH variable is used to determine the search path for man pages and isn't always present on a system. This variable is important if you have recently added man pages that aren't showing up in the man command searches and output. The correct directories might have to be added to the variable contents. When the variable MANPATH is not present, or if it contains nothing when queried, the file /etc/man.config (/etc/man.conf in some distributions) is used to set the various options for the man command's environment.

The /etc/man.config file contains settings that affect the man page environment and experience. The following is a list of important and useful options that might appear on the exam:

➤ MANPATH—The variable values that are read as locations for man pages.

➤ NOCACHE—This keeps the man command from creating caches of found data, ensuring slower but more up-to-date results.

➤ PAGER—Usually set to /usr/bin/less, this is the application that shows the man page on the console. You can also set this to the more command, which limits the functionality.

➤ CMP—This variable, when set, tries to reduce the duplicate search returns (in other words, it shows found strings or commands only once in the output).

➤ COMPRESS and COMPRESS_EXT—These set the compression program and extension; all man pages are compressed by gzip by default.

➤ MANSECT—This sets the order of man page searches.

Action Keys in man

You normally use the man command for a single target, as in finding the documentation for the ls command:

```
man ls
```

This returns the following (truncated for brevity) output:

```
LS(1)                     User Commands                    LS(1)

NAME
       ls--list directory contents

SYNOPSIS
       ls [OPTION]... [FILE]...

DESCRIPTION
  List  information  about  the FILEs (the current directory by
default).  Sort entries alphabetically if none of -cftuSUX nor --sort.

  Mandatory arguments to long options are mandatory for short options too.

   -a, --all
```

When you're in a man page, several keystrokes can help immensely including ctime, which lets you search down the man page for a particular string:

```
/ctime
```

This finds the first occurrence of the string ctime. By default, searching in the man pages is case insensitive—for example, it finds both word and WORD.

Additionally, when searching for a string, after you've found it, you can press the N key to find the next occurrence in the man page (down the man page). In addition, you can use the N key to move to successive previous occurrences (back up the page).

To move around the man page, you can use one of two keys: The spacebar key moves you down one screen at a time, and the Enter key moves you down one line at a time. The B key moves you back up the file one screen at a time, and in some cases the Home key takes you to the top of the man page.

Lastly, the Q key quits the man page. (It's considered extremely lame to get stuck in the man pages, if you do briefly, do it quietly.)

Getting More Out of man

Many sysadmins and users don't take the man command any further than the actions mentioned in the previous section, missing out on some very useful alternatives to the stock command.

For example, let's say you needed more information on the crontab file, which is edited when you run the crontab -e command. If you just type

```
man crontab
```

all you get is the crontab (1) man page, which isn't the one you wanted. To see a list of all the man pages found for your search term, use the find search function (-f), like so:

```
man -f crontab
```

This returns the output shown here:

```
crontab (1)          --maintain crontab files for individual users (V3)
crontab (5)          --tables for driving cron
```

That's much better; now you can specify the crontab (5) page and get the right information:

```
man 5 crontab
```

If you run the **whatis crontab** command, you'll see a similarity with the **man -f crontab** output, which appears on the exam in questions.

Another great option to the man command is the -k, or keyword search function, which is much more expressive and verbose than the -f option. To find all the man pages that have the word crontab in the description, use the following command:

```
man -k crontab
```

This returns the following (truncated for brevity) output:

```
/etc/anacrontab (5) [anacrontab]--configuration file for anacron
anacrontab (5)      --configuration file for anacron
crontab (1)         --maintain crontab files for individual users (V3)
crontab (5)         --tables for driving cron
```

Notice that the /etc/anacrontab entry was included, as was the anacrontab page. The -k option indiscriminately searches for any instance of the search term, including as a part of another term.

Just like the previous Exam Alert, if you run the **apropos crontab** command, you'll see a similarity with the **man -k crontab** output; they are in fact identical.

Another way of seeing all the man pages associated with a particular string or command is to use the -a option, which loads each found page successively. You can press the Q key to quit and load the next available page until all the found pages are exhausted. For example, to view all the pages found for crontab, you'd type the following:

```
man -a crontab
```

whatis Apropos?

The whatis and apropos commands by default show the same information as the man -f and man -k commands. These two commands pull their contents from the whatis database, sometimes kept in /usr/share/man/whatis, but often in the /var/cache/man/index.db file.

This file can be updated by the mkwhatis (sometimes named makewhatis) command on most distributions, but Debian doesn't include it.

Additional Documentation

An additional set of documentation appears in the /usr/share/doc directory tree. The following optional directories are sometimes in the /usr/share/doc directory structure:

➤ /usr/share/doc/program1—Docs for program1

➤ /usr/share/doc/FAQ—FAQs for programs

➤ /usr/share/doc/HTML—Docs in HTML

➤ /usr/share/doc/HOWTO—All the HOWTOs

➤ /usr/share/info—Files used by the info command

The **info** command appears on the exams in only a short cameo role as the preferred documentation reader or method of presenting documentation for the FSF (Free Software Foundation).

Web and Third-Party Documentation

LPI makes somewhat of a big deal about third-party documentation, be it the Linux Documentation Project, newsgroups, or mailing lists.

The Linux Documentation Project

The primary documentation site for Linux is The Linux Documentation Project (http://www.tldp.org). This site is considered the first place to send newbies, but it also gets a lot of traffic from old hands looking for resources to solve problems, learn new topics, or to contribute to the effort.

The LDP offerings consist of

➤ **HOWTOs**—Regular HOWTOs are medium to extensive documents about topics such as the Linux kernel, networking, and so on. Mini-HOWTOs are shorter, sometimes downright terse, documents about more focused topics such as three-button mouse configurations.

➤ **Guides**—Longer, more bookish documents provide in-depth coverage on particular topics, such as system administration, bash scripting, and so on.

➤ **FAQs**—Groupings of frequently asked questions about Linux topics. These are more interactive than a HOWTO. Few of these are available, however.

You'll likely see questions about the site URL for the LDP, questions about the acronym that represents the repository for Linux information on the Web (LDP), and the full name of the site (Linux Documentation Project).

Usenet Resources

There seems to be very little on the exams about the Usenet resources, but two things come up about the LPIC exams with regard to this topic:

➤ `www.deja.com`—This used to be the site that allowed you to access the text of Usenet through a search engine, which was very useful for those without access to a news feed. It's now `groups.google.com`, and you might see questions about this resource on the exam.

➤ `comp.os.linux`—Considered to be *the* root of Linux Usenet resources by many, this group is a great place to lurk and find a lot of good information.

Expect exam questions about these resources. Investigate them thoroughly, and you'll learn a lot about Linux in the process and do better on the exam.

Communicating with Users

A final piece of the documentation on a system is to let your users know about system events (other than saying, "Get off the system; it's going down!") via several programs and files.

The Issue Files

When a user looks at the text-mode login screen, he is viewing the contents of the file /etc/issue. The /etc/issue file usually contains the information shown here:

```
Red Hat Linux release 7.3 (Valhalla)
Kernel \r on an \m
```

The user typically sees this expressed as the output:

```
Red Hat Linux release 7.3 (Valhalla)
Kernel 2.4.18-3 on an i686
dellbert login:
```

Modifying the /etc/issue file to include a standard legal disclaimer and notice that all unauthorized use of the system is illegal is not only a good idea, but also can legally keep the system administrator out of trouble with auditors and investigators.

A /etc/issue.net file is the functional equivalent to the /etc/issue file, but it is used only to display information when a user connects to the system via Telnet. This file is not shown to SSH users or users connecting to the system via NFS or another network file-sharing protocol, such as SMB/CIFS.

 On the exam, watch out for the **issue** and **issue.net** files. If you don't know what they contain, or what types of remote clients show their contents, you'll miss questions.

Message of the Day

The /etc/motd file is typically a plain-text file shown to console and remote console users after they log in, connecting either via Telnet or SSH clients.

Modifying /etc/motd and then logging in displays something similar to the following:

```
Red Hat Linux release 7.3 (Valhalla)
Kernel 2.4.18-3 on an i686
login: rbrunson
Password: xxxxxxxxx
This is the motd file
[rbrunson@dellbert  rbrunson]
```

Use this as a method of communicating with users about system events, the help desk email and phone number, and so on.

Writing to Users

The write command is used to communicate directly with a user who is logged in to the system, with the following syntax:

```
write rbrunson /dev/pts/2
```

In this syntax, the username rbrunson is a user logged in (verified by the w or who command) and /dev/pts/2 represents the user's console or port on which you can communicate with them.

When you press Enter to execute the command, a message appears on rbrunson's console that he is receiving a message from the root user on console /dev/tty1 at 15:51. Then when the root user types a message and presses Enter, that text appears on the user's console. The conversation is ended when the sender presses Ctrl+D.

Talking to Users

The talk command is useful for two-way communication with a user, allowing for what is essentially a chat session between two users.

The talk command works locally on the machine with logged-in users or from machine to machine, as long as the users are logged in with the target username.

To initiate a talk session with the user snuffy who's logged in to the console of the server/machine, you would type the following command as the root user:

```
talk snuffy tty1
```

This pops up a message on snuffy's console that a connection is requested by the root user on the machine and tells snuffy to type talk root@localhost and press Enter. This puts the root user and snuffy into a chat mode, with the root user's information on the top of the screen and snuffy's replies on the bottom of the screen.

You might have to set the mesg options to allow messages to appear on your screen. The mesg y command sets the console to allow connections and messages. However, it causes all sorts of system and other user spam to show up, so you might want to set it to mesg n.

Additionally, you have to enable the ntalk daemon via the chkconfig utility. Or you might need to edit the /etc/xinetd.d/talk script so the line that contains disabled = yes reads disabled = no. This enables the daemon to start a request for a talk session.

You will see **motd** and the **issue** files on the exam, and reportedly **write**, **talk**, and **mesg** appear sporadically.

Lastly, the wall, or write all, command sends a message to all the users on the system consoles and remote consoles.

To send a wall message to every user that the system is going down in 5 minutes, you would use

```
wall "System going down in 5 minutes"
```

Exam Prep Questions

1. Which command with options shows identical output to the command `man -k`? Fill in the blank below with the command and any options and arguments that show the same output:

The correct answer is `apropos program`. There are no alternative answers.

2. Due to a change in your agency's status as a defense contractor, you now must have warning and login messages that contain certain legal text and are shown to any user who connects to the system with a login session. Which of the following accomplishes this? (Choose all that apply.)

   ❏ A. `/etc/login.defs`
   ❏ B. `/etc/issue`
   ❏ C. `/etc/motd`
   ❏ D. `/etc/issue.net`

Answers B, C, and D are correct because they are designed to show text to users either before or right after a login to the system. Answer A is incorrect because the `/etc/login.defs` file's contents are not shown to the user before or after login.

3. What is the full path of the directory where the `man` pages for section 1 can be found? Fill in the blank below with the full path and name of the directory:

The correct answer is `/usr/share/man/man1`. There are no alternative answers.

4. Which of the following resources is considered to be a part of the Linux Documentation Project? (Choose all that apply.)

   ❏ A. HOWTOs
   ❏ B. Guides
   ❏ C. OpenDoc
   ❏ D. FAQs
   ❏ E. Usenet

Answers A, B, and D are correct because they are all part of the Linux Documentation Project. Answer C is incorrect because OpenDoc is a programming interface that allows independent portions of a document to function as a whole. Answer E is incorrect because Usenet is not part of the LDP.

5. What is the full path and filename of the file that is shown to users connecting via Telnet sessions, but not SSH sessions? Fill in the blank with the full path and filename:

_____

The correct answer is /etc/issue.net. There are no alternative answers.

6. Which methods allows the root user to notify other users that a system event will occur but does not allow them to respond? (Choose three.)

- ❏ A. wall
- ❏ B. talk
- ❏ C. gaim
- ❏ D. write
- ❏ E. motd

Answers A, D, and E are correct because they all allow the root user to communicate with the other users. motd is not a program but a file that is shown at login; however, it does notify users of system events if that text is entered. Answer B is incorrect because the talk program is interactive and allows the user to respond. Answer C is incorrect because gaim is not part of a Linux system by default and allows for two-way communication.

7. You need to see multiple man pages that all concern a particular command or name of a file. Which command shows you successively all instances of the man pages for tarfoo?

- ○ A. man -k tarfoo
- ○ B. man -f tarfoo
- ○ C. man -c tarfoo
- ○ D. man -a tarfoo

Answer D is correct because only man -a tarfoo successively shows the actual man pages to the user. Answer A is incorrect because man -k tarfoo shows every instance of the word tarfoo in all man page descriptions, not the actual pages. Answer B is incorrect because man -f tarfoo shows a list of the man pages that contain the discreet word tarfoo but not the actual man pages. Answer C is incorrect because man -c tarfoo is a formatting option and is not designed to display a set of successive pages.

8. What is the full path and filename of the file that is used to configure the man command variables and settings? Fill in the blank below with the full path and filename:

_____

The correct answer is /etc/man.config. The alternative answer is /etc/man.conf.

9. What is the name of the variable or option in the man configuration file that sets the viewer application? Fill in the blank below with just the value:

_____

The correct answer is **PAGER**. There are no alternative answers.

10. When viewing a man page, which of the following strings searches forward for a string **PROMPTING**? (Choose all that apply.)

- ❏ A. `?/PROMPTING`
- ❏ B. `:$s/Prompting/p`
- ❏ C. `/prompting`
- ❏ D. `^PROMPTING`
- ❏ E. `/PROMPTING`

Answers C and E are correct because the man pages are case-insensitive by default, so both return the desired text. Answer A is incorrect because a `?` in front of the `/PROMPTING` searches for `/PROMPTING`. Answer B is incorrect because it's a fake search with sed-like syntax. Answer D is incorrect because the `^` character searches for the text at the beginning of the line, but there needs to be a `/` character to initiate the search.

12

Managing Users and Groups

Terms you'll need to understand:

✓ Password database
✓ Profile
✓ Session
✓ User account
✓ User environment

Techniques you'll need to master:

✓ Adding users and groups
✓ Modifying users and groups
✓ Removing users and groups
✓ Locking or disabling accounts
✓ Managing password files
✓ Repairing password files

The Importance of User and Group Management

The importance of user and group administration cannot be emphasized enough. Your system is a target and users are the bullets in the gun. All an attacker has to do is get a user to give the attacker his username or password and she can attempt penetration.

This chapter covers one of the really interesting areas of system administration—supporting users and groups, enabling access, setting their default profiles and home directories, and putting the whack on them when they misbehave.

How the Kernel Understands Users and Groups

User and group accounts are not known to the kernel by the name we use and see, but by the user ID (UID) and group ID (GID) associated with the name. Two tables of static numbers in the kernel represent the 65,536 users and 65,536 groups that are possible on a Linux system.

The only association between the username and the UID is the entry in the /etc/passwd file that defines that user. The only association between the group name and the GID is the entry in the /etc/group file that defines that group.

 NOTE   Users must have a username entry in the **/etc/passwd** file to log in to the system. Users cannot log in as their UID, either; only the username is accepted.

What Accounts Are What?

The /etc/passwd file contains a number of service accounts, all of which are assigned UIDs that range from 0 to 100. Some of the more interesting (and exam-worthy) are shown here:

➤ **0**—The root user on the system

➤ **1**—The bin user, which is responsible for some system binaries and non-login accounts

➤ **48**—The apache user, which the HTTPD daemon runs as

➤ **99**—The nobody account, which is used for many things, particularly for anonymous access on FTP and HTTP servers, but also to map root accounts that attempt NFS access to shares that have been configured to deny access to the root user

Junior Sysadmins

I normally assign my junior sysadmin and server operator accounts UIDs in the 101–200 range, just to differentiate them from the other users and to make keeping track of them easier.

There is no difference between the UIDs permissions other than the **root** user (UID 0); all the rest are simply users.

Normal User Accounts

Typical users are assigned UIDs ranging from 500 to 60,000. This is fine for a single system, but it can cause problems in larger environments.

There are many reasons to start your users at the five-digit UID mark—in other words, with UIDs from 10,000 to 60,000. Chief among these reasons is having multiple systems that users log on to and having enough users that you pass the 500–999 mark. It's much neater and more organized to have the users who range across your wide area network with five-digit UIDs, such as 10001, for the purpose of using NFS and NIS.

If you can, force the use of a standardized UID and GID structure across all your enterprise systems. If you have more than 100 users, consider using NIS for managing how users log on to their systems.

NIS is outside the scope of this discussion and not on the LPI Level 1 objectives but is a great way to centralize account and password management across all machines in your environment.

User Entries in /etc/passwd

The user's entry in the /etc/passwd file consists of the following:

```
ross:x:500:100:Ross Brunson:/home/ross:/bin/bash2
```

The entries in the /etc/passwd file are as follows:

➤ ross—The username; this must be eight or fewer characters and should be lowercase.

➤ x—The password is stored in the /etc/shadow entry for this user; otherwise, it would be a garbled-looking long encrypted password string.

➤ 500—The user's UID. This is how the system sees the user. It doesn't see it by the name; that's only resolved on demand for showing it to the user.

➤ 100—The user's primary group, this group is forced onto all created objects as the group owner, except in situations where ownership inheritance has been set.

➤ Ross Brunson—This field is a description field (also known as the G.E. Common Operating System [gecos] for historical purposes). It can be blank or have a comment or full name in it. If you want the username to appear by default, place an & character in the field.

➤ /home/ross—The home directory field, this is optional (the user is dropped in the root directory on login) and by default points to a directory in /home that matches the username.

➤ /bin/bash2—The shell field, this is optional. If it's blank, the system assigns the /bin/sh shell to the user's login (/bin/sh is a symlink to /bin/bash).

 You might be asked about what information must be in the **/etc/passwd** user entry on the exam. The simple process of elimination will show you that the username, password, UID, and GID must be in the entry, but the description, home directory, and shell are optional.

Special Login Files

Several files affect the user's login experience and define when a user can log in and from where.

These files are as follows:

➤ /etc/login.defs—This file defines the user defaults, including entries for mail, password complexity and limitations, UID and GID min and max, and whether the user's home directory is created by default.

➤ /etc/nologin—When used as a shell for a user's account, this program displays a message that the account is unavailable and exits with a nonzero exit code. If the `/etc/nologin.txt` file exists, the contents of that file are shown instead of the normal message.

➤ `.hushlogin`—This file, if created in the user's home directory, does not do a mail check and displays the last login information or the message of the day to the user.

➤ `/etc/securetty`—This restrictions file specifies from where the root user is allowed to log in. If it does not exist, root can log in from any `tty`.

➤ `/etc/usertty`—This restrictions file is for normal users on systems that don't use pluggable authentication modules (PAMs, most current systems) and is used to set the login `ttys`, days, times, and systems the user can connect from.

➤ `/bin/false`—If the user's shell is set to `/bin/false`, the user cannot log in. `false` exists solely to exit with a non-zero value. This is best used for system accounts that should never be logged in to.

➤ `/etc/motd`—After a successful login, the `/etc/motd` file contents are displayed, right before the user's shell is executed. This is a great place for warning and legal messages to be displayed.

➤ `/etc/issue` and `/etc/issue.net`—These are displayed to console and Telnet users, respectively. These files are covered in more detail in Chapter 11, "Using Linux and GNU Documentation."

 Watch for questions about the files listed here. Questions focus on what happens when a file exists, if it's assigned as a shell, or what shows on a user's screen when she logs in to the system.

What Groups Are What?

Groups are easier to manage, there being correspondingly less of them, and their usage is simpler, too. A couple of interesting points must be made about groups on Linux. Without this understanding, you'll go nuts trying to use groups the wrong way.

Groups come in only one type—a grouping of users. No nesting of groups is possible in Linux or Unix. Users are assigned to groups in two methods:

➤ **Primary**—A GID appears in the `/etc/passwd` file entry in the fourth field, and this group is made the group owner of all created objects for this user.

NOTE

> The primary group for a user is special; if a user is assigned a primary group in the **/etc/passwd**, she does not have to be listed as a member in the **/etc/group** file because the GID in the **/etc/passwd** entry supersedes secondary group membership.

➤ **Secondary**—The user's name appears in the `/etc/group` entry for that group, the user is a member of that group, and she gets access to the resources that group is the group owner of.

> A group assigned as a primary group to any user cannot be deleted because doing so would orphan the user's account and cause untold problems for you and the user.

Groups are organized in much the same way that users are as far as the GID numbering group ID (GID) associated with the name. Two tables of static. Some interesting accounts are listed here:

➤ **0**—The root group; anyone who is a member of this group may have access to resources that are restricted to the root account.

➤ **1**—The bin group is similar to the bin account.

➤ **100**—The users group is where you can place normal users and then give them access to resources by assigning that group ownership of things that all users should have access to.

> The **wheel** group is not implemented by default on Linux systems. On BSD-related systems, a user cannot use the **su** command unless her account is a member of the **wheel** group, even if she knows the root password! Linux does not use this, but the group is there for compatibility.

A special situation exists primarily on Red Hat machines, in which a user account is created without a specific primary group assigned. In this case, the system creates and assigns a group whose GID matches the numerals in the user's UID, or the next incremented number available.

This is a security feature. If you have created a user and haven't assigned her a primary group, the system might assign her the users group as a primary group. This is a security risk because this user might be a contractor or an auditor and by default should not have access to the users group resources.

Debian creates the user with the primary group set to the users (100) group.

Group Entries in **/etc/group**

The entries in the /etc/group file are much simpler and shorter than the ones in the password file.

Group files consist of the following fields:

users:x:100:ross,snuffy

The entries in a group file consist of the following:

➤ users—The name of the group, which should be eight or fewer characters and lowercase.

➤ x—Again, the shadow passwords are kept in a different file. The group passwords are in /etc/gshadow.

➤ GID—This is the system's number for this group and is resolved with the group name for user viewing convenience.

➤ ross,snuffy—Users in the group are listed one after the other separated with a comma (,); no spaces should occur.

Group Passwords

Because users can have a only single primary group, if they need to create an object that has to be assigned another group as the group owner, users can change their primary group for a particular login session with the newgrp command.

The newgrp command doesn't alter the /etc/passwd file or even the /etc/group file; it just swaps out the primary group for the user in memory. Because users could change their primary group, you should have a security mechanism in place to keep them from changing their group to one they should not be using. A password can be assigned to the group with the gpasswd command, but there is only one password and you'll have to give it to every user who needs to use this functionality.

My recommendation is to use the SGID bit to set group ownership inheritance and stay away from group passwords.

Adding Users and Groups

Now that the ground rules are laid out, and the special situations with users and groups are outlined, the next task is to intelligently add users and groups to your system.

Although you can edit the /etc/passwd file directly and then run passwd to add a user to the system, it's not considered elegant by any means. One of the reasons to use the commands outlined here is that you might not be the only person accessing these files at a given time.

Adding Users with **useradd**

The /usr/sbin/useradd command is used to automate user additions, whereas the /usr/sbin/adduser script is a friendlier front-end (so the author claims) that simplifies the process. On some distributions, the adduser file can be a link to the useradd program.

 The exam focuses on the **useradd** command and doesn't include the **adduser** script.

Rather than show the syntax for the command, let's add a user to show how it works.

To add a user with the defaults, you would type

```
useradd snuffy
```

On a Red Hat machine, this creates the user snuffy with the next available UID, the GID set to a newly created group with that username as the group name, the same value as the UID for the GID, and a copy of the /etc/skel directory properly set up as the directory /home/snuffy.

On a Debian machine, this same command creates the user snuffy with the next available UID, the GID set to the users (100) group, and no created home directory.

To set up the same user on the Debian system, you'd have to specify the -m option to create the user's home directory. A more complex example is to create a user named ulogin with a particular home directory, a specific UID, a specialized skel or template directory, the user's group set as the primary group, and the user's full given name as the comment. To do this you would type

```
useradd -m -d /home2/ulogin -u 2112 -k /etc/skel_mktg -g 100 -c
➥"Ursula K. Login" ulogin
```

This creates the user with all the specialized information. On a Red Hat machine the /bin/bash shell is auto-supplied, whereas on a Debian machine the shell is blank by default, causing the system to assume the /bin/sh (a link to the /bin/bash) shell.

Other important useradd options are as follows:

➤ -D—Running useradd with this option displays the defaults contained in the /etc/default/useradd file.

➤ -e—This sets an expire date on the user; after that date the account is disabled (an * in the password field in the /etc/passwd file).

➤ -G—This sets secondary group membership at the account creation, something that is usually done afterward with the usermod command.

➤ -f—This is the number of days after the password has expired that the user can still log in. This is set to -1 by default; setting it to 0 disables the account when the password expires.

➤ -o—This allows the creation of a user with a nonunique UID. This is very dangerous and not recommended.

➤ -s—The full path and filename of the shell must follow the -s option.

The **useradd** Defaults

The useradd defaults are kept in /etc/default/useradd and can be altered with the use of the -D option followed by what needs to be updated. For example, to change the default shell from /bin/bash to /bin/sh, you would type this:

```
useradd -D -s /bin/sh
```

Debian uses this file. Using useradd -D -g 10 sets the file to a default group of wheel, and adding a user on Debian with the defaults picks this up. Red Hat uses the defaults except for the group, which you can force using the -n option to useradd, such as

```
useradd -mn snuffy
```

This causes the default Red Hat behavior to be excepted, and it picks up the default group from the defaults file.

Adding Groups with **groupadd**

The groupadd command is much simpler than useradd, with less options and shorter command lines. To add a group named somegroup with the defaults, you would type the following:

```
groupadd somegroup
```

To add a group with a particular GID, you would type

```
groupadd -g 1492 somegroup
```

Modifying Users and Groups

Creating users and groups is one thing, but being able to make them fit a changing system environment is another thing. Typically, you'll be adding and removing users from secondary groups, locking and unlocking accounts, and even changing a password expiration now and then.

Modifying User Accounts with usermod

To modify a user account with usermod, you need to decide which of the following options is needed:

➤ -c—The new description for the user.

➤ -d—The user's new home directory full path.

➤ -e—The date the user account will expire and be disabled.

➤ -f—The number of inactive days or the number of days a user can log in after the password expires.

➤ -g—The primary or initial group; single values are allowed—either the name or GID.

➤ -G—A single value or list of comma-separated values of groups the user is to be a member of.

➤ -l—The user's new login name. This does not affect the home directory name, and you might want to change that to reflect this new name.

➤ -s—The user's new shell full path and filename.

➤ -u—The user's new UID, with the home directory and subfiles being changed to the new UID; other files must be changed by hand.

➤ -L—This locks a user's account by altering the /etc/shadow file and prefixing the current encrypted password with an exclamation point (!).

➤ -U—This removes the lock on the user's account by removing the ! from in front of the encrypted password in the /etc/shadow file.

Another way to lock and unlock the user's account is to use the **passwd** command and its **-l** and **-u** options to accomplish the locking and unlocking. Be aware that if you're not using shadowed passwords, only the **usermod -L** and **usermod -U** commands will work properly; the **passwd -l** and **passwd -u** commands depend on shadowed passwords being present.

Modifying Groups with groupmod

groupmod has fewer options than usermod, and few reasons exist to use the command. It's primarily for altering the group's name and GID, not the group contents.

To modify a group's GID, you would type this:

```
groupmod -g 101 users
```

You should think twice before altering the GID of a group because you could orphan a lot of important files if you do. You must look in the /etc/passwd entries to see which users' primary groups will be affected. You should not attempt to change the GID of a group that has a user member currently logged in. On some machines, removing or orphaning the primary group of a user defaults to the staff (50) group.

Removing Users and Groups

Removing users and groups isn't difficult, but several options need attention. Removing accounts from the system isn't like on a Windows machine. Linux accounts can be re-created easily. Remember that Linux uses tables of static UIDs and GIDs, not SIDs.

Removing Users

Say a user has left the company and you are faced with either deleting the user account and leaving the user's home directory in place for his replacement or purging the system of the user by removing his account and home directory in one step.

Removing a user without affecting his home directory is simple. You just type the following:

```
userdel snuffy
```

To remove the user along with his home directory (the one configured in the /etc/passwd entry), you type this:

```
userdel -r snuffy
```

You cannot delete a currently logged-in user, so you must find out why he is still logged on. In some extreme cases, you must do a who to find out whether he is logged in and then do a ps aux ¦ grep snuffy to find out his login shell's PID. Before you kill his shell, use usermod -L snuffy to lock the account; then use kill -9 PID to log him off the system.

> Remember that deleting a user and his home directory with the **userdel -r** command only removes the account entry in **/etc/passwd** and the actual home directory as specified in **/etc/passwd**. It does not delete that user's owned files anywhere else on the system—that requires root user intervention and probably the **find** command.

The reason you shouldn't just remove a user's account and home directory is that usually either important files or important evidence exists in that directory. If you are planning to replace the user, keep the directory and just delete the user account. This leaves the home directory looking very strange with only a UID where the username was:

```
drwxr-sr-x   2 1002     staff       4096 Mar 18 07:17 snuffy
```

This is actually not a bad thing to see because it just means that the user who owned this home directory was deleted. However, because the home directory still belongs to the UID 1002 and the old user's login name was set as the directory name, you have everything you need to re-create the user or set up a new user.

Removing Groups

Essentially, all you have to do is confirm that the group has no members or isn't a primary group for any user account and it can be deleted at will. To delete a group, you would type the following:

```
groupdel grpname
```

> The majority of the questions on the exam focus on the **useradd**, **usermod**, and **userdel** commands. There isn't much to ask about the group commands, but there might be a couple of questions about them in the fill-in-the-blank questions just to see whether you're paying attention.

The Shadow Suite

Another important piece of your Linux machine with regard to security, users, and groups is its password database and the (hopefully!) installed Shadow Suite.

The Shadow Suite isa set of authentication tools and utilities that insinuates itself into the mix of the /etc/passwd file and user accounts. Without the use of the shadow tools, your encrypted passwords would be exposed to anyone who wanted to see them because they would be in the world-readable /etc/passwd file in field #2.

Encrypted Passwords and Shadow Fields

The following is an example of an entry with an encrypted password from an actual machine:

```
snuffy:$1$vEEOvj1b$GlzLuD9F..DjlQr/WXcJv1:501:10::/home/snuffy:/bin/sh
```

As you can see, an encrypted string appears in the second field, whereas in the next example, with shadow passwords, the encrypted string is replaced with x:

```
snuffy:x:501:10::/home/snuffy:/bin/sh
```

When shadow is installed, the system stores encrypted passwords in the /etc/shadow file for user accounts and the /etc/gshadow file for group accounts.

The fields in the /etc/shadow file contain the user's account password and other important information. An example of a shadow file entry would be

```
marty:2M@nY$3cR3Ts:11263:0:99999:7:5:2:
```

The fields in the /etc/shadow file are as follows:

➤ marty—The user's login name

➤ 2M@nY$3cR3Ts—An encrypted password string

➤ 11263—The days since January 1, 1970, that have elapsed since the password was last changed

➤ 0—The days that must elapse before the password *can* be changed (0 effectively allows immediate changes)

➤ 99999—The days before the password *must* be changed, (99999 effectively disables the need to change the password)

➤ 7—The number of days before the password expires when the user will be warned

➤ 5—The number of days before an account is disabled

➤ 2—The number of days since an account has been disabled

The last field in the file is reserved for future use and is not tested or much talked about.

shadow File Permissions

The permissions on the shadow files (shadow and gshadow) are important and appear on the exam. Because the shadow files aren't world-readable, and only the system updates them, your passwords are much safer than without shadow installed.

The shadow file permissions are prominently featured on the exam, as are the passwd and group files. Here is a listing of the files and permissions on both Red Hat and Debian:

```
/etc/passwd
Red Hat = -rw-r--r-- (644)
Debian  = -rw-r--r-- (644)

/etc/shadow
Red Hat = -r-------- (400)
Debian  = rw-r----- (640)
```

 As mentioned, these files and their permissions appear on the exams. It's important that you remember that Red Hat has a stricter permission setup than Debian, preserving the perverse nature of Linux and Unix.

Password Conversion

If you installed a system a few years ago, it might not have had the Shadow Suite on it; therefore, the encrypted passwords are there in the /etc/passwd file for anyone to see and possibly crack with easily available tools. If you've installed a system lately, however, the Shadow Tools are de rigueur and almost universally present.

If you had a machine that didn't have the Shadow Suite installed, you would first get the RPM or DEB file with the tools. Then, after installing it, you would have to run the tools to convert the passwords to the new file and format.

For example, if you found a passwd file in which apparently half of the accounts used encrypted passwords and half had the shadow x in the password field, you would run the command shown here:

```
pwconv
```

The pwconv command performs the following steps:

1. pwconv reads the /etc/passwd file and any existing /etc/shadow file.

2. pwconv removes any orphaned entries in the /etc/shadow that don't have a corresponding entry in the /etc/passwd file.

3. pwconv then updates any entries in the /etc/passwd file that exist in the /etc/shadow.

4. pwconv then creates any needed entries from the /etc/passwd entries in the /etc/shadow file.

5. pwconv replaces all the /etc/passwd file's encrypted passwords with a single x that means the password now resides in the /etc/shadow file entry for the user.

The pwunconv tool essentially reverses the process, removing the encrypted passwords from the /etc/shadow file and replacing the x in the /etc/passwd file with the matching encrypted password.

The grpconv and grpunconv tools are virtually identical to pwconv and pwunconv, but they act on the /etc/group and /etc/gshadow files.

Changing Passwords

Users' passwords are typically set to some easily remembered value by the root user when created, and the user is told to change them immediately.

It's important to remember who you are logged in as and what you type on the command line when changing a password. I've seen many a sysadmin change their own password instead of a user's because they were in a big hurry!

To change your own password, type

```
passwd
```

This prompts you for a password that must be entered twice for verification; then you're done. If you are doing this as a normal user, the user's current password is required before the new password will be accepted.

If you're changing another user's password, you would type the following:

```
passwd snuffy
```

Then you answer the same prompts about entering the password twice.

You can use the **pwck** command to troubleshoot the password-related files for errors. If **pwck** finds entries that don't have the right number of fields, it prompts you to delete the broken entry. Other problems it finds only show error or informational messages.

Aging Passwords

Users' passwords need to be changed frequently enough so that attackers don't have enough time to guess them. Most users want to come to work, get paid, and go home; system security is of much lower importance than convenience.

To age the passwords properly, use the `chage` command. The syntax for the `chage` command is

```
chage -option value username
```

The command acts on the /etc/shadow fields, with the following options:

➤ `-m`—Changes the `mindays` value, or how long after a password change the user must wait until it can be changed again. This is often set to 1/2 or 1/3 of the `maxdays` value.

➤ `-M`—Changes the `maxdays` value, which is the maximum number of days the password is valid.

➤ `-d`—Changes the `lastday` value, which is the number of days since January 1, 1970, since the password was last changed. Multiple date formats are allowed for readability, such as YYYY-MM-DD.

➤ `-E`—Changes the `expiredate` value, which is the number of days since January 1, 1970, that represents the day the user's account will be disabled. It also allows for the YYYY-MM-DD and other formats.

➤ `-I`—Changes the `inactive` value, or the number of days of inactivity (no logins) before the user account is locked, requiring root attention to reenable. Setting this to 0 disables the feature.

➤ `-W`—Changes the `warndays` value, or the number of days before the user must change her password. Only one warning is given until the password expires.

Thankfully, you don't have to memorize these values, other than for exam questions. Just typing `chage username` as the root user prompts you interactively for each value that can be configured for the specified user.

Users can use the -l option to view their own information, or the root user can view another user's information with this option:

```
chage -l snuffy
```

This produces the following output:

```
Minimum:            0
Maximum:            99999
Warning:            7
Inactive:           -1
Last Change:              Mar 19, 2004
Password Expires:         Never
Password Inactive:        Never
Account Expires:          Never
```

The passwd utility includes some of the previous options, such as these:

➤ -d—Disables a user account by removing its password.

➤ -n—Sets the minimum password lifetime in days.

➤ -x—Sets the maximum password lifetime in days.

➤ -w—Sets the warning number of days before the password expires.

➤ -i—Sets the number of days an account with an expired password can be inactive before it's locked.

➤ -s—Shows the user password information, such as what encryption is used and whether a password is set. This does not support multiple username targets.

skel Templates

When you use the useradd command and the -m option, a home directory is created for the user using the base directory and username. By default, the new home directory is a copy of the /etc/skel directory and its contents.

For example, useradd -m snuffy creates the home directory /home/snuffy. This home directory is copied by default from the /etc/skel directory, and the permissions are changed to suitable security for the user.

You can put just about anything in a new user's home directory by placing the files in the /etc/skel directory. It's even more elegant to create a set of /etc/skel_xxx directories to make creating certain groups of users easier.

For example, to make linking users to a shared directory easier, you might use the following steps:

1. Copy the /etc/skel directory to a new directory named /etc/skel_shared.

2. Create a symlink in that /etc/skel_shared directory that points to the /mnt/shared directory.

3. Next time you create a user, use the following syntax to specify a particular skel template directory:

```
useradd -m -k /etc/skel_shared ulogin
```

4. View the new /home/ulogin directory, and you'll see the symlink there ready for the user to cd into or double-click to get her into the /mnt/shared directory.

The user must be a member of the group that owns the shared directory, but all the rest work by default. Think about what other groups for which you could make customized **skel** directories.

Take care not to put your newly created **skel** directories under the existing **/etc/skel** structure because the entire directory tree will be copied as any default user's home directory, causing you some embarrassment.

User Variables

Next, you'll learn how to place certain limitations on a user's account.

If you wanted a user to be unable to create objects over a certain size or use too many resources, you could configure the ulimit settings for that user. The ulimit command is placed in the user's .bashrc file with one or some of the following options enabled:

➤ -c—Limits the size of core (crash dump) files

➤ -d—Limits the size of the user's process data

➤ -f—Limits the maximum size of files created in the shell

➤ -n—Limits the number of open file descriptors or open files allowed

➤ -t—Limits the amount of CPU time allowed to the user (expressed in seconds)

➤ -u—Limits the number of processes that a given user can run

➤ -v—Limits the maximum amount of virtual memory available to the shell

To check the user's ulimit settings, use this command:

```
ulimit -a
```

For the root account, this produces the output shown here:

```
unlimited
```

The `umask` is also set in the `.bashrc`, with the limitations discussed in previous chapters.

To view the `umask` value for the user, type the following command:

```
umask
```

This produces this output:

```
0022
```

To view the `umask` expressed in symbolic format, type the command shown here:

```
umask -S
```

This produces the following output:

```
u=rwx,g=rx,o=rx
```

Watch out for **umask** and **ulimit** on the exam. Remember that **ulimit** limits are related to object sizes, memory allowed, and CPU time; **umask** is specifically for setting a mask that affects the permissions of an object.

Exam Prep Questions

1. Which field in the /etc/shadow file sets the number of warning days before the user's password expires? Fill in just the numeral in the blank below:

   _____

   The correct answer is 6. There are no alternative answers.

2. If you saw the following output of the ls command, what would it indicate?

   ```
   drwxr-sr-x    2 1002    staff      4096 Mar 18 07:17 snuffy
   ```

   ○ A. The account was deleted.
   ○ B. The user's UID is missing.
   ○ C. The /etc/passwd file is corrupt.
   ○ D. The user's group is incorrect.

   Answer A is correct because this output indicates that the user's account associated with UID 1002 was deleted. Answer B is incorrect because, if the user's UID is missing, the user doesn't exist. Answer C is incorrect because the passwd file being corrupted would not cause this output. Answer D is incorrect because the user's group has nothing to do with the output, other than showing what the group owner is currently.

3. If you have created 10 accounts beginning with the UID of 501 and then deleted 501 and 504, what would the UID of the next user you create be by default? Write your answer in the blank below:

   _____

   The correct answer is 511. There are no alternative answers.

4. Which of the following fields must be in an /etc/passwd user account entry for it to be valid? (Choose all that apply.)

   ❑ A. Username
   ❑ B. UID
   ❑ C. GID
   ❑ D. Shell
   ❑ E. Home directory

   Answers A, B, and C are correct because they must exist for a valid entry in the user's account. Answers D and E are incorrect because they are optional for a valid user's account.

5. Which directory is copied by default to a newly created user's home directory when the -m option is used for useradd? Fill in the full path and name of the directory in the blank below:

   _____

   The correct answer is /etc/skel. There are no alternative answers.

6. Which command is used to set the password expiration, warning, and other /etc/shadow file field information interactively?

○ A. passwd

○ B. chpass

○ C. vipw

○ D. chage

Answer D is correct because using the chage username command *interactively* asks and sets the /etc/shadow options. Answer A is incorrect because the passwd command doesn't interactively change the options in the /etc/shadow file. Answer B is incorrect because there is no such thing as a chgpass command. Answer C is incorrect because the vipw command is used to alter the /etc/passwd file.

7. If you see a passwd file that apparently contains some encrypted passwords and what appear to be x shadow password indicators in the second field, which command would you use to attempt to fix this?

○ A. chown

○ B. pwconv

○ C. pwck

○ D. chfn

Answer B is correct because pwconv is used to convert passwd files to shadow files. Answer A is incorrect because the chown command is used to change ownership of objects. Answer C is incorrect because the pwck file checks the validity of the user accounts but does not convert them to shadow entries. Answer D is incorrect because chfn changes the finger-related information and has nothing to do with the encrypted passwords.

8. Which command enables a user to alter her primary group until they log out? Fill in the blank below with just the name of the command:

_____

The correct answer is newgrp. There are no alternative answers.

9. What are the default permissions for the Debian and Red Hat /etc/passwd files? Fill in the blank below with the three numerals that represent the octal value for the permissions:

_____

The correct answer is 644. There are no alternative answers.

10. Which command shows the user which settings are in place for the maximum allowable size of files created in the shell, if configured?

○ A. umask

○ B. dmesg

○ C. ulimit

○ D. perms

Answer C is correct because the `ulimit` command shows the maximum size of files that can be created in the shell if configured. Answer A is incorrect because the `umask` command shows the altered permissions for created objects. Answer B is incorrect because `dmesg` is for system initialization log file viewing. Answer D is incorrect because there isn't a `perms` command.

13

System Administration

. . . .

Terms you'll need to understand:

✓ Archive
✓ Compression
✓ Daemons
✓ Facilities
✓ Levels
✓ Scheduling
✓ Services
✓ Tarball

Techniques you'll need to master:

✓ Managing daemons
✓ Configuring system logging
✓ Troubleshooting system logs
✓ Scheduling jobs
✓ Compressing, uncompressing, and viewing archives
✓ Configuring system time

Managing System Services

One task that needs some more attention is how to start, stop, and perform other functions with daemons and services on your Linux box.

Daemons can be interacted with in several ways, depending on the system's distribution and the installed commands and utilities.

Controlling Your Daemons

First is the common brute-force method, which involves using the full path to the daemon in the init.d directory with a set of commands that affect the daemon. These commands and the functions they perform are set in the executable scripts that inhabit the init.d directory.

For example, to start the Samba daemon on a Debian machine, you might type

```
/etc/init.d/smb start
```

This produces the following output:

```
Starting Samba Daemons: smbd nmbd.
```

On a Red Hat machine, the same method (adding the rc.d directory to the path) produces similar output with [OK] messages on the right of the screen indicating the daemon has started.

The daemons in the init.d directory have keywords that control their behaviors, with the following being the most common among the commands:

➤ start—Starts the daemon

➤ stop—Stops the daemon

➤ status—Displays the status or state (running or stopped) of the daemon

➤ reload—Restarts and rereads the configuration files for the daemon

➤ force-restart—A combination of a SIGHUP and a SIGKILL that is used when a daemon is not responding to other signals

In some instances, the daemon itself might be the only control mechanism available. Red Hat has a service command that substitutes itself for the full path of the daemons, but Debian doesn't include such a tool. You can easily create a small script that substitutes itself for the service command, such as the following:

```
#!/bin/bash
# Service control script "sv"
/etc/init.d/$1 $2
```

This script should be set to executable with this command:

```
chmod +x sv
```

To run it, either place it in the path or prefix it with ./. The syntax to start a service is

```
sv samba start
```

kill and killall

Controlling daemons can also include using the `kill` and `killall` commands, which work on the PID and command name, respectively.

`kill` and `killall` use the same signals; other than using PIDs and names, they are functionally similar. The `kill` command is fairly simplistic:

```
ps aux ¦ grep smb
```

This returns the output shown here:

```
root   388  0.0  0.9  7324  2460  ?  S  00:38  /usr/sbin/smbd -D
```

You then take the number from the second column and supply it as the argument to the `kill` command:

```
kill 388
```

If the program doesn't respond, or it is the parent process of a zombied process, use an *absolute kill* or the kill command with a -9 option to send the SIGKILL signal, such as

```
kill -9 388
```

The `killall` command works similarly. You can name the runaway or undesired processes by the actual command that is running, which is the last column of the `ps` output.

To kill all running instances of the Mozilla browser on your machine, as root you enter

```
killall mozilla-bin
```

If, for some reason, the browser doesn't respond, use the kill command with the -9 option to send a SIGKILL or absolute kill, like so:

```
killall -9 mozilla-bin
```

This forcibly removes the processes from memory, without even allowing them time to clean up memory and disk processes. So, be aware that using the `kill` and `killall` commands to abruptly terminate processes can cause issues with memory usage over time and can even cause you to spend some quality time with fsck.

System Logging

Logs are either text or a binary data file to which events are written, usually appending later events to the end of the file. Keeping an eye on your logged events is key to good system administration, but it's not very popular unless an administrator is unusually conscientious or has been horribly burned by not checking them.

Systems that provide logins to users and services to clients and participate in your production environment especially require proper use of logging.

Types of Logging

Logging is performed in several ways on a Linux system, depending on the software generating the log messages and the system's logging configuration. The various types of logs typically generated on a Linux system are

➤ **Software logs**—Generated by running applications, these show the status of applications, errors, and warnings.

➤ **System logs**—Generated by syslogd, these report the status of disks, hardware, and system processes.

➤ **Kernel logs**—Generated by klogd, these are concerned with kernel processes, statistics, and so on.

Applications logging is the most unstructured set of logs on the system. An application can write log entries to a system facility in a standard manner or simply keep its own logs in the file system somewhere. The man page for the application should contain logging information.

Kernel and system logging are performed by the syslogd utility or one of its component pieces. The system logging functionality is provided by the syslogd daemon, whereas kernel logging is provided by the klogd daemon, either independently or in conjunction with syslogd.

Default System Log File

The default system log file is /var/log/messages and is a great place to check for the latest happenings. This log file is typically the recipient of all informational class messages generated on the system. For example, to see whether a user has attempted to log in to the system, you can use the following command to search for that user's entries in the messages file:

```
grep rbrunson /var/log/messages
```

This returns from zero to multiple lines of output similar to the following:

```
Mar 18 14:13:36 localhost  -- rbrunson[1215]: LOGIN ON tty1 BY rbrunson
```

To watch this log file, or *tail* it, log in to a separate console and run the following command:

```
tail -f /var/log/messages
```

This shows the last 10 lines of the file by default. Because you've told it to follow the log file, any new entries appear at the bottom of the console, pushing previous entries upward and eventually out of sight.

You can place log files in any location, but the majority of system log files are kept in the /var/log directory.

Facilities and Priorities

The /etc/syslog.conf file is where the logging functionality, selectors, and targets are defined. A *selector* is the combination of a facility(s) and a priority(s). A *facility* is a predefined set of categories that group messages into common sets. A *priority* is a level of message, from purely informational to extreme emergency. These lend importance to the events being logged on the system.

The facilities as defined on a Linux system are

Facility	Meaning
authpriv	Security/authorization messages (**auth** and **security** are no longer used)
cron	Clock daemon (**cron** and **at**)
daemon	System daemons without a separate facility value
ftp	FTP daemon
kern	Kernel messages
lpr	Line printer subsystem
mail	**Mail** subsystem
news	**USENET** news subsystem
syslog	Messages generated internally by **syslogd**
user	Generic user-level messages
uucp	**UUCP** subsystem

Several other facilities exist that aren't used commonly and are not included in the previous table:

➤ `mark`—This is for internal use only; by default, every 20 minutes a time mark is sent to the syslog facility to provide a time mark for reference.

➤ `local0` to `local7`—These are open for sysadmin use or can be used for particular functions by programs and daemons; however, these are marked as available for local usage.

Expect questions about which facility represents which functionality on the system. A typical example might be as follows:

Which facility for **syslogd** represents a user's login success and failure?

The answer would be **auth** or **authpriv**.

Questions of this variety might ask about any of the facilities and the type of messages they receive.

The priorities as defined on a Linux system are as follows:

Priority	Meaning
emerg	System is unusable.
alert	Action must be taken immediately.
crit	Critical conditions.
err	Error conditions.
warning	Warning conditions.
notice	Normal, but significant, condition.
info	Informational message.
debug	Debug-level message.

Expect questions about which priority represents the highest and lowest priority and which priority isn't included in the use of the * (asterisk) character. The **debug** priority isn't included when the * (asterisk) is specified, so to include it along with the rest you must specifically include it, such as

facility.debug

This sends all levels, from **debug** and above, to the desired target.

Actions

When a selector is defined, it contains at least a facility and a priority and points to an action, usually a local file located on a mounted file system, a device, or a username `glob`.

Common options for actions include

➤ **Regular file**—A real file, one that can be accessed and written to, pre-fixed with a full path and then the filename.

➤ **Named pipes**—These are real device files that link to other systems or destinations, created with the `mkfifo` command.

➤ **Terminal/console**—`/dev/tty` files and `/dev/console` are the usual destinations. Any user logged in to that console sees the messages.

➤ **Remote machine**—By prefixing the hostname of a logging host with an @, such as `@pbunyan`, log entries can be collected on a single machine.

➤ **Usernames**—A user or list of users separated by commas that will receive the messages if they are logged in.

➤ **Everyone**—Using an * (asterisk) character sends messages to all logged-in users. This is typically reserved for emergency or catastrophic system messages.

You'll be tested on whether a message shows up on the console with **/dev/console** or using the **xconsole** pipe (**/dev/xconsole**). This is represented in the **syslog.conf** by the action l/**dev/xconsole**; it accepts any output meant for the console and sends it to the console of a shell open in the console's X session.

To use the **xconsole**, you would use the following command:

xconsole -file /dev/xconsole

Specifiers

A *specifier* is a character that replaces either one or both of the facility-priority pairing. The default behavior is to use a dot (.) to separate the facility and priority, which causes the specified priority and higher to be logged for the facility. An example of this would be the following line:

```
user.info      /var/log/userlog
```

The use of a . between `user` and `info` means that all messages of an `info` or higher priority generated by the user facility will be logged to the `/var/log/userlog` log file.

To alter this, several other specifiers have been defined. They are as follows:

➤ *—Used as a priority, this character causes all priorities of `info` and above to be logged. Used as a facility, it causes all facilities to be logged.

➤ =—This restricts the logging to the specified priority, such as `user.=crit`.

➤ !—This is used to cause a particular priority to be excluded from logging.

➤ --—A minus sign is used to prefix a target file to indicate that syslogd shouldn't flush the buffers to disk after a write. This improves performance, but if the system crashes, some logs might be lost.

Putting It All Together

Now that we've defined where logging is configured, what logging does, what facilities and levels are, and what an action and a specifier is, it's time to put all this together. Remember that you're in the `syslog.conf` file and configuring where the system log entries will be sent to.

The following are examples that occur in the real world or make a good point. I've attempted to cover every instance that might occur on the exams. The examples are arranged from simplest to most complex.

Syslog Entry Examples

To log every facility at every priority level except debug to a log file, you'd use the following:

```
*.*            /var/log/somelog
```

To log all user facility messages of warning and higher to a file named `/var/log/userlog`, you'd use the following:

```
user.warning      /var/log/userlog
```

To log all messages of info or higher priority from the user facility to all logged in users, you'd use this:

```
user.*         *
```

If a user is listed as a target and isn't logged in, the message isn't sent and no extra errors are logged as a result of the message being undeliverable.

To log all messages from the auth and daemon facilities to the console of the root user, if logged on, you'd use this:

```
auth.*;daemon.*   root
```

To log all auth messages except emerg to the console of the root user if he's logged on, you'd use the command shown here:

```
auth.!=emerg      root
```

To log all the messages from the news facility from info to crit and not alert or emerg to the console of the newsboy user, you'd use the command shown here:

```
news.!alert    newsboy
```

 The following line sends all messages (except debug) to the **tty12** console, which can be reached by pressing Alt+F12 or Ctrl+Alt+F12 to switch to the console that is defined by **/dev/tty12**:

```
*.*    /dev/tty12
```

You must HUP or restart the **syslogd** daemon to have this take effect.

Custom Log Entries

The logger command is often used in scripts to put entries into the system log facilities on demand. It has the capability to generate almost any log file entry that the system can accept, including levels of severity.

A typical logger command is used to write that a particular event was concluded, such as

```
logger Backup succeeded on host snuffy
```

The logger command can also be used to submit log entries that match facilities and are of the different severities. To submit a log entry to the user facility about a failed backup with a severity of crit, you would use this command:

```
logger -p user.crit Backup failed on host snuffy
```

Using tail -n 5 on the /var/log/messages file would display something like the following:

```
Mar 19 18:06:52 localhost network:
➥Bringing up loopback interface:  succeeded
Mar 19 18:07:05 localhost network:
➥Bringing up interface eth0:  succeeded
Mar 19 18:07:31 localhost sshd(pam_unix)[3838]:
➥session opened for user root by (uid=0)
Mar 19 20:38:39 localhost sshd(pam_unix)[4556]:
➥session opened for user root by (uid=0)
Mar 19 20:53:39 localhost root:
➥backup failed on host snuffy
```

Security Log Files

Several log files affect system security, particularly the capability to query with the who, last, lastlog, and w commands.

Log File	Purpose	Related Commands
/var/log/wtmp	Login times and durations for users	last, w, updwtmp
/var/run/utmp	Current user information about logins	finger, who, login
/var/log/lastlog	Login dates, times, and durations for users	lastlog

The last command uses the files /var/log/utmp and /var/log/btmp if they exist to show information about users who have recently logged in. By default, it shows a screenful of mixed user entries, or you can restrict it to a particular user:

```
last
```

This produces output similar to

```
rbrunson tty1      Thu Mar 18 14:13 - 21:49  (07:36)
rbrunson tty1      Tue Mar 16 16:10 - 16:23  (00:12)
rbrunson tty1      Tue Mar 16 15:59 - 16:10  (00:11)
rbrunson pts/2     Tue Mar 16 15:47 - 16:10  (00:23)
```

The w and who commands are often used to determine which users are on the system, and they refer to the /var/log/wtmp and /var/run/utmp files, respectively. The main difference between the programs' output can be seen by comparing the output.

Output from the w command looks like this:

```
 3:38pm  up 1 day, 10:53,  2 users,  load average: 0.00, 0.00, 0.00
USER    TTY     FROM           LOGIN@  IDLE   JCPU   PCPU  WHAT
root    pts/0   192.168.1.100  20Mar04 34:53m 0.41s  0.01s man xconsole
root    pts/1   192.168.1.100  3:30pm  0.00s  0.19s  0.01s w
```

Output from the who command looks like this:

```
root    pts/0   Mar 20 17:46 (192.168.1.100)
root    pts/1   Apr  1 15:30 (192.168.1.100)
```

As you can see, the w command puts out a lot more information but includes two header lines, making it inherently inaccurate for counting users on the system with the wc command.

You can disable a normal user's ability to get information from the **w** and **who** commands by removing the world or other readable bit from the **/var/run/utmp** log file. The **w** and **who** commands will still run, but they will display no data if the executing user is a normal user.

The lastlog command is one of the more useful logging commands because it shows the contents of the lastlog log file, sorting the output by user ID. If a user has never logged in, though, it prints `**Never logged in**` instead of port and time information.

 The **lastlog** command shows the **/var/log/lastlog** log file, which is a Unicode file that contains a lot of binary code and information and should be viewed primarily with the **lastlog** command. If you mess up your terminal's formatting by using **cat** on this file, use the **reset** command to reset your terminal.

To show a list of users who have logged in, particularly to check that system accounts have not been cracked and logged in to the system, use the following command:

```
lastlog | grep -iv "never logged in"
```

This produces output similar to the following:

```
Username      Port     From           Latest
root          pts/1    192.168.1.100  Thu Apr  1 15:30:52 -0500
rbrunson      tty1                    Thu Mar 18 14:13:36 -0500
```

The use of the `grep` command's `-v` option causes all the lines that match the search term to not be shown, leaving you with a list of users who have logged in to the system since it was installed.

You can also limit the display of `lastlog` entries to a particular username with the `-u` username option:

```
lastlog -u rbrunson
```

This returns the following output:

```
Username      Port     From           Latest
rbrunson      tty1                    Thu Mar 18 14:13:36 -0500
```

You can also display entries that are newer than a value of days, such as entries that have occurred in the last 5 days:

```
lastlog -t 5
```

This returns the following output:

```
Username      Port     From           Latest
root          pts/1    192.168.1.100  Thu Apr  1 15:30:52 -0500
rbrunson      tty1                    Thu Mar 30 14:13:36 -0500
```

Archiving your log files can be accomplished either manually or by using the `logrotate` command. When the `logrotate` command is configured properly and run regularly, it archives, compresses, removes, and mails log files in accordance with the configuration.

The `logrotate` command uses `/etc/logrotate.conf` as its configuration file, with entries in the file allowing you to set log rotation parameters that depend on date or log size to kick off archiving, compressing, and emailing the log file to a central host if desired.

> The **logrotate** command and the **/etc/logrotate.conf** file's existence and function are tested on the exam, but their actual use is outside the objectives and beyond our discussion.

Scheduling and Running Tasks

Three main utilities schedule tasks on a Linux system, and they all have advantages and disadvantages. Any busy sysadmin will recognize the need for a scheduling tool, if only so that repetitive tasks are actually carried out on time and often enough.

The at Command

The `at` command is designed to run a task once at a specific time. The `at` command's tasks or jobs are queued up in the `/var/spool/at` directory, with a single file representing each job.

A typical `at` job is intended to take care of the one-off or very infrequent jobs that take place at odd times. For example, many sysadmins remind themselves of meetings or to perform some task with `at`:

```
at 2pm today
at> echo "take a break"
at> <EOT>
job 1 at 2004-04-02 14:00
```

You type the first line of the previous code block (`at 2pm today`) at the command line, causing the `at>` prompt to appear. Then you type the command you want to execute, press Enter, and press Ctrl+D to end the task. Ending the task shows the `<EOT>` notice, followed by a line that echoes the job's scheduling information.

The `at` command uses a variety of time specifiers, some very complex and some very simple:

➤ `midnight`—Runs the task at 00:00 on the current day.

➤ `noon`—Runs the task at 12:00 on the current day.

➤ `teatime`—Runs the task at 16:00 (at's British roots are evident).

➤ `time-of-day`—Such as 2 p.m. or 5 a.m.

➤ `date`—You can specify a time on a specific day, such as `2pm jul 23` or `4am 121504`.

➤ `now + time`—You can specify any number of minutes, hours, days, and weeks from the current time, such as `now + 30 minutes`.

at-related Commands and Files

The `at` command just starts the jobs. A couple of commands can help you manage the `at` jobs on the system, including these:

➤ `atq`—This shows the jobs in the `at` queue with the job number, date and time, and executing user (this also can be seen with `at -l`).

➤ `atrm`—This deletes at jobs by job number, which is determined by using the previous command and the syntax `atrm #` (where # is the job number).

at has a set of security files—`/etc/at.allow` and `/etc/at.deny`—which allow users to or prevent users from queuing up at jobs. If the `at.allow` file exists and contains usernames, only those users are allowed to use `at`. If the `at.deny` file exists and contains usernames, those users are denied and all others are allowed. If neither file exists, only the root user is allowed to submit at jobs.

The **batch** Command

Using the `batch` command is relatively simple; it's somewhat of an extension of the at command and shares the same `man` page. The `batch` command is used to run tasks or jobs at no specific time, but at a particular threshold of system utilization. As you can imagine, some systems are quite busy and you need to determine which jobs might need to be run with another scheduling utility if they are time-sensitive.

By default, `batch` runs jobs once at a future time when system utilization is less than or equal to 0.8 average load for the machine. This can be configured by specifying the desired utilization average with the `atrun` command, such as

```
atrun -l 20
```

This sets the threshold that `batch` will watch to an average load of 20% of system utilization, and if system utilization drops below that average, the `batch` job is run.

Submitting batch jobs is similar to at, and it even uses the at prompt and interface. To submit a compile job that will run when the system threshold is reached, you'd use the following:

```
batch
at> bigcompile
at> <EOT>
job 6 at 2004-04-02 13:19
```

You can create a job with at or batch and then cat the file by using a command such as

```
cat /var/spool/at/a000030112ea5c
```

at's spooled jobs use a prefix of the letter *a*, whereas batch jobs use the letter *b* as a prefix. When you view the file, notice all the environment settings stored in the job, including a line that exports the username that was used to submit the job.

Remember that **at** and **batch** both export a lot of information when the job is run, which goes away after that shell is closed. **at** and **batch** jobs are run in a replica of the environment that existed at the time the job was submitted.

Also, if you don't insert the full path of commands when executing them with **cron**, you will likely get error messages about missing paths, file not found, and so on.

Using cron to Schedule Tasks

The at and batch commands run jobs one time only, but the cron daemon and its associated commands and configuration files are designed to regularly and reliably execute tasks until the tasks or cron job is deleted.

cron checks every minute for any tasks that need to be run and mails any output that is produced or needs to be checked to the submitting or configured user.

cron Components

Several components of the cron environment exist, a list of which includes

➤ crond—The cron daemon, which runs in the background and watches the submitted jobs for execution times.

➤ crontab—The command that is used to view, submit, and otherwise manage the various user or system-specific crontab-configuration files.

➤ /var/spool/cron—Jobs are stored in files within this directory that match the submitting user's name, such as /var/spool/cron/root for the root user.

➤ /etc/crontab—This file sets the directories that correspond to hourly, daily, weekly, and monthly cron jobs.

On most implementations of cron, the system crontab is the same as the root user's crontab, where crontab isn't the executable that is used later, but the name of a file that is created in the /var/spool/cron directory that matches the submitting user's name.

Managing cron's Job Tables

Almost all the editing of the user or root/system's crontab files is done via the crontab command. This command has plenty of options that help edit the crontab files, including

➤ -e—Followed by a username, this allows the root user to edit that user's crontab (that is, crontab -e henry).

➤ -l—This is used to list the cron jobs submitted for the current user. You can use the -u username in addition to list a particular user's jobs.

➤ -r—This option zeros out the current user's crontab file, or you can use it with the -u username option to zero out a particular user's file.

When you use the crontab -e command to edit the current user's crontab file, the file is loaded into vi or the default editor and shown just as any regular file would be in a vi session.

Saving and exiting the crontab file after you've made changes is all that's needed to submit the crontab file to the crond process. No HUPping or restarting of the daemons is necessary.

The fact that users can configure very few daemons as normal users and the **ability to use the crontab command to configure the cron** daemon are things you should remember when answering **cron** questions on the exam.

Submitting a cron Job

Like many other areas of Linux, cron jobs can be simple and easy to understand or very complex and difficult. The level of cron entry we'll cover stops short of the mind-numbing level and focuses on simple to relatively complex entries.

A `cron` entry is normally made up of six fields, an example of which is shown here:

```
30    *    *    *    1-5    /root/script
```

This `cron` entry runs a script every 30 minutes Monday through Friday. The fields are read from the left starting with minutes, to the right ending with the command being run. Being able to properly recognize these fields is very important, and they bear some explanation:

Field	Possible Values
Minute	**0–59** (* means every minute on the minute)
Hour	**0–23** (* means every hour on the hour)
Day of Month	**0–31** (* means every day)
Month	**1–12** (* means every month; you can use names)
Day of Week	**0–7** (**0** and **7** both mean Sunday; you can use names)

Not every `cron` entry has to consist of six fields. Alternative options consist of only two fields—the date/time and the command—such as

```
@reboot /sbin/fsck
```

The @ options that are most likely to be used are

➤ `@reboot`—This runs a command only once at the machine's startup.

➤ `@midnight`—This runs a command once a day at `0 0 * * *`.

➤ `@daily`—This is the same thing as `@midnight`.

➤ `@weekly`—This runs a command once a week at `0 0 * * 0`.

➤ `@monthly`—This runs a command once a month at `0 0 1 * *`.

➤ `@annually`—This runs a command once a year at `0 0 1 1 *`.

➤ `@yearly`—This is the same thing as `@annually`.

Submitting a `cron` job with the various settings for the date and time fields is accomplished with the `crontab -e` command. Plan what you want to accomplish and then fill in the fields for that entry, being sure to separate the fields with spaces.

Let's dissect a few entries to help you understand how `cron` entries work. A simple entry that runs a script every minute of every day of every month with no restrictions on the day of the month or day of the week would look like this:

```
* * * * * script
```

Of course, this would run the script every minute of every hour all month long for the whole year.

An example of a more useful `crontab` entry would be running a script every day at 1 a.m.:

```
0 1 * * * script
```

Now, let's run that same script every 30 minutes past the hour every hour of the day:

```
30 * * * * script
```

Now, let's run the script at 10 minutes past the hour, every hour from 0900 to 1700 (9 a.m. to 5 p.m.):

```
10 9-17 * * * script
```

Let's get a little more complex and run the script every 20 minutes during the hours of 9, 12, and 15 (starting at the top of the hour each time):

```
/20 9,12,15 * * * script
```

Watch for the use of / or step values with minute or hour fields. If a minute field has a value of **/30**, the event occurs every half hour, whereas **30** means it occurs at 30 minutes after the hour but only once an hour.

If a step has a number before it and one after it (such as **1/2** in the hour field), it starts at 1 a.m. and specifies every other hour. So, it would run at 1 a.m., 3 a.m., 5 a.m., 7 a.m., 9 a.m., 11 a.m., and so on.

A more complex example includes having a script run at a particular minute every hour, from the 1st through the 15th of the month:

```
17 * 1-15 * * script
```

This can be done with days of the week, too, where this entry executes the script Monday, Wednesday, and Friday from 9 a.m. to 5 p.m. at 21 minutes after the hour:

```
21 9-17 * * 1,3,5 script
```

If a conflict occurs in which a particular job is configured to only execute from the 1st to the 15th of the month, yet it's also set to execute on Monday, Wednesday, and Friday, it will fail to execute on Monday, Wednesday, or Friday if those days of the month are outside of the 1st through 15th.

Controlling User Access to cron

Just as the at command enables you to restrict users with allow and deny files, the /etc/cron.allow and /etc/cron.deny files allow or deny access by specific users.

If the etc/cron.allow exists, all usernames in the file are allowed to use cron and all else are denied.

If the /etc/cron.deny exists, all usernames in the file are denied access to cron and all others are allowed.

Take care not to include a user's name in both the /etc/cron.deny and /etc/cron.allow files. You might decide to allow all but a few and configure those users in the deny file or deny all but a lucky few users and put their names in the allow file.

If a user's name exists in both of the files, it's misconfigured and the user will be unable to use cron.

Watch for tricky **cron** entries. In particular, remember that **cron** doesn't store the user's environment, so you might have to alter the ownership of a command or use absolute paths to make a particular script run properly.

Archiving and Backing Up

When you install a system, realize that at some future time you'll experience a glitch or problem and want to restore some or all of that system to a previous state. This requires a thorough understanding of the various commands that provide archive or backup and restore operations on your Linux systems.

You have probably heard all about how important backups are. They're sort of like seat belts for your server, but many still ignore this important task. Although the exam will cover these important tasks, it covers them from an operation and functional perspective, except for a few key questions about what is more effective or safer.

Planning a Backup Scenario

Backups and restores require a plan, and with any plan you have to ask yourself some important questions:

➤ What do I need to back up? (Files, directories, and so on)

➤ How often do I need to back up? (Daily, weekly, and so on)

➤ What media should I use? (CDR/W, tape, HD, and so on)

➤ When should I back up? (During a slow or down time, if any)

There are various methods to backing up data. You need to understand that, if a system has just been installed, every file on the system has an archive attribute set to on, or changed. This is important for when you want to do anything other than a full backup of a system. After a full backup, all the files should have the archive bit set to off; thus, any incremental backups from that point will take only new or changed files.

The differences between the backup options are important. The following list lays out the possibilities and what they do to the `archive` attribute:

➤ **Copy**—Copies files, effectively backing them up. No archive bits are reset.

➤ **Full**—Backs up all the files on the system. The archive bit is reset for all files.

➤ **Incremental**—Backs up every file that has an archive bit set (setting each bit to off). Essentially, this is a differential of new or changed files since the last full or incremental backup.

➤ **Differential**—Backs up all the files with the archive bit set since the last full or incremental, but it doesn't change the archive bit state.

Each of the backup commands handles these types of backup operations differently, and this is beyond the scope of this discussion.

Expect to be questioned about the following scenario: A full backup is done on a Friday or at month end; then a series of differential backups, a series of incremental backups, or a combination of the two is performed; and then a crash occurs. You'll need to parse the questions to find out how many tapes are required of which variety to restore the system to its state at the time of the last backup.

Backup Commands

A number of backup options are available for Linux systems. Some are more useful than others, and some act on files, whereas others work best on partitions or disks as a unit.

Backup commands on the exams include the following:

➤ `cpio`

➤ `tar`

➤ `compress` and `uncompress`

➤ gzip and gunzip

➤ bzip2 and bunzip2

Using cpio

 The **cpio** command appears extensively in the Level 2 LPI objectives. This level of the exam might ask you about the **cpio** command at only the simplest levels, such as knowing that it exists, how it works in general terms, and whether it can be used to back up a Linux system.

The cpio command actions all treat the file system as the home base. If you are copying out, it's from the file system out to another file. The same is true with copying in—it's from a file into the file system.

The cpio command has three options for acting on files and file systems:

➤ -o or --create—This copies files to an archive using a list of files typically created by the find command.

➤ -i or --extract—This copies files into the file system from an archive or a list of the archive contents.

➤ -p or --pass-through—This copies files from one directory tree to another without the use of an archive, essentially performing the same function as the cp -r command.

The cpio command accepts a list of files in a one-file-per-line format and uses this list to send the archived files to either the standard output or an archive file you specify.

cpio supports a variety of archive formats, including binary, ASCII, crc, and tar, to name the most relevant.

An example of creating a cpio archive from the files in the current directory is shown here:

```
find . "*" ¦ cpio -o > archive.cpio
```

This outputs the list of files found by this particular find command, with the cpio command taking the entirety of the files and sending them to the archive.cpio file by redirecting standard output to the file.

The **cpio** command doesn't gather files to be archived by itself, so be aware that using either the **find** or **ls** command is necessary to feed **cpio** a list of filenames. For example, if you needed to archive all the files that have an extension of **.txt** in the current directory to a **cpio** archive named **txt.cpio**, you would use the following command:

ls *.txt | cpio -o > txt.cpio

Using tar

The tar command is relatively complex, too. It's used by default to take a grouping of files and create a single container .tar file that holds the individual files. Although it's conventional wisdom that tar doesn't compress the contents, this is not true because some compression is involved.

The tar command also can utilize or snap in various archive commands, particularly the gzip/gunzip and bzip2/bunzip2 commands by the use of special option characters. This has the effect of creating a compressed archive file, typically named .tar.gz for gzip-compressed files and .tar.bz2 for bzip2-compressed files.

As Figure 13.1 shows, the tar command has three main methods that act on files or tar archives. You can remember all the possible first letters with the acronym acdrtux. Also, any tar command must start with one of those letters. A more explanatory list of the options is shown here:

➤ A—Appends tar files to an archive

➤ c—Creates an archive

➤ d—Compares an archive and a file system and reports the differences

➤ r—Appends files to the end of an archive

➤ t—Lists the contents of an archive

➤ u—Updates an archive with changed or new files

➤ x—Expands or unarchives the archive

Although the previously listed options can be used with tar, reality is more limited. Figure 13.1 explains the method that most tar commands follow.

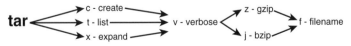

Figure 13.1   The **tar** command's methods.

As you can see, most `tar` commands create, list, or expand an archive, with the addition of the verbose option to see the full `ls -l` style output of each file. If you need to compress or uncompress an archive, the `-z` option for `gzip`/`gunzip` and the `-j` option for `bzip2`/`bunzip2` are useful. Or, it can be left out entirely when working with `.tar` files. Finally, you must specify the `-f` (for filename) option so `tar` knows to which file you are referring (remember that everything on a Linux system can be referred to as a file).

Creating tar Archives

When you're creating an archive with `tar`, you should think about what you want to archive, where you want the resulting archive to be created, and what compression if any you want to use.

To create a simple `tar` archive, the options you need are as follows:

```
tar -cf archive.tar /tarfoo
```

In this example, the `-c` option signals `tar` to create the file specified after the `-f` option, specifies the name of the file that will be created, and specifies the directory you are compressing. `tar` can compress just about anything that's a file, and everything is a file.

To create the same archive with `gzip` compression, you simply insert a `-z` option and use the letters `.gz` as the filename suffix:

```
tar -czf archive.tar.gz /tarfoo
```

This creates a compressed archive file that uses the `gzip` compression algorithms. If you want slightly higher compression, use the `-j` option (instead of the `-z` option) for `bzip2` compression.

> You will likely see questions on the exam that test your knowledge of which compression command has the highest compression. For example, using bzip2 results in a smaller archive file.

To create a `tar` archive and see a long style listing that includes ownership and permission information, use the `-v` option:

```
tar -cvf archive.tar /tarfoo
```

This produces the following output:

```
tar: Removing leading `/' from member names
tarfoo/
tarfoo /install.log
tarfoo /install.log.syslog
tarfoo /.bash_logout
```

As you can see, creating a `tar` file from a directory causes the `tar` command to strip the leading / from the full path of the objects in the archive.

If you were in the same directory as the entry for the `tarfoo` directory (the root of the system) and issued the command again, you'd see a slightly different set of messages:

```
tar -cvf /root/archive.tar tarfoo
```

This produces the output shown here:

```
tarfoo/
tarfoo /install.log
tarfoo /install.log.syslog
tarfoo /.bash_logout
```

Notice that the `tar: Removing leading '/'` from member names message is gone because you're not using absolute pathnames for the archive.

Taking Pity on the Unarchiver

It's considered proper and elegant to create `tar` archives by specifying a directory that contains the files to be archived, not just a bunch of files that are in the current directory.

For example, creating an archive of the /etc directory contents with the following command causes the archive to place the file in /etc into a folder in the archive named etc and then the files:

```
tar -cf etc.tar /etc
```

When you unarchive the `tar` file, by default it creates an etc directory in the current directory, which contains the entirety of the /etc directory you archived.

Contrast this with the nightmare that happens when you navigate to the /etc directory and create the archive from there with this command:

```
tar -cf /root/badetc.tar *
```

This archive file contains the same files as the previous one, except they aren't contained in a top-level etc directory—everything is in the top level of the archive.

Imagine what will happen to your system when you unarchive this file in the root user's home directory. You will have spewed approximately 2,400 files directly into the root user's home directory!

It really does matter where you are and which path options you use when you create or expand an archive file. It's best practice to use absolute pathnames and make sure that **tar** removes the leading / from the path when it's created.

To solve the problem of 2,400 files polluting your root user's home directory, use the following command, where badetc.tar is the offending archive file:

```
tar -tf badetc.tar ¦ xargs rm -rf
```

This command produces a list of the paths and filenames of files in the archive and uses the xargs command to feed each line of output as a filename specification to the rm -rf command, removing all the files and directories that were expanded from the badetc.tar file.

Useful Creation Options

A number of other options can be used for creating tar archives. Here is a list of the more useful and testable ones:

➤ -b—Sets the block size to fit the media to which you are archiving. This is necessary for some tape devices.

➤ -M—This specifies multiple archive targets or spreads a large archive across multiple tapes or media.

➤ -g—Creates a new format incremental backup (only those that have changed since the last full or incremental).

➤ -l—Stays on the local file system; it's used to keep from backing up the entire NFS network by accident.

➤ -L—This is followed by a number that reflects 1024 bytes, so -L 500 equals 500KB. (It's used for setting the tape length so multiple tapes can be used for an archive.)

➤ --remove-files—This is very dangerous because the specified files are removed from the file system after they have been added to the archive!

Listing Archive Files

Arguably the Rodney Dangerfield of the tar options, listing is something that typically is used after you don't get the results you wanted or realize what you've just done and want to confirm how hard it is going to be to clean up.

To list the contents of a tar archive, use the following command:

```
tar -tf archive.tar
```

This produces the output shown here:

```
etc/
etc/sysconfig/
etc/sysconfig/network-scripts/
etc/sysconfig/network-scripts/ifup-aliases
etc/sysconfig/network-scripts/ifcfg-lo
```

To list an archive that uses compression, simply insert the necessary letter between the -t and the -f options, such as the bzip2 j option shown here:

```
tar -tjf archive.tar.bz2
```

This produces the following output:

```
etc/
etc/sysconfig/
etc/sysconfig/network-scripts/
etc/sysconfig/network-scripts/ifup-aliases
etc/sysconfig/network-scripts/ifcfg-lo
```

To list an archive and see the file details for its contents, you add the -v option to the existing command to see an output of the details:

```
tar -tvjf archive.tar.bz2
```

This returns output similar to the following:

```
drwxr-xr-x root/root       0 2004-04-02 15:56:13 etc/
drwxr-xr-x root/root       0 2004-04-01 14:28:40 etc/sysconfig/
drwxr-xr-x root/root       0 2003-08-13 11:10:49 etc/sysconfig/
➥network-scripts/
```

When you create an archive with the **-v** option, a list of the files being archived is shown onscreen. When you unarchive an archive with the **-v** option, it shows a similar list of the files being unarchived.

It's only when you list an archive with the **-v** option that you get the type of output that approximates an **ls -l** command being run on the archive contents. This is an exam topic, so be ready for it.

Other Compression Utilities

Whereas the tar command is used to gather files and put them in a container, the compress, gzip, and bzip2 commands are used to compress that container. Used by themselves, they act on each file they find and replace that file with a compressed version that has an extension that indicates the file is compressed.

compress, uncompress, and zcat

Some older utilities are no longer used or have been obsoleted by the rise of gzip and bzip2. Chief amongst them is the compress utility.

The exams don't focus much on compress or its sister utility, uncompress. It's enough to know the information in this small section so you can identify a compress archive and know what to do with it.

compress, uncompress, and zcat are utilities that date back to when the tar command didn't offer the gzip and bzip2 compression options.

Creating an archive in precompression tar days was a two-step process: You archived the files in a .tar file and then ran compress, gzip, or bzip2 on the file.

Using any of the three replaced the original file with one that added an extension to the original filename that indicated it was compressed.

For example, the first step in the process is to use the following command to create a .tar file:

```
tar -cf archive.tar /tarfoo
```

This creates a file named archive.tar in the current directory. The next step is to run the compress command on the file:

```
compress archive.tar
```

This produces a file named archive.tar.z in the current directory, replacing the archive.tar file.

Using uncompress, you can then uncompress the archive.tar.z archive with the following command:

```
uncompress archive.tar.Z
```

Or, you can use the gunzip command to uncompress the file, meaning you can then recompress it with gunzip or do whatever you want with it:

```
gunzip archive.tar.Z
```

Either way, uncompressing the archive.tar.z file removes the compression and the .z extension, leaving only the original .tar file.

Another utility used in conjunction with the compress and uncompress commands is the zcat utility. You should never use zcat on a .z compressed file because it shows the contents of the file as if you had used cat on the original file and makes a lot of horrible beeping noises when the control codes in the binary file are shown onscreen.

For example, you can take a compressed file such as a copy of the /etc/ sysconfig directory contained in a file named sysconfig.tar.gz and uncompress it with the tar command and the zcat command:

```
zcat sysconfig.tar.gz ¦ tar xvf -
```

This command uncompresses a copy of the etc/sysconfig directory and its contents in the current directory, in a tree that begins with the etc directory. The use of a hyphen (-) as the file specifier in the tar command means that tar is accepting the standard output of the zcat command and sending that output directly to the tar command as a set of files to be uncompressed.

This is useful for only one or two exam questions if you find yourself on an older system or a Solaris box that offers only precompression **tar**.

Using **gzip** and **bzip2** for Compression

The gzip and bzip2 compression utilities are more up-to-date and useful than compress and zcat, and they are similar in their functions and operations. The main difference is that bzip2 offers slightly better compression than gzip, but gzip is much more widely used.

These commands replace the original file with a new file that has an additional extension, so don't delete the **.gz** or **.bz2** files that you create. They are the original files in a compressed wrapper!

To compress all the files in the current directory with gzip or bzip2, use this command:

```
gzip *
```

This replaces all the regular files (not the directories or their contents) in the current directory with the original filenames plus a .gz extension. So, if you had two files named file1 and file2 in the directory, they would be replaced with

```
file1.gz
file2.gz
```

To uncompress these files, just do the exact opposite of the compression:

```
gunzip *
```

This restores the original files.

Using bzip2 produces the same sort of results. You can issue the following command in the same directory:

```
bzip2 *
```

You would then have the following two files:

```
file1.bz2
file2.bz2
```

To uncompress these files, issue this command:

```
bunzip2 *
```

This restores the files to their original states.

 Watch for questions that ask about why you'd use either **gzip** or **bzip2** for a particular compression task (**bzip2** offers slightly better compression).

Maintaining System Time

Systems need to have the correct time for so many reasons, not the least of which are sending messages, putting entries in log files, copying files, and completing transactions in databases.

The primary source of organized time synchronization is the Network Time Protocol (NTP) protocol and suite of tools. NTP is comprised of a daemon (ntpd), a configuration file (/etc/ntp.conf), and various utilities that help maintain system time. NTP works by connecting both to peer servers and more authoritative time servers across the network and Internet.

The overall goal of NTP is to frequently compare time with peers and the upper-tier servers, so that when disconnection from an upper-tier source or network outages occur, relatively correct time can be maintained.

NTP was developed and designed to use multiple tiers of time sources. The time sources and their levels are

➤ **Tier 1**—Usually physically connected to a time-source, (the atomic clock)

➤ **Tier 2**—Hosts that communicate directly with Tier 1 sources

➤ **Tier 3**—Your local time server, or your ISP's

➤ **All else**—As many layers as you want to maintain

Figure 13.2 shows the hierarchical nature of the NTP sources.

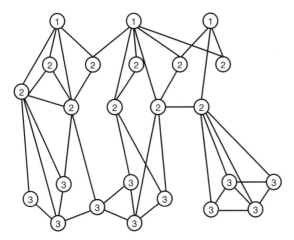

Figure 13.2 NTP server hierarchy.

NTP Files and Programs

The NTP distribution ships with everything needed to maintain system time with NTP, including the daemon and tools mentioned here:

➤ ntpd—The NTP daemon

➤ ntpq—The standard NTP query program

➤ ntpdc—A special NTP query program

➤ ntpdate—Sets the date and time via NTP

➤ ntptrace—Traces a chain of NTP servers back to the primary source

➤ tickadj—Sets time-related kernel variables

➤ ntptime—Reads kernel time variables

➤ ntp-genkeys—Generates public and private keys

A file named /etc/ntp.drift helps the NTP daemon deal with clock drift. Essentially, this file is an estimate of the system clock's frequency error (all system's have some error).

When ntpd starts, if the ntp.drift file doesn't exist, ntpd begins to watch and estimate the clock's error rate for about 15 minutes, taking a pulse of the system clock and detecting the possible frequency error rate. After about an hour, the /etc/ntp.drift file is written and ntpd functions normally. The ntp.drift file isn't referred from that point on until the next reboot.

If ntpd is started and a drift file exists, the daemon adjusts the clock relative to the drift rates in the file and begins functioning normally. Over time, the file becomes more accurate as the nuances of the clock's frequency error are better known.

If you start your NTP daemon and the system is more than 1,000 seconds out of correct time, the **ntpd** daemon errors out and the clock must be set by hand.

You can set the system time with the **date** command, and the hardware clock time can be set with the following command:

hwclock --hctosys

This sets your system clock to the value in the hardware clock, hopefully bringing it close enough to the real time that the **ntpd** daemon can take over from there.

Setting Up NTP

To determine whether the NTP package is currently installed, on an RPM-based system, use the command shown here:

```
rpm -q ntp
```

If you receive output that is similar to the following, the NTP package is installed:

```
ntp-4.1.1-1
```

Then you can edit the /etc/ntp.conf file to set the time sources; usually you need at least one line in the file to have a functional ntpd daemon:

```
server tar.foo.net
```

Be very conscious of the protocols of using someone else's time server for reference. It's considered impolite to just latch onto someone else's time server, and it's almost guaranteed to get you blacklisted or put in someone's denied file. Check out the Public NTP Time Servers page (and read the whole thing!) at **http://www. eecis.udel.edu/~mills/ntp/servers.html**.

You might need an ntp.drift file, but that is created by the ntpd daemon itself, so listing it in the configuration file might not be necessary. However, it is a good idea to put a second line in the file that matches the following:

```
driftfile /etc/ntp.drift
```

You just need to restart the ntpd daemon to begin using NTP at this point. On a Red Hat machine, you would type

```
service nptd restart
```

If you don't want to use the ntpd daemon, you can use the ntpdate command to manually set the time from an authoritative source, such as

This returns output similar to the following:

```
5 Apr 15:01:14 ntpdate[15389]: step time server
➡192.5.41.40 offset 13859.536620 sec
```

Monitoring and Changing NTP's Activities

Various programs are used to view and configure the ntpd daemon's performance and functionality.

The ntpq command is used to gather information and set values that pertain to the ntpd daemon. It's started by specifying the host for which you want to query the ntpd daemon:

```
ntpq tick.example.com
```

This drops you into an interface that begins with the prompt shown here:

```
ntpq>
```

You can type help and press Enter at this point to view the options. The ntpq command is an interactive-only tool—you can only specify the host to query on the command line, no options.

Alternatively, you can use the ntpdc command to actually configure the ntpd daemon. From the command line and interactively, ntpdc can configure many options, but care should be taken to not make configuration changes that aren't subsequently put in the configuration file. Doing so causes the ntpd daemon to revert to the old configuration after any restart or system reboot.

The ntptrace command is used as an NTP-specific traceroute, showing the path from your server to the originating time source, and the servers in between. This command is useful in troubleshooting any connection problems or server outages you might be experiencing.

Finally, you can use the tickadj command to display and manipulate the kernels' time settings via the /dev/kmem device link. tickadj is also used to cause the system to calculate slew and adjustment rates for keeping the system clock more in time with the hardware clock.

tickadj might not work with some kernels and has caused certain kernels to crash somewhat spectacularly. Use it with caution.

Exam Prep Questions

1. Which command on a Linux system queries an NTP time source from the command line given a time source? Type just the name of the command in the blank below:

   _____

   The correct answer is `ntpdate`. There are no alternative answers.

2. On a standard Debian system, what is the full path to the directory that holds the daemons that are referenced with symlinks in the runlevel directories?

   ○ A. `/etc/rc.d/init.d`
   ○ B. `/etc/rc.sysinit`
   ○ C. `/etc/rc.d/init/init.d`
   ○ D. `/etc/init.d`

   Answer D is correct because a Debian system uses the `/etc/init.d` directory to hold daemons that are symlinked to by the runlevel `start` and `kill` scripts. Answer A is incorrect because the question is about a Debian box and this is the correct answer for a Red Hat box. Answer B is incorrect because this is the system initialization script file for a Red Hat system. Answer C is incorrect because this is a spurious directory that, by default, doesn't exist on a Linux system.

3. On a default Linux system, what is the system logging facility that logs entries related to successful user logins? Enter just the lowercase facility name in the blank below:

   _____

   The correct answer is `authpriv`. The alternative answer is `auth`.

4. What is the full path name and filename of the configuration file for the syslog daemon?

   ○ A. `/etc/syslogd.conf`
   ○ B. `/etc/syslog/syslogd.conf`
   ○ C. `/etc/syslog.conf`
   ○ D. `/etc/ksyslog.conf`

   Answer C is correct because the correct file for system logging configuration is `/etc/syslog.conf`. Answer A is incorrect because the filename is incorrect. Answer B is incorrect because this file does not exist. Answer D is incorrect because this file does not exist.

5. You want to log a customized log entry for a failed backup job from a script. Which of the following will put this message onto the default logging facility? (Choose all that apply.)

❑ A. `logger -p "Backup failed on host snuffy"`

❑ B. `logger Backup failed on host snuffy`

❑ C. `logger -m Backup failed on host snuffy`

❑ D. `logger "Backup failed on host snuffy"`

Answers B and D are correct because the syntax for the logger command allows either unquoted or quoted messages. Answer A is incorrect because the `-p` option requires a priority, which is not present. Answer C is incorrect because there is no -m option for the logger command.

6. To disable the normal user's ability to get output from the `who` and `w` commands, what is the name of the log file from which you should remove the world-readable bit? Enter the full path name and filename of this log file in the blank below:

_____

The correct answer is `/var/run/utmp`. There are no alternative answers.

7. Which command will show a list of all users, whether a user has ever logged in, and the last time and date of that login?

○ A. `lastlog`

○ B. `last`

○ C. `login`

○ D. `usermod`

Answer A is correct because the `lastlog` command shows whether a user has ever logged in and the date and time of the last login. Answer B is incorrect because the `last` command shows the last few logins that occurred, but not a full list of users and data about their logins. Answer C is incorrect because the `login` command has no such capability. Answer D is incorrect because the `usermod` command has no such capability.

8. You want to run a task on the hour, every other hour starting at 1 a.m., with no other restrictions. In the blank below, enter the proper characters, separated by a single space, that make up the correct `crontab` entry to accomplish this:

_____

The correct answer is `0 1/2 * * *`. There are no alternative answers.

9. You have configured a job to run with the `batch` command, but apparently system utilization never drops as low as the default value. Which of the following commands can be used to set a custom value for the `batch` command?

○ A. `batchavg`

○ B. `atconfig`

○ C. `atrun`

○ D. `crontab`

Answer C is correct because the `atrun` command can be used to set the load average that `batch` uses as its threshold. Answer A is incorrect because there is no such command as batchavg. Answer B is incorrect because there is no such command as atconfig. Answer D is incorrect because the `crontab` command has no such capability.

10. You need to run a command that will let you take the hardware clock time and make it the system clock time before running the `ntpd` daemon. Fill in the blank below with the correct command, options, and arguments to accomplish this:

_____

The correct answer is `hwclock --hctosys`. There are no alternative answers.

Kernel Configuration and Custom Compilation

Terms you'll need to understand:

✓ Archive
✓ Compile
✓ Compression
✓ Driver
✓ Kernel
✓ Module
✓ Patch
✓ Tarball

Techniques you'll need to master:

✓ Understanding kernel options
✓ Configuring modules
✓ Patching a kernel source tree
✓ Compiling a kernel
✓ Troubleshooting kernel boot issues
✓ Repairing library issues
✓ Identifying stable kernel versions

Overview of the Kernel

The Linux kernel doesn't constitute much of what we refer commonly to as Linux. The majority of the Linux operating system is made up of software packages, daemons, and applications that are not needed to actually run the OS.

The kernel handles a multitude of things, including but not limited to, the following:

➤ Memory management

➤ Dividing up processor time amongst tasks

➤ Providing an interface for applications to talk to hardware

It's important to note that, although the Linux kernel is the lynchpin of the Linux OS, it can be compiled and recompiled for nearly any task.

The user can swap in and out of experimental kernels with just a simple reboot and a menu choice. This is difficult, if not impossible, on many other operating systems.

 Unlike when you apply service packs on Windows, when you are recompiling the kernel the system is fully functional. Until the newly compiled kernel is installed and the system rebooted, the new kernel is just another software package.

The Kernel Versions

When you start working with the kernel, it can be confusing to figure out just what the version numbers signify on the Linux kernel.

The kernel version numbers work like this:

`major.minor.patch`

Where the numbers might be

`2.6.2`

The most important version number is the middle, or minor, version. In all cases, if this is an even number, that version is considered a stable or production version. If the minor is an odd number, it's considered a development or testing version and should never be used in a production environment.

As a point of understanding, it's key to note that the kernel is in constant development, with the stable version being in production and bugfix mode, while the development version is being worked on and bug-tested.

Other examples of the versions include

➤ **2.4.12**—A stable 2.4 kernel at patch level 12

➤ **2.5.6**—A development 2.4 kernel at patch level 6

➤ **3.1.2**—A development version, not for production

If you don't know the version of your kernel, you can easily check with the uname command:

```
uname -r
```

This produces output similar to

```
2.4.18-3
```

Additionally, you can run the all-inclusive option for the uname command to get all the information about the machine uname can provide:

```
uname -a
```

This produces output similar to

```
Linux localhost.localdomain 2.4.18-3 #1 Thu Apr 18 07:37:53
➥EDT 2004 i686 unknown
```

Monolithic Versus Modular Kernels

There are advantages to having both a *monolithic* (everything compiled in) and a *modular* (essentials only, it depends on modules for additions) kernel, and indeed most distributions ship a mostly modular version of the kernel that is designed to work on most machines.

This is exactly why it's nice to be able to compile your own kernel; the ones Red Hat or Debian puts into the distributions aren't tuned for your system or, in some cases, for your level of processor. You might be running a kernel that has been tuned for and works best on a 386-class processor. Most sysadmins begin to compile their own custom kernels after they've gained a certain amount of experience and have a little extra time to experiment.

A monolithic kernel has the following advantages:

➤ It has all the necessary drivers compiled in.

➤ No load time is required for modules.

➤ It's good when you can't update or recompile.

A modular kernel has the following advantages:

➤ The necessary modules can be loaded/unloaded.

➤ It's smaller than a monolothic kernel.

➤ It's best for flexible systems.

Most Linux systems use a modular kernel or a kernel that includes less compiled-in code and relies more on external modules of code that are loaded on demand.

Modules

Essentially, a *module* is a software driver that enables interaction with hardware from the kernel or processes. If you don't want to wait for modules to load, or want the driver instantly available, compile it into the kernel.

Because the kernel is the arbiter of what has access to the hardware, modules must be made available for the kernel to load if that hardware is to be used. A module is referenced by name and assumed to be in the correct hierarchy of directories under the /lib/modules tree.

For example, you can see the current hierarchy of module directories with the following command:

```
tree -d /lib/modules
```

This returns output that's much lengthier than the following, which has been truncated for brevity:

```
/lib/modules
|-- 2.4.18-3
|   |-- build -> ../../../usr/src/linux-2.4.18-3
|   |-- kernel
|   |   |-- abi
|   |   |   |-- cxenix
|   |   |   |-- ibcs
|   |   |   |-- isc
|   |   |   |-- sco
|   |   |   |-- svr4
|   |   |   |-- util
|   |   |   `-- uw7
|   |   |-- arch
|   |   |   `-- i386
```

Module Dependencies

When you use a modular kernel, you have to depend on the modules you have created and compiled. When the kernel needs a module for something, it requests that the module and its dependencies be loaded.

This is perhaps best illustrated by Figure 14.1, which is something I constructed as an attempt to explain this multidependency process to attendees.

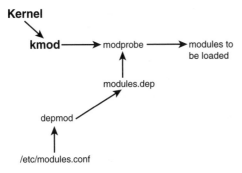

Figure 14.1   Module dependencies.

As you can see, the kernel uses the kmod process to request that the modprobe command load the necessary modules, such as in the case of a newly attached piece of hardware.

The modprobe command uses the existing /lib/modules/`uname -r`/modules.dep file to determine exactly what must be loaded and in what order to satisfy the dependencies modules might have on other modules.

The modules.dep file is built by the depmod command using the /etc/modules.conf file as its input. The modules.conf file (often known as conf.modules in the past) contains a list of variables, paths, and aliases that, when read by the depmod command, cause the modules.dep map to be built.

Watch out for questions that test your ability to remember how this complex set of commands and configuration files is read and processed. Remember that the **modules.conf** file is read by **depmod** and produces the **modules.dep** file, which is read by **modprobe** to find the right modules to load in the correct order so the **kmod** process can report a success to the kernel.

Viewing Your Modules

To see which modules are currently loaded on your system, use the `lsmod` command:

```
lsmod
```

This returns a four-column output, such as

```
Module               Size  Used by     Tainted: PF
pcnet32             15968  1  (autoclean)
ide-cd              30272  0  (autoclean)
cdrom               32192  0  (autoclean) [ide-cd]
vmhgfs              37184  4
usb-uhci            24484  0  (unused)
usbcore             73152  1  [usb-uhci]
ext3                67136  2
sd_mod              12864  6
scsi_mod           108576  2  [BusLogic sd_mod]
```

The output shows a list of four columns:

➤ **Column 1**—The module name

➤ **Column 2**—The size of the module in memory

➤ **Column 3**—The use count, or how many other modules depend on it currently

➤ **Column 4**—The list of modules that refer to the module on the current line

Notice that the `cdrom` module is referred to by the `ide-cd` module and that the `usbcore` module is referred to by the `usb-uhci` module.

Loading and Unloading Modules

If the module you want to have loaded is a single module, it's relatively simple to load with the `insmod` command. You can load a module from the `/lib/modules/`uname -r`/kernel/drivers` subdirectory with the following command:

```
insmod modulename
```

If you need to load multiple modules, or a set of modules that have interdependencies, you can use the `modprobe` command:

```
modprobe modulename
```

Your ability to unload modules is affected by whether the module is referred to by another module because modules must be unloaded in order, in much the same manner that you would remove the last box from a stack of boxes, rather than one from the middle.

The **modinfo** command is used to determine the author, license, and other information for modules. The syntax is

modinfo modulename

This returns output that lists the license, dependency, and aliases for the module.

Using modprobe to Manage Modules

The modprobe command is used for loading and unloading modules singly, in groups, or that match a particular pattern. The phrase *module stack* is used when referring to a set of modules to load or unload. To load a module with modprobe, use the command shown here:

```
modprobe modulename
```

To load a module stack (a top-level module with all its dependencies), the modules.dep file must list the appropriate relationships and you have to list only the top-level module:

```
modprobe -a modulename
```

To see everything that modprobe is doing, use the -v option and watch as it sends the needed commands and options to the insmod command to load the set of modules that are referenced together:

```
modprobe -v ide-cd
```

This produces output similar to this:

```
/sbin/insmod /lib/modules/2.4.18-3/kernel/drivers/cdrom/cdrom.o
Using /lib/modules/2.4.18-3/kernel/drivers/cdrom/cdrom.o
Symbol version prefix ''
/sbin/insmod /lib/modules/2.4.18-3/kernel/drivers/ide/ide-cd.o
Using /lib/modules/2.4.18-3/kernel/drivers/ide/ide-cd.o
```

Removing modules with modprobe is a little different than with the insmod command. modprobe reads the modules.dep file and then unloads the module or the module stack by sending the appropriate commands in the right order to the insmod command.

Also, remember that the kmod process uses modprobe extensively to load groups of modules, but kmod doesn't unload modules in the current versions of the kernel. The decision was made to retire the kerneldd process, which was used to unload modules after a specified amount of time from earlier versions of the kernel.

If you view the modules with the lsmod command, some are marked in the far right column with the word autoclean. If a module is marked as *autoclean*, that means that after about 60 seconds of inactivity, and if it's not referred to by another module, it can be cleaned out of the kernel with the modprobe -r command.

 The Red Hat distributions come with a **cron** job that runs every 10 minutes to remove modules that are marked as *autoclean*, or removable if not in use.

 If you need to specify options to loadable modules at load time, you can use the **/boot/module-info** file to set these options.

Many of the drivers on your system need to be aliased to other names for compatibility, such as aliasing Ethernet devices from the module name to **ethX** (where **X** is the number of the interface).

Patching the Kernel

After you have the system set up and running, a lot of patches and fixes might need to be applied to your system, and particularly to the kernel.

Although it's not as important in these days of widely available high-speed connections, it generally takes less time to download a patch to the kernel and apply it than it does to download the entire kernel source code for the latest patched version.

Many use the update routines that Red Hat, SuSE, and Debian provide for updating their kernels with the latest patches. Personally, I have never had the Red Hat Network, Debian's apt-get, or SuSE's Yast Online Update munge a kernel patch, but your experience might vary on this very important matter.

Overall, patching a kernel enables you to download less source and use your existing kernel .config file, instead of laboriously setting all the custom settings again and again.

When patching, remember that kernel patches are noncumulative, so if you are currently running a 2.4.18 kernel and the latest patch level is 2.4.22, you need to download and apply the patches for .19, .20, .21, and .22 (in order) to be current. Then, after downloading and applying those patches to the kernel source code, you can recompile.

The diff command is an interesting tool that enables you to take an updated tree of source code and essentially compare the new tree of code against the old tree of code and get a snapshot file that is the patch you would apply.

Using the **patch** Command

As a simple method of understanding the patch command, you can use the following set of steps to see what the patch command can do to a single file.

In this example, we'll take a commonly available file named watchdog.txt and make some changes to it, saving it as changedog.txt. Then we'll use the diff command to search the new file for items that don't exist in the old file; then we'll write those to a new file named diffdog.txt.

When the diff or patch file exists, it can be applied to the original file easily, making it match the new file.

NOTE

You must have installed the system with the kernel source packages, such as on a Red Hat 7.3 system where the package is named **kernel-source-2.4.18-3.src.rpm**.

Do the following:

1. Copy the /usr/src/linux-2.4/Documentation/watchdog.txt file to your user's home directory with the following command:

   ```
   cp usr/src/linux-2.4/Documentation/watchdog.txt ~
   ```

2. Change to your user's home directory and copy the watchdog.txt file to a new file named changedog.txt:

   ```
   cd ~
   cp watchdog.txt changedog.txt
   ```

3. Edit the changedog.txt file with vi and, as soon as you have the file onscreen, enter the following string:

   ```
   :%s/interface/connector/g
   ```

4. This changes the first term to the second term, and you can save and exit the file now with the following:

   ```
   Shift-zz
   ```

5. After the file is saved, compare the two files with the diff command:

   ```
   diff changedog.txt watchdog.txt
   ```

   This shows the following output:

   ```
   18c18
   < All six connectors provide /dev/watchdog,
   ➥which when open must be written
   ...
   ```

```
> All six interfaces provide /dev/watchdog,
➡which when open must be written
25c25
< A second temperature monitoring connector
➡is available on the WDT501P cards
- - -
> A second temperature monitoring interface
➡is available on the WDT501P cards
30c30
< The third connector logs kernel messages on additional alert events.
- - -
> The third interface logs kernel messages on additional alert events.
64c64
< The external event connectors on the WDT boards
➡are not currently supported.
- - -
> The external event interfaces on the WDT boards
➡are not currently supported.
```

6. Now create a patch file that captures the changes to a third file named diffdog.txt with the command shown here:

```
diff -Naur watchdog.txt changedog.txt > diffdog.txt
```

7. View the diffdog.txt file to see that it contains only the changes between watchdog.txt and changedog.txt.

8. Apply the patch to the original file, watchdog.txt, with this command:

```
cat diffdog.txt ¦ patch
```

9. Verify the patch was accurately applied by comparing the changedog.txt and watchdog.txt files:

```
diff changedog.txt watchdog.txt
```

10. There is no difference, and you've just used the patch successfully!

When you're patching a tree of code, it's important to remember that the application of the patch must be to the same type of object. In other words, you get better results applying a patch of a directory tree to another directory tree.

The patch command offers several options to cause the patch to be applied correctly to either an absolute path or a relative path.

If you are using a patch generated with the full paths of the source code tree /usr/src/linux, it should be applied with the full path as the target:

```
cat patchfile.txt ¦ patch /usr/src/linux
```

When you have a different source tree structure on your system, you need to strip out the leading slashes and parts of the path. For example, you might be running the patch from the /usr/src/linux-2.4 directory and should therefore use the following command:

```
cat patchfile.txt ¦ patch -p3 .
```

This applies the patch with no applied pathnames because the first / was removed with the -p1. Then usr/ is removed by the -p2 option, and finally the /linux section is removed by the -p3 option.

Additionally, if you are patching the kernel source code and the patch file is a compressed file in the gzip format, such as patch.gz, you can apply the patch without having to uncompress it:

```
zcat patch.gz ¦ patch —p0
```

If you are using the bzip2 format for a compressed patch file, such as patch.bz2, you can use the bzcat command in a similar fashion:

```
bzcat patch.bz2 ¦ patch -p0
```

Getting Kernel Source Code

When you decide to download the source code for the Linux kernel, be sure to get it either from your distribution vendor, such as a Red Hat source .rpm file, or from the http://www.kernel.org site.

It's also very important that you validate the integrity for your kernel source code, taking care to either download the gpg or PGP signature file for the package or check the MD5 checksum with the md5sum utility.

To verify the MD5 checksum of a patch file, use this command:

```
md5sum patchfile.gz
```

This returns output similar to what's shown here:

```
046dc327a0c91f06261e0012ad491792  patch.gz
```

To verify the gpg signature of a patch file, first download the patch.bz2.sign file that matches the version number of the patch code. The www.kernel.org site lists the appropriate signature files below or next to the patches. Then verify the code with this command:

```
gpg --verify patch.bz2.sign patch.bz2
```

This returns output similar to the following:

```
gpg: Signature made Fri 02 Aug 2002 08:43:34 PM EDT using DSA key ID
➥517D0F0E
```

```
gpg: Good signature from "Linux Kernel Archives Verification Key
➥<ftpadmin@kernel.org>"
gpg:                    aka "Linux Kernel Archives Verification Key
➥<ftpadmin@kernel.org>"
```

> If you see a warning about trust path issues, you can safely ignore it. This is per the kernel.org instructions, which can be found at **http://www.kernel.org/signature.html**.

> You will likely see questions about the gpg signature or the md5 checksum being used to validate kernel source code. Download the associated files and read the man pages to ensure you understand what we've covered.

Configuring the Kernel

There are three main methods for determining what is included or excluded in the new kernel you are about to compile. The following commands are run in the top-level directory of the kernel source code, and each of the options is an argument to the `make` command:

➤ `make config`—Contains a lot of yes/no questions. This is a text-based, very simple and painful way to configure the kernel because errors cause you to restart the process.

➤ `make menuconfig`—Contains a text-based menu of options that's surprisingly easy to navigate.

➤ `make xconfig`—X-based and GUI, this is the one for the recovering MCSE crowd, or the aesthetically oriented folks.

> I won't discuss the **make config** option in any detail because it's obsolete and its functionality is encompassed entirely by friendlier utilities.

make menuconfig

When configuring the options for what will or won't be in the compiled kernel, it's important to know what the little brackets and characters mean. Particularly, this is important in the `menuconfig` command, shown in Figure 14.2.

```
Linux Kernel v2.4.18-3custom Configuration
┌───────────────────────────── Networking options ──────────────────────────┐
│ Arrow keys navigate the menu.  <Enter> selects submenus --->.  Highlighted letters are │
│ hotkeys.  Pressing <Y> includes, <N> excludes, <M> modularizes features.  Press │
│ <Esc><Esc> to exit, <?> for Help.  Legend: [*] built-in  [ ] excluded  <M> module  < > │
│ module capable │
│ ┌──────────────────────────────────────────────────────────────────────┐ │
│ │ <*> Packet socket                                                       │ │
│ │ [*]     Packet socket: mmapped IO                                       │ │
│ │ <*> Netlink device emulation                                           │ │
│ │ [*] Network packet filtering (replaces ipchains)                       │ │
│ │ [ ]     Network packet filtering debugging                             │ │
│ │ [*] Socket Filtering                                                    │ │
│ │ <*> Unix domain sockets                                                │ │
│ │ [*] TCP/IP networking                                                   │ │
│ │ <M>     Threaded linUX application protocol accelerator layer (TUX)  │ │ │
│ │ [*]         External CGI module                                        │ │
│ │ [ ]         extended TUX logging format                                │ │
│ │ [ ]         debug TUX                                                   │ │
│ │ [*]     IP: multicasting                                               │ │
│ │ [*]     IP: advanced router                                            │ │
│ │ [*]       IP: policy routing                                           │ │
│ │ [*]         IP: use netfilter MARK value as routing key               │ │
│ │ [*]         IP: fast network address translation                      │ │
│ │ [*]       IP: equal cost multipath                                     │ │
│ │ [*]       IP: use TOS value as routing key                            │ │
│ │ [*]       IP: verbose route monitoring                                 │ │
│ │ [*]       IP: large routing tables                                     │ │
│ │ [ ]     IP: kernel level autoconfiguration                            │ │
│ │ <M>     IP: tunneling                                                  │ │
│ │ <M>     IP: GRE tunnels over IP                                        │ │
│ │ [*]       IP: broadcast GRE over IP                                    │ │
│ │ [*]     IP: multicast routing                                          │ │
│ │ [*]       IP: PIM-SM version 1 support                                 │ │
│ │ [*]       IP: PIM-SM version 2 support                                 │ │
│ │ [ ]     IP: ARP daemon support (EXPERIMENTAL)                          │ │
│ └v(+)────────────────────────────────────────────────────────────────┘ │
│                                                                            │
│              ┌────────────────────────────────────────────┐              │
│              │  <Select>      < Exit >      < Help >       │              │
└──────────────┴────────────────────────────────────────────┴──────────────┘
```

Figure 14.2   The **menuconfig** command.

Figure 14.2 shows Legend options. The bullets explain these in more detail.

➤ [ ]—Square brackets indicate a toggle on/off option. Pressing the space-bar inserts an asterisk in the brackets, marking this option as on, or to be compiled into the kernel.

➤ [*]—This is a toggle option turned on.

➤ < >—Greater-than/less-than brackets indicate an option that can be turned on (<*>) or off (< >) or can be set to support modules (<M>) in a three-way toggle.

Experiment with the options, toggling on and off the various selections; quit without saving your config file.

The only valid kernel parameter configuration commands are **make config**, **make menuconfig**, and **make xconfig**. The usual ./**configure** and anything else you've not used in this session are simply distracters.

make xconfig

The most graphically oriented of the kernel configuration commands is the xconfig command. (Actually, these are not really utilities or commands, but targets in the makefile for the kernel—just play along.) Its interface is similar to the `menuconfig` command but more pleasing to the eye, as Figure 14.3 shows.

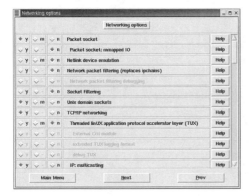

Figure 14.3 The **xconfig** command.

As you can see in Figure 14.3, options for compiling items in or leaving them out, or even making them available as a module, are provided and simplified to a set of radio buttons. This command is probably the easiest way to reconfigure or set options for the kernel.

Saving your kernel configuration file is important. When you are done with the various commands, you are asked whether you want to save the configuration file, which you of course do if you're ready to compile.

The only configuration file for the kernel is the **.config** file that is generated by the **make config**, **menuconfig**, and **xconfig** targets. Files such as the **kernel.conf**, which is used to configure logging, are not valid for the kernel.

The **.config** file is located (after configuration is completed) in the **/usr/src/linux-2.4** directory on a Red Hat system, which can differ for other distributions.

Steps to Compile a Kernel

Kernel recompilation is difficult to document so that it will work for all machines, more so than any other process. The set of steps is lengthy, and instead of trying to get it to work on every odd machine out there, we'll just go for the understanding and exam point instead.

The author has gotten this to work many hundreds of times on many different machines, so he's very aware of the pitfalls of trying to present a one-size-fits-all set of steps.

To begin compiling, you must be in the root directory of the kernel source code, usually in /usr/src/linux or /usr/src/linux-2.4 (for a 2.4 kernel). You should copy this to another tree, keeping your original tree unchanged by your experiments:

1. Copy the /usr/src/linux-2.4 tree to a new one called /usr/src/ linux-2.4-lpic with the command shown here:

   ```
   cp -r /usr/src/linux-2.4 /usr/src/linux-2.4-lpic
   ```

2. Change into the /usr/src/linux-2.4-lpic directory.

3. Run the make menuconfig command.

4. Navigate to the File Systems menu selection and press Enter.

 You're just going to change a couple of things. The items aren't of consequence—just that you do them and recompile the kernel.

5. Put the cursor over the Minix fs Support selection and press the space-bar twice to unselect it, or press it however many times until the < > brackets are empty.

6. Press the Esc key until you are back to the main menu.

7. Navigate to the Amateur Radio Support selection and press Enter.

8. Unselect the Amateur Radio Support selection to turn it off complete-ly by pressing the spacebar until the [ ] brackets are empty.

9. Press Esc until you are back to the main menu.

10. Navigate to the < Exit > selection with the left or right arrow key and press Enter.

11. When asked whether you want to save your new kernel configuration, click Yes and press Enter.

12. Ignore the instructions to run the make dep command. Instead, confirm that the .config file exists in the current directory with the command shown here:

    ```
    ls -a .config
    ```

    This returns output similar to the following:

    ```
    -rw-r--r--    1 root     root        36157 Apr  8 17:56 .config
    ```

13. Now you begin compiling the kernel with the command to make all the dependencies (all those modules you left selected):

```
make dep
```

14. When this is done scattering lines of output onscreen, clean up after any previous compile sessions with the following command:

```
make clean
```

15. This takes a couple of minutes; then it's time to do the actual compilation of the kernel:

```
make bzImage
```

Four possible options can be used when compiling the kernel:

➤ **lilo**—Used to not only make the image, but also to install it as the default entry in LILO's menu. This kernel is uncompressed.

➤ **zlilo**—Similar to **lilo**, but using compression.

➤ **zImage**—Makes a compressed kernel using the **gzip** compression option.

➤ **bzImage**—Makes a compressed kernel using the **bzip2** compression option.

Remember that kernels are commonly compressed with **gzip**, such as the **make zImage** command. It might make sense from a English perspective that **make bzImage** would use **bzip2** to compress the kernel, but the reality is that **bzImage** produces a larger compressed kernel than **zImage**.

16. Make the modules needed by this kernel; it will likely take a number of minutes, and up to several hours on a slower machine:

```
make modules
```

The making and installing of modules are the two most frequently forgotten steps in the lengthy kernel compilation process. Make a checklist of the steps so you remember them.

17. After the modules are finished compiling, install the new modules with the following command:

```
make modules_install
```

This command overwrites the current modules, although we've not changed anything that would cause a problem. Take care when doing this and never do it on a production machine.

18. When this installation is finished, install the new compressed kernel into the boot loader. Copy the compressed image to the /boot directory with the following command:

```
cp /usr/src/linux-2.4-lpic/arch/i386/bzImage /boot
```

19. Now move the bzImage kernel file to its new name with this command:

```
mv /boot/bzImage /boot/vmliunuz-2.4.18-lpic
```

If you are using the same system except for compiling the new kernel, you don't have to update the **System.map** file. If you do have to, some quality time with the man pages and Google is in order because it's more complex than we can cover here.

20. If you're using LILO, you need to edit the /etc/lilo.conf file and copy the existing Linux image to a new entry.

21. All you need to do to enable the new entry is change the filename that follows the image=kernelname section to the new filename.

22. Save and exit the /etc/lilo.conf file.

23. Rerun the lilo command with the verbose option to see what's being done:

```
lilo -v
```

This returns output similar to what's shown here:

```
Reading boot sector from /dev/sda
Merging with /boot/boot.b
Mapping message file /boot/message
Boot image: /boot/vmlinuz-2.4.18-3
Mapping RAM disk /boot/initrd-2.4.18-3.img
Added linux *
/boot/boot.0800 exists - no backup copy made.
Writing boot sector.
```

24. Reboot and test the functionality of your new kernel, being sure to keep your vi cheat sheet handy so you can refer to it when you troubleshoot any errors you make in the configuration files.

Remember that kernel and system initialization messages can be viewed with the **dmesg** command or by using the **less /var/log/dmesg** command. The **/var/log/ boot.log** log file consists almost entirely of service startup messages, not kernel-related messages.

25. If the new kernel doesn't work, check the steps again and make sure that you haven't mistyped anything.

Be very certain what steps are used in compiling a new kernel and which are not. Remember that you used the **dep**, **clean**, and **bzImage** (**zlilo**, **bzlilo**, and **zImage**) modules and **modules_install** in this session.

Exam Prep Questions

1. You need to load a module named `module1.o` into your running kernel. The module fails to load properly when you issue the following command:

   ```
   insmod module1
   ```

   Which command would you use to load the module `module1.o` and its dependencies? Fill in the blank below with just the command name:

   _____

   The correct answer is `modprobe`. There are no alternative answers.

2. Which command unloads a single unreferenced kernel module? (Choose the simplest answer.)

   ○ A. `modprobe`
   ○ B. `rmmod`
   ○ C. `rmautoclean`
   ○ D. `modunload`

   Answer B is correct because `rmmod` is the simplest command that unloads the module. Answer A is incorrect because `modprobe` is used to unload groups of modules, although it will unload a single module. Answer C is incorrect because there is no such command as rmautoclean. Answer D is incorrect because there is no such command as modunload.

3. What is the name of the file that contains all the options for compiling a kernel? Fill in the blank below with just the name of the file:

   _____

   The correct answer is `.config`. There are no alternative answers.

4. Which of the following commands is valid to produce a compiled kernel? (Choose all that apply.)

   ❑ A. `make bzImage`
   ❑ B. `make lilo`
   ❑ C. `make zImage`
   ❑ D. `make gzlilo`
   ❑ E. `make zlilo`

   Answers A, C, and E are correct because they are valid targets for making a compressed kernel. Answers B and D are incorrect because they are not valid targets to make a compiled kernel.

5. After compiling your new kernel and configuring it in the boot manager, you reboot and get a number of messages saying `module not found`. What is the most likely cause of the problem?

  ○ A. You forgot to make the modules.

  ○ B. You didn't run `lilo`.

  ○ C. You didn't copy the compressed image.

  ○ D. You forgot to rename the kernel image.

Answer A is correct because forgetting to make the modules is a common cause of this error. Answer B is incorrect because not running `lilo` would cause you to *not* receive the error messages. Answer C is incorrect because not copying the compressed kernel image wouldn't cause module errors. Answer D is incorrect because `lilo` would complain about a missing kernel image when run.

6. You need to create a compressed kernel that is larger than the traditional `zImage` option can handle. Fill in the blank below with the command line that would produce this kernel, including any necessary options or arguments:

_____

The correct answer is `make bzImage`. There are no alternative answers.

7. You need to determine the version of your kernel and use that version in a script file. Which command line would complete the following command?

`cd /lib/modules/`

Fill in the blank with the correct string to cause the command to read the proper directory and use it to transfer to that directory:

`cd /lib/modules/`_____

The correct answer is `` `uname -r` ``. There are no alternative answers.

8. Which of the following commands reads the `/etc/modules.conf` file and produces a dependency list that is stored in the `modules.dep` file in the correct directory for the kernel version?

  ○ A. `conf.modules`

  ○ B. `modprobe`

  ○ C. `depmod`

  ○ D. `ldmodules`

Answer C is correct because `depmod` reads the `/etc/modules.conf` file and produces a dependency file named `modules.dep`. Answer A is incorrect because `conf.modules` is the old name of the `modules.conf` file and is not a command. Answer B is incorrect because `modprobe` is used to load and unload modules in groups. Answer D is incorrect because it is not a valid command.

9. You need to determine the license and author information for a particular module. Which command shows information about a given module? Fill in the blank with just the command name:

_____

The correct answer is `modinfo`. There are no alternative answers.

10. Which of the following commands is valid to determine the authenticity or validity of a compressed archive of kernel source code or kernel patch code? (Choose all that apply.)

   ❑   A. `rpm -K`

   ❑   B. `md5sum`

   ❑   C. `pgp`

   ❑   D. `gpg`

   Answers B and D are correct because the `md5sum` and `gpg` commands are used to establish the validity or authenticity of compressed archives of kernel code and patches. Answer A is incorrect because the `rpm -K` command helps verify an RPM package file, not compressed archives of code. Answer C is incorrect because there isn't a command named `pgp` on a Linux system.

Linux Shells and Scripting

Terms you'll need to understand:

✓ Alias
✓ Environment
✓ Exporting
✓ Loop
✓ Options
✓ Quoting
✓ Variable

Techniques you'll need to master:

✓ Declaring a variable
✓ Exporting a variable
✓ Writing and customizing scripts
✓ Setting and removing shell options
✓ Creating and listing functions
✓ Manipulating SUID rights

Writing Scripts

Thankfully, you don't have to be much of a programmer or script-writer to fulfill the objectives of the LPIC Level 1, and the author is a prime example of that subset of quite competent sysadmins who are not programmers, nor does he feel that you have to be one. The questions you'll be answering on the exam will be about simple scripting—little tasks that make life easier.

Writing a Simple Script

The easiest way to understand what makes up a script is to examine a simple one. The following example contains everything a simple script should have:

```
#!/bin/bash
# This is a simple script that can be used to display
# any files in long format, and pause the output.
ls -al *.$1 ¦ more
```

This simple script contains the following:

➤ **Line 1**—A string that causes the script to be run specifically with the /bin/bash shell. (Also known in the parlance as a *shebang*, as in "the whole shebang." It's not on the exam, but it's essential lingo.)

➤ **Lines 2 and 3**—Comments that describe what is about to happen. This is often left out, but it's advisable so you can remember what you did later. Everything after a # symbol is part of the comment and is ignored.

➤ **Line 4**—The meat of the script, this is the command that will be run.

You can also look at a script as being constructed of any set of commands that you would type in the same order or sequence repeatedly. I'll spend 30 minutes getting a script to work that will save me 30 seconds, but that's 30 seconds 20 times a day for 30 years!

Executing a Script

Although you execute scripts by typing their names on the command line, you can cause a script to be executed in a couple of ways:

➤ sh script—If the script is not executable, use the shell to interpret the script's contents. On the command line, prefix the script with the shell you want to use.

This script doesn't need to have a shebang (**#!/bin/sh**) line or be an executable file because the shell uses it as an argument and supplies all that.

➤ `#!/bin/bash` and `chmod +x script`—The `#!/bin/bash` characters should be the only thing on the first line of the script, and you should set the script executable with the command `chmod +x` *script* and then execute the script on the command line.

Unless the script is in your path somewhere, you need to choose how to execute the script, either by prefixing it with **./** (such as **./script**) or by using the full path (such as **/home/rbrunson/script**).

You might find a script or command on your system that executes but a long `ls` listing of the file shows a weird permission pattern, such as

```
---s--x--x    1 root     root        14657 Apr 19  2002 /usr/bin/sudo
```

Although the `sudo` program is a bit of an extreme example, the use of the `s` (Set User ID [SUID] bit) in the fourth position means that, if a normal user has an `x` or execute bit in the other position, she can run this program is if she were the root user and assume the permissions of the root user.

Watch for the inclusion of long **ls -l** file listings on the exam. They don't just put them in there for show! Inspect the output very closely; usually a special bit in a particular position will be essential to the right answer.

Setting files with the SUID or SGID bit turned on is a potential security risk, and your system might be compromised if you set these bits for the wrong files.

It's best to run the following command right after you install a system:

find / -perm +7000 -exec ls -l {} \; > /root/install-specialbits.txt

Then on a regular basis run the following command:

find / -perm +7000 -exec ls -l {} \; > /root/`date +%Y-%m-%d_specialbits.txt`

Then **diff** the latest file against the original file to see what has changed. You should investigate thoroughly any new files that have the SUID or SGID bit set.

Using Positional Parameters

We cover the use of variables later in this chapter, but a special set of variables exists for every program or script that is run. These are called *positional parameters*. A positional parameter is a variable named with a single numeral, such as $1, $2, and $3. The $ symbol is how you access and expand the variable on the command line.

Positional parameters are typically numbered from 1 to 9 (any of these numbers can be used) and begin after any options for the program. For example, to specify three color options for a program, you would use the positional parameters:

```
command blue red green
```

In this command, the command stands alone, while blue becomes $1, red becomes $2, and green becomes $3.

These parameters are useful when you want to have an overall script that can be customized by what you specify as an input variable, such as

```
#!/bin/bash
# filename: au
# Create a user, username read from $1, shell from $2
useradd -m -s /bin/$2 $1
```

You then run the script with the arguments $1 and $2 being the target username and shell:

```
./au rbrunson sh
```

You can then run it many times with different usernames and shell values. This is a very simple example; use your imagination to make this much more useful.

The positional parameter $? shows the most recently executed program's status. It shows a value of 0 if it succeeded without errors and a non-zero value if it had errors or failed to execute.

The final positional parameter to discuss is $0, which reflects the name of the script or program that is running. For example, if you ran the script script1, the $0 would echo back script1:

```
#!/bin/bash
echo "$0 is the program"
```

Testing for Conditions

The `test` command is useful for comparing the dates of files, whether something is newer or older than another, or even that a file exists and is of a particular type. To test whether an object exists on the file system, the `-f` option is used, followed by the full path and name of the object being tested.

The `test` command can handle a large set of test conditions. A useful smattering is shown here:

➤ `x = y`—This compares `x` with `y` and, if true, returns an exit status of `0`.

➤ `x != y`—This compares `x` with `y` and, if they're not equal, returns an exit status of `0`.

➤ `x -eq y`—If `x` is equal to `y`, such as two variable numeric values, it returns an exit status of `0`.

➤ `x -ge y`—If `x` is greater than or equal to `y`, it returns an exit status of `0`.

➤ `x -ne y`—If `x` is not equal to `y`, it returns an exit status of `0`.

➤ `-r file1`—It tests that `file1` exists and is readable.

➤ `-w file1`—It tests that `file1` exists and is writable.

➤ `-u file1`—It tests that `file1` exists and has the SUID bit set.

Of course, more options are available, but you get the idea that `test` is useful for determining the status of files and returning exit statuses based on what it finds.

As an example, to test for the existence of the `/etc/passwd` file, you would use the following command:

```
test -f /etc/passwd ; echo $?
```

The `test` command looks to see whether the `/etc/passwd` file exists; then `echo` shows that the previous command exited with a status of `0` if it was true, and the file was found.

Having Users Make Variables

Many times the best person to fill in the value of a variable is the user running the script. I like to have the user do as much work as possible, leaving me to have more time to make up scripts she can run.

The `read` command is the primary tool I use to have a user type in the contents of a variable that will exist only inside or during the execution of a script.

The read command syntax is read followed by a variable name. The variable name can be any combination of upper- and lowercase characters, but take care not to overwrite system variables.

The following script is a simple illustration of the read command:

```
#!/bin/bash
# This script asks the user their first and last name
# then echoes back their full name
echo "What is your first name?"
read fname
echo "What is your last name?"
read lname
echo "Your full name is $fname $lname"
```

If this command is run and I type in my information, the session looks like this:

```
What is your first name?
ross
What is your last name?
brunson
Your full name is ross brunson
```

You can also declare multiple variables on the command line with the read command, such as

```
read var1 var2 var3
```

The system waits until you type in something and press Enter; then you can echo them back. I entered the following:

```
first last middle
```

This was followed by me pressing Enter.

If you echo the variables, you get all the values in whatever order you wanted them in, such as

```
echo var1 var3 var2
```

The system shows the following output:

```
first middle last
```

Watch for the use of **bash** built-in commands, such as the **read** command, in scripts. You don't need to know the path for a built-in because it's already there if you're running **bash**.

Scripting Constructs

Various scripting constructs can be used to process more than one command or handle sets of data rather than a single instance.

if/else Statements

A fairly simple tool to use, an `if/else` statement essentially tests a condition and performs an action if that condition is true. The syntax for an `if` statement is fairly simple:

```
if list
    then list
    else list
fi
```

The word `list` can be a variety of items, such as if a file or directory exists, or based on exit codes from commands.

For example, the following script attempts to determine whether a particular file is still on the system and, if true, echoes something to the console. Otherwise, it echoes another statement to the console:

```
if [ -d "~/.ssh" ]
  then
    echo "You've used ssh on this machine"
  else
    echo "You've never used ssh on this machine"
fi
```

The for Loop

A `for` loop is used to do a task a specific number of times, or for as many items as it's found in a location. `for` loops start with the keyword `for` and typically include a range or a found number of items.

For example, to perform a task five times in a loop, you might use the following in a script:

```
for n in 1 2 3 4 5
    do
        echo $n
    done
```

This basically executes the `echo` statement five times, echoing the iteration number each time it loops.

You can also embed other commands inside a loop, such as the `seq` command with the `-w` option. Here's an example:

```
for n in $(seq -w 1 20)
 do
    echo $n
done
```

This loop could do just about anything you wanted it to do for as many iterations as necessary. The `seq` `-w` command and option give you a set of numbers padded with leading zeroes if the range goes to more than one character.

NOTE   I use this loop to print a sequence of numbers for creating files that have a specific number of lines in them, mostly for examples in class, but the principle is the same for anything you'd want to do repeatedly.

while and **until** Statements

A `while` or `until` statement performs a particular task while a value is less than or greater than a particular value or until the incrementing value reaches a particular threshold; then it exits. Typically, a `while` or `until` statement includes an action that increments or decrements a counter until the threshold or exit value is reached.

An example of a `while` loop is shown here:

```
#!/bin/bash
value=0
last=33
while [ $value -lt $last ]
do
        echo $value
        value=`expr $value + 1`
done
```

As you can see, the loop uses the `$value` variable to store the value that will be increased in the `do` section. While this value is still less than 33, the loop continues. (You'll find that it starts at a value of 0 and goes to 32; if you want it to start at 1 and go to 32, make `value=1`.) Here's an example:

```
#!/bin/bash
value=0
upper=33
until [ $value -ge $upper ]
do
        echo $value
        value=`expr $value + 1`
done
```

This until loop is similar to the previous while loop. It simply declares a value, declares an upper limit to reach, and then starts echoing its progress to the screen until it has done the task 33 times, or from 0 to 32.

Customizing the Shell Environment

The shell section for the 102 exam consists mostly of how to get things running, shell variables, quoting of text and variable expansion, setting some settings in the shell itself, and so on. The majority of the material for the shell takes place in the objectives for the 101 exam.

Execution Precedence

The order in which items are processed and executed in the shell is important, not only for deciding what you should use as a tool for accomplishing a task, but also for deciding when you need to save time by loading necessary scripts as functions or having things execute in a particular order.

The bash shell sets the following order of execution or precedence:

➤ **Aliases**—Any alias is executed first, even before a command in the path with the same name.

➤ **Keywords**—These include if, for, case, while, until, and function.

➤ **Functions**—A defined function in memory.

➤ **Built-in commands**—These include alias, break, cd, echo, exit, help, kill, trap, type, and so on.

➤ **Executables**—Scripts and binary executables that are in the PATH variable. The first one found is executed, and all others are ignored.

As we work through the chapter, keep an eye out for the various items that are executed and in what order.

Environment Variables

Environment variables are useful for writing scripts or having data that stays in the machine's memory for the duration of a login, or a particular part of a program or session.

Creating Variables

Creating a variable on the command line is as simple as naming it and putting a value in it. A *variable* is a location in memory populated by declaring the variable with a value. The variable name can be almost anything and is accessed by preceeding the name with a $ symbol.

To declare a variable named VAR1 with a value of SomeData, you would use the command shown here:

```
VAR1=SomeData
```

This is entered at the shell prompt and tells the system, literally, to add a variable (a memory location that's named) of VAR1 and put the text string SomeData in that variable. You use the echo command to see that this succeeded:

```
echo $VAR1
```

Variables are case-sensitive, so you must refer to the variable with the same name as you declared it with. To be more specific, VAR1, var1, and Var1 are all different variable names.

When you echo a variable, the name of the variable name must have a $ character in front of the variable, so the shell knows that what follows is a variable.

Exporting Variables

After you have created a variable, that variable's data is available to the shell in which it was created, unless you export that variable. *Exporting* a variable means that it and its data are now available to all the child processes of the current or parent shell.

The easiest way to export a variable is to declare and export it with the following command:

```
export VAR1=value
```

This does in one step what the following two commands do:

```
VAR1=value
export VAR1
```

After the variable has been exported, it can be used in scripts or programs that are run in the non-originating or parent shell.

Removing Variables

Variables can be removed or left in place. The main reasons you remove a variable are to keep it from interfering with future iterations of scripts and to clean up the memory artifacts.

You don't have to actually remove variables; you can remove the variable's value, effectively putting a null string in the value of the variable:

```
export VAR1=
```

This sets the VAR1 variable to have a null value, but it's still in the environment of the user who exported the variable.

To remove the variable entirely, you use the unset command, like so:

```
unset VAR1
```

You can confirm that VAR1 is gone by running the following command:

```
export ¦ grep VAR1
```

This returns no output, proving that VAR1 is gone.

Using Variables in Scripts

When you are writing scripts, you'll often want to declare a variable for use in the script or pull the values from common or user-created variables in the shell environment.

For example, you might want to create a variable named STRING, populate that variable with the value cheese, and then use it in your scripts. To use this variable's value, you first have to declare and export the variable to make it available for subshells and programs to use (if you don't export it, the script you write will not see the variable or its value):

```
export STRING=cheese
```

Quoting and Variables

Using quotes around a variable is often done when you need to have the variable coexist in an echoed statement or some sort of human language or plain English message that is sent to the console or written to disk.

Quote characters and special characters cause a particular output to occur. The characters we'll use consist of

➤ "—Double quotation marks allow variable expansion but protect a string by causing everything between them to be counted as a unit.

➤ '—Single quotation marks disallow all variable expansion and print exactly what's between the single quotation marks.

➤ \—Backslashes are used to escape a single character, such as a $ symbol. For example, a Windows path that includes \\server\share would have to be entered as \\\\server\\share to show up right.

How to Use Double Quotation Marks

Double quotation marks are used to surround a string being echoed or to cause that string to be treated as a single string with variable expansion.

For example, if you wanted to have a string that was echoed to the console and reported the user's name, you would use a command like this:

```
echo "Your username is $USER"
```

This produces the following output:

```
Your username is root
```

Double quotation marks allow expansion of variables, while letting you also use apostrophes or what would otherwise be seen as a single quotation mark:

```
echo "You've logged on as $USER"
```

This produces the output shown here:

```
You've logged on as root
```

If you left off the double quotation marks, the previous `echo` command would produce the following output:

```
>
```

This is the continuation prompt, and it's trying to tell you that it was expecting another single quotation mark, so keep typing! You can exit this with the Ctrl+C keystrokes.

In addition, when using a single quotation mark or apostrophe inside double quotation marks, after you've surrounded the string with the double quotation marks, all single quotation marks are treated as apostrophes, without exception, no matter how many you use inside the double quotation marks.

Remember, double quotation marks allow variable expansion; allow the use of apostrophes as punctuation instead of as single quotation marks; and usually surround a string, treating it as a discrete unit that will be echoed.

How to Use Single Quotation Marks

The primary use for single quotation marks is to cause a string or set of characters to be treated strictly as those characters, with no expansion, no substitution—just the characters.

You don't have to use single quotation marks for an entire string unless you need to. Just the literal section can be surrounded with single quotation marks, leaving the rest of the string to contain variables and so on:

```
echo The cost for $USER access is '$150.00'
```

This produces the following output:

```
The cost for root access is $150.00
```

If you've other concerns that would lead you to surround an entire string with double quotation marks, using a backslash to except out the single quotation mark might be a better idea, depending on whether you have other instances in the same string that need escaping or quoting:

```
echo "You've incurred \$150.00 in access charges"
```

This produces the following output:

```
You've incurred $150.00 in access charges
```

Expect some interesting strings of text in exam questions that cover this topic, such as **echo** statements that are fed to **cat** commands, single and double quotation marks inside each other, single backslashes that should be doubles, and so on.

Shell Aliases

An *alias* is an alternative for a command and is typically used by visiting Windows users who need to substitute commands such as dir, cls, and ren for their Linux alternatives.

How Aliases Work

A *shell alias* enables you to substitute a single command string for another longer command or set of commands, saving time and typing for frequently used command strings.

Shell aliases are set either in the bash configuration files or on the command line with the `alias` command. You can remove aliases set in the configuration files for the duration of your session or completely remove ones that were set with the `alias` command by using the `unalias` command.

Aliases can contain any character and incorporate variables and metacharacters (`*?.`) for filename expansion, but when you use an alias once, the commands returned are not expanded further if they match an alias.

For example, aliasing the `mv` command to `mv -i` does not further expand the `mv` in `mv -i`. In other words, you don't have to worry about aliasing commands with a name that is included in the alias itself because it won't become a recursive loop.

Viewing, Setting, and Removing Aliases

Aliases are set in the system's `/etc/bashrc` or in the user's `~./bashrc`. To view your currently set aliases, run the `alias` command:

```
alias
```

This returns output similar to the following:

```
alias cp='cp -i'
alias ls='ls —color=tty'
alias mv='mv -i'
alias rm='rm -i'
alias vi='vim'
```

An alias consists of an alias name followed by an `=` character and then the command the alias refers to in single quotes, such as

```
mv='mv -i'
```

To define an alias from the command line, you would use the command shown here:

```
alias cls='clear'
```

The `alias` command takes the alias name cls (which is a DOS command to clear the screen) and assigns the command in single quotation marks (`clear`) to be executed when you type the alias name and press Enter.

To remove an alias, you simply use the `unalias` command followed by the name of the alias to remove:

```
unalias cls
```

Running the `alias` command again to view your alias definitions shows that the alias is indeed removed from memory and not set to a null value like a variable would be.

To cause an alias to be momentarily escaped, you can prefix the command you know or suspect to be aliased with a backslash character. The actual command that was superseded by the alias is run instead:

```
\ls
```

 Watch for this sort of thing on the exam; you'll have to know how to make, delete, escape out (**\cmd**), and otherwise display aliases or troubleshoot a broken or incorrectly defined alias as part of the questions.

Examples of Using Aliases

An example of a useful alias is one named `mvi` that loads all the files in the current directory into `vi`:

```
alias mvi='vi *'
```

Another thing you can do with an alias is make a shortcut for commands like `tar`, such as the following examples that compress a directory into an archive or uncompress an archive:

```
alias t='tar -czvf'
alias ut='tar -xzvf'
```

This enables you to create a compressed `tar` file of a directory with fewer keystrokes, such as

```
t sometar.tgz somedir
```

Uncompressing an archive file is also made simpler:

```
ut sometar.tgz
```

Another useful set of aliases centers around the `ls` command, particularly making two-letter aliases that perform more complex `ls` functions:

```
alias ll='ls -l'
alias ld='ls -ld'
alias lf='ls -F'
```

The ll alias substitutes for the ls -1 command, making long listings much easier; the ld alias, on the other hand, shows a directory entry's long listing, not the contents of the directory. Finally, the lf alias helps you determine the file type on terminals that don't support color.

Watch for questions about aliases, such as **ll** and **lf**, or how to create them.

The ls command's -F option supports suffixing entries with various characters that denote the file type:

➤ /—Directory entries are suffixed with a forward slash, such as etc/.

➤ *—Executable files are suffixed with an asterisk, such as scriptfile*.

➤ @—Symbolic links are suffixed with an @ symbol, such as rc.d@.

➤ =—Sockets are suffixed with an equal symbol, such as gpmctl=.

➤ ¦—Fifos or pipes are suffixed with a ¦ symbol, such as initctl¦.

It's only after you have pressed the Enter key that your command string is checked for the presence of matching words to the aliases defined in your shell. If you try to get too tricky with an alias, you'll either get an error or end up creating or deleting things you need. For more complex tasks, see the section "Shell Functions."

Watch for questions that test you on troubleshooting nonfunctional or circular alias commands and aliases that are defined for common commands. Also, watch for questions about how to cause an alias to be ignored.

Shell Functions

A *shell function* incorporates the functionality of shell aliases and includes the capability to recursively perform tasks, break tasks up into chunks that are more readable, and in general perform the same functionality as a script but from memory rather than from disk.

A function incorporates all the capabilities of an alias and adds the capability to be recursive or perform loop iterations and arguments to the commands in a function.

Functions are executed at the same level or in the current shell. No new shells are used, allowing the function full access to the shell's variables and settings.

How a Function Works

Declaring a function can be done on the command line, the syntax of which is as follows:

```
function funcname () { cmd -opts args }
```

A function can also be defined as a multiline entity by using a script file to hold common functions, rather than declaring them on the command line. For example, to declare the script funky, you can put the following into a script file and then use the source or . commands to make the function active:

```
funky ()
{
    ps;
    ls —color=tty -ld;
    who
}
```

Viewing, Setting, and Removing Functions

To see the functions defined for your user, use the declare command:

```
declare -F
```

This returns output similar to the following:

```
declare -f funky
declare -f fish
declare -f iliad
```

The declare command can also be used to see the contents of a particular function, such as

```
declare -f funky
```

This returns output similar to this:

```
funky ()
{
    ps;
    ls —color=tty -ld;
    who
}
```

To see everything that can be easily pulled about a particular function, use the type command:

```
type -all funky
```

This returns output similar to the following:

```
funky is a function
funky ()
{
    ps;
    ls —color=tty -ld;
    who
}
```

To set a function in memory, you use the format discussed previously. The following example does three simple and separate tasks that must be delimited by a semicolon (;) character, particularly including the last one after the who command.

This command declares the function funky:

```
funky () { ps ; ls -ld ; who ; }
```

Executing this function is simple; you just enter it on the command line:

```
funky
```

This returns output similar to what's shown here:

```
  PID TTY         TIME CMD
 4960 pts/3    00:00:00 bash
 5609 pts/3    00:00:00 ps
drwxr-x—-  17 root     root           8192 Apr 14 15:01 .
root     tty1      Apr  8 17:26
root     pts/1     Apr 14 14:41 (192.168.1.100)
root     pts/0     Apr  8 17:31 (:0)
root     pts/2     Apr 12 14:42 (:0)
root     pts/3     Apr 14 14:44 (192.168.1.100)
```

The components of a function can be anywhere from simple to very complex, with just about anything that a script can contain being valid for a function.

Removing a function is relatively simple: If it has been defined in a file such as the .bashrc, you can unset the function for only the current login session with the following command:

```
unset funky
```

No output is returned—the function just disappears and returns again upon the next login shell.

To remove a function defined on the command line, the same command string is used. A simple logout and login again also refreshes the original session.

Functions are usually defined in the .bashrc file for a given user or in the /etc/bashrc file for all users. The syntax is exactly the same as on the command line, and functions are typically defined after any aliases because aliases are capable of being included in functions.

 Expect some questions about functions on the exam, including what a function is; how to create, modify, and remove them; how to view them; and what the correct syntax of a function is comprised of.

Understanding Shell Levels

One of the mysteries I want to clear up in this section is what happens to variables that are declared and exported when the shell exits.

For example, take the situation where you have an environment variable named CHEESE with a value of wensleydale and then you run a script where the same value is exported with a different value. It's important to know what happens to the value of the original, and also to the value of the latest exported version of the variable.

Here's how it works, step by step:

1. Open a shell session.

2. Declare and export the variable CHEESE with the following command:

   ```
   export CHEESE=wensleydale
   ```

3. Echo the value of CHEESE with the command shown here:

   ```
   echo $CHEESE
   ```

   This returns the following output:

   ```
   wensleydale
   ```

4. With the assurance that your variable contains the right value, create and save the following script in vi or your favorite editor:

   ```
   #!/bin/bash
   # filename = scriptfile
   echo \$CHEESE is set to $CHEESE
   export CHEESE=gouda
   TYPE=$CHEESE
   echo "The $TYPE is very good"
   echo \$CHEESE is set to $CHEESE
   ```

5. Now set the file to be executable:

   ```
   chmod +x scriptfile
   ```

6. Run the script with the following command:

```
./scriptfile
```

This produces the following output:

```
$CHEESE is set to wensleydale
The gouda is very good
$CHEESE is set to gouda
```

7. Finally, echo the value of $CHEESE again:

```
echo $CHEESE
```

This produces the output shown here:

```
wensleydale
```

Let's deconstruct this script, so you can see what happened to the original value and why it's still there, even though you exported a different value for $CHEESE. Let's take the script line by line:

➤ **Line 1**—The shebang that sets which shell to use

➤ **Line 2**—A comment reminding you what the filename is

➤ **Line 3**—The echo of the original value of $CHEESE

➤ **Line 4**—The tricky export of the new value for $CHEESE

➤ **Line 5**—The incorporation of $CHEESE as the value for $TYPE

➤ **Line 6**—An echo showing that the new values work

➤ **Line 7**—An echo of the damning evidence, or so it appears

The key to all this tomfoolery with variable values and exporting of those values is to remember that the use of the export command makes the exported variable and its value available to the current shell and all subshells. In other words, when you run the script, it runs in a subshell of the current shell, which is why the original value for $CHEESE is available to the script. However, when you exit the script (and the subshell), the exported value of $CHEESE declared within the script goes away with the subshell, leaving the original value of $CHEESE.

This concept is key for the exam. You will be tested on your knowledge of how subshells and variable exports work. Many mistake the export of a variable as being the equivalent to making that variable absolute throughout the system, when it's really available only for the current shell and subshells.

There is almost always another way to do something in Unix and Linux, so I must finish with how you can execute a script in the current shell. If you remember the concept of sourcing, or using the `source` command to take a script and make its variables active for your current shell, that is the method you can use to run a script file in the current shell, if necessary. For example, you can run the script `scriptfile` in the current shell with either of these two command strings:

```
source  scriptfile
.  scriptfile
```

Outside of sourcing configuration files so their contents act on the current shell, you'll probably not see or use sourcing to run scripts.

Exam Prep Questions

1. What would you call the feature of the `bash` shell that allows a string to be typed that would then call another string that contains variables and recursive actions and is contained in memory?

   ○ A. Script

   ○ B. Alias

   ○ C. Function

   ○ D. Program

   Answer C is correct because only a function has the necessary capabilities, particularly recursive actions such as looping. Answer A is incorrect because a script is not contained in memory; it's on disk. Answer B is incorrect because an alias has most of the features but doesn't allow recursive actions. Answer D is incorrect because a program is binary and exists on disk until executed.

2. Enter in the exact command string used to declare an alias named `mm` that executes the following commands:

   ```
   ps ; file *
   ```

   _____

   The correct answer is `alias mm='ps ; file *'`. There are no alternative correct answers.

3. On a Linux system installed with the default shell, you need to execute a shell script that contains variables, aliases, and functions by simply entering its name on the command line. What should be the first line of the script? (Choose all that apply.)

   ❑ A. Nothing

   ❑ B. `#/bin/csh`

   ❑ C. `#!/bin/sh`

   ❑ D. `exec=/bin/bash`

   ❑ E. `#!/bin/bash`

   Answers A, C, and E are correct because the features mentioned as being in the script are all related to the `bash` shell. Either you use answer E to specifically set it or you allow the default of `bash` to be used by not specifying a shell, and on a default Linux system, `/bin/sh` is a link to `/bin/bash`. Answer B is incorrect because the syntax is incorrect for the string and the `csh` shell won't do what the question requires. Answer D is incorrect because the line is incorrect and means nothing in a shell script.

4. You need to reference the script being executed from within the script itself. Which string would represent this? Fill in the blank below with the exact string, including any prefixes or suffixes:

_____

The correct answer is **$0**. There are no alternative correct answers.

5. You are using the scripting statement **case** in a script and keep getting a message such as the following:

```
script1: line 10: syntax error: unexpected end of file
```

What would be the most effective addition to the script you can make in attempt to fix it? Fill in the blank below with the exact characters you would use:

_____

The correct answer is **esac**. Alternative answers are **fi** and **done**.

6. When executing with the **bash** shell, what is the most accurate order of precedence? (Choose the best answer.)
   - ○ A. Built-in, keyword, alias, program, function
   - ○ B. Alias, keyword, function, built-in, program
   - ○ C. Function, alias, keyword, program, built-in
   - ○ D. Program, function, built-in, alias, keyword
   - ○ E. Keyword, built-in, alias, function, program

   Answer B is correct because the order is alias, keyword, function, built-in, and then program. Answers A, C, D, and E are incorrect because they don't follow the correct order.

7. A value that's held in a variable needs to be available to all subshells of the current shell. Which command would you run? Fill in the blank below with just the command name:

_____

The correct answer is **export**. There are no alternative correct answers.

8. You want to have the following message show on the console exactly as it appears here:

```
You've spent $192.68 on our site so far, Thank you!
```

Which of the following command strings accomplishes this? (Choose two.)

- ❑ A. `echo 'You've spent $192.68 on our site so far, Thank you!'`
- ❑ B. `echo "You've spent \$192.68 on our site so far, Thank you!"`
- ❑ C. `echo "You've spent '$192.68' on our site so far, Thank you\!"`
- ❑ D. `echo "You've spent $192.68 on our site so far, Thank you!"`
- ❑ E. `echo You\'ve spent \$192.68 on our site so far, Thank you\!`

Answers B and E are correct. Answer B is correct because the `$` symbol needs to be escaped specifically, but the ! symbol is handled by the double quotation marks enclosure. Answer E is correct because the \ symbol is used to escape the characters that must appear as themselves only. Answer A is incorrect because the use of three single quotation marks leaves one of them unmatched, and a syntax error will occur. Answer C is incorrect because single quotation marks inside a pair of double quotation marks are treated as apostrophe characters. Answer D is incorrect because double quotation marks allow for variable expansion, causing `$192.68` to be displayed as `92.68` because no value or even variable is filling the `$1` positional parameter spot.

9. You need to remove from memory the function named `conjunction`. What single command would you use to accomplish this? Fill in the blank with just the command name:

_____

The correct answer is `unset`. There are no alternative correct answers.

10. After running the `tarfoo` command, you inspect the output and decide that either an alias or function is being executed, not the `tarfoo` command. To guarantee that you are executing the desired command and not anything else, what could you attach to the command name? Fill in the blank with the entire string to execute the `tarfoo` command itself:

_____

The correct answer is `\tarfoo`. There are no alternative correct answers.

Linux Printing

Terms you'll need to understand:

✓ Filter
✓ Print job
✓ Print queues
✓ **printcap**
✓ Printer
✓ Spool

Techniques you'll need to master:

✓ Managing printers and queues
✓ Submitting print jobs
✓ Prioritizing and promoting print jobs
✓ Printing multiple copies of print jobs
✓ Installing local and remote printers
✓ Troubleshooting print problems

Linux Printing Overview

The LPI exams don't place much importance on the subject of printing and only cover the lpd or RFC 1179 BSD-style printing options.

That's not to say that printing isn't important and can occupy many hours of a sysadmin's busy life either by troubleshooting or configuring how users can print their jobs. Although you'll see few questions about the topic, a thorough understanding of the topic is a required job skill for any Linux/Unix sysadmin.

How lpd Printing Works

The lpd or BSD-style of printing uses several components to make up the environment in which printing is performed. Those components are shown in Figure 16.1.

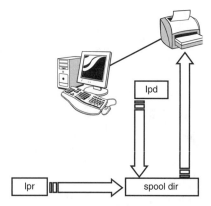

Figure 16.1 Linux **lpd** printing.

In Figure 16.1, the set of steps being performed are

1. A user submits a print job with the lpr command.

2. The job is sent to the local machine's spool directory for the target printer.

3. The lpd daemon senses the print job and scoops it up for delivery to the target printer.

4. The print job is formatted with the appropriate filter; if it's an ASCII or a Postscript job, it's left unaltered.

5. The job is delivered to the printer for printing.

The lpd daemon or server follows an algorithm to cause the printing to happen, loosely defined as follows:

1. Open the print device (or make a socket connection to the remote host the printer is on).

2. Initialize the printer with the correct strings (these vary greatly between printers).

3. If configured to, send a banner to the print device or socket.

4. Send the print job data file to the print device or socket.

5. Send print job termination strings to the print device or socket.

6. Close off the print device or socket.

Again, this process is loosely what happens; it's almost impossible to give a typical printer session when so many parameters and different printer situations could occur.

The Printer Capabilities File

The lpd printing style uses a printer capabilities file named /etc/printcap for printer definition and initial configuration. This file is editable only by the root user but is readable by all users, particularly to allow them to read it when attempting printing.

An example of the /etc/printcap is shown here, with notes as to the lines in the following list:

```
hplaser:\
        :ml=0:\
        :mx=0:\
        :sd=/var/spool/lpd/hplaser:\
        :af=/var/spool/lpd/hplaser/hplaser.acct:\
        :sh:\
        :lp=/dev/lp0:\
        :if=/usr/share/printconf/util/mf_wrapper:
```

The previous printer definition contains the following entries:

➤ hplaser—The name of the printer.

➤ ml—The minimum allowable characters in a print job.

➤ mx—The maximum allowable job size in KB. 0 means the size is unlimited.

➤ sd—The spool directory to be used for the printer.

➤ af—The accounting file (mostly for chargebacks for usage).

➤ sh—The shell used by filters,; it defaults to /bin/sh.

➤ lp—The device or pipe that data is sent to (for local system printers).

➤ if—The filter used on each file (much like a printer driver).

The printcap file's entries each describes a particular printer. As shown in the previous example, entries are typically broken up into many individual lines, each of which contains a setting and the value(s) that corresponds to that setting. The use of the backslash character at the end of these lines simply means to begin the next field on the next newline. A printcap entry could be one long line of fields, but that would be difficult to parse for humans.

Red Hat and Debian differ on what you can use to configure printers. The Red Hat distribution has had many changes in what is used as a tool to add and remove printers, including printconf, printtool, and recently the duo of redhat-config-printer-tui and redhat-config-printer-gui.

Debian, on the other hand, defaults to an editor for its printer configuration, unless you're running X or not using the lpd or BSD-style of printing—for instance, if you're using Common Unix Printing System (CUPS).

NOTE | We don't cover either CUPS or LPRNG in this discussion; they are both excellent but beyond the scope of this book.

Remote Printing Entries

When you are printing to another host across the network, the same set of tools and daemons is present; however, some are on another machine, such as in Figure 16.2.

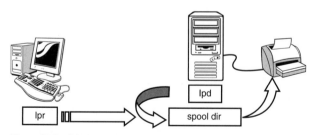

Figure 16.2   Printing to a remote printer.

As you can see, the host on the left is submitting a print job and the process is the same as the process shown in Figure 16.1, but it has been simplified for readability.

The host submitting the print job has a couple of special settings in the
/etc/printcap entry for the remote server's printer. rm is for remote machine
and rp is for remote printer. A typical remote printer entry is shown here:

```
remoteptr:\
        :ml=0:\
        :mx=0:\
        :sd=/var/spool/lpd/remoteptr:\
        :af=/var/spool/lpd/remoteptr/remoteptr.acct:\
        :sh:\
        :rm=192.168.1.2:\
        :rp=brother:\
        :lpd_bounce=true:\
        :if=/usr/share/printconf/util/mf_wrapper:
```

Notice that no local lp=/dev/lp line appears in this configuration. The
rm=192.168.1.2 and rp=brother lines take its place and send the print jobs submitted to this printer to the remote system's lpd daemon for submission into
the brother printer's spool directory.

The **rm** and **rp** entries are likely to be on the exam, so make sure that when you're
shown an **/etc/printcap** print-out, that you look carefully to see where the printer
points and what other parameters are present.

Printing Command Overview

Several commands are used in the lpd style of printing. The following table
lists them, and examples are presented in the later sections.

Command	Description
lpd	The **lpd** daemon itself. All printers defined on the system get an instance of **lpd** to themselves.
lpr	Used to submit print jobs. **lpr** uses the default printer if none is specified.
lpq	Used to query the default printer, specific printers, or all printers.
lprm	Used to remove print jobs from the default, specific, or all queues.
lpc	Used to configure the **lpd** daemon and printers either from the command line or interactively.

The original version of **lpd** and its associated utilities offered a small subset of the
commands in use today with later versions of **lpd** and LPRNG. Some of the options
covered here are a result of the widespread use of the LPRNG printing package,
but noting them as such would be tiresome and bring nothing to the goal of exam
readiness.

Each command is shown with its syntax and various examples in the following sections, including any exam alerts to clue you in to what to expect.

The lpd Daemon

The lpd daemon is the main process that oversees the printing programs and tasks. The daemon is located in /usr/sbin and referenced by a script in the /etc/rc.d/init.d directory for Red Hat and the /etc/init.d directory for Debian.

The syntax for lpd is

```
lpd -option parameter
```

The /etc/lpd.conf file might be present for later versions of lpd (and LPRNG) to hold the default configuration parameters. This file is read before the /etc/printcap is read, and any conflicting parameter settings between the two take on the latest applied value, such as banner settings or the shell used for running the filters.

Print Filters

Print filters are subcommands or filtering programs that help the lpd process and format submitted print jobs for the destination print device.

Typically, lpd and the /etc/printcap configuration reference any or all of three types of filters:

> **OF**—Output filters are used for banner generation, initialization, and the termination strings that are sent to the print device.

> **Data**—Uses a lowercase character to identify a file type and then loads the appropriate filter type defined in the /etc/printcap to process the date.

> **Pipe**—If a printcap device is noted by a pipe followed directly by a program name, such as ¦someprog, the device being printed to is the actual program noted, which then has access to the real print device.

Print filters come in many varieties, the most common being apsfilter, magicfilter, and Red Hat's über-filter. These filters are relatively complex, and thankfully the only knowledge needed on the exam at this level is that they exist, what their names are, and their locations on the system:

> apsfilter—Used mostly for converting print jobs to the PostScript format, its configuration files are in the /etc/apsfilter or /usr/local/etc/ apsfilter directory.

➤ `magicfilter`—Very configurable, this filter uses the magic numbers contained in the print files, particularly the file type and formatting that can be detected.

➤ Red Hat's `printtool`—This utility does several operations for you, taking the place of or organizing the processing of print jobs using the various other filter options.

Printing with lpr

The `lpr` command is used almost exclusively to print on a Linux system, either from the command line or as the subcomponent of a graphical print routine such as a word processor. The alternative is to have the application directly call the functions the `lpr` command uses.

Print jobs submitted with `lpr` take the following form:

```
lpr -option value filename
```

lpr Command Options

`lpr` offers a number of options with which to specify print jobs:

➤ `-b`—Forces the submission of a literal job; no filtering is done.

➤ `-K` and `-#`—Followed by a numeric value, these cause multiple copies to be printed.

➤ `-P`—Followed either by a space and a printer name or directly by a printer name, this option specifies the printer to be printed to.

➤ `-v`—Makes the process more verbose, showing extra information in some cases about the print job.

Printing a job to the default queue is simple; you use the command shown here:

```
lpr file2print
```

To print to a specific printer, such as one that is not the default, you use the following command:

```
lpr -P hplaser file2print
```

Interestingly, you can leave out the space between the -P for the printer and the actual printer name itself, so the following command works identically to the previous example:

```
lpr -Phplaser file2print
```

To print more than one copy of a document, use the following command:

```
lpr -K3 file2print
```

This is identical to this command:

```
lpr -#3 file2print
```

 Be aware that **lpr** accepts standard input like other commands, such as printing the contents of four files with the following command:

cat file[1-4] | lpr -P hplaser

This reads the contents of **file1**, **file2**, **file3**, and **file4** and then sends that output as a single print job to the printer **hplaser**.

Monitoring Print Jobs with lpq

After you or others have submitted a print job to the queue, the lpq command is used to monitor the progress or status of those print jobs.

lpq is a read-only or informational tool; it cannot be used to alter anything about your machine's printing configuration or do anything to the listed print jobs. Several other commands, which are covered next, are used for those tasks.

The lpq command syntax is as follows:

```
lpq -option value
```

lpq Command Options

lpq offers several options to control how information is presented:

➤ -a—Used to specify that all print queues should be queried.

➤ -P—Followed by a value for the printer name, it's used to specify a particular printer to query.

➤ -l—Used for verbose output.

➤ -L—Increases the verbosity of output to an alarming level, simulating debug information.

➤ -t—Followed by a value of seconds, this displays the specified queues, waits the length of the sleep time, and displays the queue's information again until it's interrupted by a Ctrl+C.

Examples of Using lpq

lpq is usually the first utility you should run if you're not sure that printing is occurring properly. It gives you quick and precise information and can be used to troubleshoot if you use the -L option for increased verbosity.

To show the jobs in the default queue, use the command shown here:

```
lpq
```

This returns output similar to

```
Printer: hplaser@localhost
 Queue: 1 printable job
 Server: pid 23462 active
 Unspooler: pid 23463 active
 Status: IF filter 'mf_wrapper' filter msg - '' at 14:39:13.726
 Rank    Owner/ID           Class Job Files          Size Time
active root@localhost+461    A     461 /etc/printcap   997 14:39:13
```

NOTE As you can see, a lot of information is already in an **lpq** query. I won't torture you (and the editorial staff!) with the output from the most verbose options because it would fill a couple of pages.

To view a queue other than the default, such as the brother queue, use this command:

```
lpq -P brother
```

This produces this output:

```
Printer: brother@localhost
 Queue: no printable jobs in queue
 Status: brother: Ready
```

Additionally, you can view all the print queues with either the -a or -all option, such as

```
lpq -a
```

This returns output similar to

```
Printer: hplaser@localhost
 Queue: no printable jobs in queue
 Status: hplaser: Update_status: no identifier for 'hfA461' at 14:43:53.544
Printer: brother@localhost
```

```
Queue: no printable jobs in queue
Status: job 'root@localhost+397' error 'aborting operations'
➥at 15:18:58.800
```

If you use the -all option, the returned messages are more verbose, separating the information returned to a series of lines with one status message on each line.

lpq often appears in simple questions that test your knowledge of its existence. The **-P**, **-a**, and **-all** options might appear, too.

Removing Print Jobs with **lprm**

The lprm command is used to remove, or *dequeue*, print jobs from any of the print queues.

Requests to remove print jobs with the lprm command take the following form:

```
lprm -option value keyword
```

Most **lprm** removal commands use the job ID of * or **all**, which means to act upon all jobs that can be removed by the user executing the command.

lprm Command Options

lprm differs from the other lp commands in certain ways. If you have two queues that have print jobs in both queues, running the lprm command acts on the default queue's first job and removes it.

lprm offers a number of options with which to remove print jobs:

➤ -a—Removes all files from any and all spools that are modifiable by the user (can be used with the all keyword to specify all jobs in all queues).

➤ -P—Used for specifying a printer, this must be followed by a printer specifier, which is usually a name such as hplaser.

➤ -U—Used to remove a job with a specific user ID.

➤ -D—Contains debugging options.

➤ -V—Provides print version information.

Print jobs are often removed by job IDs but can be specified by the following types of information:

➤ `all`—This keyword affects all jobs in the default queue.

➤ ID—A number representing the print job ID, or several IDs separated by spaces.

➤ User ID—A user's ID, such as `rbrunson`.

➤ `*`—Like all the others, it affects all jobs in the queue.

Examples of Using **lprm**

To remove just the first listed print job in the default queue, use `lprm` by itself:

```
lprm
```

To remove just job 33 from the default queue, use this command:

```
lprm 33
```

To remove jobs 33 and 144 from the default queue, use the following command:

```
lprm 33 144
```

To remove just the first job from all queues, use

```
lprm -a
```

To remove all the jobs from the default queue, use

```
lprm all
```

To remove all jobs from all queues, use the command shown here:

```
lprm -a all
```

 The exam will test your knowledge of which options and specifiers are used to remove certain types of jobs, such as **-a**, **all**, and possibly a combination of the two.

Monitoring Print Jobs with **lpc**

The `lpc` command is used to configure and control `lpd`, its child printers, their configuration settings, and the state of operations.

lpc is quite different from the rest of the lp commands. It can be used either in command-line or interactive (like ftp's interface) mode.

The lpc command syntax is as follows:

```
lpc -option value
```

lpc Command-Line Options

The options used with lpc can be only on the command line; otherwise, you can use some of the options along with the internal commands while in the lpc interface. Options for lpc include

➤ -a—An alias that stands for -Pall or that affects all queues.

➤ -P—If followed by a printer name or all, this affects the specified printers. If no specifier is set, it affects the default queue.

➤ -s—Followed by either the name or IP of the server the desired printer is on.

➤ -v—Shows version information about lpc.

➤ -U—Followed by the username to perform the actions as.

➤ -D—Followed by debugging options.

Internal lpc Options

The lpc interface is similar to the ftp commands. Here you simply execute the lpc command and then are put into an interface where options and configuration settings are specified.

The lpc command and options are entered in two ways. They can be entered on the command line, like so:

```
lpc status all
```

This yields the following output:

```
Printer Printing Spooling Jobs Server Subserver Redirect Status/(Debug)
hplaser@localhost   enabled  enabled   0    none    none
brother@localhost   enabled  enabled   0    none    none
```

Or they are entered in the interface, like so:

```
lpc>status all
```

This yields the following output:

```
Printer Printing Spooling Jobs Server Subserver Redirect Status/(Debug)
hplaser@localhost   enabled  enabled    0    none    none
brother@localhost   enabled  enabled    0    none    none
```

lpc has a lot of internal options, some of which are used on the command line and are covered in the examples section. We'll not cover all lpcs options because there isn't room and most aren't on the exam. Instead we'll cover the options most likely to appear on the exam.

Internal options for lpc include

➤ ?—Shows help for the lpc interface.

➤ defaultq—Shows the default queue.

➤ defaults—Shows the configuration defaults for all parameters.

➤ disable—Disables printing to the print queue(s) you specify. (This does *not* delete the printer; it still exists but just does not print.)

➤ enable—This enables printing to the printer again.

➤ exit or quit—Quits the interface.

➤ hold—Causes jobs to be held when submitted, and they must be released to print with the release command. It's used with a job ID, such as hold 25.

➤ kill—This is usually followed by a printer name or the keyword all. This kills the printer daemon that governs the printer(s) specified.

➤ client—Shows the local machine's printcap file and configuration information for troubleshooting help.

➤ move—This allows a job to be moved from queue to queue, which is useful when a printer dies or someone wraps copier labels around the corona wire.

➤ redirect—Sends jobs that were submitted to a printer to another printer; it's essentially print job forwarding.

➤ start—Starts the printer and is followed by either a printer name or all.

➤ status—Prints the status for the printer or all printers, with one line of output per printer.

➤ topq—This is a very useful command and is followed by the printer name and the job ID. It moves that print job to the top of the print queue, causing it to be printed next.

➤ up—Followed by a printer name or all, this command brings up all printers and makes them available for printing.

Examples of Using **lpc**

There are two methods of using lpc—interactive (with the interface and lpc> prompt) and noninteractive (where you type the lpc option parameter and press Enter to execute).

To use lpc interactively, just enter

```
lpc
```

You are presented with the following prompt:

```
lpc>
```

To use lpc noninteractively, you enter the command, with any options, as shown here:

```
lpc status all
```

This returns output similar to

```
Printer Printing Spooling Jobs Server Subserver Redirect Status/(Debug)
hplaser@localhost   enabled  enabled   0    none     none
brother@localhost   enabled  enabled   0    none     none
```

To bring up all the printers, use the following command:

```
lpc up all
```

This returns output similar to what is shown here:

```
Printer: hplaser@localhost
server process PID 24938 exited
hplaser@localhost.localdomain: enabled and started
Printer: brother@localhost
server process PID 24947 exited
brother@localhost.localdomain: enabled and started
```

To bring a print job to the top of the queue, you should view the print jobs first with

```
lpq
```

This returns output that contains the print job IDs:

```
Printer: hplaser@localhost
 Queue: 4 printable jobs
 Server: pid 2795 active
 Unspooler: pid 2796 active
 Status: waiting for subserver to exit at 09:02:17.548
 Rank   Owner/ID            Class Job Files          Size Time
active root@localhost+794     A   794 /etc/printcap   997 09:02:15
2      root@localhost+811     A   811 /etc/printcap   997 09:02:16
3      root@localhost+813     A   813 /etc/printcap   997 09:02:17
4      root@localhost+815     A   815 /etc/printcap   997 09:02:17
```

You can then decide to promote print job 815 to the top of the queue with the following command:

```
lpc topq hplaser 815
```

This returns output similar to

```
Printer: hplaser@localhost
hplaser: selected 'root@localhost+815'
kill server process PID 2795 with User defined signal 1
hplaser@localhost.localdomain: started
```

Then you can confirm that job 815 was sent to the top of the queue with this command:

```
lpq
```

This returns output similar to the following:

```
Printer: hplaser@localhost
 Queue: 4 printable jobs
 Server: pid 2795 active
 Unspooler: pid 2796 active
 Status: waiting for subserver to exit at 09:03:08.971
 Rank   Owner/ID             Class Job Files          Size Time
 1      root@localhost+815     A   815 /etc/printcap   997 09:02:17
 active root@localhost+794     A   794 /etc/printcap   997 09:02:15
 3      root@localhost+811     A   811 /etc/printcap   997 09:02:16
 4      root@localhost+813     A   813 /etc/printcap   997 09:02:17
```

As you can see, the command did promote job 815 to the top of the queue, as requested. Use this for emergency print jobs, to get little memos out before 500-page PDF files, and so on.

Additional Printing Commands

Several other commands don't really come with the lpd suite but are present for use when printing. The following lists some commands that are likely to appear on the exam and that you can use in real life:

➤ mpage—The mpage command is used for printing multiple print pages per sheet of paper when using PostScript printers.

➤ lp—The lp command is used with later versions or variations of the lpd daemon, notably the LPRNG printing suite. lp is normally a symbolic link back to the lpr command and is used most often by homesick Solaris sysadmins.

➤ lpstat—If you see the lpstat, lpinfo, or lpmove command on the exam, they are being used by the exam writers as a distractor, or incorrect answer. These commands aren't used by lpd and are often on the system as symlinks made by a sysadmin.

Watch for the commands associated with the **lpd** daemon versus ones for the **lp** printing service on System V machine Unix versions, such as Solaris and AIX. Only **lpd** commands or links to them are correct answers on the exam.

Printer Security

The last exam-related situation that needs coverage for printing is security for print jobs or the ability to print. This is accomplished in two methods— either putting a group ownership on the spool directory or by limiting the printing capability by the host submitting the print job.

By default, all hosts on your network can print to any printer, but by setting the parameters and entries in the /etc/hosts.lpd file, you can control who can and cannot print to a server's printers.

To clarify, if you need to print to a remote host that restricts printer usage via the **/etc/hosts.lpd** file, your hostname must be added to that file to allow your host's processes to print to the remote host's printers.

The /etc/hosts.lpd file is very simple. The typical entry in the file is either an unqualified hostname or a fully qualified domain name, the presence of which means that the host is allowed to print on that server's printers.

An example of a functional /etc/hosts.lpd file is as follows:

```
bruce.example.com
geddy.example.com
zakk.example.com
192.168.1.201
```

In the file shown here, only the listed hosts can submit print jobs across the network to this host's printers. The /etc/hosts.lpd file allows hostnames or IPs.

Watch for the missing step in a printer configuration on the exam. If the printcap file (**/etc/printcap**) is correctly configured and the host still can't print to a remote server, you need to add an entry for the printing host to the remote server's **/etc/hosts.lpd** file.

Exam Prep Questions

1. You are configuring a user's printer settings for a remote server. Which parameter should be present in the /etc/printcap printer definition to successfully deliver print jobs to a remote host? (Choose two.)

   ❏ A. remote=
   ❏ B. rpm=
   ❏ C. rp=
   ❏ D. rmc=
   ❏ E. rm=

   Answers C and E are correct because the rm=hostname and rp=printername parameters are needed for sending remote print jobs. Answers A, B, and D are incorrect because no options by those names exist in the /etc/printcap file specification.

2. You need to allow a host named ishmael in your local domain to print on your host's lpd daemon print queues. In the blank below, enter the exact syntax that will allow printing for this host, if put in the /etc/hosts.lpd file:

   _____

   The correct answer is ishmael. There are no correct alternative answers.

3. Which of the following command lines promotes all print jobs on the queue brother that belong to the user llaffer to the top of the queue?

   ○ A. lpc -P brother topq llaffer
   ○ B. lpc topq brother llaffer
   ○ C. lpc brother topq llaffer
   ○ D. lpc topq -Pbrother llaffer

   Answer B is correct because the lpc command's topq option syntax is lpc topq *printer user*. Answer A is incorrect because lpc doesn't use the -P *printer* syntax and the order is incorrect. Answer C is incorrect because the topq option must be used before the printer name. Answer D is incorrect because neither the -P*printer* nor -P *printer* syntax works with lpc.

4. Which file on a remote host should be configured to allow your host to print to its already functioning printers? Fill in the blank below with the full path and filename of the appropriate file:

   _____

   The correct answer is /etc/hosts.lpd. There are no correct alternative answers.

5. Which command prints two copies of the file to the default printer? (Choose all that apply.)

❑   A. `cat hosts ¦ lpr -#2`

❑   B. `for 1 in 2 lpr > hosts`

❑   C. `lpr -P -count 2 hosts`

❑   D. `cat hosts > lpr ; cat hosts > lpr`

❑   E. `lpr -K2 hosts`

Answers A and E are correct because only the `-#` and `-K` options are capable of printing multiple copies from `lpr`. Answer B is incorrect because, even though the loop might work, you can't print with this command because you get either a syntax error or a continuation prompt waiting for more input. Answer C is incorrect because there isn't any such parameter for `lpr`. Answer D is incorrect because it only sends (twice) the contents of the `hosts` file to a file named `lpr` in the local directory and does not print the `hosts` file.

6. Which command with any options, keywords, or parameters removes just the first queued print jobs on all print queues but does not remove multiple print jobs from any of the queues? Fill in the blank below with the exact command string that accomplishes this task:

_____

The correct answer is `lprm -a`. There are no correct alternative answers.

7. What is the full path and filename of the spool directory for the printer `hplaser` on a system that uses the standard `lpd` printing daemon and the default locations?

○   A. `/usr/spool/lpd/hplaser`

○   B. `/var/spool/hplaser`

○   C. `/var/spool/lpd/lp`

○   D. `/var/spool/lpd/hplaser`

Answer D is correct because the `lpd` daemon default base directory for printer spools is `/var/spool/lpd` and you just have to add the printer name to complete the answer. Answer A is incorrect because the default base for the spool directory isn't in the `/usr` tree. Answer B is incorrect because the base directory is `/var/spool/lpd`. Answer C is incorrect because the name of the printer is `hplaser` and there is no indication in the question that it is named `lp`, even though that might be an alias for the printer.

8. Which of the following is true about the standard `lpd` daemon and its associated processes on a default system? (Choose all that apply.)

   - ❏ A. `lpd` uses a single instance for all defined printers.
   - ❏ B. `lpd` uses one subprocess for each printer defined.
   - ❏ C. `lpd` jobs are sent directly to the print device.
   - ❏ D. `lpd` uses the `/etc/hosts.lpd` for printer definitions.
   - ❏ E. `lpd` conforms to the BSD style of printing.

   Answers B and E are correct because the `lpd` daemon uses a subprocess for each defined printer and follows the BSD style of printing. Answer A is incorrect because the `lpd` daemon uses multiple subprocesses, one per defined printer. Answer C is incorrect because `lpd` print jobs are sent to the spool directory and then are sent to the print device. Answer D is incorrect because `lpd` uses the `/etc/hosts.lpd` file for printing security and the `/etc/printcap` file for printer definitions.

9. Which of the following commands prints the file **spackle** on the printer **hplaser**? (Choose all that apply.)

   - ❏ A. `lpr -P hplaser -F spackle`
   - ❏ B. `lpr -Phplaser spackle`
   - ❏ C. `lpc printer=hplaser file=spackle`
   - ❏ D. `lpr -p hplaser spackle`
   - ❏ E. `lpr -P hplaser spackle`

   Answers B and E are correct because the `-P` option can be followed either directly by the printer name or a space and then the printer name. Answer A is incorrect because there should not be a `-F` parameter in the `lpr` command line. Answer C is incorrect because the `lpc` command does not submit print jobs. Answer D is incorrect because there must be a capital *P*, not a lowercase *p*, in the printer name option.

10. Which command, with any needed options and parameters, shows you the most information about the default `lpd` print queue without using the debugging options? Fill in the blank below with the appropriate command:

    _____

    The correct answer is `lpq` `-L`. There are no correct alternative answers.

11. If your system is using the BSD style of printing and has two printers defined and active, you will see multiple instances of the _____ daemon or service running. Fill in the blank below with just the daemon name:

    _____

    The correct answer is `lpd`. There are no correct alternative answers.

Basic Networking

Terms you'll need to understand:

✓ Broadcast address
✓ DHCP
✓ IP (Internet Protocol)
✓ Network address
✓ Network interface
✓ Network mask
✓ PPP
✓ Routing table

Techniques you'll need to master:

✓ Understanding basic networking
✓ Identifying hosts on a network
✓ Determining addresses
✓ Viewing, changing, and verifying interface configurations
✓ Configuring IPs manually or statically
✓ Configuring gateway addresses
✓ Viewing, changing, or correcting routing table entries
✓ Troubleshooting network problems
✓ Configuring a PPP client
✓ Initializing and connecting via a PPP link

Conceptual Overview of Networking

An Internet Protocol (IP) is a unique address or locator for a host on a network or on the Internet. All machines and internetworking devices that communicate via Transmission Control Protocol/Internet Protocol (TCP/IP) have an IP they are known by and communicated through.

To understand how all this works, think of the Internet, which is a large network made up of many interconnected smaller networks. The smallest building block of a network is the *host*, or any machine that has an IP and could respond to a ping.

Hosts are considered standalone unless they are connected to a network, and a logical grouping of hosts on a network is usually known as a *subnet*.

The difference between a subnet and a segment is that a *subnet* is a logical grouping of hosts, based on their addressing, whereas a *segment* is usually a physical grouping of hosts that are attached to the same wire, hub, or switch.

When trying to understand the concepts of networks and hosts, think of a network as a street that has houses on it that represent hosts. If you wanted to find a particular house, you could very well go to that street and begin looking up and down it at the house numbers. Figure 17.1 illustrates a network as a street and hosts as houses.

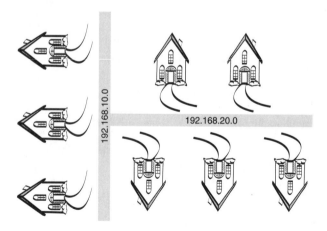

Figure 17.1 Networks and hosts.

Following the analogy of networks being streets and hosts on those networks being houses on the streets, an intersection between two streets would be similar to a *router* or *gateway* between networks.

In this day of subnet calculators and IBM's Linux Watch, the temptation would be to skip some of this information. None of this is blue-sky knowledge; it's all applicable to the exam and in most cases to real-life work on a daily basis for a network sysadmin.

Necessary Configuration Information

To participate in more than a single subnet or network, a host needs to have three things:

> **IP**—Assigned either statically or dynamically, the address must be valid to work.

> **Network mask**—Each logical network or subnet has a particular network mask that helps define where one section of addresses ends and another begins. This is also known as the *subnet mask*, particularly in a Microsoft environment.

> **Gateway address**—Like a door leading out of a room, a gateway address is the local IP associated with a network card or interface on a gateway or router device. Hosts configured with this address as the default gateway send traffic to this address when they need to access remote hosts.

IPs

An IPV4 IP consists of 32 bits grouped in four octets of 8 bits, with each octet separated by a dot. This is also known as a *dotted quad*. A particular IP, such as 192.168.10.100, would be expressed as the bit values shown here:

```
11000000.10101000.00001010.01100100
```

Bits in an octet have a specific value, and each octet's bits have the values shown in Figure 17.2.

128	64	32	16	8	4	2	1

Figure 17.2 Bit values in an octet.

When a bit in an octet is turned on, that value is added to any other bit values that are turned on to make a decimal number. With the way the bits are arranged, there is only one bit pattern to make any given number.

It might help to visualize these bits as a bank of light switches, each representing a particular value of watts. For example, if you had a bank of light switches with corresponding wattage, you would turn on the switches for 64, 32, and 4 to produce 100 watts of light. Figure 17.3 shows how this would look.

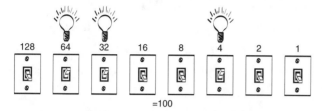

Figure 17.3 The light switch analogy.

Typically, you'll be working with IPs that have been assigned by a higher authority—either your IT department or corporate headquarters, or even an Internet service provider (ISP).

Networks and Hosts

The basic tenet of all networking with IPs is that there will be two portions to any given address that are assigned. Using the previous streets = networks and houses = hosts analogy, you could look at a host's address, such as 192.168.1.200, as being broken up into two parts: the street or network address (192.168.1) and the house or host address (.200).

Just as houses on the same street use that street as part of their addresses, a host address is treated as belonging to the network address it shares with the other hosts that belong to that network.

Address Class Ranges

Five address class ranges are defined by a request for comment (RFC 1918). An address class range is defined by the bit pattern of the first two or three bits in the first octet. This is important because the address class determines the number of hosts that are possible by default for each of the resulting networks.

A request for comment (RFC) documents specifications for Internet standards. As a draft for a particular specification is evaluated, it goes through a process that ends with it becoming an RFC, which is similar to a standard but is often treated as a very firm suggestion.

The five address classes are as follows:

➤ **A**—From 1 to 126; each of these encompasses 16,777,216 host addresses. There can be 126 Class A networks.

➤ **B**—From 128 to 191; each of these encompasses 65,536 host addresses. There can be 16,382 Class B networks.

➤ **C**—From 192 to 223; each of these encompasses 254 host addresses. There can be 2,097,150 Class C networks.

➤ **D**—From 224 to 239. This range is reserved for such activities as multicast and is not usually available for host addresses.

➤ **E**—From 240 to 254; this range is reserved for future use.

For those who are asking where the 127 range is, the designers saw fit to leave the entire 127 range for loopback or local host networking only. Yes, that's 16,777,216 addresses all so someone can ping his local host to see whether IP is working!

NOTE   Remember that when looking at the massive expanse of IPs available for Class A and Class B address ranges, those are typically broken up into many smaller networks by the use of custom subnet masks, which are covered later in the chapter.

Using the Bits to Determine Class

If you look at the bit pattern for the first octet of an address that's a Class A, you'll see the first bit must always be off because no Class A address is above a 126 in the first octet:

1 = 01000000

In a similar fashion, a Class B address cannot have the first bit in the first octet on. All Class B addresses range from 128 and higher:

128 = 10000000

By the same token, no Class C address can exist without the first two bits in the first octet set to on. All Class C addresses range from 192 and higher:

192 = 11000000

Network Masks

I've long said that one way to understand IPs and their partner network (or subnet) masks is to think of every IP as consisting of two pieces: a network section and a host section. The network mask sets where network bits end and host-assignable bits begin.

For each class, the point at which a network mask stops is where the network portion of an address ends and the host-assignable portion begins. For example, if you take the address 192.168.1.200 and a default subnet mask, the first three octets represent the network and the last octet is where hosts can be assigned.

Address class ranges come with their own built-in default subnet mask; only one can be the default per range:

➤ **A**—255.0.0.0 or /8 for the number of bits that represent the network mask

➤ **B**—255.255.0.0 or /16 for the number of bits that represent the network mask

➤ **C**—255.255.255.0 or /24 for the number of bits that represent the network mask

LPI follows the industry in its use of either fully spelled-out network masks (**255.255.255.0**) or using abbreviated notation (**/24**) to represent any network mask assigned to a host or set of hosts. The number 24 relates to the number of bits used for the subnet mask.

Be prepared to solve questions that use either method of expressing the network mask.

Using Default Network Masks

As previously mentioned, the place where the network portion of an address ends is where the subnet mask bits stop. If you have a network address such as 192.168.10.0 and a default subnet mask of 255.255.255.0 or /24, a single network (192.168.10.0) exists and the remaining 8 bits that are outside the network portion are available for assignment to hosts.

It might help to express the network address and then the network mask as a set of bits, like so:

```
11000000.10101000.00001010.00001010      (The IP)
11111111.11111111.11111111.00000000      (The Subnet Mask)
```

Because the network mask is a /24, or default Class C network mask, you can easily see where the network begins and ends and what's usable for host addresses. The boundary in this example is the last dot, leaving 8 bits worth of addresses for this single network assignable to hosts.

Gateway Addresses, or "Do I Dial 9?"

Gateway addresses were previously mentioned as an important part of the host's networking configuration. If a host needs to communicate on the greater network, it must have a portal or door to the network, typically known as a *default gateway*, or *gateway*.

When a host wants to communicate with another host on a network, it inspects the other host's network address to determine whether that host is on the local network or on another network. If the host exists on the local network, it can be contacted directly; otherwise, a default gateway or other router must be used.

Effectively, it's as if you needed to make a phone call to another person and needed to find out whether she was in the same building (local, just dial it) or outside the building (other network, dial 9 first and then the number).

The host uses its network mask to determine whether it needs to send traffic targeted to a remote host to the router for further delivery or whether it can just communicate on the local network to deliver the traffic to the target host.

For example, if you have an IP of 192.168.10.10 and your target host has an IP of 192.168.11.10, (and both use the /24 default network mask), your machine will look at your IP/mask as such:

```
11000000.10101000.00001010.00001010
11111111.11111111.11111111.00000000
```

It will then apply the same network logic to the target host, such as:

```
11000000.10101000.00001011.00001010
11111111.11111111.11111111.00000000
```

The network mask is expressed by the digits in the first three octets, and the last eight digits represent the difference between the network portions of the host's addresses. If there is even a single bit of difference inside the bits that make up the network mask, the host has to "dial 9," or send the traffic to the configured route or default gateway to have it further delivered.

Broadcast Addresses

All IP networks use the concept of a broadcast to send traffic that is designed to impact all hosts on that network. For example, if you have a small Class C network represented by the address 192.168.10.0 and a default subnet mask of 255.255.255.0, the network address is 192.168.10.0 but the broadcast address for every host on that network is 192.168.10.255. No matter how small or large, all networks include the concept of the broadcast address, which is not assignable to any host.

Custom Network Masks

The art of custom subnetting is fading, but you'll have to know how to do at least a Class C custom subnetting problem in your head to determine whether a host has a bad gateway address or how many hosts are possible on a particular network, given the defaults and a custom network mask.

Determining a Custom Network Mask

We'll discuss two scenarios. In one, you are creating the subnet map and determining the custom network (subnet) map, and in the other, you're solving how many hosts can fit on the network you are assigned.

Scenario 1: Custom Subnetting from Scratch

You are the sysadmin of a small company, and your boss wants to plan a set of networks for your main office and a few other locations. He arranges to rent a Class C network from your network reseller and tells you that you need to have six networks with as many hosts as possible on those networks.

Your task is to define a new network mask that will be applied to every host on the entire network. All subnets must have a network address, broadcast address, and gateway address, plus as many hosts as possible from the remaining addresses.

Because you know that you are dealing with a Class C network, you can assume that your default network mask that covers 24 bits will allow you to do your custom subnetting in the last 8 bits left over.

 Typically, you would be doing host addressing in the last octet, but because you're breaking up a single network into multiple smaller networks, bits from the last octet are stolen or used from the highest value end (128), leaving fewer bits for hosts per resulting subnet.

You know that your network address information is as follows:

Class C address	=	192.168.33.0
Network mask	=	Default (255.255.255.0)
Subnets needed	=	6
Hosts needed	=	As many as possible

Here are the steps you need to perform:

1. Convert the number of networks (6) to binary = 00000110.

2. Turn all the bits after the 4 bit to on = 00000111.

3. Flip the entire octet from end to end = 11100000.

4. Add the bits together to get the new custom network mask:

   128 + 64 + 32 = 224 (the new subnet mask)

5. Start at 0 and use the LSB (least significant bit) or 32 as the increment for the networks (keep in mind that a network's 0 and 224 might be network and broadcast addresses and thus invalid for use, depending on your networking hardware):

 The network addresses (0, 32, 64, and so on) are not assignable as host addresses. The first odd-numbered address (1, 32, 64, and so on) on each of these new networks is the first possible host address.

Network	Address Range
0	192.168.33.1—192.168.33.31
32	192.168.33.33—192.168.33.62
64	192.168.33.65—192.168.33.94
96	192.168.33.97—192.168.33.126
128	192.168.33.129—192.168.33.158
160	192.168.33.161—192.168.33.190
192	192.168.33.193—192.168.33.222
224	192.168.33.224—192.168.33.254

6. You can now assign these ranges to the networks that you build, with each representing 30 host addresses, a network address, and a broadcast address.

The previously listed network numbers represent the subnet or network to which you are assigning hosts. The network address, such as 192.168.33.32, is not assignable to a host. It isn't even assigned anywhere—it's agreed upon by the hosts on the network and the custom network mask.

Additionally, the first and last networks (192.168.33.0 and 192.168.33.224) are traditionally not seen as valid for assigning hosts to, unless the networking equipment supports it. Because I can't predict the hardware capabilities, we'll use the most common and compatible method.

The address range represents the numbers assignable to hosts, with one exception: The last or odd number on each range is the broadcast address and is not assignable to a host. It's used to address all hosts when broadcasts are sent over the network.

Scenario 2: How Many Hosts on a Network?

Another situation that might occur is that you are a new consultant for a small company and part of the initiation ritual seems to be setting you down in a cube with a workstation and a slip of paper that has your IP and an abbreviated notation network mask on it and having you discover your default gateway and other IP information.

The IP information you've been given is 10.30.200.120/26, and your gateway is supposed to be the last host-assignable IP on your network.

 You can convert the **/26** into a standard subnet mask by dividing 26 by 8; each 8 becomes a **255** and the remainder of 2 becomes a **.192**. In other words, convert the 26 into the number of bits in a subnet mask starting from the leftmost bit and moving right.

To solve this, you should do a quick subnetting problem, such as

1. The 10.30.200.180 address is a Class A address, but the network mask of 26 translates into a 255.255.255.192, or a very small chunk of the original 10.0.0.0 network.

2. Turn the 192 into the bit values = 1100000.

3. The smallest bit is 64, so the subnets increment by 64, starting at 0.

Network	Address Range
0	10.30.200.1–10.30.200.63
64	10.30.200.65–10.30.200.127
128	10.30.200.129–10.30.200.191

4. After you have your network (180 falls in the 129–191 network) you can stop, unless you just have to finish the networks.

Your network address is 10.30.200.128, the first addressable host IP is 10.30.200.129, the last addressable host IP is 10.30.200.190, and the broadcast address is 10.30.200.191. There are 62 host IP addresses on your subnet.

Be prepared to reread questions to see if they want to know all IPs on a network or whether you leave out the router and broadcast address. If you're asked for the number of IPs that could be assigned to hosts, it's always an even number; if you are to disregard or leave out the router/gateway address, it has to be an odd number.

Managing Interfaces

A Linux machine has a default interface called the *loopback* or *local interface*. The device appears as lo (that's a lowercase *L*, not a one) and can be configured like other interfaces, with the main difference being that the loopback is never going to connect to a network. The loopback interface is only there so your machine can have IP bound to an interface even if it's not otherwise configured to use a network card.

Real life, bosses, and the exam will require you to be able to set your IP via the interface configuration files or even statically configure the interface from the command line.

Viewing IP Information

The primary tool for viewing your IP information is the ifconfig command. By default, ifconfig shows all active interfaces, including the loopback interface: lo.

To display the interfaces on a Linux machine, you would enter the following command:

```
ifconfig
```

This produces output similar to the following:

```
eth0      Link encap:Ethernet  HWaddr 00:0C:29:66:DE:2D
          inet addr:192.168.1.73 Bcast:192.168.1.255 Mask:255.255.255.0
          UP BROADCAST RUNNING MULTICAST  MTU:1500  Metric:1
          RX packets:162318 errors:0 dropped:0 overruns:0 frame:0
          TX packets:97324 errors:0 dropped:0 overruns:0 carrier:0
          collisions:0 txqueuelen:100
          RX bytes:242424213 (231.1 Mb)  TX bytes:6835983 (6.5 Mb)
          Interrupt:10 Base address:0x1080
```

```
lo          Link encap:Local Loopback
            inet addr:127.0.0.1  Mask:255.0.0.0
            UP LOOPBACK RUNNING  MTU:16436  Metric:1
            RX packets:58 errors:0 dropped:0 overruns:0 frame:0
            TX packets:58 errors:0 dropped:0 overruns:0 carrier:0
            collisions:0 txqueuelen:0
            RX bytes:4020 (3.9 Kb)  TX bytes:4020 (3.9 Kb)
```

In the previous output, you see a wealth of information, particular of note is the eth0 interface. Pay attention to the following information:

➤ Link encap—Either Ethernet or Token. It indicates the type of link you are using. This might show up as local for loopback interfaces.

➤ HWaddr—The Media Access Control (MAC) or burned-in-address. In any case, it's the 48-bit physical address of the interface hardware.

➤ inet addr—The address assigned to the interface.

➤ Bcast—The broadcast address for the network this machine is on; it's entirely dependent on the network mask.

➤ Mask—The network mask, or how the system knows the logical network it's on.

➤ Interrupt—The machine interrupt the interface uses.

➤ Base address—The I/O address through which the interface communicates.

Also note the receive (RX) and transmit (TX) statistics and collisions that might exist for a particular interface. I've not mentioned the local interface; it's there but doesn't impact the machine's network presence.

 If you see any output from the **ifconfig** command on the exam, inspect it very carefully for configuration errors, collisions, and whether the interface state is up or down. LPI doesn't use screen real estate lightly, so that information will be key to the answer to the question, whatever it is.

Red Hat Interface Configuration

On a Red Hat machine, the /etc/sysconfig/network-scripts directory contains the scripts that are used to configure and bring up and down the interfaces on the machine.

For example, if you have an eth0 interface you need to configure with a static IP and other configuration, you can choose to run netconfig—one of the redhat-config-network-* utilities—or just edit the files themselves. Figure 17.4 shows the netconfig command's interface. These utilities are good

enough to stand on their own (and don't appear on the exam), so let's discuss
how to edit the file to configure the interface.

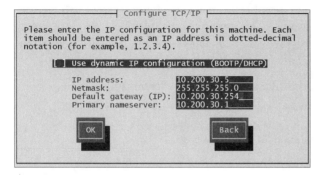

Figure 17.4   The **netconfig** interface.

 None of the graphical utilities Red Hat includes in the various versions of Red Hat
Linux are tested, the editing of the files and possibly **netconfig** being the extent of
the exam's mention of utilities for configuration of interfaces.

To display the ifcfg-eth0 file, you would use the command shown here:

```
cat /etc/sysconfig/network-scripts/ifcfg-eth0
```

With a static configuration, you would see output similar to

```
DEVICE=eth0
ONBOOT=yes
BOOTPROTO=static
IPADDR=192.168.1.73
NETMASK=255.255.255.0
GATEWAY=192.168.1.1
```

If the interface is configured for DHCP, you would see output similar to this:

```
DEVICE=eth0
ONBOOT=yes
BOOTPROTO=dhcp
```

Whichever method you decide to use can be implemented by editing this file
and setting the parameters you desire. The parameters are self-explanatory,
with the possible exception of the BOOTPROTO parameter. The BOOTPROTO parameter, when set to either static or dhcp, tells the network daemon how to configure this interface, either by reading the other parameters in the ifcfg-eth0
file or by using DHCP to get the address.

Debian Interface Configuration

Debian uses a different style of configuring interfaces: Instead of several smaller scripts or configuration files, Debian uses the /etc/network/interfaces file for all interfaces. Although Debian doesn't include the netconfig utility by default, the netcardconfig program is included in some Debian distributions and does roughly the same tasks.

To see the contents of this file, use the following command:

```
cat /etc/network/interfaces
```

This produces output similar to the following:

```
# /etc/network/interfaces -- configuration file for ifup(8), ifdown(8)
# The loopback interface
# automatically added when upgrading
auto lo eth0
iface lo inet loopback
iface eth0 inet static
        address 192.168.15.5
        netmask 255.255.255.0
        network 192.168.15.0
        broadcast 192.168.15.255
        gateway 192.168.15.2
```

Each interface defined in the interfaces file starts the keyword iface, then the name of the interface, the type of address (inet for IP, ipx for IPX, and inet6 for IPv6) and then the method for the interface (either static or dhcp).

After configuring the interfaces file with the correct parameters, it's recommended to restart the network daemon with the command shown here:

```
/etc/init.d/networking restart
```

This restarts the networking and brings the interfaces down and back up again.

Notice that the Debian interfaces file contains the gateway address but doesn't use uppercase letters like Red Hat does. Nor does Debian use an equal sign (=) between the parameter and the value in the interfaces file. Debian also uses the scripts as an input or source file, whereas Red Hat actually executes its configuration scripts.

It's important to note that, although Debian does primarily use the previous method, an instance of the file **/etc/sysconfig/network-scripts/ifcfg-eth0** is often found on the Debian machine. You'll need to read the documentation for your distribution or method to determine what relationship exists between the two. You can safely assume that this won't be an issue on the exam.

Viewing and Configuring Gateway Addresses

The default gateway is used for sending traffic to an interface that is the doorway or gateway to the rest of your networks, hence the name. A default gateway is necessary because you don't want to have static routes on all your machines for every destination network—that would be unwieldy and quickly become outdated.

Viewing the Default Gateway

To view the default gateway configured on your machine, you can use either the route command or the following command:

```
netstat -r
```

This displays output similar to

```
Kernel IP routing table
Destination  Gateway       Genmask        Flags  MSS Window   irtt Iface
192.168.1.0  *             255.255.255.0  U      40  0        0 eth0
127.0.0.0    *             255.0.0.0      U      40  0        0 lo
default      192.168.1.2   0.0.0.0        UG     40  0        0 eth0
```

This is an important set of output. Without a properly configured default gateway, your machine is capable of reaching hosts only on your local network.

The line that begins with 192.168.1.0 is the actual network address of your subnet or network. An address will appear in the output that is on the same network and that represents the actual IP of the router that provides the gateway functionality; in this case, it's on the last line and is 192.168.1.2.

Beware of any questions or answers that try to trick you into thinking that the actual IP of the gateway is 0.0.0.0. It's not; that's just the method that IP addressing schemes use to represent the default gateway when you are looking for a destination network for which a route isn't configured.

Configuring a Default Gateway

As you have seen in the configuration files for both Red Hat and Debian, a valid GATEWAY or gateway parameter and a value of an IP can configure a valid gateway for the interface.

On a Red Hat machine, you can edit either the /etc/sysconfig/network file or the /etc/sysconfig/network-scripts/ifcfg-eth0 file and add the GATEWAY entry:

```
GATEWAY=10.0.0.1
```

Debian uses the actual /etc/network/interfaces file to set each individual interface's gateway value.

On both types of systems, you can add a default gateway manually with the following command:

```
route add default gw 10.0.0.1
```

It's very important to note the syntax for the previous command, line by line:

➤ route—The route command, which is used for many things related to establishing, viewing, and removing routes to other networks.

➤ add—Used to add the default gateway. Other options include del to delete a particular route.

➤ default—The default gateway is the one that is used if no other route exists or matches the target address.

➤ gw—Notes that the entry is a gateway to the rest of the networks and traffic should be routed through this interface.

➤ 10.0.0.1—Replaced with your gateway address, or the resolvable domain name of the host that provides this functionality.

 Expect to troubleshoot, configure, or fill in the blank on a question about a default gateway. This type of question appears several times on the exam, as either fill-in-the-blank or multiple-choice (and often both) stated slightly differently.

Local Name Configuration

Local name configuration is a mish-mash of different files, most notably of which are

➤ /etc/hosts

➤ /etc/resolv.conf

➤ /etc/nsswitch.conf

These three files are used to configure how local name resolution occurs. Figure 17.5 shows the relationship between these files and how they use each other to resolve the name for a host to which a client software application needs to connect.

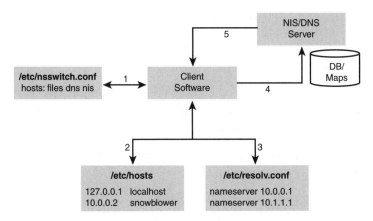

Figure 17.5   Name resolution diagram.

The numbered steps in Figure 17.5 represent the steps that would be followed during a normal name resolution. The following examples show how different variations would work on a system with this configuration.

For example, we have issued the following command on a host with the sample configuration shown in Figure 17.5:

```
ping snowblower
```

When a name is used instead of an IP, the client software asks the system to resolve that name. The system follows these steps:

1. The system first refers to the /etc/nsswitch.conf file and the hosts: line for the order in which it should look for the name's resolution. In Figure 17.5, the hosts: line is set to first look at the local files, then dns, and then nis:

    ```
    hosts: files dns nis
    ```

2. The system looks in the file /etc/hosts for the resolution of the name snowblower to an IP; in this case, it finds a matching entry with an IP of 10.0.0.2.

3. The system returns the IP to the client and the name resolution portion of the transaction is complete.

As a more complex example, let's see what happens if we issue the following command on a host that has the previous configuration:

```
ping shpdoinkle
```

The system follows the same general set of steps, with an addition:

1. The system first refers to the /etc/nsswitch.conf file and the hosts: line for the order of resolution.

2. The /etc/hosts file is inspected for a matching entry.

3. When none is found, the /etc/nsswitch.conf file is read and the next option for resolution is found to be dns.

4. The system then reads the /etc/resolv.conf file for the name server entries, with an upper practical limit of three expected.

5. The system queries the first found name server for the resolution of the name. If the name is resolved, resolution is halted. If the first name server doesn't reply in a reasonable amount of time, it tries the next configured name server until no entries remain; if no resolution is found, it fails.

6. If the name is resolved, the system returns the IP to the client and the name resolution portion of the transaction is completed.

As a summary, the steps taken to resolve a name depend on the order of the options in the /etc/nsswitch.conf file. Those entries are queried and any matching results are returned to the requesting software, where any errors are handled and the name resolution is complete.

 Just because an entry in the local files resolves a hostname to an IP doesn't mean that the IP is the correct one for the target host! A prime troubleshooting topic on the exam is having name resolution problems for hosts right after switching to using domain name services (DNS) for name resolution. The host does not query further if a resolution is made.

Other name resolution-related files can be used on a Linux system, but most are, by default, not on the Red Hat or Debian systems you'll see these days:

➤ /etc/hostname—Used to statically store the fully qualified domain name, such as snowblower.brunson.org.

➤ /etc/networks—Used to map a network name to an otherwise IP-related network, more often used in Solaris environments than Linux.

➤ /etc/host.conf—Similar in function to the /etc/nsswitch.conf file. It sets the order in which resolution sources are searched (this file is overridden by /etc/nsswitch.conf).

Network Configuration Utilities

A number of commands are used to view, configure, or troubleshoot your network configuration, including

➤ `ifconfig`—Used to set and display the host's IP address and network mask

➤ `route`—Used to set and display the host's routing and gateway information

➤ `dhcpcd`, `dhcpclient`, and `pump`—Used (variously) to initiate, release, or renew the client's DHCP-assigned address(es)

➤ `host`, `nslookup`, and `dig`—Used to look up DNS names and return information about the targeted host

➤ `hostname`—Used to set or view the host's hostname; other name utilities can create name-related links to this file

➤ `netstat`—Used to view information about the networking subsystem, statistics, and attached hosts/ports

➤ `ping`—The simplest way to establish that a host is alive and responding; essentially a network "hello"

➤ `traceroute`—Used to determine the path, names, and statuses of the routing devices that a set of traffic uses to reach a given remote host

➤ `tcpdump`—Used to capture and inspect the contents of packets from the network

Network Utility Examples

Many of the previously listed utilities are quite complex and robust programs and could be the subject of a much longer book. This section consists of quick examples and (very!) relevant exam tips for these utilities.

The **ifconfig** Command

The `ifconfig` command is used primarily to view or set the IPs for a host. You can set everything but the default gateway with this command, including the bringing up or activation of the interface.

To set up the `eth0` interface to communicate on the `192.168.33.0` network with an IP of `192.168.33.2` and a network mask of `255.255.255.0` and to activate the interface, you would use the following command:

```
ifconfig eth0 192.168.33.2 netmask 255.255.255.0 up
```

ifconfig displays the working or activated interfaces for the system. If any are down or not activated, they can be shown with the **-a** switch—for example

ifconfig -a

The route Command

The route command was featured earlier in this chapter for the purposes of adding default gateways, but it's also used in defending your system from an attack in progress.

When you have a host that is being denial-of-service attacked, or some sort of denial of service is being attempted, the quickest action you can take is to add a route that causes any responses to the attacker's IP to be routed through the loopback address, effectively causing your system to misroute the traffic to that host.

To stop a particular host from attacking a server, open a shell on the server and enter the following (where 10.1.1.69 is the attacker's IP) command:

```
route add 10.1.1.69 lo
```

Any of the traffic that your host would have sent in return to the attacking host is now sent to the loopback network, where it times out and the attacking host times out and gives up on your poor server.

Obviously, this is not a long-term solution, but try this on your local network with the ping command from a host and type the previous command on the host being attacked. You'll see that the attacking or pinging host suffers a time-out very quickly.

 Although not directly attached to the **route** command, if you need to turn on IP forwarding on a host, one of the ways is to echo a 1 into the file **/proc/sys/net/ipv4/ip_forward**. This effectively turns on the forwarding of traffic between the different interfaces on the machine. For example:

echo 1 > /proc/sys/net/ipv4/ip_forward

DHCP Client Tools

This section assumes that you know how to use DHCP and that you understand that IPs are leased from the DHCP server by the client for a specified period of time, timing out and expiring unless renewed by the client utilities mentioned in this section.

When you use DHCP to assign IPs in a Linux environment, the interface configuration files are read at network initialization.

Depending on the distribution, to cause an interface to request a DHCP address, one or more of the following DHCP-related programs must be present:

➤ dhcpcd

➤ dhcpclient

➤ pump

dhcpcd (DHCP Client Daemon) runs on the client to help configure the client's IP and watch the lease time-out period, requesting a new address lease when needed for the client.

The /sbin/dhcpcd daemon is typically invoked from the startup scripts or from the /sbin/ifup script's reading and executing of the commands in the /etc/sysconfig/network-scripts/ifup script on a Red Hat machine and the /etc/network/interfaces script on a Debian machine.

If you need to immediately renew or refresh your client's address lease, you can restart, or *hup*, the **dhcpcd** daemon with the following command:

dhcpcd -k

This kills and restarts the daemon, causing it to either recontact the DHCP server and get a new lease or reconfirm the old one.

The dhclient program is used by some distributions as a method of getting a DHCP lease, using the dhclient.conf file for configuration including its time-out and retry values. The dhclient command attempts to obtain a lease for all interfaces that are set up to use DHCP, keeping the lease information in the dhclient.leases file.

Using dhclient is very simple. If you need a new address, restart the network services and run

dhclient

The pump command is another of the possible variations you can use to obtain a DHCP lease.

To obtain a new address with pump, you'd use the command as such:

pump

Of course, after running the available client tool, it's best to confirm that an address was actually obtained or renewed with the ifconfig command.

The **host**, **nslookup**, and **dig** Commands

The host, nslookup, and dig commands are another trio of commands that are used for a particular function—name lookups or troubleshooting of hostname or fully qualified domain names.

The host command is simple and has little use other than to return the resolved IP for a hostname:

```
host Brunson.org
```

This returns the output shown here:

```
brunson.org has address 192.168.1.1
```

You can use options to gather further information about the targeted host or domain, but they aren't tested.

The nslookup command is used to retrieve or troubleshoot information about a host or domain and can mine the DNS server specified for nearly any record or information that is available. Interestingly, nslookup is being deprecated and possibly retired in favor of the dig command.

To query a particular host with nslookup, you can use either the command-line or interactive mode. To use the command-line mode to resolve the host www in the brunson.org domain, you would use the following command:

```
nslookup www.brunson.org
```

This returns the following output:

```
Note:  nslookup is deprecated and may be removed from future releases.
Consider using the `dig' or `host' programs instead.  Run nslookup with
the `-sil[ent]' option to prevent this message from appearing.
Server:        192.168.33.2
Address:       192.168.33.2#53
Non-authoritative answer:
www.brunson.org canonical name = brunson.org.
Name:    brunson.org
Address: 207.238.213.12
```

The interactive mode is used when you are going to be setting a different server to query other actions that are easier to accomplish inside the program. If you've used ftp interactively or the lpc program and its interface, nslookup has a similar layout and function.

The latest darling of the Linux community, as far as name resolution and troubleshooting go, is the dig command. dig is usable in a command-line mode or batch mode for larger sets of target servers.

When you use `dig`, follow this syntax:

```
dig server name type
```

The `server` is the domain or server IP you are querying for information. Typically, you would use the `server` section only if you needed to specify a particular one. The `name` is the actual domain or host you are searching for, such as `lpi.org`. The `type` allows you to specify whether you want to see MX, SIG, A, or ANY record types.

Using `dig` is relatively simple. To find just the MX records (mail server) for the `brunson.org` domain, you would use the following command:

```
dig brunson.org MX
```

This returns the output shown here:

```
; <<>> DiG 9.2.4rc2 <<>> brunson.org MX
;; global options:  printcmd
;; Got answer:
;; ->>HEADER<<- opcode: QUERY, status: NOERROR, id: 41375
;; flags: qr rd ra; QUERY: 1, ANSWER: 1, AUTHORITY: 2, ADDITIONAL: 3
;; QUESTION SECTION:
;brunson.org.                   IN      MX
;; ANSWER SECTION:
brunson.org.            3598    IN      MX      0 brunson.org.
;; AUTHORITY SECTION:
brunson.org.            1835    IN      NS      NS3.INDYSERV.NET.
brunson.org.            1835    IN      NS      NS4.INDYSERV.NET.
;; ADDITIONAL SECTION:
brunson.org.            1835    IN      A       207.238.213.12
NS3.INDYSERV.NET.       167293  IN      A       207.238.213.33
NS4.INDYSERV.NET.       167293  IN      A       207.238.213.34
;; Query time: 65 msec
;; SERVER: 192.168.33.2#53(192.168.33.2)
;; WHEN: Wed May 12 11:31:16 2004
;; MSG SIZE  rcvd: 141
```

The output for a `dig` query is structured, consisting of the following:

➤ HEADER—This contains information about the `dig` environment and options.

➤ QUESTION—This section simply echoes back your query.

➤ ANSWER—This section is the reply to your query.

➤ AUTHORITY—This section shows the servers that are the authoritative name servers for the requested target.

➤ ADDITIONAL—This is a catch-all section, typically displaying the name servers for the target.

➤ STATISTICS—This section shows you how much time it took in milliseconds or seconds to answer the query as well as the date and time of the query.

 Expect to see **host** and **dig** on the exam, particularly the ability to see a particular type of host with the **dig** command.

Hostname Utilities

The hostname command is used to view and set the host and domain names for a system. The hostname can be set by this command, or it can be set in the boot process by various scripts depending on the distribution and version.

The hostname command is linked to the following commands:

➤ domainname

➤ dnsdomainname

➤ nisdomainname

➤ ypdomainname

➤ nodename

The nodename link to hostname isn't present on some systems, and it might be missing entirely in later distributions. You can also use options to the hostname command to show information, such as the following command:

```
hostname --fqdn
```

This returns similar output to the following:

```
localhost.localdomain
```

Using netstat

The netstat command is useful for determining statistics for network interfaces, connections to and from the local machine, and a lot of other information.

Using netstat without any options outputs a list of the open sockets on the system, but the most useful output is produced when you use options or combine them for richer information and troubleshooting.

netstat has lot of options; the most relevant of the options include

➤ -t—Shows TCP statistics

➤ -r—Shows the routing table

➤ -a—Shows all the sockets on all functioning interfaces

➤ -c—Shows a refreshing (every 1 second) view of statistics for usage

➤ -p—Shows the name and PID of the program related to each socket (very useful!)

To see all the interfaces usage statistics, you would use this command:

```
netstat -s
```

This returns output similar to

(Output truncated for space)

```
Ip:
    216167 total packets received
    0 forwarded
    0 incoming packets discarded
    216092 incoming packets delivered
    104652 requests sent out
    80 dropped because of missing route
```

netstat is also used for viewing the routing table for the system, otherwise shown by the route command:

```
netstat -r
```

This returns output similar to the following:

```
Kernel IP routing table
Destination  Gateway        Genmask        Flags  MSS Window  irtt Iface
192.168.1.0  *              255.255.255.0  U       40 0          0 eth0
127.0.0.0    *              255.0.0.0      U       40 0          0 lo
default      192.168.1.1    0.0.0.0        UG      40 0          0 eth0
```

The final and most exam-related situation netstat is used for is the detection and troubleshooting of connections to and from your machine.

The output from the next command is voluminous, so I've truncated it to a usable portion, while maintaining a reasonable facsimile of what you will see on your system.

The output from netstat is divided up into a number of columns, including

➤ Proto—The protocol used, typically TCP or UDP.

➤ Recv-Q—The bytes not yet received by the service or client attached to the socket.

> Send-Q—The bytes not yet acknowledged by the remote host.

> Local Address—This is your machine, the address, and the port number or name of services.

> Foreign Address—The address and port number of the remote end of the connection, or the other user's machine.

> State—Typically, this is set to ESTABLISHED if a connection is or has been recently active; otherwise, it might be TIME_WAIT when it's almost done processing packets and LISTEN when the socket is a service/daemon waiting for a connection.

To see what your system has for connections, you would use the following command (using head and line numbering to keep the output manageable):

```
netstat -a ¦ head -n 20
```

This returns output similar to the following:

 In the following output, I've added line numbers to the left of each line to make referring to the output simpler and more direct.

```
1  Active Internet connections (servers and established)
2  Proto Recv-Q Send-Q Local Address     Foreign Address _____  State
3  tcp     0      0   *:pop3s            *:*                       LISTEN
4  tcp     0      0   *:netbios-ssn      *:*                       LISTEN
5  tcp     0      0   *:sunrpc           *:*                       LISTEN
6  tcp     0      0   192.168.15.5:domain *:*                      LISTEN
7  tcp     0      0   *:ssh              *:*                       LISTEN
8  tcp     0      0   *:smtp             *:*                       LISTEN
9  tcp     0      0   *:7741             *:*                       LISTEN
10 tcp     0      1   192.168.15.5:36651 206.235.223.112:smtp     SYN
11 tcp     0     48   192.168.15.5:ssh   192.168.15.1:4417        ESTABL
12 tcp     0      0   192.168.15.5:36619 www.certmag.com:www      ESTABL
13 0              1   192.168.15.5:36657 206.235.223.112:pop3     SYN
14 tcp     0      1   192.168.15.5:36653 206.235.223.112:pop3     SYN
15 tcp     0      0   192.168.15.5:36594 moviesunlim:www          ESTABL
16 tcp     0      0 192.168.15.5:36595   moviesunlim:www          ESTABL
```

Key items in the output listed previously are

> **Line 6**—The 192.168.15.5:domain in the Local Address column and a state of LISTEN represent a name server (typically Bind) listening for DNS queries on the local machine.

> **Line 10**—This is the beginning stage of connecting to the remote SMTP server from this machine with an email client, hence the SYN state.

▶ **Line 11**—The `192.168.15.5:ssh` in the Local Address column shows this is the daemon side of an `ssh` connection, with the foreign address of `192.168.15.1:4417` being the connecting client.

> Expect to see **netstat** output and to be asked to pick the client and server sides of the right connections on the exam. This is important for real-life situations, too, because it's always a good idea to know who's connecting to the network you are responsible for!

▶ **Line 12**—This is a Web client on the local machine attaching and requesting data from a site on the remote machine, as are Lines 15 and 16.

▶ **Lines 13 and 14**—These are a POP3 connection from the local machine to the remote machine.

> Use **netstat -c** to show **netstat** output continuously, and use **netstat** in cron tasks to keep track of what's happening to a host during off-hours.

The ping Command

The `ping` command uses Internet Control Message Protocol (ICMP) `ECHO_REQUEST` and `ECHO_RESPONSE` packets to determine whether a host is functioning, or is at least able to respond to a ping.

`ping` is used for many things, including finding if a host is available, if a network can be reached, if a gateway is functioning, and so on.

`ping` is the simplest and easiest way to determine whether a host is alive, and it can show up to nine devices with the `-R` option. If you need to determine the route taken by a set of packets, it's more useful and accurate to use the `traceroute` command, covered next.

To determine whether a host is functioning (or at least responding to an ICMP request), use this command:

```
ping 192.168.1.1
```

This returns output similar to

```
PING 192.168.1.1 (192.168.1.1) from 192.168.1.73 : 56(84) bytes of data.
64 bytes from 192.168.1.1: icmp_seq=1 ttl=150 time=9.23 ms
64 bytes from 192.168.1.1: icmp_seq=2 ttl=150 time=0.774 ms
64 bytes from 192.168.1.1: icmp_seq=3 ttl=150 time=0.715 ms
64 bytes from 192.168.1.1: icmp_seq=4 ttl=150 time=11.3 ms
```

When using `ping`, watch the time it takes to return the ECHO_RESPONSE. If you see anything higher than 1000ms, you might be experiencing some congestion between your host and the target. Some latency is to be expected. The best method is to periodically measure the response time; any large variation from the norm might indicate an issue.

 When you use **ping**, **traceroute**, and other utilities that typically accept either a hostname or an IP as the target, it's important to remember that DNS might not be present or configured and that the speediest method is to use the **-n** option to not have it resolve the hostname.

Using traceroute

The `traceroute` command is used primarily to troubleshoot and view the route taken between two hosts. If you are a sysadmin and your users can reach internal hosts but not Internet destinations, your primary tool will be `traceroute`.

`traceroute` uses three UDP packets to map the set of devices between the source and target hosts. The first set of three packets has a time to live (TTL) of 1, which is decremented when the packets reach the first device on the way to the target host.

When a packet's TTL reaches 0, the packet is expired and a message is sent to the originating host to that effect. The host then sends three more packets with a TTL of 2, which make it past the first device and die at the second one. This continues for as many devices as it takes to reach the target host.

The `traceroute` command output is useful for determining the number and statuses of the devices between your host and a target host.

To see the routers between your host and another (but not show the resolved names for speed), you could use the following command:

```
traceroute -n brunson.org
```

This shows output similar to the following:

```
traceroute to brunson.org (207.238.213.12), 30 hops max, 38 byte packets
 1  66.23.145.1   15.741 ms   15.020 ms   15.200 ms
 2  66.70.95.221  11.532 ms   12.271 ms   15.714 ms
 3  66.66.180.41  58.104 ms   57.294 ms   59.119 ms
 4  66.109.15.109 58.019 ms   57.665 ms   56.713 ms
 5  66.109.3.157  56.701 ms   59.802 ms   57.235 ms
 6  66.109.3.130  60.236 ms   94.471 ms   227.276 ms
 7  206.223.123.33  88.672 ms   126.281 ms   59.622 ms
 8  165.117.200.193  170.647 ms   129.370 ms   123.876 ms
 9  165.117.200.122  51.481 ms   58.137 ms   57.667 ms
10  165.117.192.26  59.002 ms   57.756 ms   58.730 ms
```

```
11   165.117.200.66   63.039 ms   62.622 ms   62.201 ms
12   165.117.192.38   61.137 ms   53.314 ms   115.764 ms
13   165.117.200.45   82.695 ms   93.937 ms   94.976 ms
14   165.117.192.18   93.599 ms   97.354 ms   93.501 ms
15   165.117.200.1   102.788 ms   116.023 ms   110.338 ms
16   165.117.192.2   91.001 ms   116.288 ms   123.706 ms
17   165.117.200.6   127.074 ms   188.887 ms   110.655 ms
18   165.117.175.133   111.660 ms   133.583 ms   129.227 ms
19   165.117.48.182   132.952 ms   110.658 ms   175.021 ms
20   165.117.178.84   130.887 ms   99.306 ms   135.562 ms
21   67.95.172.210   120.904 ms   132.106 ms   203.681 ms
22   207.238.213.12   150.149 ms   132.494 ms   111.996 ms
```

If you see a series of * (asterisks) where a return time should be, that's an indication that the router is either configured to not return ECHO_REQUESTs from traceroute or it's too busy or even down and can't respond. That is typically the bottleneck or problem that caused you to start troubleshooting in the first place.

When you're troubleshooting a user's access problem, it can be a number of things, the most likely of which are

> **User can't connect to anything**—This is a local IP or network mask problem. If she can't even ping someone on her local network, her machine is the problem.

> **User can see her network, but not others**—This is a problem with her default gateway. The only path out of her network is misconfigured.

> **User can see internal network, but not Internet**—This is usually a firewall or even DNS problem. If she can ping Internet sites by IP, but not name, it's definitely DNS.

For all these instances, use ping first. Then, if you can't find the problem or it's outside your area of responsibility, use traceroute.

Using tcpdump

The tcpdump utility is used to capture and display packets from a network. Either you can search the output in real time by redirecting the captured data to grep or the data can be written to a file for later searching.

tcpdump has a dizzying array of options to choose from; the man page for most versions rivals the bash man page. A couple of half-hour sessions with a few machines and the tcpdump man page will have you past the dangerous stage and able to use tcpdump properly for troubleshooting and security assessments.

To use tcpdump to capture all the data going across your local network and put that data in a file, you would use the command shown here:

```
tcpdump -w capturefile.cap
```

This does not display real-time output to the screen but captures the packets on the network to the file named `capturefile.cap`. Take great care not to leave this capture process running for extended periods of time because filling up your system's root partition can crash the machine or make it unavailable.

To view the data contained in the capture file, such as FTP packets, you would use the following command:

```
tcpdump -r capturefile.cap dst port 21
```

This shows output similar in format to

```
01:42:27.452770 192.168.1.101.2659 > 192.168.1.2.ftp:
➡S 2841408587:2841408587(0) win 64240 <mss1460,nop,nop,sackOK> (DF)
01:42:27.452935 192.168.1.101.2659 > 192.168.1.2.ftp:
➡ . ack 2413194434 win 64240 (DF)
01:42:27.567524 192.168.1.101.2659 > 192.168.1.2.ftp:
➡ . ack 50 win 64191 (DF)
01:42:31.216098 192.168.1.101.2659 > 192.168.1.2.ftp:
➡ P 0:13(13) ack 50 win 64191 (DF)
```

Although **tcpdump** shows up on the exam objectives, I've never seen a question more complex than asking which utility you might use to see the contents of packets, nor have my attendees, of which there have been hundreds. So, don't spend too much time worrying over **tcpdump** for the exam.

To get a refresher on how PPP works, see Chapter 4, "Linux and Hardware," which discusses PPP. The exams both have PPP items on them, but that section covers the objectives and more.

Exam Prep Questions

1. If your IP is **192.168.33.35** and your network mask is **/28**, what is the
address of your local network?

   ○ A. **192.168.33.16**

   ○ B. **192.168.33.32**

   ○ C. **192.168.33.0**

   ○ D. **192.168.33.64**

   Answer B is correct because the network is a Class C; therefore, the
   network mask of **/28** causes the LSB to be 16, and networks are incremented by 16, making the **192.168.33.35** address's network address
   192.168.33.3 2. Answer A is incorrect because that is the first valid network but not the one your IP resides on. Answer C is incorrect because
   192.168.33.0 is the default network if you were using a **/24** network
   mask. Answer D is incorrect because it's two networks past the one
   your IP is on.

2. You need to view a user's routing information on his workstation.
Which command, with any needed options, would you use to accomplish this? Write your answer on the blank below:

   _____

   The correct answer is **route**. An alternative is **netstat -r**.

3. Your boss wants you to create a subnet scheme that gives your company eight networks with at least 10 hosts per network. Which subnet
mask for a Class C leased network address would meet those
objectives?

   ○ A. **255.255.255.192**

   ○ B. **255.255.255.224**

   ○ C. **255.255.255.240**

   ○ D. **255.255.255.248**

   Answer C is correct because, with the number of networks needed, a
   240 subnet mask is needed and allows for at least 10 hosts per network.
   Answer A is incorrect because a **192** subnet mask allows for only 4 possible networks. Answer B is incorrect because a **224** subnet mask allows
   for only 8 possible networks, but with the loss of the first and last subnets, a 224 subnet mask really means that 6 networks are usable.
   Answer D is incorrect because a **248** subnet mask allows for enough
   networks (32) but not enough hosts per network.

4. A user is complaining that she can't reach a Web mail site she frequents, but she can reach other hosts on your networks and on the Internet. Which command would show you where the problem is occurring? Fill in the blank with just the most appropriate command name:

_____

The correct answer is `traceroute`. There are no correct alternative answers.

5. When a user tries to access a server that has recently had its IP changed, he gets a message stating `host not found`. Which of the following commands shows the relationship between that server's IP and the MAC address of its interface on the network?

- ○ A. `ping`
- ○ B. `arp`
- ○ C. `host`
- ○ D. `nslookup`

Answer B is correct because it shows the IP-to-MAC mapping for a particular host. Answers A, C, and D are incorrect because they have nothing to do with the IP-to-MAC mapping.

6. You are configuring a system and need to set your `eth0` interface to have a default gateway with the address `192.168.33.1`. Fill in the blank with the exact command and options to accomplish this from the command line:

_____

The correct answer is `route add default gw 192.168.33.1`. There are no correct alternative answers.

7. You want to find the mail servers for a particular domain but not see all the address records. Which of the following commands can accomplish this? (Choose all that apply.)

- ❏ A. `nslookup`
- ❏ B. `host`
- ❏ C. `resolver`
- ❏ D. `dig`

Answers A, B, and D are correct because they all can be used to show MX records or the names of the mail servers. Answer C is incorrect because there isn't a command on a default machine named `resolver`.

8. On a Red Hat machine, you need to edit a file that will set the order for how names are resolved. Fill in the blank with the full path and filename for this file:

_____

The correct answer is `/etc/nsswitch.conf`. There are no correct alternative answers.

9. Which of the following is a valid entry for resolution methods on the
hosts: line in the /etc/nsswitchconf file? (Choose all that apply.)

☐ A. files

☐ B. ylwpage

☐ C. dns

☐ D. nis

Answers A, C, and D are correct because they all are valid resolution
methods on the hosts: line in the /etc/nsswitch.conf file. Answer B is
incorrect because there isn't a method named ylwpage.

10. You need to capture data packets from the network for later analysis.
Fill in the blank below with only the command name that will accomplish this on a default machine:

_____

The correct answer is tcpdump. There are no correct alternative
answers.

Network Services

Terms you'll need to understand:

✓ Aliases
✓ Caching
✓ Lookup
✓ Share
✓ Smart host
✓ Wrappers

Techniques you'll need to master:

✓ Configuring and managing network services
✓ Configuring and managing services on demand
✓ Configuring and operating Sendmail
✓ Configuring and operating Apache
✓ Configuring and operating NFS and Samba
✓ Setting up and configuring name services
✓ Setting up and using Secure Shell

Network Services

This chapter is specifically designed to help you configure and manage the services or daemons installed by default on a standard Linux server.

Some of the services covered in this chapter are complete book topics in themselves. LPI's exam objectives (which I must follow and expand upon) don't cover such in-depth knowledge but focus on the ability to configure and manage most basic functions of these services.

The 102 exam assumes you have passed the 101 exam, which means you have a certain level of proficiency with installation and basic configuration. Building on that base of knowledge are the 102 requirements to do basic configuration and management tasks for the various services a typical departmental server would provide.

Providing Services on Demand

A Linux server can run about any service. Therein lies one of its greatest strengths, and for a weak-willed sysadmin, one of its greatest weaknesses. If you configure your server to provide too many services that run constantly, performance will suffer.

The three strata of service configuration for a server are

➤ **Always on**—This level is for services that should be running because clients will expect their presence.

➤ **On demand**—This level is for periodically used services, those that should be present but not on using RAM and CPU constantly.

➤ **Off or disabled**—This level represents those services that you're not going to run regardless, such as ISDN services on an Ethernet-connected server and so on.

Using **inetd** and **xinetd**

The older of two services, the inetd daemon is intended to provide services upon client demand. The idea behind inetd is to provide a method to start and run services on demand, particularly to start the service on receipt of a client connection request. The inetd configuration file (/etc/inetd.conf) contains a line for each service inetd controls.

The xinetd service is the newer of the two services and provides more atomic control, using a main configuration file (/etc/xinetd.conf) to point to a directory (typically /etc/xinetd.d) that contains a single text configuration file for each controlled service, such as /etc/xinetd.d/telnet.

> Writing about **inetd/xinetd** without switching back and forth in a confusing manner is difficult; therefore, I cover both in one section, splitting into notes and tips when needed or when one deserves more attention. The two services are very similar, with the main difference being the layout of the configuration files.

Although having standard services capable of being started on demand is advantageous, many services require the starting of multiple child processes or the generation of various security keys that make them less likely candidates for being run on demand.

> Some services are **httpd** (which needs to start several to many child processes), **ssh** (which needs to generate keys and so on), and **ssl** (which can also require the generation of keys when starting).

A number of services are governed by inetd/xinetd; the more familiar of these include

> ➤ finger—It's used to provide user login information and is considered to be a security risk.

> ➤ imap—It's a daemon that enables users to store their email on a server rather than download it to a client. This is often moved to a full-time service.

> ➤ ktalk/ntalk—These are used to provide chat/instant messenger–type services; they're not needed very often.

> ➤ rsh/rexec/rlogin—The very unsecure r services, these should be disabled and replaced by ssh and scp.

> ➤ telnet—It's another unsecure service, but one that is frequently used for providing a shell session to a remote client.

> ➤ wu-ftpd—The most common of the FTP daemons that are present in many distributions, this is often migrated to a full-time service.

If a service is important enough to be available and running, you probably should not have the service governed by inetd/xinetd. Migrate the service into the init.d service directory and start it in the appropriate runlevels via ntsysv, chkconfig, or update-rc.d.

If you look carefully on the Net, you'll see that the **auth** or **identd** service has been historically configured to run under the governance of **inetd**.

inetd Configuration Files

inetd is much older than xinetd, and the main difference between the two is the structure of the configuration files.

inetd uses a single configuration file, typically the /etc/inetd.conf file. This file contains comments that begin with # and entries that each define a single service. An example of a couple (many more exist) of typical lines from /etc/inetd.conf is shown here:

```
ftp      stream  tcp   nowait  root  /usr/sbin/in.ftpd      in.ftpd
telnet   stream  tcp   nowait  root  /usr/sbin/in.telnetd   in.telnetd
```

The lines shown here are broken up into the following fields and definitions:

➤ **Service name**—This name must match a valid service name entry in the /etc/services file.

➤ **Socket type**—This can be any of stream, dgram, raw, rdm, or seqpacket.

➤ **Protocol**—This is one of the protocols defined in the /etc/protocols file; typically it's either tcp or udp.

➤ wait **or** nowait **parameter**—Use the wait parameter for single-threaded servers that grab the socket and operate until timeout; use nowait for multithreaded servers that free up the socket when not active.

➤ **User/group**—The user or group this service should run as, giving you the ability to restrict a risky service to an account that's not root.

➤ **Server program**—The full path and name to the program that will provide the service.

➤ **Server argument(s)**—Any parameters the service might need to run properly.

If the service is to be controlled by hosts.deny and hosts.allow or TCP wrappers, the server program should be /usr/sbin/tcpd and the server argument should then be the full path and name of the service tcpd will be watching over. This is true only for inetd—not xinetd. You can learn more about this in Chapter 19, "Security."

If you have been running **inetd** and are converting to run **xinetd**, the most important file is **/etc/inetd.conf**, which contains entries that define which services should be provided on demand. These lines should form the basis of the new **xinetd** configuration. Red Hat includes a utility named **inetdconvert** that can help with this process.

xinetd Configuration Files

The xinetd daemon initially uses the /etc/xinetd.conf file to set a few daemon configuration settings and the defaults that will be picked up by all xinetd's governed services and to specify the include directory. (These defaults are overridden by any settings in the individual service configuration files.)

The include directory is typically /etc/xinetd.d, which contains a single text file for each governed service. The service configuration files contain the definition of a service and any special settings that need to be set for correct functioning.

Figure 18.1 shows the relationships between the components of the xinetd services and files.

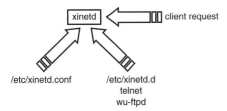

Figure 18.1   How **xinetd** works.

As you can see, xinetd reads /etc/xinetd.conf and gets its configuration, including the include directory location; then it waits for a client request for one of its services. When a client request arrives, xinetd looks at the packets and finds the target port/service and looks that service up by name in the /etc/xinetd.d directory. This directory contains one file per service, named exactly as the service name appears in /etc/services.

The /etc/xinetd.conf file is simple by nature:

```
# Simple configuration file for xinetd
# Some defaults, and include /etc/xinetd.d/
defaults
{
        instances               = 60
        log_type                = SYSLOG authpriv
        log_on_success          = HOST PID
        log_on_failure          = HOST
        cps                     = 25 30
}
includedir /etc/xinetd.d
```

The file contains a few lines that set the default limitations for the services governed by xinetd. If an individual service has a conflicting setting in its configuration file, that individual file setting takes precedence.

 You're likely to see questions about how to have a service run as a different user, which is accomplished by editing the service's configuration file and changing the user line.

Several of these lines bear defining:

➤ instances—This sets the total number of daemon instances allowed; this daemon is limited to 60 instances.

➤ cps—This limits the number of connections per second allowed through xinetd. Any more than the maximum (25) causes the service to be disabled for 30 seconds and then check whether it can accept more connections.

➤ The other settings are log related, logging the host and PID for successful connections and just the host for unsuccessful connections

An individual service configuration file from the /etc/xinetd.d directory such as telnet would contain

```
service telnet
{
        disable = yes
        flags           = REUSE
        socket_type     = stream
        wait            = no
        user            = root
        server          = /usr/sbin/in.telnetd
        log_on_failure  += USERID
        access_times     =  08:00-17:00
        only_from       =  snowblower
}
```

These files contain a number of settings:

➤ service—This keyword must be followed by the service name, such as telnet.

➤ disable—Values include yes (which disables the service and no connections are accepted) and no (which doesn't disable or enables the service for connections).

➤ flags—Many and varied flags exist; the most common is REUSE, which allows the port and service to accept multiple connections.

➤ `socket type`—This can be `stream`, `dgram`, `raw`, `rdm`, or `seqpacket`.

➤ `wait`—Use the `wait` parameter for single-threaded servers that grab the socket and operate until timeout; use `nowait` for multithreaded servers that free up the socket when not active.

➤ `user`—The user or group this service should run as, giving you the ability to restrict a risky service to an account that's not `root`.

➤ `server`—This is the full path and filename of the server or daemon program that is run when a client requests a connection.

➤ `log_on_failure`—This can also be `log_on_success`, and values include `HOST`, `USERID`, and `PORT`, to name a few options.

➤ `access_times`—This setting lets you set access timeframes for the service, such as from 8 a.m. to 5 p.m. in the previous file.

➤ `only_from`—This can be a list of hostnames, IPs, globs of addresses, and defined networks by name from the `/etc/networks` file.

To enable a service governed by `xinetd`, such as the previous `telnet` service, you would use the following command:

```
chkconfig telnet on
```

This changes the previous file to contain the following line:

```
disable = no
```

The service is now enabled and can accept requested connections. Changes to the file for a service don't require any restarting of services or `xinetd`; those changes take place for the next and subsequent instances of the service whose file you changed.

> If you edit the **/etc/xinetd.d/telnet** file by hand, the **xinetd** service might have to be restarted for the change to take effect. This is done automatically by the **chkconfig** command.

To disable the service completely from being initiated and governed by `xinetd`, you would use this command:

```
chkconfig telnet off
```

This disables the service and `xinetd` ignores requests for this service from this point on.

inetd must be restarted after a new configuration is written to the /etc/inetd.conf file, but xinetd reads the service configuration files in /etc/xinetd.d dynamically and requires restarting only if you change the /etc/xinetd.conf file.

Using TCP Wrappers for Securing Services

If you want to protect your on-demand services, use TCP wrappers as one of the layers of protection for seldom-used services.

The common concept of using TCP wrappers is that only services in the /etc/inetd.conf file can be wrapped or protected, but that's untrue. The TCP wrappers package includes a library called libwrap.a that an increasing number of Linux services reference for security. Although it used to be true that a service must be included in /etc/inetd.conf so that tcpd could govern it, many can directly use the libwrap.a library and the allow/deny files for protection.

inetd and TCP Wrappers

When used with inetd, the concept of using TCP wrappers is to place a controlling daemon with instructions as to who's allowed and denied in front of each service that runs on your machine. Most services in the era of widespread inetd usage didn't have any built-in protection, so they were configured to be run as parameters of the tcpd daemon.

tcpd is set up to refer to the /etc/hosts.allow and /etc/hosts.deny files for the hosts that are allowed and denied access to services protected by tcpd.

xinetd and TCP Wrappers

If you are using xinetd or running a current distribution of Linux, many of the services are developed to use the libwrap.a library, finally divorcing TCP wrappers from the inetd.conf file.

In the case of current distributions and xinetd, any service capable of referencing libwrap.a has the potential to benefit from the protection that the hosts.allow and hosts.deny files provide.

Additionally, if you wanted to run a set of services that were both secure and fast, you'd use TCP wrappers and a standalone daemon, instead of putting the service under `inetd` or `xinetd` control. Anytime you put services behind `inetd` or `xinetd`, they must be started to function, and that means a small though noticeable delay—often enough that a client request times out.

The **hosts.allow** and **hosts.deny** Files

The two tables that affect which clients can connect to which services (provided the service uses `libwrap.a` or is controlled by `inetd/xinetd`) are `/etc/hosts.allow` and `/etc/hosts.deny`.

The format of a typical `hosts.allow` or `hosts.deny` file is as follows:

`daemons: hosts : option : option`

Daemons or services can be specified several ways, including

➤ `ALL`—This means just that, all services.

➤ `service`—A single service name affects only that service.

➤ `daemon,daemon`—Multiple daemons affected by an entry should be separated by spaces or commas.

Hosts can be specified by many methods, including

➤ `hostname`—This affects a single unqualified hostname, typically from the local domain.

➤ `hostname.example.com`—This affects a resolvable, fully qualified hostname, typically from a remote domain.

➤ `@group`—This is used by NIS to denote a Net group and is unlikely to appear on the exam.

➤ `10.1.1.0/255.255.255.0`—This notation affects the hosts `10.1.1.1`–`10.1.1.255`. The `/xx` notation for bits can be used, too, such as `/24` to denote a default Class C subnet mask.

➤ `/path/filename`—This causes the listed file (full path and filename) to be referred to as the list of hosts that will be affected.

Wrapper Read Order

The following rules are important to understand when using TCP wrappers to protect services:

➤ **The `/etc/hosts.allow` file is read and parsed first**—Any matches in it cause access to be allowed, skipping the `/etc/hosts.deny` file entirely.

> ➤ **The TCP wrapper files are read each time a service is requested**— Therefore, any changes to the `hosts.deny` and `hosts.allow` files are immediately used.

> ➤ **The files are read sequentially**—This means that two conflicting entries in the same file cause the first one to be matched, ignoring the second and subsequent entries.

> ➤ **The files are read only if they exist**—If they don't exist, no rules can be applied, allowing complete access for services as far as TCP wrappers are concerned.

The most important point about how these files are processed is the order in which rules are matched from the files.

Format of hosts.allow and hosts.deny

It's important to choose what you want to deny or allow with the following guidelines:

> ➤ **Deny by default**—You deny all host access to all services by inserting an entry that reads ALL: ALL in the `/etc/hosts.deny` file; then you can allow any specific hosts with entries in the `/etc/hosts.allow` file.

> ➤ **Allow by default**—If you trust everyone more than not, don't have an allow file and just put the bad hosts or domains in the deny file.

> ➤ **Mix and match**—The most complex style, this is when you don't have a clear delineation of good and bad. You should carefully inspect the allow files for lines that invalidate your deny rules.

Sample Configurations

The simplest configuration for the allow and deny files is for a networked workstation, such as the configuration shown here in the `/etc/hosts.deny` file:

```
ALL: ALL
```

The presence of an `/etc/hosts.allow` file in this example is unnecessary because we're denying everyone, so no allow rules are needed.

The next example in the `/etc/hosts.allow` file allows all hosts but denies a domain and then excepts out a single host in that denied domain:

```
ALL: somehost.example.com
```

In the `/etc/hosts.deny` file, you'd also use

```
ALL: .example.com
```

Another way to accomplish the preceding is to not have the `allow` file present and in the `deny` file have the following line:

```
ALL: EXCEPT somehost.example.com
```

To have more granular control of who can access services, you can use service names to deny and allow access to just that service. The following `deny` file entry allows access to all services but `telnet`:

```
telnetd: ALL
```

Conversely, the following example allows DNS and `sendmail` access from any host but no access to any other services from any host:

In the `/etc/hosts.allow` file, you'd use

```
named: ALL
sendmail: ALL
```

In the `/etc/hosts.deny` file, you'd use

```
ALL: ALL
```

 Expect to see lines from **hosts.deny** and **hosts.allow** as examples and to be asked to determine what is happening. Also expect to be queried about how to have a speedy set of services while still maintaining another level of security on those services.

Using Rule Options

Remember that the allow and deny files have the possibility of four configuration fields:

```
daemons: hosts : option : option
```

The real strength of using TCP wrappers comes out when you use the option fields to add characteristics to the entries that control access to services.

Options can be a single keyword or take the form of keyword values when using programs or utilities that need arguments.

For example, if you wanted to log the fact that a host had attempted to access one of your services configured to be denied, you might use the following line in the `/etc/hosts.deny` file:

```
service: badhost : severity auth.info
```

This entry not only denies the host access to the service, but also logs to the auth facility any messages that are severity level info or higher when the denial occurs.

Two useful keywords in the option fields are twist and spawn.

You use the twist keyword when you want to booby-trap what would appear to be a service with another program or action.

For example, if you wanted to cause a message to be sent back to an offending host that tries to use your finger daemon, you might employ the following entry in the /etc/hosts.deny file:

```
in.fingerd: ALL : twist /bin/echo "421 Buzz off!"
```

This sends a standardized message to the host's console telling it access is denied.

The last keyword we'll cover is spawn. Often you'll want to allow some host to connect to a service, but at the same time be notified of the access.

For example, to be notified every time someone accesses telnet so you can email him with an SSH FAQ and scolding note to stop using telnet, you would use the following entry in the access file:

```
in.telnetd: ALL : spawn /bin/echo `date` from %h ¦ mail root
```

This works for just about any service, as long as it can use the TCP wrappers or can be configured to work from inetd or xinetd.

If you spawn a command, it runs the command as a child of the current shell, but if you use twist to run the command, it replaces the current process with the command you run.

Watch carefully for denial file modifications, such as **twist** and **spawn** statements. Being able to verify which entries are valid or invalid is essential.

sendmail, Bloody sendmail

If there's a topic in the world of Unix and Linux that can cause otherwise competent sysadmins to mutter invectives in frustration, it's sendmail and its configuration files.

Thankfully, you won't have to configure a sendmail server at a level deeper than aliases for users, forwarding email to users, and tools for determining what mail is queued for local and remote delivery.

The three main tasks that make up a full-featured email environment are as follows:

➤ **MTA**—Message transfer agent

➤ **MDA**—Mail delivery agent

➤ **MUA**—Mail user agent

MTAs transport messages between servers similar to how an interstate trucking company might deliver goods between depots. Examples of MTAs include sendmail, postfix, and exim.

MDAs deliver messages from the server to the user's account, similar to how goods in a store are taken from the shipping dock and put on the shelves for customers. Examples of MDAs include procmail and mail.

MUAs enable the user to get his email from the system, similar to how a customer might go to a store to pick up groceries. Examples include evolution, pine, mutt, and kmail.

> It's important to know that **sendmail** uses Simple Mail Transfer Protocol (SMTP) and communicates via port 25 with other **sendmail** or SMTP servers.

sendmail Configuration Files

It would be hard to name a more complex configuration than sendmail's /etc/mail/sendmail.mc and /etc/sendmail.cf files. When even the author of sendmail calls these files complex, you know it's going to be a tough configuration.

> You'll not be required to perform much configuration of these files as a part of your preparation for the LPI exams. The only things you'll need to know are what the configuration files are named, where they are kept, and how to disable relay options for the server.

The most important configuration files for sendmail are as follows:

➤ /etc/mail/sendmail.mc—The source configuration file, which is compiled into the /etc/sendmail.cf file.

➤ /etc/sendmail.cf—This is the configuration file read and used by the sendmail daemon.

> ➤ /etc/sendmail.cw—This file should contain the list of domains the sendmail server should accept and keep mail for, as opposed to forwarding the mail.

The sendmail.cf File

"The lines of text in a sendmail.cf file have been described by some as resembling modem noise, and by others as resembling Mr. Dithers swearing in the comic strip *Blondie*"—Bryan Costales

Both the sendmail.cf and sendmail.mc files are much too complex for this venue, but some mention of them and how they are read and used by sendmail will be helpful.

First, you edit the /etc/mail/sendmail.mc file and insert the configuration parameters and rules you need for your email environment. Next, you compile the .mc file with the m4 macro processor, such as

```
m4 sendmail.mc > /etc/sendmail.cf
```

This produces the compiled or processed sendmail.cf file.

Every time sendmail is started, it rereads the /etc/sendmail.cf file. It's not recommended to edit the sendmail.cf directly.

If you do need to disable SMTP relay for a host, you can edit either the **/etc/mail/sendmail.mc** or **/etc/sendmail.cf**, but you must then restart **sendmail** to have it take effect.

Smart host is a particular entry in the sendmail configuration that has shown up multiple times in discussions about the exam.

A *smart host* is typically used as a focal point for getting mail to hard-to-reach hosts, such as behind a corporate firewall. In today's environment, it's much more likely that a firewall or security host will be the control point for a domain's worth of hosts.

Hosts that are not reachable from the wide area Internet can be especially difficult to send mail packets to, so a smart host is either on the firewall itself or a part of the demilitarized zone (DMZ)—a quasi-secure area between an internal firewall and a gateway to the Internet.

Aliasing and Forwarding Mail

When you have an organization and particularly a Web presence for which you are providing email, certain aliases or nicknames should be routed to another address.

For example, if you run an e-commerce site or use the Web for product support, you might have accounts set up for support, sales, comments, and information. Someone must check those accounts often because the email will build up and customers will be unsatisfied otherwise.

A more elegant solution is to define aliases in the /etc/aliases file for those names instead. In the alias entry you can configure which live users will receive any email that is sent to those aliases.

Defining an Alias

To configure an alias, you edit the /etc/aliases file and add an alias that matches the following format:

```
alias_name: name1, name2, name3
```

For example, to define the alias support and have emails sent to support@example.com be sent to peter, paul, and maria, you would add a line to the /etc/aliases file that looked like this:

```
support: peter, paul, maria
```

To update sendmail with the new contents of the aliases file, you just have to run one or the other of the following commands:

```
newaliases
```

or

```
sendmail -bi
```

You don't have to restart **sendmail** to have it reread the **/etc/aliases** file. If you change other **sendmail** configuration files, you have to restart it, but not for aliases.

Forwarding Email for Users

Sometimes a user cannot receive email from her usual system, and leaving the user out of the loop or letting her email inbox swell to quota-busting proportions isn't a wise idea.

To cause any email that would be otherwise read by the user on her system to be sent to another email address, such as an external address accessible to the user from home, you or the user can create a file named `.forward` in her home directory.

The `.forward` file is extremely simple and is usually made up of a single line that contains the email address to which the user's email should be sent. To create a `.forward` file that sends mail from `snuffy`'s account to his home email, you could use the following command:

```
echo snuffy@homemail.net > /home/snuffy/.forward
```

This creates a file named `.forward` in `/home/snuffy` and causes email sent to `snuffy` to be forwarded to that email address.

 Remember that only the **root** or a suitable user with permissions can change the **/etc/aliases** file, but every user has the ability by default to create a **.forward** file, possibly forwarding email inappropriately.

sendmail-Related Utilities

It's worth mentioning that `sendmail` is controlled like any other service, either via the Red Hat `service` command or directly from the daemon itself.

For example, to restart `sendmail` using the full path to the daemon on a Debian system, you would use this command:

```
/etc/init.d/sendmail restart
```

The two locations at which mail is queued for delivery are

➤ `/var/spool/mqueue`—Undelivered remote mail is stored in this directory, waiting until the remote host can receive the data.

➤ `/var/spool/mail`—Undelivered local user mail is stored in this directory. The mail is contained in a single text file named after the user account.

 Remember that the **/var/spool/mail** location is a directory, and the user's mail is stored in a file within that directory.

To view unsent or queued mail, you would use the `mailq` utility, like so:

```
mailq
```

This produces the output shown here:

```
/var/spool/mqueue is empty
```

A useful utility for finding out how much action **sendmail** is getting is **mailstats**. If I run **mailstats** on my simple Red Hat server, I get the following output:

Statistics from Wed Aug 13 15:43:03 2003

M	msgsfr	bytes_from	msgsto	bytes_to	msgsrej	msgsdis	Mailer
9	100	114K	100	114K	0	0	local
T	100	114K	100	114K	0	0	
C	100		100		0		

Apache

As previously mentioned, none of the services we cover in this chapter or LPI covers in its objectives require full installation, just configuration and mild maintenance after the distribution is installed. This holds true for Apache: The exams treat Apache as if it were already installed and needs only to be configured.

How Apache Runs

Apache doesn't just run a single process but runs a main process and then other child processes that take care of Web requests from clients.

Apache's structure makes it ill-suited to run on demand from inetd or xinetd. The startup time required for main and child processes often causes the client request to time out with an error message.

On a Red Hat machine, Apache runs as the httpd process with the main process's owner set to the root user and the children processes running as the user apache.

On a Debian 3.x machine, Apache runs with the main process's owner set to the root user and the children processes running as the www-data user.

Using apachectl

As important as Apache is, you should have a front-end controller for it, which the apachectl utility performs well as.

apachectl options include

➤ start—Starts the httpd daemon

➤ stop—Stops the httpd daemon

> restart—Restarts the httpd daemon (also causes Apache to reread its configuration file)

> fullstatus—Reports the status (requires lynx and the mod_status module to be present and compiled into Apache)

> graceful—Restarts and lets current connections finish

> configtest—Checks syntax in the /etc/httpd/conf/httpd.conf file

Most sysadmins use apachectl either from the shell to immediately affect the Apache server or from a script to cause actions that occur as part of normal maintenance.

 When you want to shut down Web services but not disconnect currently connected users, use the **apachectl graceful** command. It's designed to allow current connections to finish while disallowing new connections. This is much more acceptable on the users' end than a cold stop is.

Apache Configuration Files

In the past, Apache used two configuration files in contrast to today's main configuration file:

> access.conf—Used to control access to directories and other access-related configuration

> srm.conf—Used to set directives or parameters for the server

Some instances of Apache use any or all of the files, depending on how old the server is and how much trouble the consolidation to a single configuration file was perceived to be.

Apache's main configuration file in later versions is /etc/httpd.conf. Several years ago, the decision was made to move the plethora of configuration files that gathered in the /etc directory tree's root to reside in their own named directories. This means that on a Red Hat machine, the httpd.conf file is located in

/etc/httpd/conf/httpd.conf

On a Debian machine, the file now typically is located in

/etc/apache/httpd.conf

 If you're asked on an exam to choose which files are considered to be configuration files for Apache, all three of the **access.conf**, **srm.conf**, and **httpd.conf** files are valid and possible choices. If you're asked to choose all that apply, all three would be correct. If you're asked for a single answer, only **httpd.conf** is valid.

Apache Directives

The httpd.conf file contains configuration parameters called *directives*.

Important Apache directives are listed in Table 18.1. These vary by distribution, vendor, and date.

Table 18.1 Apache Directives	
Directive and Example	**Explanation**
ServerAdmin ross@brunson. org	Sets the administrator's address for error messages generated by the server.
DocumentRoot /var/www/html	Sets the location where html content can be found.
ServerRoot /etc/httpd	Sets the location of the files needed for server configuration.
Servertype standalone	Sets the mode for use with **inetd/xinet**. The default is standalone.
MinSpareServers 5	Sets the minimum number of spare servers in RAM. These are used to handle surges in requests for pages.
MaxSpareServers 15	Sets the maximum number of spare servers in RAM for handling surges in requests for pages.
StartServers 5	Sets the number of child servers started with the server.
MaxClients 150	Sets the maximum number of clients that will be served; all others get a **server busy** message.
Listen 192.168.10.2:80	Sets the IP and port Apache listens to. The default is to bind to **eth0** and port **80**.
Alias /img/ /usr/share/img/	The **Alias** directive redirects a user to another directory, even if it is on another file system.
Redirect Old_URL New_URL	Useful for when an obsolete URL still gets traffic; it redirects it to another URL.
DirectoryIndex index.html index.htm index.shtml	Sets the names that will be searched for (in order) and loaded to provide an index for the directory/site.
UserDir public_html	Sets the document root for a user's Web site. The **/home/username/public_html** directory must be world-readable and the user's home directory must be set to **711**. The site is accessed with the URL **http://www.example. com/~username**.

Watch for directives and valid values on the exam; LPI loves to ask the file locations and filenames, also.

Network File System

Network File System (NFS) was originally developed by Sun Microsystems and now is the default option for sharing files and data over a network for Unix and Linux systems.

Nearly every Linux system has the necessary client or server files and utilities to support NFS. Typically, the NFS client software is installed by default and the NFS server software is installed but not started.

NFS runs over Remote Procedure Call (RPC) and its adherence to published standards makes it possible to communicate with any client or server that follows the standards properly, including Apple, Windows, and any other system that has NFS software loaded.

NFS is used by a server to share a file system with other systems via the NFS protocols and software. When a system uses or mounts a remote file system to the local system, it appears to be a part of the local file system structure.

 Remember that NFS doesn't deal with users; it allows hosts to connect to other hosts and makes a bridge across the network that a user can then travel across to attempt to get access to the resources being shared.

NFS Daemons

The NFS packages include a client, a server, and configuration files. The daemons include

➤ portmap—This daemon is used by all daemons that communicate via RPC.

➤ rpc.nfsd—The NFS server daemon.

➤ rpc.mountd—This daemon handles any share mounting requests received from clients.

➤ rpc.rquotad—Allows the querying and setting of quotas from the local system, acting on a remote share's configured quotas.

➤ rpc.lockd—When files are requested for editing or use, this daemon notes this and denies use for other clients appropriately.

➤ rpc.statd—Used by rpc.lockd to manage locks that remain after or from a system crash on the server side.

Exporting File Systems

When exporting or sharing a file system, the NFS daemon allows clients to view what's available and request a mount for any shares defined in the /etc/exports file, depending on the restrictions for each share.

An exports file consists of a set of single-line entries that each defines a share by full path and then the access particulars that restrict the share.

By default, all shares defined are to be shared with any system as read-only. In other words, if you have a single line in the /etc/exports file that only has the full path of a directory, that share would be open for all clients with a restriction of read-only by default.

An example of an exports file follows:

```
/pub      (ro) *.brunson.org(rw)
/home     192.168.0.0/24(rw)
/docs     dellbert(ro)
```

The first line (/pub) shares (or exports for mounting by other hosts) the directory /pub with explicit read-only (ro) permissions for all hosts. Then it allows any host that can be resolved as being a member of the zones that belong to brunson.org to mount the share with the possibility of having read/write access to the resources shared.

The second line (/home) uses a glob (IP ending in a wildcard) to allow a range of hosts to connect to the share. The use of a network number and a network mask means the range of hosts that can access this resource is 192.168.0.1–192.168.0.255 (because of the 24-bit network mask, 8 bits of hosts remain).

The third line (/docs) is restricted only to the host dellbert with read-only access.

The key point in the **/etc/exports** file is the exact placement of the glob and the access permissions. If even a single space separates the glob on line 2 (**192.168.0.0/24**) from the access permissions (**rw**), exactly the opposite of what was intended is achieved. A space here means the glob was restricted to read-only and that every other host is granted read/write access to the share.

Exports File Client and Address Options

You can address clients and addresses in the /etc/exports file in several ways. The following lists the options for the second field, or the address glob:

➤ **No name**—If it's only a list of options or permissions, any client can attach.

▶ **Single name**—This must be followed immediately by options in parentheses, such as host1(rw).

▶ **Wildcards**—You can use ? and * to sub for single characters and portions of the fully qualified domain name, such as 192.168.1.* and *.brunson.org.

▶ **NIS group**—You can use @nisgroup as a group option, such as @domusers.

▶ **IP/Net globs**—This can be a single IP or networks with or without masks, such as 192.168. and 192.168.33.0/24.

Making Shares Active

When you've finished editing the /etc/exports file and want the NFS shares to be available on the network, you can simply enter the following command:

exportfs -a

This command updates the NFS server daemon with the contents and entries in the /etc/exports file, without having to restart the NFS server.

If you wanted to reexport a single share, such as one you'd changed the options for, you could do so by specifying that share when running the exportfs command:

exportfs -o rw dellbert:/usr/share/man

This exports the share with the new options, which should also be in the /etc/exports file.

To simply export a temporary share, you can specify the entire share on the command line, but it must be reexported if the system is rebooted or NFS services are stopped:

exportfs -o no_root_squash dellbert:/public

The use of the no_root_squash option allows the root user to use the share as the root user, instead of being denied or mapped to the nobody account (which happens by default).

Mounting NFS Shares

Mounting an NFS share is similar to mounting a local file system. The mount command is used, with any options, a device (in this case a *host:/share*), and the mount point:

mount *host:/directory* */mount_point*

This would look like this:

```
mount dellbert:/home /mnt/client1
```

To have your system mount remote file systems automatically, you can edit the /etc/fstab and place an entry there to have it be mounted during the system's startup (when the system runs a mount -a):

```
dellbert:/home /mnt/data   nfs   rw  0  0
```

Be aware of **/etc/fstab** entries that are invalid or **mount** commands that include *host:/share* as the device. If you're not careful, you might think that a valid NFS share is a wrong answer or distracter.

Samba

Samba is a 32-bit suite of programs that enable a Linux machine to function as a Windows-compatible file and print server and a Windows NT 4.0 domain controller.

The exam objectives on Samba are very sparse. We'll stick to the objectives and put some tidbits in to help you out.

The Samba package consists of client and server components, with the server-side function provided by

➤ smbd—SMB/CIFS server, file, and printer sharing

➤ nmbd—Name resolution and browsing name proxy services

You need to know specifically that nmbd provides all the name resolution, browsing, and WINS support that Windows clients on a Linux network could need. When any of that is needed, that functionality is provided by the nbmd daemon.

The smbd daemon provides all the file and printer sharing functionality for the Windows clients on a Linux network. Although Linux clients can use Samba tools to access Windows resources via SMB/CIFS, and even each other via the same protocols, the majority of clients are Windows machines with Samba running on the Linux server to provide common resources to those clients.

Samba's Configuration File

The Samba daemons are configured with the file /etc/samba/smb.conf. This file used to reside in the /etc directory but, like many others, has been moved in the last couple of years to its own directory structure.

 If you see questions about the **smb.conf** file on the exam, it might appear as **/etc/smb.conf** or **/etc/samba/smb.conf**, but never as a choice between the two in the same question.

This file consists of three sections, all of which are important:

➤ **Global**—For options that affect the server environment and defaults for shares that don't have specific options.

➤ **Homes**—Thought to be for user home directory shares, Homes auto-provisions and creates user home directory shares for valid users.

➤ **Printers**—Not needed in later Samba versions because all printers are loaded automatically, it's now used for specific printer options or printer security.

The smb.conf file has more than 300 options.

 You can edit the **smb.conf** file directly or use a tool called Samba Web Admin Tool (SWAT). Take great care using SWAT, though, because it removes any customized configuration you might have added!

Entries in the smb.conf file typically take the following form:

```
keyword = value
```

Take great care when editing the file, and be sure to run the testparm command to check the syntax of your newly configured smb.conf file for errors.

Important smb.conf Entries

The following section covers the basics and includes anything reputed to be on the exams, with a few extra items to help you.

Important `smb.conf` entries include

➤ `workgroup`—The value takes the form of a NetBIOS workgroup or domain name, with the same restrictions.

➤ `server string`—The value is a description only, such as `I'm really a Linux box!`.

➤ `hosts allow`—The value is a host glob or IP range that effectively restricts the use of Samba services to those hosts.

➤ `guest account`—This provides a mapping to an account with functionality equivalent to the Windows guest account.

➤ `security`—The values here can be `share`, `user`, `server`, and `domain`, depending on the level of security you need.

➤ `password server`—This points all queries for authentication to a Windows domain controller by name, IP, or an asterisk (*) that uses a broadcast for the nearest domain controller.

➤ `interfaces`—The value here should be the IPs of the local interfaces you want Samba to listen and work with. Delete or remove this entry to service all interfaces.

➤ `local master`—With a value of yes, this causes the Samba server to participate vigorously in the local master browser elections.

➤ `domain master`—If set to yes, this causes Samba to also participate in the elections for the domain master browser, sometimes beating out any and all Windows domain controllers!

➤ `domain controller`—The value should be the local domain controller name or IP, used when the Samba server is a domain member.

➤ `wins support`—Either yes or no. If it's yes, the Samba server performs WINS (Windows Internet Name Server, a poor man's DNS) and accepts NetBIOS Name + IP registrations, queries for name resolution, and releases of the mappings.

➤ `wins server`—The value is the IP of the WINS server the Samba server is configured to query, and it should not point to the Samba server itself.

 Take great care to test your configuration with the **testparm** command because it prints the sections and their shares and displays a list of the options that are current for the Samba server.

Setting Up a Simple Samba Server

To show how easy Samba is to configure, the next section is a quick setup of Samba to share a single directory for a user, including setting up the user for access. Follow these steps:

1. Edit the /smb.conf file and add the following share to the end of the file:

```
# A share usable only the user snuffy
[snuffydir]
   comment = a private share for snuffy
   path = /usr/share/snuffy
   valid users = snuffy
   public = no
   writable = yes
   printable = no
```

 The comment is just that—the path is a valid path that **snuffy** has access to, the valid users are **snuffy**, the **public** keyword keeps other users out of that directory, the **writable** keyword allows **snuffy** to change the files therein, and **printable** being set to **no** means that no print job will be accepted into the directory.

2. Save and exit the file.

3. Run testparms to check the file.

4. Start Samba with /etc/rc.d/init.d/smb start (on Red Hat).

5. Confirm the service's start.

6. Add the user snuffy with the following command:

   useradd -m snuffy

7. Set the password for snuffy with the following command:

   passwd snuffy

   (Enter the password twice.)

8. Add the existing user to the Samba password files with the command shown here:

   smbadduser snuffy:snuffy

   (Enter the password twice.)

 The first instance of the name **snuffy** represents the Linux user **snuffy**; the second **snuffy** after the colon represents the Samba user or the connecting Windows client user.

9. Go to a Windows client, map a share to the \\server\snuffydir share, and be sure to supply snuffy's username and password when prompted.

10. Access the share.

Monitoring SMB Connections

After you've connected to the share, copy an MP3 file or media file to the server. Then double-click it to run or listen to the file.

When the file is playing, run the smbstatus commandto see what the user is doing. I often use this tool to see what's going on with the server and to see what users are listening to:

```
smbstatus
```

This returns output similar to

```
Samba version 3.0.2a-Debian
PID    Username      Group        Machine
- - - - - - - - - - - - - - - - - - - - - - - - - - - - - - - - - - - - -
 1268   rbrunson     users        wideboyxp (192.168.33.1)

Service     pid    machine      Connected at
- - - - - - - - - - - - - - - - - - - - - - - - - - - - - - - - - - - - -
rbrunson     1268   your-fulkl1oh2q  Sun May 23 21:36:26 2004
Locked files:
Pid    DenyMode    Access     R/W      Oplock        Name
- - - - - - - - - - - - - - - - - - - - - - - - - - - - - - - - - - - - -
1268   DENY_NONE  0x20089     RDONLY    LEVEL_II
➥/home/rbrunson/Ghost Of Freedom.mp3   Sun May 23 21:36:33
```

smbstatus shows statistics and file locks for whichever users are accessing via Samba on your server.

Samba Client Connections

The vast majority of access using Samba is from Windows clients to Samba servers (typically running Linux or Unix), not the other way around.

For the odd instance when you need to determine that a server is advertising itself properly or to grab a file from a Samba server or Windows server and put it on a Linux client, you can use the smbclient command.

smbclient provides an FTP-like interface when run interactively, and it can run in command-line mode, such as the following command:

```
smbclient -L localhost
```

(Press Enter when prompted for a password.)

This returns output similar to the following:

```
Anonymous login successful
Domain=[WORKGROUP] OS=[Unix] Server=[Samba 3.0.2a-Debian]

        Sharename       Type      Comment
        ---------       ----      -------
        IPC$            IPC       IPC Service (knpxvm server
➥(Samba 3.0.2a-Debian))
        ADMIN$          IPC       IPC Service (knpxvm server
➥(Samba 3.0.2a-Debian))
Anonymous login successful
Domain=[WORKGROUP] OS=[Unix] Server=[Samba 3.0.2a-Debian]

        Server                  Comment
        ---------               -------
        KNOPPIX33               knpxvm server (Samba 3.0.2a-Debian)
        WIDEBOYXP

        Workgroup               Master
        ---------               -------
        WORKGROUP               KNOPPIX33
```

The `-L` option is similar in function to using the `net view \\server` command on a Windows server.

When you find the share's names on the target server, you can easily mount the share on a Linux system. You could mount the share from the command line or, even better, put an entry in the `/etc/fstab` file to have it mounted automatically.

Here's an example of syntax for the `fstab` entry:

```
//server/share       /mnt/mtpt    smb     user=user    1  1
```

Watch for questions about the **smbd** and **nmbd** daemons, whether they use port 139 and NetBIOS to communicate with SMB/CIFS clients, and the sections of the **smb.conf** file.

Domain Name System

DNS is how names are resolved to IPs across networks. As you saw in the discussion of name resolution in Chapter 17, "Basic Networking," a host can refer to a number of sources to resolve a name for which it needs to know the IP.

At its simplest, a DNS server provides name resolution for hostnames to IPs, with a slightly more complex operation being to provide confirmation of a host's belonging to a particular domain.

There isn't much information involving DNS that is required to function at the LPIC1 level. A broad discussion of the many areas encompassed by DNS is impossible in this format, so we'll concentrate on the basics and some areas you'll see that might be a surprise.

Components of DNS

The primary components of DNS include the DNS server daemon, named, the /etc/named.conf file (for version 8 and above) or /etc/named.boot (for version 4), and the zone files that define a zone or domain.

Typically, the Berkley Internet Name Domain (BIND) package is included when the distribution is installed, or at least when the typical server installation is selected.

The typical configuration includes the following files:

> **Zone files**—These are typically named with the zone name and .db, such as example.db, and map the hostname to an IP.

> **Reverse zone files**—These are named oddly, with a reversed network address followed by .in-addr.arpa. So the name for the 192.168.33.0 network would be 0.33.168.192-in.addr-arpa and contain a reverse mapping of the IP to the hostname.

> **named configuration files**—The /etc/named.conf or /etc/named.boot files depending on the version; these contain the parameters for the DNS daemon and point to the correct zone and hints files.

> **Hints files**—These files contain the root server information, which is referred to if the server can't find a resolution through its data or configured servers.

Types of DNS Servers

DNS servers come in three main types and functions:

> **Master**—The authority for a domain or zone, it contains the physical files that define that domain.

> **Slave**—Used to provide load balancing and name resolution for far-flung networks or hosts, it receives zones only from the master.

> **Cache**—Used to cache resolved requests for a longer time than other servers, it can query only other configured servers. It has no zone or domain files itself.

The exam objectives require you to know a little about both BIND v4 and BIND v8, particularly the differences between the files, their names, and what's in the files.

The **named.*** Files

The following is an example of the two files—/etc/named.boot for BIND v4 and /etc/named.conf for BIND v8:

```
Example of BIND v4 /etc/named.boot file:
; bind configuration file
directory /usr/local/named
primary    somecoll.edu            db.somecoll
primary    33.168.192.in-addr.arpa   db.33.168.192
primary    0.0.127.in-addr.arpa     db.0.0.127
cache      .                db.cache
```

The version 4 file is simple and direct, beginning with a comment and then getting into the configuration.

The lines in this file define the following, in order:

➤ directory—The directory that contains the configuration files mentioned in the following lines.

➤ primary—The first primary entry defines this server as the primary or master server for the somecoll.edu domain; then it references the actual zone file (db.somecoll.edu) where the zone information is kept.

➤ primary—The second primary entry defines the reverse lookup for the zone that uses network 192.168.33.0.

➤ primary—The final primary entry defines a local 127.0.0.0 reverse lookup zone, a common part of most configurations.

➤ cache—This entry defines that the cache for the server exists and is named db.cache.

When you know what's in the file and how it looks, you're ready to compare it with the v8 file.

Here's an example of the BIND v8 /etc/named.conf file:

```
// bind configuration file
options {
        directory "/usr/local/named";
};
zone "somecoll.edu" in {
        type master;
      · file "db.somecoll";
}
```

```
zone "33.168.192.in-addr.arpa" in {
        type master;
        file "db.33.168.192";
}
zone "0.0.127.in-addr.arpa" in {
        type master;
        file "db.0.0.127";
}
```

The BIND v8 file is more complex and has a lot more formatting, appearing more like a C or C++ file source file than the plain-text keyword/value entries in the v4 configuration file.

Rather than put you through a line-by-line comparison, suffice it to say that where you would use a single-line entry in a v4 file, the v8 file uses blocks defined by a keyword such as options or zone and a set of parameters completely encased in curly brackets as the value for the keyword.

 Expect to see one or the other of these files in your exam experience, with various questions about what the role of the server is and which networks the zones might be serving. A careful inspection of the examples will tell you all you need to know for the exam, and more.

Zone and Record Types

A *zone* is an organization unit that is similar to a domain. A quick run-through of the various types of zones will help you determine what the role of a server is:

➤ **Master**—A master zone contains the information needed to resolve the hostnames to IPs and is considered an authority on the domain.

➤ **Slave**—A slave zone is a copy or replica of a master zone and is used for traffic management or load balancing. It can only receive zone information from a master, not update a master.

➤ **Forward**—This zone type simply points to another server, typically an ISP or a higher-echelon corporate DNS server for resolution; it doesn't do any resolution itself.

➤ **Hint**—A hint zone is used to locate a root server so a query that is not resolvable by the local servers can be resolved.

BIND uses several resource record types. The one you're most likely familiar with is an A, or address, record, which is simply a hostname and IP record.

The most common and useful record types are

➤ **SOA**—A start of authority record defines the zone and sets the portion of a domain or set of domains a zone covers.

➤ **NS**—A name server record defines which servers are responsible for which zones.

➤ **A**—An address record is a mapping of a hostname to an IP.

➤ **PTR**—A pointer record is a mapping of an IP to a hostname.

➤ **MX**—A mail exchanger record sets the server to which SMTP connections should be made for email transfer.

➤ **CNAME**—A canonical name record is a simplistic method of load balancing; multiple CNAME records for www should point to different hosts containing the same data and randomize between them.

➤ **TXT**—A text record is for keeping notes and comments about your configuration. It has no other meaning outside of the zone file.

Watch for questions about which type of record performs a particular function, with a focus on A, PTR, NS, and SOA record types.

Even though the SSH objective is covered in this chapter, I have also included it in Chapter 19, "Security," for flow and appropriateness. Please see Chapter 19 for the full coverage of SSH.

Exam Prep Questions

1. On a default install of a Linux server, regardless of the distribution version, what are the easiest methods to disable `telnet` but not uninstall or remove the service? (Choose two.)

   ❑ A. Comment `telnet` out of the `/etc/inetd.conf` file.

   ❑ B. Delete the `/etc/rc.d/init.d/telnet` file.

   ❑ C. Rename all `SXXtelnet` links in the `/etc/rc` or `/etc/rc.d` directory.

   ❑ D. Run `chmod 554 /etc/xinetd.d/telnet`.

   ❑ E. Nothing; it's not enabled by default.

   Answers A and E are correct because the `telnet` daemon isn't enabled by default if using `xinetd` and can be easily commented out of the `inetd.conf` file. Answer B is incorrect because deleting daemons from the system is inadvisable if you ever think you'll need to use them again. Answer C is incorrect because it would take too long to rename the links so that's not the easiest method. Answer D is incorrect because you wouldn't be disabling the `telnet` daemon with this solution; you'd be setting its permissions.

2. Which file could contain a list of shared directories on a typical Linux server system? Enter the full path and name of the file:

   _____

   The correct answer is `/etc/exports`. There are no correct alternative answers.

3. Which of the following services would you be least likely to configure to be governed by the Internet super server?

   ○ A. FTP

   ○ B. DNS

   ○ C. SSH

   ○ D. Telnet

   Answer C is correct because the SSH daemon or service uses encryption and keys that need to be generated, making it slower to start than the other choices. Answers A, B, and D would be reasonable to have governed by the Internet super server because they don't take a proportionally long time to start.

4. Which file should you edit to configure your `smbd` and `nmbd` daemons? Enter the full path and name of the file:

   _____

   The correct answer is `/etc/samba/smb.conf`. An alternative answer is `/etc/smb.conf`.

5. You've set up a service to use TCP wrappers for protection, but a host that should be denied gets through to the service anyway. What is the most likely cause of the problem?

   ○ A. The host is spoofing an allowed address.
   ○ B. The host has an `allow` entry in `/etc/hosts.allow`.
   ○ C. The TCP wrappers service must be started.
   ○ D. The service cannot use TCP wrappers.

   Answer B is correct because the `/etc/hosts.allow` file is read first and any entry that allows the host to connect would take precedence. Answer A is incorrect because, if the host is spoofing an allowed address, TCP wrappers won't be of any help. Answer C is incorrect because there isn't a TCP wrappers service, and most services use the `libwrap.a` library, not `tcpd`. Answer D is incorrect because you just configured the service for use with TCP wrappers.

6. Which commands (with any options) cause a `sendmail` daemon to recognize newly added aliases without restarting the service? Enter them in the blank below:

   _____

   The correct answer is `newaliases`. An alternative answer is `sendmail -bi`.

7. Which of the following resolves NetBIOS names to IPs? (Choose all that apply.)

   ❑ A. DNS
   ❑ B. WINS
   ❑ C. IEN
   ❑ D. NMBD

   Answers B and D are correct because they both are implementations of the WINS functionality—with WINS on Windows and NMBD on Linux. Answer A is incorrect because DNS resolves hostnames and IPs, but not NetBIOS names and IPs. Answer C is incorrect because IEN stands for Internet experimental note and has nothing to do with the question.

8. Undelivered mail for local system users is stored in which directory? Enter the full path of the directory:

   _____

   The correct answer is `/var/spool/mail`. There are no correct alternative answers.

9. Which of the following is a valid entry for resolution methods on the hosts: line in the /etc/nsswitch.conf? (Choose all that apply.)

❏   A. files

❏   B. ylwpage

❏   C. dns

❏   D. nis

Answers A, C, and D are correct because they all are valid resolution methods on the hosts: line in the /etc/nsswitch.conf file. Answer B is incorrect because there isn't a method named ylwpage.

10. Which command (with any needed options) shows you the SMB server information for the host 192.168.33.44? Fill in the blank below with the exact string to query the server for the share and workgroup information:

_____

The correct answer is smbclient -L 192.168.33.44. There are no correct alternative answers.

Security

Terms you'll need to understand:

✓ Chain
✓ Firewall
✓ Host security
✓ Masquerade
✓ Rule
✓ Secure shell
✓ TCP wrappers

Techniques you'll need to master:

✓ Configuring hosts for security
✓ Setting and changing user password options
✓ Finding security risks
✓ Verifying package authenticity
✓ Configuring basic **ipchains**
✓ Configuring basic **iptables**
✓ Viewing current **iptables**' configurations
✓ Setting up and configuring SSH
✓ Signing in, copying files, and setting boot options for SSH

Using TCP Wrappers to Secure a Service

Though covered in detail elsewhere, TCP wrappers are an important part of system security and require a quick review.

The majority of system services or daemons use the libwrap.a library for TCP wrappers functionality. The concept of TCP wrappers is to use a set of allow and deny files that wrap daemons in a protective sheath that keeps unwanted hosts from even contacting the daemon. TCP wrappers cannot protect from a host that is spoofing itself as a known or permitted host—that is where usernames, passwords, and other security measures come into play.

Remember that TCP wrappers depend on the /etc/hosts.allow and /etc/hosts.deny files for configuration. If a host or an address should be permitted to contact a service, an entry can be placed in the /etc/hosts.allow file to specifically allow that host to contact the service, or you can just leave the service open and not wrap it with protection.

It's when you have a more complex set of rules or policies that mandate that some hosts have access to particular services or that some other hosts don't have access that the real utility of using both an allow and a deny file becomes apparent.

 Keep in mind that any host you permit to have access in the **/etc/hosts.allow** file will have access, regardless of what entries are in the **/etc/hosts.deny** file!

Allow and Deny Files

The syntax used in the /etc/hosts.allow and /etc/hosts.deny files is fairly simple. For example, to deny access to all services from all hosts but the machine Mortimer, you would use an /etc/hosts.allow file with the following entry:

```
ALL: mortimer.example.com
```

Then in the /etc/hosts.deny file, you would have this entry:

```
ALL: ALL
```

Take care to plan out what is the most common rule for access to the system being configured: Is it a mostly open system or a mostly closed system? If the system is a mostly open one, you'd effectively reverse the previous setup, allowing all hosts access to all services but a few that are specifically mentioned in the /etc/hosts.deny file.

 Remember to check the syntax of your **allow** and **deny** files with **tcpdchk** and then use the **tcpdmatch** utility to predict how a particular client's requests will be handled with your current configuration.

Understanding Permission Problems

When you install a distribution, a number of files are set with special bits or permissions, mostly to make it easier for normal users to accomplish mild setup tasks.

You should run a find command that shows these files right after you install the system and then keep that output in a file in a different location for referral later.

One of the first changes to your system that a hacker or cracker will make is to set permissions on certain programs to allow an otherwise normal user special or root privileges.

As a reminder, the special bits that can be set for files include

➤ **SUID**—Represented by the numeral 4, the Set User ID special bit allows processes to run with the permissions of the file's owner.

➤ **SGID**—Represented by the numeral 2, the Set Group ID special bit allows processes to run with the permissions of the file's group owner. If it's set on a directory, it forces group ownership inheritance for all objects created in that directory.

➤ **Sticky**—On a program it causes the program to be nonswappable in memory, and on a directory it keeps any nonowners from deleting files in the directory.

It's important to know how to find the files on the system that have special bits set. In particular, the SUID and SGID special bits are used to gain access to elevated levels of capability and could be disastrous if set on utilities such as passwd, shutdown, and useradd.

Finding Files by Permissions

It's important to periodically run a find command to see which special bits are set on which files. To find all the files on your entire system that are owned by the root user with any special bit set and mail that list to yourself, you would use the following command:

```
find / -user root -perm +7000 -exec ls -l {} \; ¦ mail -s
►"Files that have any special bit set" root
```

This command finds the files that have any sort of special bit set, produces an ls -l listing from each, and sends an email that has the entire listing of files to the root user with the subject line in quotation marks.

When you use the -perm option with permissions, it matters whether you use a + or a - symbol or don't use one at all. If you are searching for a particular permission setting, such as all the files that have an exact permission setting, you would use the command shown here:

```
find / -perm 4777
```

This command finds only files whose permission trios and special bit match exactly the permissions specified. If you use the + and - symbols to search for special bits, the - symbol means to look for the exact combination of special bits that match the first numeral, such as 6, which would be 4 and 2—or SUID and SGID. To find any or all of the bits that are set that match the first numeral, you use the + symbol.

Once a week, run the same report again and then compare the first one with subsequent reports with the diff command to see what has changed. I'd suggest automating this with a script.

You'll probably see questions about the **find** command and the permissions, so be prepared to parse the commands to see which perform the specified tasks.

Validating Package Integrity

Another important aspect of system security is to keep your systems up-to-date with the latest security patches and fixes. You should subscribe or follow the announcements from your distribution's vendor.

Keeping systems up-to-date is hard work, particularly if you do it by hand. However, most vendors offer some sort of automated update tool, the premier and easiest to use being Debian's Automated Package Tool (APT) repositories.

On the commercial side of Linux distributions, several vendors offer online updates, most of them for a fee. Red Hat offers the Red Hat Network (RHN), which is an excellent tool and worth paying for if you run Red Hat for a living. SuSE/Novell offers an online update via YAST, and Mandrake has its Mandrake Online offering.

If you do choose to update packages by hand, never install a security-related package without verifying the package is what it appears to be.

Validation Methods

The two main methods of verifying package authenticity are the MD5 checksum that's calculated and included in the package and a GNU Privacy Guard (GPG or GnuPG) signature for the file.

The MD5 checksum included in a package can be checked easily by running the command shown here:

```
rpm -K gentoo-0.11.39-1.fr.i386.rpm
```

The command produces output similar to the following:

```
gentoo-0.11.39-1.fr.i386.rpm: md5 (GPG) NOT OK (MISSING KEYS: GPG#E42D547B)
```

The MD5 checksum in the package is there to be compared against when you run the validation on the package, so it's never supposed to be missing. Someone could have altered the checksum after modifying the package, though, so you should check whether the vendor or package maintainer has a separate .md5 file for the package.

The other mechanism for checking package authenticity is the GPG, which is essentially a method of signing the package with the developer or maintainer's GnuPG key, thus guaranteeing authenticity.

In the previous example you see that the GPG signature is NOT OK; then a listing of the missing key (GPG#E42D547B) is shown. The gentoo file manager is available from http://www.obsession.se/gentoo/ or from the gentoo. sourceforge.net project page, but the missing GPG key is not easy to find.

If I have a hard time finding the developer's key, I usually get GPG to do the heavy lifting for me and refer to the MIT PGP site (http://pgp.mit.edu) for help.

For example, to attempt to retrieve the developer's GPG key from the MIT site, I ran the following command:

```
gpg --recv-keys --keyserver pgp.mit.edu E42D547B
```

This returned the following output:

```
gpg: requesting key E42D547B from pgp.mit.edu ...
gpg: key E42D547B: public key imported
gpg: Total number processed: 1
gpg:               imported: 1
```

A quick listing of the keys that exist in my public-key key ring is accomplished with this command:

```
gpg --list-keys
```

This returns output similar to

```
/root/.gnupg/pubring.gpg
pub   1024D/2D3F3D03 2004-04-08 Ross Brunson (monkeyboy) <ross@brunson.org>
sub   1024g/DD8ED7C6 2004-04-08
pub   1024D/DB42A60E 1999-09-23 Red Hat, Inc <security@redhat.com>
sub   2048g/961630A2 1999-09-23
pub   1024D/E42D547B 2000-07-03 Matthias Saou (Thias)
➥<matthias.saou@est.une.marmotte.net>
sub   1024g/40043CA7 2000-07-03
```

As you can see, the third key in the ring is from the developer of the gentoo file manager. If I now run the same validation command that previously failed, it should work:

```
rpm -K gentoo-0.11.39-1.fr.i386.rpm
```

This returned the following output:

```
gentoo-0.11.39-1.fr.i386.rpm: md5 gpg OK
```

You'll need to know both ways to check signatures for the exam; the equivalent of the **rpm -K *package*.rpm** command is to use the **--checksig** option, like so:
rpm --checksig gentoo-0.11.39-1.fr.i386.rpm

Both **-K** and **--checksig** return the same output.

Secure Shell

By this time, you are probably aware that the Telnet protocol is essentially clear-text and shouldn't be trusted for important sessions and tasks. The Secure Shell (SSH) suite includes a protocol, a daemon, and client utilities that make your host-to-host shell sessions much more secure—about as secure as being at the physical console.

One of the features that makes SSH desirable as a remote protocol is its end-to-end encryption, which encrypts not only the username and password, but also all communications.

The SSH suite replaces telnet, as well as rsh, rexec, rcp, and other unsecure utilities. You can use SSH to connect for a shell session, or you can use the scp command to remotely transfer files through the secure pipe that SSH builds between the hosts.

SSH Components

SSH includes a number of programs and files:

➤ ssh—Used for remote shell sessions on another host, it replaces telnet, rsh, and rexec.

➤ scp—Used for remote copying operations, it replaces rcp.

➤ sshd—The SSH daemon.

➤ ssh-agent—Runs as a wrapper to the user's session and provides authentication when requested.

➤ ssh-add—Loads the user's key(s) into the agent.

The SSH package configuration files are somewhat scattered. SSH daemon and global configuration files are kept in the /etc/ssh directory, with local or user-specific configuration files being kept in the ~/.ssh directory for the currently logged-on user. The global configuration files include

➤ /etc/ssh/sshd_config—The main configuration for the sshd daemon.

➤ /etc/ssh/ssh_host_key—This file, the ssh_host_dsa_key, and the ssh_host_rsa_key are in the same directory and are the private parts of the host's key structure and should be protected from public view. The permissions for these files are 600, or rw for the root user and no permissions for anyone else.

➤ /etc/ssh/ssh_host_key.pub—This file, the ssh_host_dsa_key.pub, and the ssh_host_rsa_key.pub are in the same directory and are the public parts of the host's key structure. These must be world-readable and write-only by the root user, or set to 644.

➤ /etc/nologin—This isn't a part of SSH. However, if it's present, no one can log in via SSH except the root, which sees only the contents of the /etc/nologin file and is denied access.

A couple of special file pairs affect how SSH works, particularly the /etc/ssh/ssh_known_hosts and ~/.ssh/known_hosts files.

The global (/etc) file is used to check the public key of a host attempting to attach via SSH, and the local (~) file is the file from which the client gets the public key of the remote server. If a new connection is begun to a previously unknown host, the user sees a message informing him that the host is an unknown host and asking whether he wants to store the host's key in his known hosts file. If the user answers in the affirmative, the host's public key is added to the ~/.ssh/known_hosts file.

The global (/etc) file should be world-readable and root-writable. The local (~) file must be owned by and writable for the user.

The second special file pairing is the /etc/ssh/sshrc and ~/.ssh/rc files.

The global file (/etc/ssh/sshrc) is used to set global login-time initialization for users' SSH sessions. Anything that should be run (for all users) after the users complete authentication and before they get their shells should be in this file.

The ~/.ssh/rc file is functionally identical to the /etc/ssh/sshrc file, but it affects only an individual user. If this file does not exist, the /etc/ssh/sshrc file is used.

A couple of files affect only a particular user's environment, such as the ~/.ssh/authorized_keys file. This file is used to store the public keys that can be used for logging as this user. These are matched with the keys presented by an ssh or scp client upon login request.

The second file that affects only a user's environment is the ~/.ssh/environment file. This is used for setting options that affect the user's SSH shell environment.

Using SSH Client Utilities

The SSH client utilities are very versatile, with a number of options available to customize the experience. You'll just need the basics for the exam, but I've included a few fun things I've picked up along the way.

Using the SSH Client

The SSH client is used to replace the RSH and Telnet programs specifically. Its syntax is as follows:

```
ssh -l username remotehost
```

If you don't specify a username with the -l option, SSH assumes you want to use the account you are logged on with presently.

For example, I could attach to the host mp3server as the user snuffy with this command:

```
ssh -l snuffy mp3server
```

If I have not connected to this server before, I get a message similar to what's shown here:

```
The authenticity of host 'mp3server (192.168.33.44)' can't be established.
RSA key fingerprint is 73:4f:fa:b0:42:a4:3a:a8:64:2c:ad:26:1d:b1:21:e0.
Are you sure you want to continue connecting (yes/no)?
```

If I answer with yes, the host's public key is added to my ~/.ssh/known_hosts file and looks something like this:

```
192.168.3.44 ssh-rsa AAAAB3NzaC1yc2EAAAABIwAAAIEA1gFIB9VQpFKWAZUzNM+ac/
➥U81Tk9R8OCFfUkegVJXwj6
➥nqCISPyV2iJwaukcVVaVAQ+JR3EhvOvh4PhoSg4yzBSUkJ8aUBYoRSGj7PCD+vyWyi1922HG
➥xWbWooMBAO/Was8I7N0zQ6jxDO9qNOHcrIFeU7qbOCrKjQDM08HQjk0=
```

Using the scp Client

Rather than work with RCP or FTP, most of my file transfer work is with SCP. The scp command uses the SSH protocol and encrypts the files sent from one host to another host.

For example, if I wanted to transfer file1 from my root user's home directory on my machine to the same location on a host named remotehost, I would use the following command:

```
scp /root/file1 root@remotehost:/root/file1
```

This would prompt me with the RSA key question and then the password, and then it would transfer the files. The output from a file transfer looks like this:

```
root@192.168.1.73's password:
mypubkey.txt  100% |*********************| 1379  00:00
```

You can copy from your host to another as shown previously, copy from that one to yours by reversing the source and target specification, or even transfer from one remote host to another completely remote host—all from your host. The following recursively copies the /data directory and all its contents from remote1 to remote2 after prompting you for the password for both hosts:

```
scp -r root@remote1:/data root@remote2:/data
```

Another use of the SSH protocol is to log in to a host and use SSH to forward the output from an X client back to your display. This is the default behavior for the SSH client, but it can be specifically invoked with the -x option if your environment has that option set to off.

Using SSH Sans Password Prompts

SSH allows for skipping the password prompt when signing on between computers, which can be convenient if you use the SSH or scp clients frequently and don't mind the possibility that someone could sit down at your accidentally unlocked station and have her way with your network!

There has been a lot of talk about why it's important to delete **.rhosts** files from user directories. Basically, if you have a user that has a hostname in her **.rhosts** file and that host also has the user's hostname in its **/etc/hosts_equiv** file, that user can log in without a password! This would be a security risk, so my advice is to delete these files with the following command:

find /home -iname .rhost -exec rm -f {} \;

This deletes all **.rhosts** files it finds in users' home directories and does not prompt you for each deletion.

When I need to enable SSH usage without a password, here are the set of steps I take. I have two machines, fattyre and murphy, both of which are Linux workstations with the necessary SSH software loaded as per the defaults. This demonstration assumes that fattyre and murphy are both in each other's hosts files or resolvable via DNS.

Here's how you can enable SSH usage without passwords:

1. Log in to fattyre as the root user.

2. For this example, use a new user named user1. Create it with the following command:

```
useradd -m user1
```

3. Set user1's password with the passwd command to whatever you want:

```
passwd user1
```

4. Switch to the user1 user account with the following command:

```
su - user1
```

5. Enter the password for user1.

6. Create and set the permissions for the .ssh directory with the following command:

```
mkdir .ssh ; chmod 700 .ssh
```

7. Generate an RSA key:

```
ssh-keygen -b 1024 -t rsa
```

8. When prompted for the location for the file, press Enter to accept the default.

9. When prompted for a passphrase, enter the following:

```
seatec astronomy
```

10. Reenter the passphrase when prompted.

11. Change into the .ssh directory and set the permissions on the id_rsa.pub file with these commands:

```
cd .ssh ; chmod 644 id_rsa.pub
```

12. Copy the id_rsa.pub file to a new file called authorized_keys:

```
cp id_rsa.pub authorized_keys
```

 The next steps take place on the host **murphy**.

13. Ensure you can contact the host fattyre with a ping:

```
ping fattyre
```

14. Sign on to the host murphy as the root user.

15. Add a user named user2 with the following command:

```
useradd -m user2
```

16. Set the password for user2:

```
passwd user2
```

17. Enter the password twice to confirm it.

18. Switch to the user2 account with this command:

```
su - user2
```

19. Enter user2's password.

20. Make a directory and set its permissions with the following command:

```
mkdir .ssh ; chmod 700 .ssh
```

 The next steps take place on the host **fattyre**.

21. Connect to the murphy host as user2:

```
ssh -l user2 murphy
```

22. When prompted about the RSA key, answer yes and then enter user2's password.

23. While logged in as user2 on the host murphy via SSH, copy the authorized_keys file from the fattyre host with the following command:

```
scp user1@fattyre:~/.ssh/authorized_keys ~/.ssh
```

The output of the scp program should look similar to this:

```
authorized_keys  100% |*************************| 236  00:00
```

24. Exit user2 on the host murphy and return to being user1 on fattyre.

25. On fattyre as user1, invoke the ssh-agent as a wrapper to your shell with the command shown here:

```
ssh-agent $SHELL
```

26. Add your key to the agent:

```
ssh-add
```

27. When prompted for the passphrase, enter **no more tears**.

28. You'll then see output similar to this:

```
Identity added: /home/ssha/.ssh/id_rsa (/home/ssha/.ssh/id_rsa)
```

29. Now try to log in as user2 on murphy, and watch what happens:

```
ssh -l user Murphy
```

30. You shouldn't see any password prompt; you should see only the confirmation of where you last logged in from:

```
Last login: Wed May 26 13:46:55 from fattyre
```

If you do see a prompt for the passphrase, enter **no more tears** as you did before.

That's all it takes to get two accounts and machines set up to use SSH utilities without having to enter anything but the `ssh-agent` command along with the passphrase.

Remember that **ssh-agent** resides in memory and wraps a security blanket around your shell session, answering any SSH-related security requests for you. The **ssh-add** utility is for adding your key information into the agent and doesn't have to be run again as long as your key information remains the same.

Using Firewalls for Security

The progression of firewall or security utilities in Linux ranges from the early days with `ipfwadm` and `ipchains` to the latest version of firewalling, called `iptables`.

The exam objectives mention either **ipchains** or **iptables**, and you need to know the differences between the two:

➤ **iptables** uses only one chain's rules on a packet, whereas **ipchains** uses multiple, making it more complex to understand what's happening.

➤ The **DENY** target was changed to **DROP**. Both simply discard the packet.

➤ The order of rules in a chain matters more with **iptables** than with **ipchains**. **iptables** requires you to be more orderly or exact when specifying options.

➤ **OUTPUT** and **INPUT** chains are now separated. Traffic going out of a interface does not see the **INPUT** chain with **iptables**, whereas **ipchains** matches packets against both chains.

This is not, by any means, all the changes, but it's good enough to help you distinguish which is being asked about on the exam. Besides, most people report that the questions include which firewall option is being tested.

Although a firewall is important for security, using one also makes it easy to use nonpublic addressing inside the firewall, with only a small set of leased addresses on the outside of your organization.

The use of internal addressing or addresses that cannot be routed on the public Internet introduces yet another layer of security. An attacker cannot send an attack across the public Internet addressed to an internally addressed host because the routers in between will reject the traffic.

Understanding Basic iptables

When you are running a firewall on a workstation, it's typically not for protection of outside hosts; it's to keep bad things from happening to your machine.

The simplest method on a Red Hat machine is to run the setup program (and select Firewall Configuration to run the lokkit program). In later versions, use the redhat-config-securitylevel program.

The interface enables you to set simple firewall rules that disallow any traffic other than the services you configure it to accept (see Figure 19.1).

```
lqqqqqqqqqqqqqqqqqqqu Firewall Configuration - Customize tqqqqqqqqqqqqqqqqqqqqk
x                                                                            x
x You can customize your firewall in two ways. First, you can select to      x
x allow all traffic from certain network interfaces. Second, you can allow   x
x certain protocols explicitly through the firewall. Specify additional      x
x ports in the form 'service:protocol', such as 'imap:tcp'.                  x
x                                                                            x
x Trusted Devices: [ ] eth0 [ ] irlan0                                       x
x                                                                            x
x Allow incoming:   [ ] DHCP        [ ] SSH        [ ] Telnet                x
x                   [ ] WWW (HTTP) [ ] Mail (SMTP) [ ] FTP                   x
x                   Other ports                                              x
x                                                                            x
x                            lqqqqk                                          x
x                            x OK x                                          x
x                            mqqqqj                                          x
x                                                                            x
mqqqqqqqqqqqqqqqqqqqqqqqqqqqqqqqqqqqqqqqqqqqqqqqqqqqqqqqqqqqqqqqqqqqqqqqqqqqqj
```

Figure 19.1 Firewall configuration interface.

The other and more complex method is to use the iptables command line to customize your rules for the allowing and denying of packets for the system.

It's when you run a firewall or boundary router with a firewall function on it that life and iptables gets much more interesting.

 Thankfully, the rules for **iptables** are not an exam item because it could take many pages along with much head-scratching and hmm'ing to get even seasoned but innocent sysadmins to understand how to write effective **iptables** rule sets. A thorough understanding of what's going on will more than suffice, along with the ability to view your configuration.

For our purposes, a firewall that uses iptables is effectively made up of the following:

➤ **Chains**—Sets of rules that affect traffic.

➤ **Rules**—A criteria that attempts to match packets and send them to a target. If no match is found, the packet is inspected by the next rule in the chain.

➤ **Target**—It's ACCEPT, DROP, QUEUE, or RETURN. A matched packet is accepted, dropped, queued for another chain, or returned to the parent chain.

iptables's Three Chains

An understanding of the three chains or paths that can be controlled on a machine with iptables is essential to good security because you want to ensure that all interfaces are covered properly with the right chain rules.

I have seen a few attempts to graphically represent the way iptables's chains interact and protect a machine. However, I've had to come up with my own to explain it to customers and attendees in my boot camps.

Figure 19.2 is my attempt at graphically showing how the chains protect a machine.

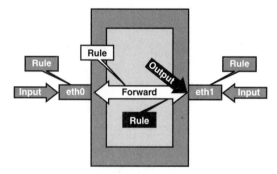

Figure 19.2   How **iptables** chains work.

As you can see, the left side of the machine has an interface named eth0 and the right side has an interface named eth1. In our examples, I treat eth0 as an internal and trusted network and treat eth1 as an external and untrusted network.

You need to understand how the different paths to, from, and across the iptables-protected firewall work.

Figure 19.2 shows three types of chains, and each chain has its own set of rules that make up the chain:

➤ **INPUT**—An input chain exists wherever there is an interface that can accept traffic. Each input chain affects only traffic entering the interface and destined for that local interface.

➤ **OUTPUT**—An output chain exists for the entire machine and affects only traffic that is generated on the machine, such as a client application attempting to send a request to either interface.

➤ **FORWARD**—A forward chain affects only traffic attempting to cross from interface to interface on the machine.

The example in Figure 19.2 has four rule points, two inputs, one output, and one forward. If the machine had only one interface, it would have three rule points: one intput, one output, and one forward. If it had three interfaces, it would have five rule points: three inputs, one output, and one forward.

Chains are sets of rules, and rules specify what to do with a packet that matches the rules criteria. Rules typically take the form of a packet criteria and a target, with each rule being examined in turn and order. If a packet doesn't match a rule, it goes on to be inspected by the next rule.

Using the **iptables** Command

Three table types exist for `iptables`: mangle, nat, and filter. Unless you're quite advanced in your use of `iptables`, the filter table is where you'll spend 99% of your time. All commands that don't include a `-t` option followed by mangle or nat affect filter by default.

The tables that exist for `iptables` include

➤ **Mangle**—This table is used to set the type of service, time to live, and mark targets. Essentially, it's used to alter packets for special routing and `iptables` purposes.

➤ **Nat**—The nat table is used only for network address translation (NAT) traffic. NAT is used when you have an internal set of hosts and an external network and want to have the addresses matched and translated, effectively masking your internal network from the external world.

➤ **Filter**—The default table, and the one that contains the prebuilt chains input, output, and forward.

To view the filter table on your machine, use the following command:

```
iptables -L
```

This returns the following output:

```
Chain INPUT (policy ACCEPT)
target    prot opt source              destination
Chain FORWARD (policy ACCEPT)
target    prot opt source              destination
Chain OUTPUT (policy ACCEPT)
target    prot opt source              destination
```

To view the nat or mangle table, you just have to include the `-t` option followed by the desired table type:

```
iptables -t mangle -L
```

For the exam, you'll need to know which commands show the different tables, by using the **-t tabletype** option.

Configuring an **iptables** Chain

You'll not see any chains on the exam, but it would be a shame to come this far without actually configuring the firewall for a machine.

Examples of simple rules that accomplish tasks include

```
iptables -A INPUT -s 223.107.1.101 -j DROP
```

This rule drops all traffic from just the IP of a particular host, such as one that keeps trying to break into something on one of your public servers.

Another example would be having to block an entire network from accessing your public server with the following command:

```
iptables -A INPUT -s 223.107.1.0/24 -j DROP
```

This rule blocks every host on the Class C network mentioned. The slash notation (/24) means that 254 host addresses are being blocked.

Another handy rule is to deny a particular service from use by a block of addresses, such as Telnet:

```
iptables -A INPUT -s 223.107.1.0/24 -p tcp
➡--destination-port telnet -j DROP
```

 You could also use the port number 23 to block the addresses. The previous use of the name Telnet depends on that service being defined in the **/etc/services** file.

Let's say you want to secure your firewall system from any connection to hosts that you didn't initiate. This is handy when you are using private addresses and don't want people following your address back to the firewall and trying to break in. You'd use the following:

```
iptables -A INPUT -i eth0 -p tcp --syn -j DROP
```

This causes any computer that initiates a connection to eventually time out waiting for a TCP synchronize packet because you're dropping it at the interface. If you initiate the connection (and it hasn't done the same thing to you!), your systems can connect to the remote host just fine.

The problem with the previous rule is that it drops everything, and you might want to keep an SSH port and perhaps a Web server listening on that machine.

In this case, you can use an exception to the DROP we used, even though it takes two lines to accomplish the two open ports. The order of the rules in the chain is unimportant for our example.

To block all but port 80 (www) on your system, you would use the command shown here:

```
iptables -A INPUT -i eth0 -p tcp --syn --destination-port ! 80 -j DROP
```

To add another port, such as 22 (ssh) to the chain, you would use the following command:

```
iptables -A INPUT -i eth0 -p tcp --syn --destination-port ! 22 -j DROP
```

If you show the filter table contents, you'll see that both rules are there and will be active for this session:

```
iptables -L
```

This returns the following output:

```
Chain INPUT (policy ACCEPT)
target prot opt source     destination
DROP   tcp  -- anywhere anywhere   tcp dpt:!http flags:SYN,RST,ACK/SYN
DROP   tcp  -- anywhere anywhere   tcp dpt:!ssh flags:SYN,RST,ACK/SYN

Chain FORWARD (policy ACCEPT)
target     prot opt source                destination
Chain OUTPUT (policy ACCEPT)
target     prot opt source                destination
```

Now that you've seen some good examples of how to use the iptables command to protect your system, be sure to save the rules you've defined with the iptables-save command.

When run, the iptables-save command (present on Red Hat and Debian) saves the contents of your iptables tables to the /etc/sysconfig/iptables file. Upon reboot of the system, the table rules are restored automatically by the iptables-restore command.

On a Debian machine, the iptables-save function can be automated by saving the rules with this command:

```
iptables-save > firewall.txt
```

Then, in your startup scripts you can restore the configuration with this command:

```
iptables-restore < firewall.txt
```

Be aware of logic-based questions for firewalls, such as where you'd put a rule to deny internal users access to an outside resource (on the input chain for the internal interface).

Also watch for questions that want to know the different types of firewall options available for Linux, such as **ipfwadm**, **ipchains**, and **iptables**.

Exam Prep Questions

1. When a user on **host1** uses the SSH client to successfully connect to **host2** for the first time, which file is updated with SSH-related information?

   ○ A. `~/.ssh/known_hosts` on **host1**
   ○ B. `/etc/ssh/known_hosts` on **host2**
   ○ C. `~/.ssh/authorized_keys` on **host2**
   ○ D. `/etc/ssh/authorized_keys` on **host1**

   Answer A is correct because, when a user connects to a host for the first time via SSH, the RSA host key is copied to that user's local `.ssh/known_hosts` file. Answer B is incorrect because the `known_hosts` file exists only in user configurations. Answer C is incorrect because the `authorized_keys` file on **host2** has nothing to do with this connection. Answer D is incorrect because `authorized_keys` files are used only in user configurations.

2. You are ordered to deny access to the Telnet service on your server for the host **snuffypc** and to use the TCP wrappers files and utilities to accomplish this. In the blank below, write the full path and filename to the file that should contain this entry:

   _____

   The correct answer is `/etc/hosts.deny`. There are no alternative correct answers.

3. You are the root user on your managed systems. You need to send `/root/file6` from **host1** to **host3** in the same location, but you're on **host2**. Which of the following commands accomplishes the task? (Choose all that apply.)

   ❏ A. `scp root@host1:~/file6 root@host3`
   ❏ B. `scp root@host1:/root/file6 root@host3`
   ❏ C. `scp root@host1:/root/file6 root@host3:~`
   ❏ D. `scp root@host1:file6 root@host3`

   Answers A, B, and D are correct because they all copy the file properly from **host1** to **host3**. Answer C is incorrect because the addition of the `:~` to the end of the **host3** target causes an error trying to write a file to a directory that can't be resolved.

4. You've just downloaded a security fix from a vendor's site and want to validate the package's integrity. Fill in the blank below with the command and necessary option (no filename) to accomplish this on a Red Hat or RPM-based system:

   _____

   The correct answer is `rpm -K`. An alternative answer is `rpm --checksig`.

5. You've just downloaded a new public key and imported it into your GPG key ring. Fill in the blank below with the command and any necessary options that will show you the contents of your key ring:

_____

The correct answer is `gpg --list-keys`. There are no alternative correct answers.

6. One of the systems you manage is acting funny, leading you to believe some files might have special bits set that allow standard users to run important utilities as root. Which of the following search commands shows you all files that have any combination of special bits set?

   ○ A. `find / -perm -7000`

   ○ B. `find / -perm +7000`

   ○ C. `find / -perms 7000`

   ○ D. `locate --permissions=rws`

Answer B is correct because the `+7000` means to look for any combination of special bits that are set when using the `-perm` option for `find`. Answer A is incorrect because it finds only files that have all the special bits set. Answer C is incorrect because it finds only files that have the permissions `---s------`. Answer D is incorrect because the `locate` command doesn't have a `--permissions` option.

7. You suspect a broken firewall rule on a system is preventing access from other hosts. In the blank below enter the command with any necessary options and arguments that show you the rules defined for the filter table:

_____

The correct answer is `iptables -L`. An alternative answer is `iptables -t filter -L`.

8. You need to be able to attach, via a shell session, to other hosts over a secure and encrypted connection and to log on to the remote system without entering a password every time. Which of the following is the program or utility that directly makes this possible?

   ○ A. `ssh-add`

   ○ B. `ssh-keygen`

   ○ C. `ssh-agent`

   ○ D. `.ssh/authorized_keys`

Answer C is correct because `ssh-agent` wraps around the current shell and provides requested credentials, enabling you to not enter a password for a connection. Answer A is incorrect because it is used to load the user's key into the `ssh-agent`, but it doesn't run otherwise. Answer B is incorrect because it's used to generate the user's private and public keys but isn't otherwise used. Answer D is incorrect because the `.ssh/authorized_keys` file is not a program or utility.

9. A security situation requires you to create a 1K RSA public/private key combination for your currently logged-in account. Fill in the blank below with the correct command, with any necessary options and arguments, to accomplish this:

_____

The correct answer is `ssh-keygen -b 1024 -t rsa`. There are no alternative correct answers.

10. What has the `DENY` target from `ipchains` been changed to in the `iptables` firewalling tool? Fill in the blank with the exact name of the new target:

_____

The correct answer is `DROP`. There are no alternative correct answers.

Practice Exam 101

1. With a Linux 2.2 kernel-based machine that has a configuration of 133MHz, 32MB of RAM, and a 1GB hard drive, what is the maximum swap that should be configured?

   ○ A. 512MB
   ○ B. 256MB
   ○ C. 128MB
   ○ D. 64MB

2. Which of the following devices is least likely to work on a default install of a Linux system?

   ○ A. ISDN TA
   ○ B. Cable modem
   ○ C. Analog modem
   ○ D. PCI modem
   ○ E. Win modem

3. When partitioning a disk with more than 1,024 cylinders, which of the following could affect the system's capability to boot?

   ○ A. The location of **lilo.conf** on disk
   ○ B. The location of **/boot** on disk
   ○ C. The location of **/var** on disk
   ○ D. The disk transfer rate

4. How many storage devices can be used on a 16-bit SCSI system, excluding the controller?

   ○ A. 8
   ○ B. 10
   ○ C. 12
   ○ D. 16
   ○ E. 15

5. What would be the device name of the second SCSI disk on your system? Fill in the blank below with the full path and filename of the device file:

_____

6. What is the device file for the first logical drive in the extended partition of the secondary master IDE drive? Fill in the blank below with the full path and filename:

_____

7. Fill in the blank below with the full command line to begin partitioning the second SCSI drive on your system using the most common disk partitioning tool:

_____

8. Fill in the blank below with the full path and filename of the second serial port on a Linux system:

_____

9. What does the command `rpm -e tarfoo --allmatches`" accomplish? (Choose the best answer.)
   - A. It verifies all instances of the `tarfoo` package's existence on the system.
   - B. It enhances the `tarfoo` package's installation.
   - C. It enables the `tarfoo` package.
   - D. It removes all instances of the `tarfoo` package from the system.

10. What happens when the following command is issued? (Choose all that apply.)

```
rpm -Uvh snafoo-10.14.i386.rpm
```

   - A. The `.rpm` file is verified.
   - B. If installed, the package is upgraded if the file is a newer version.
   - C. If not installed, the package is installed from the file.
   - D. An error occurs because a package specifier was not included in the command line.

11. Which utility would be used to verify the checksum of a downloaded archive file?
   - A. `verify`
   - B. `chksum`
   - C. `md5sum`
   - D. `chkrpm`
   - E. `pkgchk`

12. Which operation of the `make` utility cannot be performed as a normal user?

   ○ A. `mrproper`
   ○ B. `clean`
   ○ C. `dep`
   ○ D. `depends`
   ○ E. `install`

13. You are on a Linux system and need to install all the RPM packages in the current directory on the local machine. Fill in the blank with the necessary command, options, and arguments:

   _____

14. You need to remove the `tarfoo` package regardless of any dependencies it might have or break. Fill in the blank below with the command, options, and arguments to accomplish this. There are at least two possible answers:

   _____

15. Before installing the `rtfm-foo.rpm` package on your system, you want to verify that a bug from the last version has been fixed. Fill in the blank below with the command, options, and arguments to display a revision history for the package:

   _____

16. You need to display the build host, licensing, and authorship information from a particular package. Which of the following shows this information? (Choose all that apply.)

   ❑ A. `rpm -q package --info`
   ❑ B. `rpm -ql package`
   ❑ C. `rpm -q --provides package`
   ❑ D. `rpm -qi package`

17. As a regular task, your boss has told you to generate a list verifying the state of all configuration files in all packages on a system, which you will redirect to a report file. Which of the following commands produces the needed output to populate the report file? (Choose two.)

   ❑ A. `rpm --verify`
   ❑ B. `rpm -ql package`
   ❑ C. `rpm -Vac`
   ❑ D. `rpm -qi package`
   ❑ E. `rpm -Va --configfiles`

18. You have downloaded a security update from a vendor's Web site and want to see whether it has been signed properly with the public key signature of the vendor or the author. Fill in the blank below with just the command and options (no package filename) needed to accomplish this for a `.rpm` package:

    _____

19. When installing a Red Hat system, what is the default boot loader? Fill in the blank below with the acronym that represents the boot loader, not the full name:

    _____

20. Your senior system administrator gives you access to a package cache of RPM packages that contain fixes for your server. What command, including any needed options and arguments, causes only installed packages to be upgraded and any uninstalled packages to be ignored? Assume you are at the shell prompt and in the package cache directory and write your answer in the blank below:

    _____

21. Which directory tree of an installation might have to be separated to avoid boot problems with a large hard drive? Fill in the blank below with the full path and filename of the directory tree:

    _____

22. With 500 users and several attached printers, which portions of your system would be most advantageous to isolate from the root file system? (Choose two.)
    - ❏ A. `/tmp`
    - ❏ B. `/root`
    - ❏ C. `/home`
    - ❏ D. `/usr`
    - ❏ E. `/var`

23. After installation and X configuration, your system reboots and won't complete the boot process. To bring the system to maintenance mode and fix the problem on a default Linux system, fill in the blank below with the exact boot parameters to accomplish this:

    _____

24. To change all lowercase characters in a file to uppercase, which command would you use? (Choose all that apply.)
    - ❏ A. `tr 'a-z' 'A-Z' file`
    - ❏ B. `tr [a-z] [A-Z] < file`
    - ❏ C. `tr "a-z" "A-Z" file`
    - ❏ D. `tr 'a-z' 'A-Z' < file`
    - ❏ E. `tr {a-z} {A-Z} > file`

25. You sign on to the system as the **root** user and immediately issue one of the following commands. Which of the following commands moves all the contents of the /**A** directory to the existing and empty /**B** directory using the least keystrokes possible?

    ○ A. `mv /A/* /B`

    ○ B. `mv /A/ /B`

    ○ C. `mv /A /B`

    ○ D. `mv /A/* .`

26. What does the command **kill -HUP 1354** do?

    ○ A. Removes the process **1354** completely and immediately from memory

    ○ B. Kills the process **1354**, allowing cleanup of memory

    ○ C. Restarts the process **1354**, rereading its configuration files

    ○ D. Restarts the process **1354** abruptly, resetting its associated modem

27. You're going to be running a script named **myscript1** as a **cron** task and need to have it execute without sending any output whatsoever to the console of any logged-in user. Which of the following commands can accomplish this?

    ○ A. `myscript1 > file1.out 2>&1`

    ○ B. `myscript1 > file1.out 1>&2`

    ○ C. `myscript1 > file1.out 1> /dev/null`

    ○ D. `myscript1 1&2> file1.out`

    ○ E. `myscript1 1> /dev/null > file1.out`

28. Which of the following commands shows you only the middle 10 lines of a 30-line text file named **tarfoo**?

    ○ A. `head -n 11-20 tarfoo`

    ○ B. `head -n 20 tarfoo¦ tail`

    ○ C. `tail -n 11-20 tarfoo`

    ○ D. `cat tarfoo¦ pr -n 11-20`

    ○ E. `nl -n 11-30 tarfoo`

29. You've exported the variable **BLARG** with a value of **number**. What is the result of the following command?

`# cat 'echo "$BLARG" '`

    ○ A. "`A Syntax Error has occurred`"

    ○ B. `cat: number not found`

    ○ C. `cat number`

    ○ D. `echo number`

    ○ E. `cat: echo "$BLARG" : no such file or directory`

30. How can you execute two commands, the second one being executed only if the first one returns a nonzero (program execution failed) exit status?

   - ○ A. `command1 || command2`
   - ○ B. `command1 && command2`
   - ○ C. `command1 $$ command2`
   - ○ D. `command1 @@ command2`

31. What best describes what is happening in the following command?

   `bar < foo | tarfoo`

   - ○ A. `bar`'s output is sent to `tarfoo`, and `tarfoo`'s output is written to `foo`.
   - ○ B. `bar` and `foo` are sent to `tarfoo` as input, and the output is shown on the console.
   - ○ C. `bar` reads `foo` as standard input and pipes the resulting output to the program `tarfoo`.
   - ○ D. `bar` overwrites `foo` with standard output and the result is sent to the program `tarfoo`.

32. You've executed a command that doesn't send any indication of success or failure to the console. What single command could you execute immediately afterward to determine the exit status?

   - ○ A. `echo $EXIT`
   - ○ B. `echo $1`
   - ○ C. `echo $?`
   - ○ D. `exitstatus`

33. Your boss wants you to take a large file that contains only text source code and prepare it for a review by formatting it for printing with header information and numbering for every line of the original file, regardless of its content. Which of the following accomplishes this? (Choose two.)

   - ❑ A. `pr -n codesamp`
   - ❑ B. `cat codesamp | nl | pr`
   - ❑ C. `pr < codesamp | tac | nl`
   - ❑ D. `nl -ba codesamp | pr`
   - ❑ E. `cat file | pr > nl`

34. Which command, when used with the proper options, shows the latest entries to a log file on a continuing basis?

   - ○ A. `head`
   - ○ B. `syslog`
   - ○ C. `crontab`
   - ○ D. `logrotate`
   - ○ E. `tail`

35. You are the `root` user on a system and you've found a file named
`-TMPFILE-` in the `/tmp/user1` directory. This file needs to be removed so a
program can function properly. You are in the `/tmp/user1` directory.
Which of the following commands removes the file? (Choose all that
apply.)

❑ A. `rm ./-TMPFILE-`

❑ B. `rm \-TMPFILE-`

❑ C. `rm "-TMPFILE-"`

❑ D. `rm [-TMPFILE]`

❑ E. `rm -- -TMPFILE-`

36. Because of usernames being different lengths, when you display output
from a tab-separated file, the columns are not aligned. Which command most efficiently replaces the tabs with spaces?

○ A. `expand`

○ B. `vi`

○ C. `convert`

○ D. `tr`

○ E. `sed`

37. You're logged in as the superuser and your current directory is
`/usr/local/appname`. You want to navigate to `/home/rbrunson/subdir1` without using any absolute pathnames (starting with /). Which of the following commands accomplishes this task? (Choose all that apply.)

❑ A. `cd ~/subdir1`

❑ B. `cd ../../../home/rbrunson/subdir1`

❑ C. `cd ~rbrunson/subdir1`

❑ D. `cd ../../home/rbrunson/subdir1`

❑ E. `cd $HOME/subdir1`

38. In `vi`, which keystrokes represent the following actions: down, right,
up, left? (Choose the best answer.)

○ A. hjkl

○ B. lkhj

○ C. lhjk

○ D. jlkh

○ E. jklh

39. After executing a program in a shell session, you don't get any messages, the command seems to have exited normally, and it produces no
extra output. Which of the following is the most likely representation
of the program's exit status?

○ A. `1`

○ B. `127`

○ C. `202`

○ D. `0`

40. You are compiling a large program and want to have it continue the compile and installation process while you're gone for the evening. Which of the following executes the commands needed but stops if an error occurs?

    ○ A. `./configure $$ make $$ make install`
    ○ B. `./configure ¦¦ make ¦¦ make install`
    ○ C. `./configure && make && make install`
    ○ D. `./configure @@ make @@ make install`
    ○ E. `./configure ^^ make ^^ make install`

41. You are performing a system backup with a command that has failed in the past and want a second command to run only in the event that the first fails. Which of the following causes this to happen?

    ○ A. `backup1 ; backup2`
    ○ B. `backup1 & backup2`
    ○ C. `backup1 && backup2`
    ○ D. `backup1 ¦ backup2`
    ○ E. `backup1 ¦¦ backup2`

42. When writing a book, an author needs to search the entire **chapter 5** file for all instances of a single asterisk (*) and see output on the screen that tells him what the lines are that contain the asterisks. Which of the following accomplishes this? (Choose all that apply.)

    ❑ A. `grep '*' chapter5`
    ❑ B. `grep \<*\> chapter5`
    ❑ C. `grep "*" chapter5`
    ❑ D. `grep \* chapter5`
    ❑ E. `grep {*} chapter5`
    ❑ F. `grep * chapter5`

43. You need to create a hard link in the current user's home directory named **tarfoo** to the existing file **/backup/home_user_foo2**. Which command accomplishes this?

    ○ A. `ln -s /backup/home_user_foo2 ./tarfoo`
    ○ B. `ln /backup/home_user_foo2 tarfoo`
    ○ C. `cp – hlink /backup/home_user_foo2 tarfoo`
    ○ D. `dd if=./tarfoo of=/backup/home_user_foo2`

44. The user **snuffy** has set his home directory to read-only. You inspect the permissions of his **home** directory and find that you need only to set it writable for the owner to fix the problem. Which of the following accomplishes this?

    ○ A. `chmod 740 /home/snuffy`
    ○ B. `chmod 711 /home/snuffy/*`
    ○ C. `chmod u+w /home/snuffy`
    ○ D. `chmod o+rwx /home/snuffy`

45. While taking over for a departed sysadmin, you find the following line in a script:

    ```
    cp * ~tfoo
    ```

    What is this line supposed to accomplish? (Choose the best answer.)

    ○ A. It copies all files in the current directory to a subdirectory named **tfoo** in the current user's **home** directory.

    ○ B. It copies everything in the current directory to the current user's **public_html** directory.

    ○ C. It produces a syntax error.

    ○ D. It copies everything in the current directory to the **home** directory of the user **tfoo**.

    ○ E. None of the selections.

46. You have a server that houses a number of users and is also your primary email server. Due to several users backing up their laptops to the server and causing space problems for email, you have decided to institute quotas. If you require a 100MB quota for the users' **home** directories and a 50MB quota for the users' mail, what must be true about these two directory trees?

    ○ A. They must be on separate drives.

    ○ B. The special bit 4 must be set on each directory to enable quotas.

    ○ C. They must be correctly entered in the **/etc/qtab** file.

    ○ D. The directories must be at least on separate partitions.

47. While looking at a script that's designed to make an **ext2** file system on a device, you find the following line:

    ```
    mkfs.ext2 -b 1024 -m 5 /dev/hdb1
    ```

    What does the **-m** option specify?

    ○ A. That each inode can have up to 5MB associated with it by default

    ○ B. That the reserved percentage for the **root** user is 5% of the file system

    ○ C. That metadata will be journaled for the file system

    ○ D. That the last mounted directory will be retained for utilities that request the last mount point

48. On a Red Hat machine, what would be the correct permissions for the **/etc/passwd** and **/etc/shadow** files, respectively?

    ○ A. 644 and 400

    ○ B. 640 and 640

    ○ C. 644 and 440

    ○ D. 644 and 600

49. Which feature of a system restricts users' space usage on a file system–by–file system basis if their kernel has support for it? Fill in the blank below with the lowercase name of the feature only:

    _____

50. On a Debian machine, what would be the correct permissions for the `/etc/passwd` and `/etc/shadow` files, respectively?

    ○ A. 644 and 440
    ○ B. 644 and 600
    ○ C. 644 and 400
    ○ D. 644 and 640

51. You need to conserve time and space for backups on a busy server, so you decide to not back up two particular directory trees. Which of the following is the most likely *not* to change on a regular basis? (Choose two.)

    ❑ A. `/usr`
    ❑ B. `/etc`
    ❑ C. `/home`
    ❑ D. `/dev`
    ❑ E. `/root`

52. You need to have a set of users that will create files that have read and write permissions for the owner and group but no permissions whatsoever for any other user. Which value should you set for each of these users in their `~/.bash_profile` files?

    ○ A. `umask 007`
    ○ B. `umask 022`
    ○ C. `umask 027`
    ○ D. `umask 054`

53. As a normal user, you find that you cannot create files above a certain size. When you contact your system administrator, she tells you that the _____ has been set, effectively restricting your ability to create large files. Choose the missing word from the following:

    ○ A. `umask`
    ○ B. `unalias`
    ○ C. `noclobber`
    ○ D. `ulimit`
    ○ E. `unset`

54. After moving a large number of small files to your system, you need to determine the percentage of inodes free and used. Which command would best accomplish this?

    ○ A. `du`
    ○ B. `fsck`
    ○ C. `df`
    ○ D. `tree`
    ○ E. `dumpe2fs`

55. To see a summary of the space used by the /home directory tree, which of the following commands would you use?

   - A. df -h
   - B. du -sh /home
   - C. freespace /home
   - D. dirs /home

56. Choose the steps that need to be performed to enable user quotas on a given file system. The list need not include every action—just the ones listed that must be performed.

   - A. Add the string usrquota to the fourth column of the /etc/fstab.
   - B. Run the edquota command.
   - C. Run the quotacheck command.
   - D. Remount the file system.
   - E. Run the quota command.

57. Your system has two parallel ports and you've attached a device to the second one as listed on the rear panel of the system. Fill in the blank below with the full path and filename of the device file that represents this port:

   _____

58. You have hooked a modem to the existing third serial port and want to configure it. Fill in the blank below with the full path and filename for the device file that points to the serial port in question:

   _____

59. You are using a workstation as a master for rolling out identical workstations for a lab. Which command would duplicate the /dev/hda disk block by block to an identical disk that's present as device /dev/hdb? Fill in the blank below with the simplest string to accomplish this:

   _____

60. You need to configure xscreensaver to time out in 30 seconds. What is the name of the file that you can edit to accomplish this? (Choose two.)

   - A. /etc/ssaver.conf
   - B. /etc/X11/xinit/scrnsaver.conf
   - C. .xscreensaver
   - D. .Xdefaults
   - E. .xssaverrc

61. Which file is used to store the program customizations during a user's session?

   - A. Xresources
   - B. .Xdefaults
   - C. .Xsession
   - D. xrdb

62. You need to configure where fonts are located on your system, which uses version 4 of the XFree86 system. Which section of the X configuration file would this be located in?

   ○ A. `Device`
   ○ B. `FontPath`
   ○ C. `Files`
   ○ D. `Display`

63. Which of the following is a window manager? (Choose all that apply.)

   ❑ A. Xfce
   ❑ B. Afterstep
   ❑ C. IceWM
   ❑ D. FVWM
   ❑ E. BlackBox

64. Once started, X doesn't look like it's displaying the color depth you specified. Which utility, when run in an xterm or shell session under X, shows the color depth for your current display settings?

   ○ A. `xvidtune`
   ○ B. `xset`
   ○ C. `xdepth`
   ○ D. `xwininfo`

65. You need to configure a custom X login screen for your users that shows a company logo and welcome text. Which of the following is used to accomplish the task? (Choose two.)

   ❑ A. `Xresources`
   ❑ B. `Xsession`
   ❑ C. `xdm-config`
   ❑ D. `XF86Config`

66. A user complains that her system will run X but defaults to a very low resolution. Which file can you edit to change the resolution?

   ○ A. `/etc/X11/xinit/xinitrc`
   ○ B. `/etc/X11/XF86config`
   ○ C. `/etc/X11/xfconfig-4`
   ○ D. `/etc/X11/serverconfig`

Answer Key 101

1. C

2. E

3. B

4. E

5. `/dev/sdb`

6. `/dev/hdc5`

7. `fdisk /dev/sdb`

8. `/dev/ttyS1`
(Alternative: `/dev/cua1`)

9. D

10. B, C

11. C

12. E

13. `rpm -i *.rpm`

14. `rpm -e tarfoo --nodeps`
(Alternative: `rpm -e`
`--nodeps tarfoo`)

15. `rpm -qp --changelog rtfm-foo.rpm`
(Alternative: `rpm -qp`
`rtfm-foo.rpm --changelog`)

16. A, D

17. C, E

18. `rpm --checksig` (Alternative:
`rpm -K`)

19. `grub` (Alternative: `GRUB`)

20. `rpm -F *.rpm` (Alternative:
`rpm --freshen *.rpm`)

21. `/boot`

22. C, E

23. `linux 1` (Alternative:
`linux single`, `linux S`, `Linux s`)

24. B, D

25. A

26. C

27. A

28. B

29. E

30. A

31. C

32. C

33. A, D

34. E

35. A, E

36. A

37. B, C

38. D

39. D	**53.** D
40. C	**54.** C
41. E	**55.** B
42. A, C, D	**56.** A, C, D
43. B	**57.** `/dev/lp1`
44. C	**58.** `/dev/ttyS2`
45. D	**59.** `dd if=/dev/hda of=/dev/hdb`
46. D	**60.** C, D
47. B	**61.** B
48. A	**62.** C
49. `quota`	**63.** A, B, C, D, E
50. D	**64.** D
51. A, D	**65.** A, C
52. A	**66.** B

1. Answer C is correct because the 2.2 kernel recommendation was twice the size of swap up to 128MB. Answer A is incorrect because it's well above the amount of recommended swap for a 2.2 kernel machine. Answer B is incorrect because it's still twice the recommended amount of swap for a 2.2 kernel. Answer D is incorrect because, even though it's twice the size of RAM, with a machine this slow, it's wise to configure the maximum amount of swap.

2. Answer E is correct because Winmodems are dependent on the Windows operating system or functionality. All other modem types listed are compatible or can be configured out of the box for use with Linux, so answers A, B, C, and D are incorrect.

3. Answer B is correct because the /**boot** directory would have to be on a small partition at the beginning of the disk to avoid any cylinder 1024 issues. Answer A is incorrect because the **lilo.conf** file is used by the **lilo** command only when setting up or refreshing the boot information. Answer C is incorrect because the location of /**var** has no relation to the cylinder 1024 problem. Answer D is incorrect because the disk transfer rate has no relation to the cylinder 1024 problem.

4. Answer E is correct because a 16-bit SCSI system fits 15 devices, not including the controller. Answers A, B, and C are incorrect because they are too few (8, 10, 12) devices. Answer D is incorrect because it is too many (16) devices.

5. Answer: `/dev/sdb` (There are no alternative correct answers.)

6. Answer: `/dev/hdc5` (There are no alternative correct answers.)

7. Answer: `fdisk /dev/sdb` (There are no alternative correct answers.)

8. Answer: `/dev/ttyS1` (An alternative correct answer is `/dev/cua1`.)

9. Answer D is correct because the command is used to remove all instances of the `tarfoo` package, most likely after getting an error message about multiple short package names being found for `tarfoo`. Answer A is incorrect because it does not verify the existence of any packages on the system. Answer B is incorrect because there isn't an enhancement option for `.rpm` packages. Answer C is incorrect because there isn't an enable option for `.rpm` packages.

10. Answers B and C are correct because the `-U` option is for upgrading installed packages or installing a package that is not currently installed. Answer A is incorrect because verification is done with the `-v` option. Answer D is incorrect because the command is correctly formatted.

11. Answer C is correct because the `md5sum` command is used to verify the MD5 checksum of a file. Answer A is incorrect because the `verify` command is used to verify certificates for SSL operations. Answer B is incorrect because there isn't a chksum utility on a standard Linux box. Answer D is incorrect because there isn't a chkrpm utility on a standard Linux box. Answer E is incorrect because `pkgchk` is a Solaris utility and isn't on Linux systems.

12. Answer E is correct because the `make install` command typically installs binaries into protected system directories. All other answers are incorrect because they can be run by non-`root` users.

13. Answer: `rpm -i *.rpm` (There are no alternative correct answers.)

14. Answer: `rpm -e tarfoo --nodeps` (Alternative answer: `rpm -e --nodeps tarfoo`)

15. Answer: `rpm -qp --changelog rtfm-foo.rpm` (Alternative answer: `rpm -qp rtfm-foo.rpm --changelog`)

16. Answers A and D are correct because either `-q --info` or `-qi` returns the information page in a package. Answer B is incorrect because the `-l` option only lists the files contained in or installed by the package. Answer C is incorrect because the `--provides` option only lists the capabilities of the package, not the requested information.

17. Answers C and E are correct because both verify all files in all packages on the system and print to the console the state of the files found, with a **c** denoting configuration files. Answer A is incorrect because the **--verify** command needs either **-a** or **--all** to be valid. Answer B is incorrect because it queries a package only for the files in it. Answer D is incorrect because it queries a package only for the information page for a package.

18. Answer: **rpm --checksig** (Alternative answer: **rpm -K**)

19. Answer: **grub** (Alternative answer: **GRUB**)

20. Answer: **rpm -F *.rpm** (Alternative answer: **rpm --freshen *.rpm**)

21. Answer: **/boot** (There are no alternative correct answers.)

22. Answers C and E are correct. Answer C is correct because **/home** contains the user home directories and, with 500 users, the usage would be considerable. Answer E is correct because **/var** contains all printer spool directories and logging, which with 500 users and several attached printers will see a lot of activity. Answer A is incorrect because **/tmp** sees a lot of use but its files are temporary and the entire system uses **/tmp**. Answer B is incorrect because the **root** user's home directory should see less usage than **/var** and **/home**. Answer D is incorrect because **/usr** is often static or mounted from a remote source and therefore changes less often than others.

23. Answer: **linux 1** (An alternative answer is **linux single, linux S, Linux s**.)

24. Answers B and D are correct because the **tr** command needs to have a < redirect to function and either putting the characters in [] ranges or surrounding them with single quotation marks will work. Answer A is incorrect because it doesn't contain the necessary < redirect. Answer C is incorrect because it doesn't contain the necessary < redirect and surrounding the ranges by quotation marks won't accomplish the task. Answer E is incorrect because it has a > redirect rather than a < redirect.

25. Answer A is correct because it accomplishes the task of moving the contents via the trailing **/*** and the full path of the target directory. Answer B is incorrect because it moves the **/A** directory to **/B** as a subdirectory, not its contents as specified. Answer C is incorrect because it does exactly the same thing as Answer B. Answer D is incorrect because you cannot assume that you are in the **/B** directory unless specified; if you're in any other directory, the files will not be copied correctly.

26. Answer C is correct because the **-HUP** or **SIGHUP** signal is used to restart a process, causing it to reread its configuration files. Answer A is incorrect because, to accomplish a complete and immediate kill, a **-9** or **SIGKILL** signal is required. Answer B is incorrect because a **-15** or **SIGTERM** signal allows for cleanup of memory and an orderly shutdown of the process. Answer D is incorrect because nothing about the process states it's associated with a modem, nor will a simple kill (**SIGTERM**) do anything abruptly.

27. Answer A is correct because it alone correctly captures STDOUT with the > to file1.out and also correctly captures STDERR with the 2>&1. Answer B is incorrect because the 1>&2 results in all the output being sent to the console. Answer C is incorrect because it still allows STDERR to reach the console. Answer D is incorrect because it puts the first command into the background and attempts to execute the 1&2> string. Answer E is incorrect because it allows STDERR to reach the console.

28. Answer B is correct because using head with -n 20 and the filename reads the tarfoo file and sends the first 20 lines to the tail command, which automatically shows the last 10 lines of any input. This results in lines 11–20 being shown onscreen. Answer A is incorrect because ranges aren't allowed with the head command, so 11-20 produces an error about an invalid number of lines. Answer C is incorrect because tail doesn't support ranges either and causes a similar error to Answer B. Answer D is incorrect because it causes pr to attempt to number lines in a file named 11-20. Answer E is incorrect because it causes an error about invalid line number formats.

29. Answer E is correct because cat is attempting to use the echo statement as a file input, in which the variable $BLARG is being interpreted as a file. Answer A is incorrect because no syntax errors occur but a file error does occur. Answer B is incorrect because the value of $BLARG isn't being read by cat, just the name of the variable. Answer C is incorrect because cat can't see the value number, only the variable name. Answer D is incorrect because cat can't see the echo number, only the variable name.

30. Answer A is correct because separating two commands with double pipe symbols (¦¦) causes the second command to attempt to execute only if a nonzero value is returned from the previous command. Answer B is incorrect because, if command1 executes with a nonzero exit status, command2 is not attempted. Answer C is incorrect because the $$ characters are shorthand for the PID of the current shell. Answer D is incorrect because the @@ characters are interpreted as a parameter or argument to command1.

31. Answer C is correct because bar must be a program, with foo being read as input, and the output is being sent to tarfoo, which is also a program. All other answers are wrong because of the order of execution and because the pipe from the first program sets bar < foo to the second program, tarfoo.

32. Answer C is correct because the variable $? stores the previously executed command's exit status. Answer A is incorrect because there is no system variable named $EXIT. Answer B is incorrect because the variable $1 is a positional variable for the command line. Answer D is incorrect because exitstatus isn't a variable.

33. Answers A and D are correct because only the use of `pr -n` and `nl -ba` numbers every line of the original file. Answer B is incorrect because it does not number every line of the original file. Answer C is incorrect because it doesn't number every line of the original file and the use of `tac` reverses the file from top to bottom. Answer E is incorrect because it doesn't number every line of the original file.

34. Answer E is correct because only it can follow a log file with the use of `tail -f logfile`. Answer A is incorrect because the `head` command doesn't show the latest entries of a log file; it shows the file from the top down. Answer B is incorrect because there isn't a `syslog` command on a standard Linux system. Answer C is incorrect because the `crontab` command is used to configure a user's `cron` task table, not to read log files. Answer D is incorrect because the `logrotate` command is used to archive log files, not read the latest entries.

35. Answers A and E are correct because the use of the `./` before the file-name substitutes the full path of the filename and the `--` characters are specifically used in the `rm` command to allow removal of files that start with a `-`. All other answers are incorrect and return errors because the `rm` command interprets the filename as a set of options that begin with a dash (-) and not a filename.

36. Answer A is correct because the `expand` command is designed to replace tabs with spaces in files. Answer B is incorrect because, even though `vi` could be used, it's not the most efficient method. Answer C is incorrect because the `convert` command is used to convert graphics formats. Answer D is incorrect because `tr` is not the most efficient tool for this task. Answer E is incorrect because `sed` is not the most efficient tool for this task.

37. Answers B and C are correct because both cause you to end up in the `/home/rbrunson/subdir1` directory. Answer A is incorrect because you're not `rbrunson`, so unless there is a `/root/subdir1` directory, an error results; also, the answer doesn't take you to the correct directory any-way. Answer D is incorrect because it doesn't go back up the tree to the `/` of the system; it attempts to `cd` into `/usr/home/rbrunson/subdir1`. Answer E is incorrect because the `$HOME` variable does not expand out to `/home/rbrunson`; it expands to `/root`.

38. Answer D is correct because the keystrokes jlkh represent the pattern down, right, up, and left. All others are incorrect because the order is wrong.

39. Answer D is correct because the exit status of `0` indicates success. All other answers are incorrect because any nonzero value for an exit code indicates failure or an error.

40. Answer C is correct because the double **&&** symbols allow the next program to execute only if the previous program's exit status was zero, and the process stops or fails if any of the commands has a nonzero exit status. Answer A is incorrect because the **$$** symbols represent the current shell's value. Answer B is incorrect because the **¦¦** symbols do the exact opposite of what's desired; they don't execute the next command if the previous one succeeded. Answer D is incorrect because the **@@** symbols are treated as an argument to the first command. Answer E is incorrect because the **^^** characters are treated as an argument to the first command.

41. Answer E is correct because only the **¦¦** symbols cause the second backup program to run if the first fails. Answer A is incorrect because it causes both to attempt to be run regardless of their individual exit status. Answer B is incorrect because it puts the first backup into the background and still executes the second one. Answer C is incorrect because it causes the second backup to execute if the first succeeds, counter to what is needed. Answer D is incorrect because it sends the output from the first backup program to the second backup program as standard input, which does something but not what's intended.

42. Answers A, C, and D are correct because they correctly find lines that contain an asterisk. Answer B is incorrect because it causes **grep** to look for the string \<*\>, not just an asterisk. Answer E is incorrect because the curly brackets don't signify a range; if they were square brackets, it would find the asterisk. Answer F is incorrect because the naked asterisk is expanded into every filename in the current directory by the shell before **grep** can search with it.

43. Answer B is correct because it creates the hard link needed. Answer A is incorrect because it's a symbolic link being created and is backward. Answer C is incorrect because the **cp** command doesn't have a --hlink option. Answer D is incorrect because **dd** doesn't create hard links.

44. Answer C is correct because it alters just the bit needed to give **snuffy** write access to his **home** directory. Answer A is incorrect because it assumes that you know what the permissions are and can set, not alter, them. Answer B is incorrect because it too assumes that you know the permissions. Answer D is incorrect because it adds read, write, and execute to all the permission trios for **snuffy**'s home directory.

45. Answer D is correct because the **~tfoo** string is shorthand for the user **tfoo**'s **home** directory. Answer A is incorrect because the string would have to be ~/tfoo for this to be correct. Answer B is incorrect because the string would have to be ~/**public_html** for this to be correct. Answer C is incorrect because no syntax error occurs if the user **tfoo** exists. Answer E is incorrect because Answer D is correct.

46. Answer D is correct because quotas are on a file system–by–file system basis and conflicting quotas cannot be configured on the same partition. Answer A is incorrect because they don't have to be on separate drives, just separate file systems. Answer B is incorrect because the special bit 4 (SUID) has nothing to do with this situation. Answer C is incorrect because there is no /etc/qtab file on a standard Linux system.

47. Answer B is correct because the reserved percentage is set with the `-m` option followed by a percentage value in numerals. Answer A is incorrect because it's a description of the `largefile4` option, which isn't specified. Answer C is incorrect because the `ext2` file system doesn't do journaling, so metadata isn't journaled. Answer D is incorrect because the description is indicative of the `-M` option's behavior.

48. Answer A is correct because a Red Hat machine has the `/etc/passwd` file set to 644 and the `/etc/shadow` file set to 400. All other answers are wrong because of either permission being set incorrectly.

49. Answer: `quota` (There are no alternative correct answers.)

50. Answer D is correct because a Debian machine has the `/etc/passwd` file set to 644 and the `/etc/shadow` file set to 640. All other answers are wrong because of either permission being set incorrectly.

51. Answers A and D are correct because the `/usr` directory tree contains mostly binaries and reference files and the `/dev` directory tree is mostly static after the server is set up properly. Answer B is incorrect because anytime a user is added or a service is configured, the `/etc` directory is changed and the server is a busy system. Answer C is incorrect because, if there are any users at all, the `/home` directory changes frequently. Answer E is incorrect because the `root` user's home directory can change frequently, and on a busy system you'll spend a good amount of time as the `root` user.

52. Answer A is correct because a `umask` of `007` creates files with the permissions set to `660` by default. Answer B is incorrect because `022` is the default and creates files that are set to `644`. Answer C is incorrect because it creates files that are too restrictive—they should be set to `640`. Answer D is incorrect because a `umask` of `054` produces files that have permissions of `622`.

53. Answer D is correct because the `bash ulimit` option is capable of restricting a user's ability to create files above a certain size. Answer A is incorrect because the `umask` only has to do with masking out permissions. Answer B is incorrect because `unalias` is used solely to remove aliases. Answer C is incorrect because the `noclobber` option is for restricting a user's ability to overwrite existing files with > redirection. Answer E is incorrect because `unset` is for removing arrays that have been set.

54. Answer C is correct because the `df` command, when used with the `-i` option, shows the number of used and free inodes for all mounted file systems. Answer A is incorrect because the `du` command shows information only about files on a file system, not file systems. Answer B is incorrect because the `fsck` command is capable of warning you only if a serious lack of free inodes exists, and only when it's run. Answer D is incorrect because the `tree` command only shows files and directories in a tree-like manner. Answer E is incorrect because the `dumpe2fs` command shows many things, but not inode exhaustion or usage.

55. Answer B is correct because only the `du -sh /home` command shows the information needed, with the `-sh` showing a summary in MB/GB of the space usage for the `/home` directory and its contents. Answer A is incorrect because `df -h` shows space usage only on a file system level. Answer C is incorrect because there isn't a freespace command on a default Linux machine. Answer D is incorrect because the `dirs` command is for remembering frequently used directories, not showing file usage.

56. Answers A, C, and D are correct because, of the answers listed, they *must* be performed before quotas are enabled for a file system. Answer B is incorrect because it doesn't have to be run to enable quotas but should be run to set users' quota constraints. Answer E is incorrect because the `quota` command is for users to query their disk usage and quota statuses.

57. Answer: `/dev/lp1` (There are no alternative correct answers.)

58. Answer: `/dev/ttyS2` (There are no alternative correct answers.)

59. Answer: `dd if=/dev/hda of=/dev/hdb` (There are no alternative correct answers.)

60. Answers C and D are correct because both can be edited to set the desired result. Answer A is incorrect because there is no such file on a default Linux system. Answer B is incorrect because there is no such file on a default Linux system. Answer E is incorrect because there is no such file on a default Linux system.

61. Answer B is correct because during a user's session the `.Xdefaults` file is used to store program customizations. Answer A is incorrect because the `.Xresources` file is only used to load the user's program customizations once when X is started. Answer C is incorrect because `.Xsession` is not related to user customizations. Answer D is incorrect because `xrdb` is the X server resource database utility and has nothing to do with user program customizations.

62. Answer C is correct because the `Files` section is where the FontPath setting is located. Answer A is incorrect because fonts are not a device. Answer B is incorrect because the question is looking for the section and not the keyword for the fonts' location. Answer D is incorrect because there isn't a Display section in the configuration file.

63. Answers A, B, C, D, and E are correct because all are valid X window managers.

64. Answer D is correct because only the `xwininfo` utility shows the current color depth. Answer A is incorrect because `xvidtune` shows the resolution and positioning setting but not the color depth. Answer B is incorrect because `xset` is used to refresh or set parameters in X, not show the color depth. Answer C is incorrect because `xdepth` doesn't show the color depth for the display.

65. Answers A and C are correct because together they are used to configure a customized login screen that can contain graphics and customized welcome text. Answer B is incorrect because the `Xsession` command and `.Xsession` file are used to start the user's session after logging in from `xdm`. Answer D is incorrect because the `XF86Config` file doesn't have any settings that affect a customized login screen for users.

66. Answer B is correct because only the `XF86Config` file is used to set the resolution for X. Answer A is incorrect because the `xinitrc` file is used as a parameter for the `xinit` process and is used to set keymaps and resources, among other settings. Answer C is incorrect because the case is incorrect; it should be `XF86Config-4`. Answer D is incorrect because `serverconfig` isn't a file; it's a directory.

Practice Exam 102

1. Which option to the `modprobe` command causes modules so marked to be removed or unloaded from memory if they haven't been used for a period of time?
   - ○ A. `autoclean`
   - ○ B. `inactive`
   - ○ C. `remove`
   - ○ D. `timeout`
   - ○ E. `holdoff`

2. Which of the following is not a valid `make` command during a kernel recompile?
   - ○ A. `make dep`
   - ○ B. `make clean`
   - ○ C. `make xconfig`
   - ○ D. `make modules`
   - ○ E. `make gzlilo`

3. Which of the following is a valid compilation option for the Linux kernel?
   - ○ A. `make zImage`
   - ○ B. `make zlilo`
   - ○ C. `make bzImage`
   - ○ D. `make lilo`

4. You need to load a particular module and all its dependencies with one command. Fill in the blank below with just the command name to accomplish this:

   _____

5. You're on a Debian system and need to create a rescue disk for system restore. Fill in the blank below with the complete command to create a rescue disk on your system. The kernel filename is `/boot/vmlinuz`:

_____

6. A piece of software that's registered by the CPU requires you to know the exact version of your Linux kernel. Write the command, with any needed options, that will show you just the kernel version:

_____

7. You need to boot your system to a state in which maintenance to disk subsystems can be performed. Which of the following accomplishes this? (Choose all that apply.)
   - ❏ A. `linux 1`
   - ❏ B. `linux 3`
   - ❏ C. `linux 4`
   - ❏ D. `init S`
   - ❏ E. `init s`

8. After making a change to the `/etc/lilo.conf` file, you decide to install the LILO bootstrap code to the default location. Which of the following is the default location for installing the LILO bootstrap code?
   - ○ A. `/boot/map`
   - ○ B. First sector
   - ○ C. `/boot/boot.b`
   - ○ D. MBR

9. Your system is running an older version of Linux and providing services on demand to clients that attach. Which file contains the on-demand services configuration information on this machine?
   - ○ A. `/etc/services`
   - ○ B. `/etc/inetd.conf`
   - ○ C. `/etc/xinetd.conf`
   - ○ D. `/etc/sysconfig`

10. A setup step for a system utility says to take your system to the level that will present you with a text-based login prompt and that the machine be fully functional. Fill in the blank below with the exact command to run as root to accomplish this task:

_____

11. You've just edited the `/etc/inittab` file to secure your system from being rebooted by the Ctrl+Alt+Del keys. Other than rebooting the system, which command can you run to refresh the `/sbin/init` process with the new settings? Fill in the blank below with the exact command string needed:

_____

12. You have mistakenly sent a print job to the default queue on your system and want to delete just that job. Which of the following commands removes just the first print job from the default queue?

    ○ A. `lprm -a`
    ○ B. `lprm all`
    ○ C. `lprm -Pdefault`
    ○ D. `lprm`

13. When you arrive at a meeting, two of your engineers are arguing about which command to use when printing multiple copies of a particular document. After logging on to your Linux system, you use the `history` command to show the two command strings you have recently used to print three copies of a document. Which two of the following are similar to the commands you used?

    ❑ A. `lpr -K 3 codesamp`
    ❑ B. `lpr -C 3 codesamp`
    ❑ C. `lpr -count 3 codesamp`
    ❑ D. `lpr – copies 3 codesamp`
    ❑ E. `lpr -# 3 codesamp`

14. You receive a request from a junior sysadmin to set up a host to print from a spool that's defined on your system. You already have an `/etc/printcap` file that contains the printer information he is using to print to your printer. Fill in the blank with the full path and filename of the file you will need to alter to enable his host to begin printing to your spools:

    _____

15. You try to use the `whatis` and `apropos` commands on your system and receive an error message that indicates a necessary file is missing. What is the command you can run to create this shared file?

    ○ A. `makewhatis`
    ○ B. `makeapropos`
    ○ C. `makeinfo`
    ○ D. `makeman`

16. Which option to the `man` command shows you a list of single-line entries containing a description of the command you are searching for?

    ○ A. `man command`
    ○ B. `apropos command`
    ○ C. `whatis command`
    ○ D. `whereis command`

17. While searching the `man` pages for the `port` command, you get several pages of results to a single command. Which command is the most likely to return this type of results? (Choose all that apply.)

   ❑ A. `apropos port`
   ❑ B. `man -a port`
   ❑ C. `whatis port`
   ❑ D. `man -k port`
   ❑ E. `whereis port`

18. In which section of the `man` pages is the `man` page that details the layout of the user's `crontab` file found? Fill in the blank with the exact command, options, and arguments to display the `man` page for this entry:

   _____

19. You know that a particular command you want to know more about has multiple `man` pages in different sections. You know the page you want exists because you've seen it before. Fill in the blank below with the exact command and options to show you all the individual `man` pages for the file `tarfoo`, one after another:

   _____

20. A friend needs to know more about Linux and wants to know what the official documentation site for the Linux operating system is. You tell her to visit a URL. Fill in the blank with the complete URL, starting with the characters `www`:

   _____

21. You are new to Linux, have heard about shell functions, and want to see them in action. Which command shows you all the available functions for your shell but not their contents? Fill in the blank below with the exact command and any needed options:

   _____

22. Which file disables normal user logins for the system if created and restores the ability to log in if deleted? Fill in the blank below with the full path and filename:

   _____

23. You run a script that includes an export of a variable. Upon exit of the script, you run an `echo` statement to see the value of that variable. What is the value for the variable?

   ○ A. The value from the script is still there.
   ○ B. The value is set to `0`.
   ○ C. The value is empty or `null`.
   ○ D. The value is set to `NULL`.

24. You have a script that runs properly when submitted as an **at** job but that returns errors about the path and files not being found when used in a **cron** job. What can you do to fix the problem?

    ○ A. Use the full paths to all commands.

    ○ B. Set the user running it to **root**.

    ○ C. Export the user's environment.

    ○ D. Move the script to the / of the system.

25. In which instance is a user connecting to a system shown the contents of the /**etc**/**issue.net** file?

    ○ A. When he connects via FTP

    ○ B. When he connects via **ssh**

    ○ C. When he connects via NFS

    ○ D. When he connects via Telnet

26. You want a series of commands that will prompt the user for arguments to run in the current shell, not in a subshell of the current shell. What would you use to make this happen?

    ○ A. An alias

    ○ B. The .**inputrc** file

    ○ C. A function

    ○ D. A script

27. You're nervous about running out of backup tape space, so you decide to monitor your very average server for a month to see which file system types don't need to be backed up consistently. Which partition/file system would you be least likely to back up or restore?

    ○ A. /**etc**

    ○ B. /**home**

    ○ C. /**usr**

    ○ D. /**var**

28. Which of the following commands can be used to change the user's password expiration information? Specifically, you want to force the user to change her password every 60 days. (Choose all that apply.)

    ❏ A. **passwd -x 60 user1**

    ❏ B. **chage -M 60 user1**

    ❏ C. **passwd +x 60 user1**

    ❏ D. **useradd -e 60 user1**

    ❏ E. **usermod -f 60 user1**

29. While performing routine maintenance, you find that most of the first 30 or so entries in the system's /etc/passwd appear to contain encrypted passwords instead of the shadow suite's x character in the password field. Which command should you run to fix this situation?

    ○ A. `passwdconv`
    ○ B. `pwconvert`
    ○ C. `passwd -conv`
    ○ D. `pwconv`
    ○ E. `passwd -mx5`

30. You're unhappy with the default settings for the `useradd` command and want to alter them to suit your environment. Which of the following is the full path and filename of the file in which these defaults are stored?

    ○ A. `/etc/defaults/useradd`
    ○ B. `/etc/sysconfig/useradd`
    ○ C. `/etc/.useradd`
    ○ D. `/etc/default/useradd`
    ○ E. `/etc/login.defs`

31. You have a standard server environment that users log in to via SSH and Telnet for various tasks. The users were created with the default account properties. All the following files exist both for the system and all users. During a user's login session, which is the last file to be read, executed, or sourced?

    ○ A. `/etc/profile`
    ○ B. `~/.bash_logout`
    ○ C. `~/.bashrc`
    ○ D. `~/.bash_profile`
    ○ E. `/etc/.profile`

32. You want to run a system script every 20 minutes starting at the top of the hour, from 8 a.m. to 6 p.m. every weekday. Fill in the blank below with the exact string to accomplish this, given the script name `script1` (use spaces, not tabs, to separate the fields):

    _____

33. You want to enable users to enter their own `cron` jobs on the system. What is the full path and filename of the file into which you would enter their usernames to cause this to happen?

    ❑ A. `/var/spool/cron/cron.accept`
    ❑ B. `/etc/sysconfig/crontab`
    ❑ C. `/etc/cron.allow`
    ❑ D. `/etc/cron.ok`

34. On a per-user basis, which file is used to store the aliases that are used · to shorten or replace commands you type? Fill in the blank with the fully qualified path and filename for the currently logged-in user:

_____

35. While filling in for another sysadmin, you find a couple of entries in the /etc/shadow file for a system that have an exclamation point (!) in front of the encrypted password for the user. Which two commands are the most likely to have caused this to happen?

- ❏ A. usermod
- ❏ B. chfn
- ❏ C. passwd
- ❏ D. chattr
- ❏ E. chpasswd

36. You have entered a single **at** job on the command line and want to confirm that the job has been submitted properly to the system. Fill in the blank below with the single command (no options) that shows the list of **at** jobs that exist for the system:

_____

37. You need to determine what the group membership of a particular user is currently, prior to modifying the user's group membership.

Fill in the blank below with the command you would use to see just this information for the user **snuffy**:

_____

38. You want to configure all messages of any category from the **syslogd** system logging daemon to come to a particular console for active monitoring. Fill in the blank below with the full path and filename of the configuration file for the **syslogd** daemon:

_____

39. You need to communicate with all logged-in users immediately, so you use the **wall** command. Of the users whose monitors you can see, all but one gets the message, even though all are logged in to the same server and you can see them with the **w** or **who** command. Fill in the blank below with the command and option used by the uninformed user to deflect these messages:

_____

40. On a system you have inherited, the `syslog.conf` file contains the following entry:

    ```
    *.crit     |/dev/xconsole
    ```

    To show the messages that are configured, what must you also do? (Choose all that apply.)

    - ❏ A. Run the `/dev/xconsole` application.
    - ❏ B. Run X.
    - ❏ C. Run `xconsole`.
    - ❏ D. Run `Xconsole &`.
    - ❏ E. Do nothing.

41. You want to configure `syslog` to show you all the messages that pertain to users' logins, successful or unsuccessful. Which facility or category of `syslog` messages should be configured to accomplish this?

    - ○ A. `login`
    - ○ B. `auth`
    - ○ C. `user`
    - ○ D. `daemon`
    - ○ E. `secure`

42. You need to be aware of all the priorities of messages that aren't for bug testing or debugging for the user facility of the `syslog` daemon. Which of the following entries in `syslog.conf` accomplishes this in the simplest manner?

    - ○ A. `Debug is always shown`
    - ○ B. `user.=info`
    - ○ C. `user.!debug`
    - ○ D. `user.debug`
    - ○ E. `user.*`

43. You are configuring your system to use NTP for an authentic time source. Which keyword is prefixed to a time source in the `/etc/ntp.conf` file entries?

    - ○ A. `source`
    - ○ B. `server`
    - ○ C. `tier1`
    - ○ D. `fudge`
    - ○ E. No keyword is needed.

44. You currently run a system that has three configured NICs on the same address range. You want this server to be the gateway between your corporate network and two internal testing networks. Which single command is capable of configuring the IP address information needed to accomplish this from the command line?

  ○ A. `netstat`
  ○ B. `iwconfig`
  ○ C. `default`
  ○ D. `ifconfig`
  ○ E. `route`

45. You own a small business and to save money you have your nephew install the Linux system that will become your firewall. The system has two identical NICs that he configured properly and that can `ping` both internal and external addresses. Which additional step must be performed before you can use the system for an access point to reach the Internet from your internal network?

  ○ A. `set +1 ip_firewall`
  ○ B. `cat 1 > /proc/forward`
  ○ C. `echo 1 >  /proc/sys/net/ipv4/ip_forward`
  ○ D. `echo 1 ¦ /proc/sys/net/ethernet`

46. Your use of `traceroute` for troubleshooting is typically very fast, but lately traces have taken many minutes and the output contains a few asterisks (*) where some of the routers' names used to be. Which option could you use to speed up your queries?

  ○ A. `-0`
  ○ B. `-p`
  ○ C. `-n`
  ○ D. `-t`
  ○ E. `-f`

47. After laboriously configuring dial-up for a particular user's Linux laptop, you quickly test connectivity with a particular application. What is the name of that application?

  ○ A. `setserial`
  ○ B. `minicom`
  ○ C. `hyperterm`
  ○ D. `procomm`

48. Your boss has been reading management magazines again and wants you to investigate the possibility of using a private address range for your internal network. Which of the following is a valid private address range according to RFC 1918? (Choose all that apply.)

   ❑ A. `10.0.0.0–10.255.255.255`
   ❑ B. `192.168.0.0–192.168.255.255`
   ❑ C. `172.16.0.0–172.31.255.255`
   ❑ D. `223.107.1.0–240.107.255.255`

49. Company A needs to have a *version 4.x* name server that's protected from attacks from particular address ranges but that also is as responsive as possible. Which statement should be true about this server? (Choose two.)

   ❑ A. It should run `named` under `xinetd`.
   ❑ B. It should use `tcpd` to protect `named`.
   ❑ C. It should run `named` standalone.
   ❑ D. It should have `/etc/hosts.deny` configured.
   ❑ E. It should have `/etc/hosts.allow` configured.

50. You have a demand-dialing connection that sometimes gets into a loop in which a connection is interrupted, attempts to immediately reconnect, and is rejected because the remote modem hasn't reset yet. Which option for the connection could you use to fix this situation?

   ○ A. `waitone`
   ○ B. `restart`
   ○ C. `disable`
   ○ D. `connect-delay`
   ○ E. `holdoff`

51. Which of the following is listed as a routing engine or daemon for use with Linux in a standard install of Linux? (Choose all that apply.)

   ❑ A. `ripd`
   ❑ B. `route`
   ❑ C. `bgpd`
   ❑ D. `rtnetlink`
   ❑ E. `gated`

52. A junior sysadmin has recently been cleaning up a system and now a particular daemon that used to work no longer does. She mentions something about editing a file and fixing a duplicate port problem for FTP. Which file did the junior sysadmin mistakenly edit?

   ○ A. `/etc/sysconfig/scripts`
   ○ B. `/etc/resolv.conf`
   ○ C. `/etc/services`
   ○ D. `/system32/drivers/etc/services`

53. You find one of your systems exhibits an odd traffic and usage pattern. On further inspection, you determine that a possible denial-of-service attack is originating from the address 172.16.38.125. You want to stop the attack, but leave the server otherwise functional, and update your firewall software later. Fill in the blank with the command and options/arguments to accomplish this:

_____

54. You're configuring your system to have a static IP and need to add a gateway to the system. Given the address of 10.1.2.3 for the gateway, fill in the blank below with the proper command, options, and arguments to set up the default gateway for your system:

_____

55. While setting up a mail server, you need to see the fully qualified name and IP for another server at the example.com domain. Choose an answer with the exact command, options, and arguments that will show both the name and IP for the mail server at example.com.

○ A. dig example.com MX

○ B. host -c MX example.com

○ C. nslookup example.com MX

○ D. traceroute – mail example.com

56. An installation step for a particular service asks you to disable file sharing on a Linux system. In a primarily Linux and Unix file sharing environment, which file contains a list of file systems to be shared? Fill in the blank with the full path and filename of this file:

_____

57. When configuring a Linux server to share files and printers in a mostly Windows environment, you want to cause no client-side visits and incur no licensing costs. Which service/daemon will you be running to accomplish this? (Choose two.)

❑ A. nfsd

❑ B. smbd

❑ C. tarantella

❑ D. wu-ftpd

❑ E. nmbd

58. You need to do an installation in your lab environment across the network. You're in a hurry, the files exist on a server in the /shared directory, and you want to make the fewest changes to the server as possible. Which file should you edit to cause this to happen?

   - ○ A. /etc/dfs/dfstab
   - ○ B. /etc/exports
   - ○ C. /etc/exportfs
   - ○ D. /etc/nfs/exports
   - ○ E. /proc/sys/nfs/shares

59. When configuring a new Apache server, you need to determine where content should be placed on the system. You read the httpd.conf file and find a directive that specifies where the HTML content is by default. Which of the following is the name of that directive?

   - ○ A. RootDoc
   - ○ B. DocRoot
   - ○ C. ContentRoot
   - ○ D. DocumentRoot
   - ○ E. DocPath

60. You've made a few important changes to one of the Apache servers you use for e-commerce and need to have the configuration file be reread. Which command can you use to accomplish this without aborting the current sessions?

   - ○ A. /etc/rc.d/init.d/httpd restart
   - ○ B. service httpd restart
   - ○ C. apachectl graceful
   - ○ D. killall -1 httpd

61. Which command can be used to cause your sendmail daemon to reread the list of username-to-email address mappings without restarting the sendmail daemon? Fill in the blank below:

   _____

62. Users are complaining that their email to other domains isn't being delivered but that internal email is working fine. Which command shows you the status of the queue directory for undelivered remote mail? Fill in the blank with the command name only:

   _____

63. What is the full path to the directory that contains user email? Fill in the blank with the full path and name of the location:

   _____

64. After leasing a Class C IP range from a provider, you decide that you need to have six networks with as many hosts as possible on each network. Which of the following represents the subnet mask you should choose?

   ○ A. `255.255.255.128`

   ○ B. `255.255.255.224`

   ○ C. `255.255.255.0`

   ○ D. `255.255.255.240`

   ○ E. `255.255.255.248`

65. After configuring a new set of Samba configuration parameters, you schedule the restart of the `smbd` and `nmbd` daemons with `cron` and go home for the weekend. Around the time that the `cron` job would have run, you are paged that the file and printer sharing services are unavailable. Which command should you have used to check your `smb.conf` file before leaving? Fill in the blank below with just the command name:

   _____

66. You need to transfer some sensitive files from one remote host to another. You want to accomplish this in a single command and transfer the directory and all files to the target host. Fill in the blank with just the command name and the necessary option that would accomplish this:

   _____

67. What is the parameter name that sets a Windows-compatible name for your Samba server? Fill in the blank with the exact characters to set a name of `boomer` for your host:

   _____

68. You have been ordered to provide Telnet services for a particular user. On your system you have just executed the following command:

   `chkconfig telnet on`

   Which change is made to which file? (Choose the best answer.)

   ○ A. A link is made to `telnet` in the `runlevel` directory.

   ○ B. A line is added with `telnet=on` to `/etc/services`.

   ○ C. A line is added to the `rc.sysinit` script.

   ○ D. A line in `/etc/xinetd.d/telnet` now reads `disable = no`.

69. You encounter a file whose contents contain the following entries:

```
zone "." in {
        type hint;
        file "root.hint";
};
```

What is the full path and filename of the file that contains this sort of syntax?

- ○ A. `/etc/named.boot`
- ○ B. `/etc/named.dns`
- ○ C. `/etc/named.conf`
- ○ D. `/etc/named.db`

70. You have just received a phone call from your ISP, who warns you that your leased line will be shut off if you don't disable any and all spam relaying. Which file should this change be made in if you are using Sendmail?

- ○ A. `/etc/aliases`
- ○ B. `/etc/sendmail.cf`
- ○ C. `/etc/sendmail.conf`
- ○ D. `~/.forward`

71. After unsuccessfully attempting to mount a remote server's NFS share, you want to investigate to see whether the system has the proper services and ports enabled. Fill in the blank with just the name and option to accomplish this:

_____

72. After finding a root-restricted command that has a special bit 4 (SUID) set, you embark on a quest to find all the files on your system that have any special bits set that then show on the console. Fill in the blank with the exact command, with options and arguments, to accomplish this:

_____

73. You suspect that the firewall software on your local workstation is misconfigured because it just allowed a piece of traffic that should have been denied through. Fill in the blank below with the exact command that shows the rule set for the default `iptables` table:

_____

74. While working late on a sick legacy server, you find a normal 9-to-5 user is logged on and busy listing out files on your Linux server. You don't want to permanently delete the user or affect her password, but you want to make her contact you before she can log in again.

    Before you kill the user's shell process, which can you do to accomplish this?

    ○ A. Run `passwd -1`.

    ○ B. Run `usermod -L`.

    ○ C. Put an `*` in the password field in `/etc/passwd`.

    ○ D. Run `touch /etc/nologin`.

    ○ E. Run `passwd -d`.

75. After reading a magazine article, you decide to disable Telnet on all your systems. Upon inspection, you find that Telnet is _____ by default on most Linux boxes. Fill in the blank with the correct word to describe the situation:

    _____

76. Every morning you run a report that shows the latest user authentication activity on your standard Linux system. The output is similar to the following:

```
root pts/2 192.168.1.103 Thu Jun 17 14:39   still logged in
root pts/1 192.168.1.103 Thu Jun 17 13:28 - 14:39  (01:10)
root pts/1 :0            Thu Jun 17 13:27 - 13:27  (00:00)
root pts/1 192.168.1.103 Tue Jun 15 16:49 - 17:07  (00:18)
root pts/1 192.168.1.103 Tue Jun 15 16:12 - 16:49  (00:37)
```

    Which log file is being read by the command you are running to display this output?

    ○ A. `/var/log/boot.log`

    ○ B. `/var/log/secure`

    ○ C. `/var/log/wtmp`

    ○ D. `/var/log/lastlog`

77. To log in to a remote server via SSH, what must the permissions on that server's `/etc/ssh/id_dsa.pub` file be, at the least?

    ○ A. 640

    ○ B. 644

    ○ C. 440

    ○ D. 400

23

Answer Key 102

1. A

2. E

3. A, B, C

4. `modprobe`

5. `mkboot vmlinuz` (Alternative: `mkboot /boot/vmlinuz`)

6. `uname -r`

7. A, D, E

8. D

9. B

10. `init 3` (Alternative: `telinit 3`)

11. `init q`

12. D

13. A, E

14. `/etc/hosts.lpd`

15. A

16. C

17. A, D

18. `man 5 crontab`

19. `man -a tarfoo`

20. `www.tldp.org`

21. `declare -F`

22. `/etc/nologin`

23. C

24. A

25. D

26. C

27. C

28. A, B

29. D

30. D

31. B

32. `*/20 8-18 * * 1-5 script1` (Alternative: `0,20,40 8-18 * * mon-fri script1`)

33. C

34. `~/.bashrc` (Alternative: `$HOME/.bashrc.`)

35. A, C

36. `atq`

37. `groups snuffy`

38. `/etc/syslog.conf`

39. `mesg n`

40. B, C

41. B

42. E

43. B

44. D

45. C

46. C

47. B

48. A, B, C

49. C, D

50. E

51. A, C, E

52. C

53. `route add 172.16.38.125 lo` (Alternative: `route add 172.16.38.125 gw 127.0.0.1`)

54. `route add default gw 10.1.2.3`

55. A

56. `etc/exports`

57. B, E

58. B

59. D

60. C

61. `newaliases`

62. `mailq` (Alternative: `sendmail -bp`)

63. `/var/spool/mail`

64. B

65. `testparm`

66. `scp -r`

67. `netbios name = boomer` (Alternative: `netbios name=boomer`)

68. D

69. C

70. B

71. `rpcinfo -p`

72. `find / -perm +7000`

73. `iptables -L` (Alternative: `iptables -t filter -L`)

74. C

75. disabled

76. C

77. B

1. Answer A is correct because the `autoclean` option allows modules so marked to be removed or unloaded from the running kernel. All the other answers are incorrect because they are from different commands or don't exist.

2. Answer E is correct because there isn't any such command as make gzlilo, although both the `lilo` and `zlilo` commands exist. Answer C is incorrect because, even though you might run `make menuconfig` or `make config`, the `make xconfig` command is a valid configuration option for the kernel recompilation. All other answers are incorrect because they are integral parts of the recompilation of a Linux kernel.

3. Answers A, B, and C are correct because all are correct commands for compiling the Linux kernel. The `zlilo` and `lilo` options are used for automating the installation into LILO's configuration file. Answer D is incorrect because it does not compile the Linux kernel.

4. Answer: `modprobe` (There are no alternative correct answers.)

5. Answer: `mkboot vmlinuz` (An alternative answer is `mkboot /boot/vmlinuz`.)

6. Answer: `uname -r` (There are no alternative correct answers.)

7. Answers A, D, and E are correct because they all result in the system entering runlevel `1`. `s` is a synonym for `1`, and `s` means that scripts will be run before runlevel `1` is entered. Answer B is incorrect because runlevel `3` produces a fully running system that permits users to access the disk. Answer C is incorrect because runlevel `4` is not normally assigned, so assuming it's a maintenance runlevel is not reliable.

8. Answer D is correct because LILO is installed by default in the master boot record. Answer A is incorrect because the `map` file is used to store system information for LILO's use. Answer B is incorrect because the first sector of the partition is a valid installation target, but it's not the default. Answer C is incorrect because the `boot.b` file is used to store the binary code that LILO writes, but not the bootstrap code.

9. Answer B is correct because the older versions of Linux used the `inetd` super server to provide on-demand services, not the `xinetd` daemon. Answer A is incorrect because the `services` file is where ports are mapped to services, but it does not provide those services on demand. Answer C is incorrect because it is the `xinetd` daemon's top-level configuration file. Answer D is incorrect because the `/etc/sysconfig` directory is not a file.

10. Answer: `init 3` (An alternative answer is `telinit 3`.)

11. Answer: `init q` (There are no alternative correct answers.)

12. Answer D is correct because only the `lprm` command by itself deletes just the current job from the default queue. Answer A is incorrect because `lprm -a` deletes the current job from all configured queues. Answer B is incorrect because `lprm all` deletes all the print jobs from the default queue. Answer C is incorrect because there is no way to specify the default with the `-P` option; it requires a printer name.

13. Answers A and E are correct because they both print three copies of the `codesamp` file. Answer B is incorrect because the `-c` option is for printer classes, not copies. Answer C is incorrect because there isn't a -count option for `lpr`. Answer D is incorrect because there isn't a --copies option for `lpr`.

14. Answer: `/etc/hosts.lpd` (There are no alternative correct answers.)

15. Answer A is correct because the `/usr/sbin/makewhatis` command creates the shared `whatis` database that's used by both the `whatis` and `apropos` commands. Answer B is incorrect because there isn't a makeapropos command. Answer C is incorrect because, although a `makeinfo` command does exist, it's for making `Texinfo` files. Answer D is incorrect because there isn't a makeman command.

16. Answer C is correct because the `whatis` command searches for the requested command and returns a single line per found result, including a description. Answer A is incorrect because the `man` command doesn't show a single line; it shows the `man` page for the command. Answer B is incorrect because `apropos` shows many lines all containing the command's name, not just a single line for the command. Answer D is incorrect because the `whereis` command shows the binary, source, and `man` page locations, but not a description.

17. Answers A and D are correct because they both show any instances in the `whatis` database for the command name you're searching for. Answer B is incorrect because `man -a` can potentially show multiple pages of output, but only if there are multiple hits for the search, and then only on a page-by-page basis. Answer C is incorrect because `whatis` shows only the `man` pages that match the command name, not as a keyword. Answer E is incorrect because `whereis` shows the binary, source, and `man` page locations, but rarely more than one line's worth.

18. Answer: `man 5 crontab` (There are no alternative correct answers.)

19. Answer: `man -a tarfoo` (There are no alternative correct answers.)

20. Answer: `www.tldp.org` (There are no alternative correct answers.)

21. Answer: `declare -F` (There are no alternative correct answers.)

22. Answer: `/etc/nologin` (There are no alternative correct answers.)

23. Answer C is correct because, when a script is run, a subshell is used. Any variables defined in that subshell are removed when the subshell is exited, even if it's exported. Answers A, B, and D are incorrect because the subshell's variables are removed upon exit.

24. Answer A is correct because `cron` doesn't store the environment of the user running the script but `at` does. Answer B is incorrect because setting the user to be `root` does not fix the path problem. Answer C is incorrect because there is no way to export the user's environment in `cron`; you should use `cron` to invoke an `at` job. Answer D is incorrect because moving the script's location does not solve the problem.

25. Answer D is correct because only a Telnet user signing on is shown the contents of the `/etc/issue.net` file. All other answers are incorrect because only Telnet users are shown the `/etc/issue.net` file.

26. Answer C is correct because a function runs its commands in the current shell. Answer A is incorrect because an alias doesn't allow arguments or requests for input—only a function does. Answer B is incorrect because the `.inputrc` file is for defining the default key bindings, among other things. Answer D is incorrect because a script is run in a subshell.

27. Answer C is correct because the /usr directory tree is often mounted from another system or shared out to other systems, in the case of a server. Unless an application or set of system files is changed, the /usr partition is relatively stable. Answer A is incorrect because every time you add, remove, or modify any of your configuration, the /etc directory contents are changed. Answer B is incorrect because the /home directory and tree is often on its own partition and should be backed up nightly if you have any user data changes. Answer D is incorrect because the data in /var includes log files, Web sites, and FTP sites, and print spools—all of which change often.

28. Answers A and B are correct because they both set the maximum number of days since the password was changed that it can be valid. Answer C is incorrect because the option needs to be a -, not a +. Answer D is incorrect because the useradd -e option is for an exact expiration date, not the number of days that a password is considered valid. Answer E is incorrect because the usermod -f option sets the number of inactive days, not the maximum number of valid days for the password.

29. Answer D is correct because the pwconv utility is used to move the encrypted passwords from the /etc/passwd file to the /etc/shadow file and replace them with an x in the password field. Answer A is incorrect because there isn't a passwdconv command on a Linux box by default. Answer B is incorrect because there isn't a pwconvert command on a Linux box by default. Answer C is incorrect because the passwd program doesn't have a -conv option. Answer E is incorrect because the passwd command doesn't have a -mx5 option.

30. Answer D is correct because the correct location is /etc/default/useradd, which is a file. Answer A is incorrect because it's default, not defaults. Answer B is incorrect because there isn't a file on a standard Linux system named /etc/sysconfig/useradd. Answer C is incorrect because there isn't a file on a standard Linux system named /etc/.useradd. Answer E is incorrect because the /etc/login.defs file is for site-specific configuration for the shadow suite.

31. Answer B is correct because the ~/.bash_logout file is read after the user initiates a sign-out via exit, logout, or Ctrl+D and typically includes the single command clear to clear the screen. All other answers are incorrect because they are used to set up the user's environment and shell, whereas the .bash_logout file is always the last file to be read or sourced in the session.

32. Answer: */20 8-18 * * 1-5 script1 (An alternative answer is 0,20,40 8-18 * * mon-fri script1.)

33. Answer C is correct because /etc/cron.allow is where you put usernames that are allowed to use the cron daemon to submit jobs. All other answers are nonexistent files on a standard Linux system.

34. Answer: `~/.bashrc` (An alternative answer is `$HOME/.bashrc`.)

35. Answers A and C are correct because they have a lock function, which is what caused the `!` in front of the encrypted password. Answer B is incorrect because `chfn` is used to change the `finger`-related information for users. Answer D is incorrect because `chattr` is used for changing the file attributes viewable by `lsattr`. Answer E is incorrect because `chpasswd` is used for setting users' passwords in batches or bulk mode.

36. Answer: `atq` (There are no alternative correct answers.)

37. Answer: `groups snuffy` (There are no alternative correct answers.)

38. Answer: `/etc/syslog.conf` (There are no alternative correct answers.)

39. Answer: `mesg n` (There are no alternative correct answers.)

40. Answers B and C are correct because you must be running X and must start the `xconsole` application to show the messages being directed to the configured target. Answer A is incorrect because `/dev/xconsole` is a pipe, not a program. Answer D is incorrect because Xconsole isn't the name of the application, nor must you run it in the background with an `&` character. Answer E is incorrect because you must be in X and must start the `xconsole` application to see these messages.

41. Answer B is correct because all authentication messages are sent to the `auth` facility. Answer A is incorrect because there isn't a login facility. Answer C is incorrect because authentication messages for users are still sent to the `auth` facility. Answer D is incorrect because the `daemon` facility is a miscellaneous or catch-all facility for daemons that don't have a particular category. Answer E is incorrect because there isn't a secure facility.

42. Answer E is correct because it most simply accomplishes sending all but `debug` to the target because `debug` is not included by default. Answer A is incorrect because `debug` is never shown unless specifically requested. Answer B is incorrect because it sends only the `info` priority messages, not `info` and higher. Answer C is incorrect because it's not the simplest method to show all but `debug` messages, although it will work. Answer D is incorrect because it sends `debug` and higher priority messages.

43. Answer B is correct because the keyword `server` is prefixed before time sources in the `/etc/ntp.conf` file. Answer A is incorrect because `source` is what is being configured, but the keyword is `server`. Answer C is incorrect because tier1 is a description of a type of server, not a keyword. Answer D is incorrect because `fudge` is a keyword that prefixes a fake server used for backup synchronization. Answer E is incorrect because you must prefix the server's address with the keyword `server`.

44. Answer D is correct because it alone can be used to configure the IP address information needed for NICs. Answer A is incorrect because it shows connections and socket information but can't change IP settings. Answer B is incorrect because it's the wireless configuration utility that's part of some distributions, but none of the NICs are specified as wireless. Answer C is incorrect because there isn't a command named default. Answer E is incorrect because the `route` command is only capable of showing or managing the routing and gateway information for a system, not setting the IP settings.

45. Answer C is correct because your nephew forgot to put a 1 in the `/proc/sys/net/ipv4/ip_forward` file so the system will forward traffic between the interfaces. Answer A is incorrect because it uses the `set` command and attempts to set a 1 to a nonexistent file. Answer B is incorrect because it has no affect on routing. Answer D is incorrect because `echo`'ing a 1 into a file isn't possible and a > redirect symbol should be used.

46. Answer C is correct because the use of `-n` with `traceroute` keeps the names from being resolved and just prints the IPs of routers it finds, speeding things up measurably. All other answers are incorrect because they don't produce the desired result.

47. Answer B is correct because the `minicom` application is a quick and easy method to determine whether connectivity is present for a Linux dial-up connection. Answer A is incorrect because `setserial` is used beforehand to set up the serial port used by a dial-up connection. Answer C is incorrect because it's a Windows application that does much the same thing as `minicom`. Answer D is incorrect because it's an older DOS application that was used for modem communications.

48. Answers A, B, and C are correct because they are specified in the RFC as private address ranges. Answer D is incorrect because it's a network that was often used in the early days of training for IP subnetting classes, even though it's a publicly addressable range of addresses.

49. Answers C and D are correct because you want `named` to run standalone for speed, but to configure the `/etc/hosts.deny` file to block the undesirable networks from attacking the server. Answer A is incorrect because running `named` under `xinetd` slows it down, mostly when it has to be started on demand. Answer B is incorrect because using `tcpd` introduces a layer of complexity and slows down `named`. Answer E is incorrect because you are denying particular networks of hosts, so the specific configuration should be in the `/etc/hosts.deny` file.

50. Answer E is correct because the `holdoff` timer option causes the connection to be delayed in reconnecting to give the other end time to reset. Answer A is incorrect because the waitone timer option doesn't exist. Answer B is incorrect because restart isn't a valid option for a connection. Answer C is incorrect because disable is not a valid option in this case. Answer D is incorrect because `connect-delay` is used only when a connection has been gracefully completed, not broken or interrupted.

51. Answers A, C, and E are correct because they are routing daemons or engines on a Linux system. Answer B is incorrect because the `route` command is simply a command, not a daemon or an engine. Answer D is incorrect because `rtnetlink` is a description of a routing socket, not a daemon or an engine.

52. Answer C is correct because the `/etc/services` file lists the services and their associated ports for the machine. Misconfiguring this file disables services. Answer A is incorrect because an /etc/sysconfig/scripts file doesn't exist on Linux. Answer B is incorrect because the `/etc/resolv.conf` file is for name resolution, not services and their ports. Answer D is incorrect because it's referring to the `c:\windows\system32\drivers\etc\services` file on a Windows system.

53. Answer: `route add 172.16.38.125 lo` (An alternative answer is `route add 172.16.38.125 gw 127.0.0.1`.)

54. Answer: `route add default gw 10.1.2.3` (There are no alternative correct answers.)

55. Answer A is correct because only the `dig` command with the `example.com` domain and the `MX` specifier show the requested records. Answer B is incorrect because the `host` command doesn't show specific servers in a domain; it shows just the resolved IP for the name queried. Answer C is incorrect because the `nslookup` command doesn't query for the `MX` record as shown and requires more options. Answer D is incorrect because the `traceroute` command doesn't have a --mail option.

56. Answer: `/etc/exports` (There are no alternative correct answers.)

57. Answers B and E are correct because they are the two components of the Samba suite, which masquerades a Linux/Unix system as a Windows server for file and printer sharing. Answer A is incorrect because NFS usage for Windows client systems requires extra software and configuration. Answer C is incorrect because Tarantella is a commercial software package and requires a license. Answer D is incorrect because the `wu-ftpd` daemon is for FTP and doesn't affect printer sharing.

58. Answer B is correct because the /etc/exports file can be edited to contain just the characters /shared to make the files available to all hosts read-only via NFS. Answer A is incorrect because this is the file that should be edited on a Solaris box to share these files. Answer C is incorrect because this file doesn't exist on a Linux box by default. Answer D is incorrect because this file doesn't exist on a Linux box by default. Answer E is incorrect because this file doesn't exist on a Linux box by default.

59. Answer D is correct because the DocumentRoot is the directive that sets the path for the content on the system. All other answers are incorrect because they are not directives in the Apache configuration file.

60. Answer C is correct because only the apachectl command gracefully (without aborting current sessions) restarts the httpd process. All other answers destructively restart the httpd process, severing current connections.

61. Answer: newaliases (There are no alternative correct answers.)

62. Answer: mailq (An alternative answer is sendmail -bp.)

63. Answer: /var/spool/mail (There are no alternative correct answers.)

64. Answer B is correct because a subnet mask of 224 means 3 bits are taken for the network, which exactly matches the requirement for six subnets. Answer A is incorrect because it allows for only two subnets. Answer C is incorrect because it doesn't custom subnet the network at all, allowing only a single network. Answer D is incorrect because it allows for more than six networks but means that instead of 30 hosts per subnet, only 14 hosts are possible per subnet. Answer E is incorrect because it allows for only six hosts per subnet.

65. Answer: testparm (There are no alternative correct answers.)

66. Answer: scp -r (There are no alternative correct answers.)

67. Answer: netbios name = boomer (An alternative answer is netbios name=boomer.)

68. Answer D is correct because the chkconfig command is used to manage the services in both the runlevels and those controlled by xinetd/inetd, and running that command turns on or sets disallow = no for the Telnet service. Answer A is incorrect because the chkconfig command shown doesn't modify the runlevel directory entries. Answer B is incorrect because the services file doesn't contain yes and no parameters. Answer C is incorrect because chkconfig doesn't affect the lines or entries in rc.sysinit.

69. Answer C is correct because the entries are from a Bind version 8 and above `named.conf` file. Answer A is incorrect because the syntax for a `named.boot` file is different; typically all entries are a single line. Answer B is incorrect because named.dns is not a recognized filename for a Linux system. Answer D is incorrect because `named.db` is a zone file for a domain called named.

70. Answer B is correct because the `/etc/sendmail.cf` file is where you specify the `NoRelay` parameter. Answer A is incorrect because the `/etc/aliases` file is for defining aliases, not relay control. Answer C is incorrect because there isn't normally an /etc/sendmail.conf file on a Linux system, although there might be an `/etc/log.d/conf/services/sendmail.conf` file for the logging of sendmail events. Answer D is incorrect because the user's forwarding file isn't designed to affect spam relaying options.

71. Answer: `rpcinfo -p` (There are no alternative correct answers.)

72. Answer: `find / -perm +7000` (There are no alternative correct answers.)

73. Answer: `iptables -L` (An alternative answer is `iptables -t filter -L`.)

74. Answer C is correct because it alone disables the user's ability to log in without altering the encrypted password or disabling all user logins. Answer A is incorrect because it alters the encrypted password for the user by prefixing it with a ! in the `/etc/shadow` file. Answer B is incorrect because it does exactly the same thing as answer A. Answer D is incorrect because creating the `/etc/nologin` file disables all user logins. Answer E is incorrect because it deletes the user's password to disable the account.

75. Answer: disabled

76. Answer C is correct because the command being run is the last command, which uses the `/var/log/wtmp` log to gather the information it presents. Answer A is incorrect because `boot.log` is used for boot messages. Answer B is incorrect because the `/var/log/secure` log file is used for reverse lookup results for SSH among other SSH-related messages. Answer D is incorrect because `/var/log/lastlog` is used by the `lastlog` command, which shows when and if users have logged in, but not the output shown previously.

77. Answer B is correct because only it allows anyone outside the user owner and group owner members to see the file. This file is used when SSH clients attempt to attach and is typically copied to the attaching user's `~/.shh/known_hosts` file. All other answers are incorrect because they don't have the permissions that enable other users to read the file upon attaching to the system.

Debian Package Management

Debian Package Architecture

Debian's package management landscape is made up of databases for tracking packages (which is kept in /var/lib/dpkg), package-related tools for package management, and package files (or .deb files).

Debian's Package Database

The package database for Debian's dpkg scheme is located in /var/lib/dpkg. Typically, three main files are in this directory: status, diversions, and available. The status file contains the states for each package that's installed. The available file is a list of the packages available from the package sources for update, and the diversions file is the list of diverted packages, or packages that weren't installed to the default locations for whatever reason.

Debian Package Files

Debian's package files are unlike the usual source or RPM packages you might be used to. A Debian package is really an ar, or archive, file that has at least a Debian binary, a control file, and a file that lists the contents of the package.

A Debian package typically contains the following:

➤ Necessary application files

➤ Metadata information

➤ Dependency information (libraries, other packages, and so on)

➤ Suggestions (alternatives to the package, or packages that would make nice companions to the package)

Debian packages use a standardized naming convention, in which the package name, version, build, and architecture are separated by underscores rather than dashes, as in the RPM name convention. Here's an example:

```
Package_version-build_architecture.deb
```

Here's a typical package that follows this convention:

```
ethereal_0.8.13-2_i386.deb
```

Debian Package Management Tools

Debian has a number of package management utilities. The four that are most frequently used and tested are

➤ dpkg

➤ dselect

➤ apt-get

➤ alien

> These utilities are covered in detail in the next few sections. The objectives require examinees to know how to install, upgrade, uninstall, and query package information, and a fair amount of long options such as **--print-avail** and a few short options such as **-i** appear on the exam.

Using **dpkg**

The dpkg command is the core package handler for Debian. It's what I jokingly call the most powerful of all the package manager tools, meaning it's full-featured while still being difficult to use.

Installing Packages with **dpkg**

The most common way to install packages is to download them from the current directory using the following command:

```
dpkg --install foobaz_5.1.1063-1_i386.deb
```

This returns output similar to the following:

```
Selecting previously deselected package foobaz.
(Reading database ... 114161 files and directories currently installed.)
Unpacking foobaz (from foobaz_5.1.1063-1_i386.deb) ...
Setting up foobaz (5.1.1063) ...
```

Sometimes you need to satisfy dependencies for a package, and it's easier to use the apt-get utility for this task. To handle a dependency for a particular package, specify that main package on the install command line first, followed by any dependencies you've identified (usually from trying to install the main package first). The command would look like this:

```
dpkg --install some_pkg.deb depend_pkg.deb"
```

Removing Packages

When you need to remove a package with the dpkg command, you can use two options. The -r or --remove option removes the package's files but leaves any configuration files intact on the disk. The other option for getting rid of packages is the -P or --purge option, which removes all the package's files, including any configuration files.

To remove a package but leave its configuration files in place, use the following:

```
dpkg --remove package_name"
```

To purge a package, including its configuration files, use the following:

```
dpkg --purge package_name
```

When a package is installed, any configuration files are noted in the **conffiles** file. This is used to determine which files are left in place during a remove action and which files should also be purged in a purge action.

Dependency Issues

When you are working with packages, a desired package installation often finds entries in the package database that conflict with the files it is attempting to install. Also, sometimes during a removal, a package has a file that other packages depend on.

In keeping with the sturdy and less-than-verbose nature of Debian, using the package tools **--force** option can lead to some truly unpleasant circumstances for your machine. Take great care when removing packages that have dependencies, and read in detail the **man** page for **dpkg**'s force section. For the exam, you'll need to know how to force an action, but not all the 20 or so forcing options.

To force the removal of a broken package that is marked in the database as requiring reinstallation, you use the following:

```
dpkg --force-reinstreq packagename
```

The `-reinstreq` is used on packages marked as requiring reinstallation, and it allows dpkg to remove that package.

Additionally, you can use the `-depends` option after `--force` to turn all those nasty error messages into dire warnings, but the tool then allows you to do whatever inadvisable action you're about to perform. Here's an example:

```
dpkg --force-depends packagename
```

Finally, you can also use the `--force-remove-essential` option. Even the most conservative and dry man page cautions that this option will likely cause the system to stop working.

If you positively must (usually on direction from the vendor or a nearby Debian guru), you can force the installation of a package, regardless of the conflicts generated with the command and options, like so:

```
dpkg --install new_pkg.deb --force-conflicts
```

If you have problems with the package or other packages after forcing past any conflicts, remember that you were warned.

Querying Packages

Packages that are currently installed can be queried for a plethora of information. In particular, you can list the existence, version, name, and a description of the package by using the `-l` or `--list` option:

```
dpkg --list krb*
```

You can use either a singular package name, such as krb5-user for the Kerberos-related package, or use the previous filename (glob of krb*) to see the following listing:

```
Desired=Unknown/Install/Remove/Purge/Hold
| Status=Not/Installed/Config-files/Unpacked/Failed-config/Half-installed
|/ Err?=(none)/Hold/Reinst-required/X=both-problems
→(Status,Err: uppercase=bad)
||/ Name                    Version              Description
+++-=======================-====================-
```

```
================================================================
pn  krayon             <none>        (no description available)
un  krb5-doc           <none>        (no description available)
un  krb5-user          <none>        (no description available)
ii  krdc               3.1.4-1       KDE Remote Desktop Client
pn  krecord            <none>        (no description available)
ii  kreversi           3.1.4-1       Reversi for KDE
ii  krfb               3.1.4-1       KDE Remote Screen Server
ii  kruler             3.1.4-1       a screen ruler and color
pn  krusader           <none>        (no description available)
```

You can check the status of a particular package or packages by using the -s
or --status option:

```
dpkg --status krdc
```

The output returned is similar to the rpm command's -qi information page.

You can see the files that were installed by a package by using the -L or
--listfiles option:

```
dpkg --listfiles coreutils
```

This results in output similar to the following (output truncated to fit):

```
/usr/bin/factor
/usr/bin/id
/usr/bin/logname
/usr/bin/pathchk
/usr/bin/printenv
/usr/bin/printf
/usr/bin/seq
/usr/bin/tee
/usr/bin/test
/usr/bin/tty
```

The use of either the -S or --search option lets you search the installed files
on disk via the package database, such as

```
dpkg -S apt.conf
```

This returns output that contains the various places an apt.conf file was
found from the database entries:

```
apt: /usr/share/doc/apt/examples/apt.conf
debconf: /etc/apt/apt.conf.d/70debconf
apt: /usr/share/man/fr/man5/apt.conf.5.gz
debconf: /etc/apt/apt.conf.d
apt: /usr/share/man/man5/apt.conf.5.gz
```

Finally, to see what details are contained in the available portion of the database for a package, you can use the --p or --print-avail option. An example
shown later in the chapter shows output from this command.

Using **dselect**

Because the dpkg utility is so easy to use, a team of programmers set about constructing a text-based GUI front end for dpkg called dselect. One of the more prolific developers in the Debian arena calls dselect "afailed experiment in C++." With the advent of the apt-get package management utility, dselect has all but dropped from mainstream use.

Using dselect, you can access packages from a variety of sources, including

➤ CD-ROM

➤ NFS

➤ Local disk

➤ Mounted disks

Although dselect encompasses support for most if not all dpkg functions, it also manages to be nearly as complex as using dpkg. It's not recommended for newcomers to the Debian package management arena.

Using **apt-get** to Manage Packages

The crown jewel of Debian's package management commands is the system known as APT or apt-get. With apt-get and properly configured sources, a sysadmin can completely automate package management, including installation, upgrades, removal, and even upgrading of the entire distribution to the latest stable distribution release.

The main configuration file for the APT suite is the /etc/apt/apt.conf file. This file is read by all the APT tools and can be set to override configuration specifications for the individual utilities.

Depending on the distribution, this file can be very small or quite large. On my testing systems, the entire file consists of three lines:

```
APT::Default-Release "testing";
APT::Cache-Limit 10000000;
Apt::Get::Purge;
```

The first line sets the default release level; in this case mine are set to the testing level, which means the packages are still in testing but not likely to go down in flames suddenly. The second entry is the cache limit that is set aside for APT's use, which is the amount of disk space set aside for the available information or the list of packages that have updates that haven't been applied yet. The third and final entry sets the default option for removal/purge operations. This setting means that configuration files are not automatically saved as in a remove operation, but are deleted with their associated packages.

Protecting Your Sources

The `apt-get` tool's sources for packages are configured in the `/etc/apt/sources.list` file. Depending on how adventurous you are, you can set your sources to the Stable, Testing, or Unstable package repository:

➤ **Stable**—Very conservative, it's a stable and well-tested set of packages and is almost paranoid in its stability. (If massive uptime is the goal, use the Stable release.)

➤ **Testing**—The release that is next in line to become the successor to the current Stable release, it still has bugs and problems, but they are non-critical. (If you want some new packages and troubleshooting fun, but a mostly stable system, choose the Testing release.)

➤ **Unstable**—The bleeding edge of development, in this version, packages can change often, features are still not frozen, and large changes might take place. (This is *not* for use on enterprise or mission-critical systems!)

I recommend looking at another system of the same release level for a sanity check and making sure that the sites you do pick are stable and up all the time.

NOTE | Often I find a package repository is down or has load-balancing problems, so I configure several sources for a particular feature or package set, commenting out the slow or down one and uncommenting the next in my list.

The source formats available for use in the `/etc/apt/sources.list` file are

➤ **CD-ROM**—Local CD-ROM drive

➤ **File**—Local directory

➤ **HTTP**—Web site

➤ **FTP**—FTP site

Updating the Package Database

The first task to accomplish when using the `apt-get` command is to get the latest package information for your release from the sources you've configured.

To get the latest package information and populate that into the available file, you use this command:

```
apt-get update
```

This returns output similar to what's shown here (output truncated severely to fit the page):

```
Hit http://ftp2.de.debian.org ../project/experimental/non-free Sources
Get:53 http://ftp2.de.debian.org ../project/experimental/non-free
➥Release [110B]
Fetched 9110kB in 51s (177kB/s)
Reading Package Lists... 96%
Reading Package Lists... Done
```

After the update function is complete, you can upgrade any packages found to be newer than your current versions.

First, it's helpful to find out what will happen to particular packages, such as your email client. To do this, you can display the package's upgrade data in the available listing with the following command:

```
dpkg --print-avail evolution
```

This returns output similar to the following:

(Output truncated heavily, evolution has a *lot* of dependencies)

```
Package: evolution
Priority: optional
Section: mail
Installed-Size: 28968
Maintainer: Takuo KITAME <kitame@debian.org>
Architecture: i386
Version: 1.4.6-2
Replaces: evolution1.3
Provides: mail-reader, imap-client
Depends: gtkhtml3.0 (>= 3.0.10), libart-2.0-2 (>= 2.3.8),
➥libasn1-6-heimdal (>= 0.6), libatk1.0-0 (>= 1.4.1),
➥libaudiofile0 (>= 0.2.3-4), libbonobo2-0 (>= 2.4.3)
Recommends: mozilla-psm (>= 2:1.3.1), gnome-pilot-conduits
➥ (>= 2.0.9), gnome-desktop-data
Suggests: gnupg, gnome-spell (>= 1.0.4)
Conflicts: evolution1.3
Size: 10201086
Description: The groupware suite
 Evolution is the integrated mail, calendar, task and address
➥book distributed suite from Ximian, Inc.
See http://www.ximian.com for more information.
```

You can see the current evolution package's information with this command:

```
dpkg --list evolution
```

This shows output similar to what's shown here:

```
Desired=Unknown/Install/Remove/Purge/Hold
¦ Status=Not/Installed/Config-files/Unpacked/Failed-config/Half-installed
¦/ Err?=(none)/Hold/Reinst-required/X=both-problems
➥(Status,Err: uppercase=bad)
¦¦/ Name                   Version                 Description
+++-=====================-=====================
➥-=============================
ii  evolution             1.3                     The groupware suite
```

To upgrade the `evolution` package to the latest version for your release, you would use

```
apt-get install evolution
```

This returns appropriate output and a question about downloading additional needed dependencies:

```
Reading Package Lists... Done
Building Dependency Tree... Done
The following extra packages will be installed:
  gtkhtml3.0 libgal2.0-6 libgal2.0-common libgtkhtml3.0-4
Suggested packages:
  gnome-spell
Recommended packages:
  gnome-desktop-data gnome-pilot-conduits
The following NEW packages will be installed:
  libgal2.0-6 libgtkhtml3.0-4
The following packages will be upgraded
  evolution gtkhtml3.0 libgal2.0-common
3 upgraded, 2 newly installed, 0 to remove and 836 not upgraded.
Need to get 11.8MB of archives.
After unpacking 4738kB of additional disk space will be used.
Do you want to continue? [Y/n]
```

Assuming you want to upgrade the package, you should answer Y for yes and press Enter.

The APT tools gather the `evolution` package, all needed extra packages previously listed, and any suggested packages; then they start the upgrade process. When the upgrade process is complete, you get a message indicating so and the shell prompt is returned.

To upgrade all the packages that have available updated packages, you can run a single command:

```
apt-get upgrade
```

To upgrade the whole distribution with one command (and a few Y answers to prompts afterward), you can use this command:

```
apt-get dist-upgrade
```

It's useful to schedule these operations with a **cron** task, but remember that you have to use the **which** command to determine the paths for the utilities mentioned in the **cron** job. **cron** doesn't store the user's environment and needs the full path to executables in many cases.

Removing a package with apt-get is relatively simple by using the following command:

```
apt-get remove krdc
```

This package doesn't have any dependencies and simply requires pressing Y and then Enter to execute. The following output is an example:

```
Reading Package Lists... Done
Building Dependency Tree... Done
The following packages will be REMOVED:
  krdc
0 upgraded, 0 newly installed, 1 to remove and 835 not upgraded.
Need to get 0B of archives.
After unpacking 381kB disk space will be freed.
Do you want to continue? [Y/n]
```

If you're about to remove something that has dependencies, you get a few screens of output that list the about-to-be-broken packages, and then you see the dire warning shown here:

```
WARNING: The following essential packages will be removed
This should NOT be done unless you know exactly what you are doing!
  coreutils debianutils fileutils gzip shellutils textutils
69 upgraded, 37 newly installed, 446 to remove and 428 not upgraded.
Need to get 73.3MB of archives.
After unpacking 1129MB disk space will be freed.
You are about to do something potentially harmful
To continue type in the phrase 'Yes, do as I say!'
 ?]
```

Obviously, removing the coreutils package does break a *lot* of packages and can disable your system. Take great care, and don't forget to enter Yes, do as I say! exactly in answer to the question, with case-sensitive characters!

Cleaning Out the Archives

The apt-get utilities typically keep local copies of .debs that have been downloaded to satisfy update or upgrade commands. The archive location of complete packages is /var/cache/apt/archives, whereas partial packages are kept in /var/cache/apt/archives/partial. These are packages that are in progress or have an unreliable and frequently down source.

After a period of updating your system, you should clean out the cache archive directories to make room for newer packages and for general maintenance.

To remove all the files in the archives, regardless of their completeness and relationship to the current system's release, use the following command:

```
apt-get clean
```

To clean out outdated files, such as previous versions that have been superseded by the current version of a package, you use this command:

```
apt-get autoclean
```

Loving the alien Command

Debian includes a package format conversion command named alien. The alien command is used to convert from alien (hence, the name) package formats to a .deb package format so the software can be more easily installed on the Debian system.

alien converts to and from the following formats:

➤ Debian (.deb)

➤ Red Hat (.rpm)

➤ Slackware (.tgz)

➤ Stampede (.slp)

To convert a .rpm file to .deb format, you would use this command:

```
alien package.rpm
```

The command works for a while and then, if successful, returns the following message:

```
package.deb generated
```

You can also have a package such as a .rpm converted and installed in a single step, with this command:

```
alien -i package.rpm
```

This converts the package to .deb format and then runs the installation routine to install that package on the system. You can verify its existence on the system with this command:

```
dpkg --list package
```

What's on the CD-ROM

This appendix is a brief rundown of what you'll find on the CD-ROM that comes with this book. The primary items you will find on your CD are the ExamSim exam simulator software for both Linux and Windows platforms and relevant readme files for the software. In addition to the ExamSim software, the CD-ROM includes an electronic version of this book in Portable Document Format (PDF), a Need to Know More? PDF file of useful resources, additional PDF file(s), and the Adobe Acrobat Reader used to display these files.

Using ExamSim

ExamSim is an exam simulator that provides two practice exams for the LPIC1 certification (LPI101 and LPI102). Each practice exam consists of about 45 questions similar to the questions of the LPI exams. About 300 questions are chosen randomly for each practice exam. So, if you start a new exam, you will get different questions every time.

You can choose from different exam modes. In Training Mode, you can select an answer button if you want to see the correct answers or you can choose to disable the timer if you want to practice the exam without timeout restrictions. In Exam Mode, you work similarly to the actual test conditions, without an answer button and with a running timer.

ExamSim is a program you can use to practice your skills for the LPIC exams. Passing ExamSim exams is no guarantee that you'll pass the actual exam, but if you work with ExamSim for a while and you pass all the tests in it, it is very unlikely that you will run into problems with the exams.

Exam Simulation

One of the main functions of ExamSim is exam simulation. To prepare you to take the actual vendor certification exam, ExamSim is designed to offer the most effective exam simulation available.

Question Quality

The questions provided in ExamSim are written to the highest standards of technical accuracy. The questions tap the content of the LPIC topic and help you review and assess your knowledge before you take the actual exam.

Interface Design

The ExamSim interface provides you with the experience of taking an electronic exam. This enables you to effectively prepare for taking the actual exam by making the test experience a familiar one. Using this test simulation can help eliminate the sense of surprise or anxiety you might experience in the testing center because you will already be acquainted with computerized testing.

Effective Learning Environment

The ExamSim interface provides a learning environment that not only tests you through the computer, but also teaches the material you need to know to pass the certification exam. Each question comes with an explanation of the correct answer and may provide reasons the other options are incorrect. This information helps reinforce the knowledge you already have and provides practical information you can use on the job.

Hardware and Software Requirements

The main goal in the development of ExamSim was to offer a program running under Linux. It would be ridiculous to exercise Linux exams using Windows. Thus, the program has been developed using Linux. Currently, there are two major alternatives to writing a graphical program for Linux:

using the qt-library (like KDE does) or using the GTK-libraries (like Gnome does). I decided to use the GTK-libraries because they are completely free and are available for Linux and Windows. After finishing the program, I ported it to Windows and it worked well. Thus there are two versions of the program—one for Linux and another for Windows.

Requirements for Linux

To run the program under Linux, you should have the GTK+ runtime environment installed. This should be no problem if you use a modern distribution. I tested the program with Red Hat 9.0, Mandrake 9.2, Slackware 9.1, SuSE 8.2, SuSE 9.0, and Debian 3.0 without any problems.

Debian users should ensure that they have a working pango installation. Debian offers to have the pango fonts managed by defoma. This is necessary to work with ExamSim. If you don't have an existing file named /etc/pango/ pengox.aliases, you should run the following command:

```
dpkg-reconfigure libpango1.0-common
```

Answer yes to the question of whether defoma should manage pango fonts.

Requirements for Windows

ExamSim runs under any Win32 version (Win95, Win98, WinNT, Win2K, and WinXP). ExamSim requires an installed and working GTK+ runtime environment (see the following installation instructions) and about 2MB of free disk space.

Installing ExamSim

Both versions of ExamSim come as self-extracting archives. Therefore, ExamSim is installable by calling just one command and following the onscreen instructions. When using Linux there aren't any instructions; the program is installed to the standard location of the Linux file system.

Install ExamSim by running the setup program on the CD.

Installation for Linux

To install ExamSim, you need root privileges. Ensure that permissions are set so that examsim-linux-1.0-setup is executable by entering

```
chmod +x examsim.setup.
```

Then execute the file:

```
examsim-linux-1.0-setup
```

The questions are installed to `/usr/local/lib/examsim/exams`; the binary is installed to `/usr/local/bin/examsim`; the configuration file is installed to `/etc/examsim.conf`; and the README file is installed to `/usr/share/doc/examsim`.

Execute the program:

```
./examsim-linux-1.0-setup
```

To start ExamSim after the installation, enter

```
examsim
```

Installation for Windows

To install ExamSim for Windows, you need administrator privileges and must have the GTK+ runtime environment installed. Installation stops if the GTK+ runtime environment can't be found.

To install the GTK+ runtime environment, execute the following:

```
GTK-Runtime-Environment-2.2.4-3.exe
```

To install ExamSim, execute the program:

```
ExamSim-Win32-1.0-setup.exe
```

To start ExamSim after the installation, go to Start, Programs and select ExamSim.

Using ExamSim

After you've installed the program successfully, it can be started by any user. In Linux, it is started by entering the command examsim. In Windows, you can use the appropriate menu entry.

Using the program is simple. A menu contains just one important entry: Exam. This submenu contains several entries:

➤ **Open Exam**—Loads a previously saved exam (this entry is available only if there is no currently active exam).

➤ **Save Exam**—Saves a currently running exam. It enables you to save an exam for later continuation. This entry is available only if there is a currently active exam that can be saved.

➤ **Start Practice Exam LPI101**—This menu entry starts the LPI101 exam simulation.

➤ **Start Practice Exam LPI102**—This menu entry starts the LPI102 exam simulation.

➤ **Quit**—This entry quits the program.

To start an exam, choose one of the existing selections. This results in a start page for the exam. Here you can select some options and then start the exam.

Available options are

➤ **Exam Mode**—Two modes are available: Training Mode and Exam Mode. In Training Mode, you can click an answer button to view the correct answers and there is no running timer by default. In Exam Mode, there is no answer button and the timer runs if you don't disable it.

➤ **Exam Options**—Here you can fine-tune your settings. You can disable the timer in Exam Mode or enable it in Training Mode. And you can disable the answer button in Training Mode. There is no way to enable the answer button in Exam Mode, however.

➤ **Examinee Name**—Here you can enter your name. This is used only to create a filename to save a running exam.

After setting all the options, you can start the exam by clicking the Start Exam button. During the running exam, you have several questions to be answered, and each question can be marked for a later review. The three types of questions are

➤ **Multiple-choice single-answer**—These questions have just one correct answer. If you check one answer, all the other answers are deselected automatically.

➤ **Multiple-choice multiple-answer**—These have various correct answers. You have to check all the correct answers.

➤ **Fill-in-the-blank**—Answers have to be written in a text entry field.

On the bottom of the screen are buttons to navigate through the exam. You can walk through all the questions using the Previous Item and Next Item buttons. If you want to end the exam, click the Grade Exam button.

After having answered all the questions or navigated to the last question, you'll see a Review Screen button. This leads you to a page where you can choose to review the questions again. You can select one of the following options:

➤ **Review Only Marked Items**—Only questions marked for review are displayed.

➤ **Review Only Unanswered Questions**—Only currently unanswered questions are displayed.

➤ **Review Marked and Unanswered Items**—This displays all the questions that are unanswered or marked for review.

➤ **Review All Items**—This starts the complete exam again.

This review allows you to change any answer of the exam again. You can navigate through the exam as you did in the first place; then it ends again with the review screen where you can choose a new criteria to review. After having finished the review, you can grade the exam by clicking the Grade Exam button. This leads you to the result page where you will find a statistic about how many questions were answered correctly, how many were wrong, and whether you passed or failed. To review the exam, you can click one of two buttons on the bottom of the screen:

➤ **Review All**—Displays the complete exam again. You will see the correct answers in green, the wrong answers in red, and your choice.

➤ **Review Errors**—Displays only the wrongly answered questions.

This review is a read-only review. You can't change any answer; you can just see which of your answers were correct and which were not. Every question provides a Show Answer button to read an explanation of which answer was correct. You can also click a Back to Grade Exam button to return to the result page where you will find an End Exam button to return to the main menu. Once there, you can start a new exam or quit the program.

Exclusive Electronic Version of the Text

As mentioned previously, the CD-ROM that accompanies this book also contains an electronic PDF version of this book. This electronic version comes complete with all the figures as they appear in the book. You can use Acrobat's handy search capability for study and review purposes.

Glossary

- -

alias

An alias can be defined for a user's shell to have a single command take the place of several commands with options and arguments.

argument

An argument is typically a file, directory, or other object that a command is being targeted to or is acting upon. See also option.

buffer

A buffer is a location in memory that contains data that has yet to be written to disk. For example, a new file that is unnamed and unsaved in vi contains the text you type in a buffer. *Buffer* is also used to describe various locations in memory that hold data.

build

A build in software terms can be a particular version or set of software, such as "the January 98 build of Apache." Or it can be used as a verb, meaning to compile and configure the software.

compile

To compile software is to build the source code into a set of binary programs, modules, and libraries. C or C++ programs are compiled, whereas Perl scripts are typically interpreted, or run like a shell script would be.

daemon

A daemon is a friendly background service or capability that is typically interacted with through a controller application or console. Daemons are typically called *services* by users transitioning from the proprietary side of software. Often the terms *daemon* and *service* are used at will to describe something such as apache or sendmail on a system.

device file

Linux accesses devices through a particular type of file called a device file. The device files are typically kept in the /dev directory, with most devices having a device file associated with them by the startup and initialization scripts.

distribution

A distribution is a collection of the Linux kernel along with a large set of utilities and applications that make up a release of Linux. Typical distributions include Debian, Red Hat, SuSE, and Slackware. More than 100 distributions are available at any given time.

driver

A piece of software that provides the communication method needed for a piece of hardware to be accessed and available to the operating system.

environment

A user's or program's environment is the settings and variables that have been loaded from the initialization scripts or inherited from the parent process of the user's shell.

export

To export a variable is to make that variable and its value available for use by all child processes of the shell in which the variable was exported.

facility

A category of system logging present in the system logging configuration. Typical facilities are user, auth, daemon, and so on.

file descriptors

File descriptors are how programs interact with each other through input and output. The typical file descriptors are 0 (or STDIN), 1 (or STDOUT), and 2 (or STDERR).

filter

Some text-processing commands are known as filters because they either filter out or add in text and features. The pr command is a perfect example of a filter; it takes the original input file and adds header and footer information, page numbers, the file's name, and the date and time to the output.

firewall

A firewall is a host that contains two or more network interfaces and filters traffic from the outside of the network to protect internal hosts.

GNU

The GNU Software Foundation's name is a recursive algorithm and an example of geek humor. The letters GNU stand for GNU's not Unix.

GPL

The General Public License (GPL) is the license under which most free and open-source software is licensed. The basic tenets of the GPL are that all changes must be made available, prominent notice must be given of changes, local modifications are allowed for competitive advantage, and no restrictions exist for copying or using GPL-licensed software.

GRUB

The grand unified boot loader (GRUB) is one of the boot loaders available for Linux and is the default for such distributions as SuSE and Red Hat.

header

A file's header is used to determine the type of the file. Some utilities, such as the `file` command, can read the file's header and compare it against a set list of file header values and report the file's type.

history

The stack of previous commands maintained by the Bash shell, the history can be viewed with the `history` command, edited with the `fc` command, and accessed with the up and down arrows.

inode

An inode is a pointer to a file on a disk. inodes are created as part of the file system and, as such, are finite in number. New files cannot be created without a free inode, even if there is free disk space.

interrupt

A hardware event generated when a device needs attention from the CPU, such as data that has been read and is available for use from a storage device.

kernel

A kernel is the most basic component of an operating system; it typically controls the scheduling of processes and performs memory management. The Linux kernel is often referred to as just *the kernel*.

level

A level or priority set is associated with every facility in the system logging configuration. A level or priority is a classification of the severity or type of message being logged. Typical priorities or levels include `emerg`, `crit`, `info`, and `debug`.

LILO

The Linux Loader (LILO) is one of the original boot loaders and is the default boot loader for most Linux distributions.

man **page**

A set of documentation that is standard on all Linux and Unix systems. man pages are not typically easy to read or search, but they constitute the most authoritative set of documentation for a system.

MBR

The master boot record (MBR) is typically the first 512 bytes of the first sector of a hard disk. The MBR is where LILO, GRUB, and other boot loaders write code that allows the choosing of from which partition to load operating system loader code.

mode

`vi` has three modes, or styles of operation: Command, Insert, and ex (or Lastline mode). These modes dictate how `vi` interprets commands and keystrokes.

module

A module is typically a piece of functionality that the kernel can call upon or have loaded to make it available for the system. Modules are similar to drivers.

Monkeyboy

See Ross.

network interface card

An Ethernet or Token Ring network interface card (NIC) is used to connect a host to the wire that leads to the network hubs, switches, and routers.

option

An option is typically preceded by a dash or double-dash and is used to cause a program or command to perform a particular function. See also argument.

package

The term *package* is used in several ways. A software package is a set of software that is a discrete application. A package file is used to describe an RPM or DPKG package file, which contains a set of software that is copied and set up on a system when the package is installed on the system.

patch

To patch software is to apply a set of changes that will bring the software to a state of better security, fix a bug, or otherwise enhance its working.

pipe

A pipe is a shell construct that sends the output of one program to the input of another.

Plug and Play

A specification that dictates how cards are detected and configured on the hardware platform.

print job

A print job is a file or set of data that has been submitted through lpr or the printing interface calls and is currently queued up for printing in the print queue.

print queue

The software and spool directory to which a printer sends a print job when it's submitted. A print queue is also known as a *print spool* or simply a *spool*.

profile

A user's profile is typically the settings, variables, and files that are copied from the /etc/skel directory to form the new user home directory. A profile can also be used to describe the set of groups and rights a user has on a particular system.

recursive

When a command or action acts on the current directory and all the contents within it, including all files and subdirectories.

redirection

The process of directing a program's output to a file or device file.

regular expression

For finding a piece of data that you
don't know the exact characters of.
Regular expressions are similar in
function to wildcards on the command line but offer much more
complexity and flexibility.

root

The top level of the file system, or
the / directory. Also the root user
of the system, who has ultimate
control over every aspect of the
system.

Ross

See Monkeyboy.

runlevel

A runlevel is a set of system capabilities and services configured to
run when that runlevel or system
state is entered. Linux uses links to
the runlevel control scripts in the
/etc/rc.d/rc0.d - rc6.d directories
on a Red Hat machine and the
/etc/rc0.d - rc6.d directories on
Debian to control what is started
and stopped in each runlevel.

session

When a user logs in successfully,
and until that user logs out of the
system, he is in what is called a session. If the user logs out and back
in again, he has initiated a different
session.

share

A share is typically a directory that
has been exported or shared out via
NFS or Samba for mounting by
other hosts.

shell

A shell is a command interpreter
that reads the keystrokes that are
entered at the command line and,
when executed, performs a number
of tasks, such as variable expansion,
wildcard substitution, redirection,
and the piping of input/output
data.

signal

Signals are how you communicate
with processes to kill them or alter
their priorities. Typical signals are
15 (or SIGTERM), 1 (or SIGHUP), and 9
(or SIGKILL). The 15 (or SIGTERM)
signal is the default.

source

What open-source software is all
about; it's the source code or files
you can inspect, change, and compile to make your own or a common version of the software.

special bits

All file system objects have the
capability to have special bits set;
these are 4 (or SUID/Set User
ID), 2 (or SGID/Set Group ID),
and 1 (or the sticky bit). Special
bits are set when a particular
action or behavior is required.

special characters

Characters that have a special
meaning within or are reserved
solely for use with the shell.
Special characters include the
asterisk, question mark, single
quotation mark, and double quotation marks, among others.

Superblock

The Superblock for a file system contains the type and location of the file system and the file system's utilization statistics, and it is replicated a number of times on the file system for backup and recovery purposes.

tarball

Typically a .tar file is an uncompressed file created by the tar command, otherwise known as a *tar file*. A tarball is typically a compressed .tar archive, with the compress command, the gzip command, or the bzip2 command.

TCP wrappers

TCP wrappers enable the administrator to configure access to daemons based on hostnames or IPs. Wrappers can be used by running the daemon through the tcpd program or by having the daemon call functions in libwrap.a directly. Entries in the /etc/hosts.deny and /etc/hosts.allow files either deny or allow access on a per-daemon basis.

variables

A variable is a location in memory that can be populated by declaring the VARIABLE=value, where value is some data or text. Exporting a variable makes that variable and its contents accessible to all child processes of the current shell.

virtual terminal

Virtual terminals use a /dev/ttyX port, where x ranges from 1 to approximately 63 to provide the capability to log in as multiple users to the same console of a machine.

Index

How can we make this index more useful? Email us at indexes@quepublishing.com

How can we make this index more useful? Email us at indexes@quepublishing.com

Y - Z

Trusted.

All Linux Professional Institute certification programs are created using extensive community input, combined with rigorous psychometric scrutiny and professional delivery. We test the whole continuum of important Linux skills - we don't just focus on small, subjective tasks. LPI exams are not simply an afterthought used to help sell something else. LPI is a non-profit group that does not sell software, training or books. Our programs and policies are designed to meet educational requirements, not marketing.

Accessible.

LPI exams are available in seven languages, at more than 7,000 locations, in more than 100 countries. You take LPI exams when you want, where you want. In addition, special exam lab events around the world make our program even more affordable. And because we don't make exclusive partnerships, LPI is supported by a broad range of testing centers, book publishers and innovative suppliers of preparation materials.

Independent.

You switched to Linux to get away from single-vendor dependence. So why trade one form of vendor lock-in for another? LPI's program follows the LSB specification, so people who pass our tests can work on all major distributions. Because of its strong grass-roots base and corporate support both inside and outside the world of open source, LPI goes beyond "vendor-neutral" to truly address community needs.

LPI is IT certification done RIGHT!

Save 20% (Valid only in USA and Canada). See back for details.

Linux Professional Institute

www.lpi.org